Emerging Labor Market Institutions for the Twenty-First Century

A National Bureau
of Economic Research
Conference Report

Emerging Labor Market Institutions for the Twenty-First Century

Edited by **Richard B. Freeman, Joni Hersch, and Lawrence Mishel**

The University of Chicago Press

Chicago and London

Richard B. Freeman is the Herbert Ascherman Professor of Economics at Harvard University. He is also program director of labor studies at the National Bureau of Economic Research and senior research fellow at the Centre for Economic Performance of the London School of Economics. Joni Hersch is adjunct professor of law at Harvard Law School. Lawrence Mishel is president of the Economic Policy Institute.

The University of Chicago Press, Chicago 60637
The University of Chicago Press, Ltd., London

Printed in the United States of America
14 13 12 11 10 09 08 07 06 05 1 2 3 4 5
ISBN: 0-226-26157-3 (cloth)

Library of Congress Cataloging-in-Publication Data

Emerging labor market institutions for the twenty-first century / edited by Richard B. Freeman, Joni Hersch, and Lawrence Mishel.
p. cm. — (National Bureau of Economic Research conference report)
Includes bibliographical references and index.
ISBN 0-226-26157-3 (alk. paper)
1. Labor market. 2. Labor unions. 3. Industrial relations. 4. White collar workers. 5. Work environment. I. Freeman, Richard B. (Richard Barry), 1943– II. Hersch, Joni, 1956– III. Mishel, Lawrence R. IV. Series.

HD5706 .E475 2004
331—dc22 2004055330

⊗ The paper used in this publication meets the minimum requirements of the American National Standard for Information Sciences—Permanence of Paper for Printed Library Materials, ANSI Z39.48-1992.

Relation of the Directors to the Work and Publications of the National Bureau of Economic Research

1. The object of the NBER is to ascertain and present to the economics profession, and to the public more generally, important economic facts and their interpretation in a scientific manner without policy recommendations. The Board of Directors is charged with the responsibility of ensuring that the work of the NBER is carried on in strict conformity with this object.

2. The President shall establish an internal review process to ensure that book manuscripts proposed for publication DO NOT contain policy recommendations. This shall apply both to the proceedings of conferences and to manuscripts by a single author or by one or more co-authors but shall not apply to authors of comments at NBER conferences who are not NBER affiliates.

3. No book manuscript reporting research shall be published by the NBER until the President has sent to each member of the Board a notice that a manuscript is recommended for publication and that in the President's opinion it is suitable for publication in accordance with the above principles of the NBER. Such notification will include a table of contents and an abstract or summary of the manuscript's content, a list of contributors if applicable, and a response form for use by Directors who desire a copy of the manuscript for review. Each manuscript shall contain a summary drawing attention to the nature and treatment of the problem studied and the main conclusions reached.

4. No volume shall be published until forty-five days have elapsed from the above notification of intention to publish it. During this period a copy shall be sent to any Director requesting it, and if any Director objects to publication on the grounds that the manuscript contains policy recommendations, the objection will be presented to the author(s) or editor(s). In case of dispute, all members of the Board shall be notified, and the President shall appoint an ad hoc committee of the Board to decide the matter; thirty days additional shall be granted for this purpose.

5. The President shall present annually to the Board a report describing the internal manuscript review process, any objections made by Directors before publication or by anyone after publication, any disputes about such matters, and how they were handled.

6. Publications of the NBER issued for informational purposes concerning the work of the Bureau, or issued to inform the public of the activities at the Bureau, including but not limited to the NBER Digest and Reporter, shall be consistent with the object stated in paragraph 1. They shall contain a specific disclaimer noting that they have not passed through the review procedures required in this resolution. The Executive Committee of the Board is charged with the review of all such publications from time to time.

7. NBER working papers and manuscripts distributed on the Bureau's web site are not deemed to be publications for the purpose of this resolution, but they shall be consistent with the object stated in paragraph 1. Working papers shall contain a specific disclaimer noting that they have not passed through the review procedures required in this resolution. The NBER's web site shall contain a similar disclaimer. The President shall establish an internal review process to ensure that the working papers and the web site do not contain policy recommendations, and shall report annually to the Board on this process and any concerns raised in connection with it.

8. Unless otherwise determined by the Board or exempted by the terms of paragraphs 6 and 7, a copy of this resolution shall be printed in each NBER publication as described in paragraph 2 above.

Contents

Preface

This volume is the culmination of a three-year project to study new institutions in the labor market. The project, "Emerging Labor Market Institutions for the Twenty-First Century," was funded by a grant from the MacArthur Foundation and was a cooperative venture of the National Bureau of Economic Research, the Economic Policy Institute, and the Labor and Worklife Program at Harvard Law School. The project was spurred by the decline of private-sector unionism in the United States and by the innovative efforts by labor activists to develop new institutions to represent workers' interest in the absence of unionism. The project spanned three years to allow time for researchers to follow the development of new institutional forms, some of which changed in the period under study.

The practitioners who created and guided some of the new institutions have not coauthored any of the papers, but they played a major role in guiding the researchers to ask and answer the most salient questions and to make use of information about their organizations. Researchers in the project learned to appreciate the problems involved in the implementation of policies to help workers and in doing so ended up thinking about the development of labor institutions differently than they had in past. In addition, the project benefited from comments by discussants and other participants at the preconference and final NBER research conference where the papers were presented.

Introduction

Richard B. Freeman and Joni Hersch

Private-sector unionism, the institution that has historically represented and advocated on behalf of workers in capitalist economies, is in decline in the United States. At this writing, union density has fallen into single digits in the private sector and shows little or no sign of reviving, despite a major effort by the American Federation of Labor-Congress of Industrial Organizations (AFL-CIO) and many affiliated unions to organize new workers. Falling union density is not unique to the United States, however. Density has dropped in several countries in the European Union (EU), Japan, New Zealand, and Australia as well.

But declines in density have a much greater impact on workers in the United States than in Western Europe or Japan and in most other countries. The reason is that the United States lacks institutional alternatives to trade unions to provide workers with collective voice. In Western Europe, falling union membership does not reduce workers' voice at their workplace because EU law provides for elected works councils at workplaces. In Japan, nonunion workers have some voice at their workplace because Japan's consensual style of labor relations creates scope for workers to express their views outside of union settings. By contrast, U.S. law makes alternative forms of collective voice difficult to attain, due to the Wagner Act's outlawing organizations weaker than independent unions. Management's fear that any form of independent collective voice will lead to full unionization makes it difficult for workers to represent themselves as a

Richard B. Freeman is the Herbert Ascherman Professor of Economics at Harvard University, director of the labor studies program at the National Bureau of Economic Research, and senior research fellow at the Centre for Economic Performance of the London School of Economics. Joni Hersch is adjunct professor and codirector of the Program on Empirical Legal Studies at Harvard Law School.

group in many U.S. enterprises. As union density has fallen in the United States, so too has the collective voice of workers.

In the face of this development, labor activists, workers, and non-governmental organizations concerned with the well-being of workers have sought to develop alternative ways to represent workers' interests. They have formed diverse nonmembership organizations (NMOs) or have altered the operations of member-based organizations, such as occupational associations, to perform some of the functions that traditional unions undertake on behalf of workers.

What is the nature of these new institutions? How do they operate? How effective have they been in providing services or voice to workers compared to unions? Do the new institutions have the breadth and scope to expand in the labor market and substitute at least in part for traditional unions, or are they likely to be limited to small niches?

These questions motivate the research in this volume. Because the new labor institutions of concern have short histories, much of the research takes a case study approach, describing the history and operation of particular innovative institutions. The purpose of the volume, however, is neither to produce definitive case histories nor to illuminate the idiosyncrasies of particular institutions. Rather, it is to understand the behavior of the new institutions within the framework of the standard economic analysis of optimizing agents. This framework directs attention at the goals of the new labor institutions—their maximands, as it were; the constraints on their actions; and the way in which they respond to parametric changes in economic and other incentives.

At the heart of this volume is the difference between membership-based nonunion organizations, where members have some direct say in the way the institution operates, and non-membership organizations, which activists form and run on behalf of workers. There is nothing new about membership-based nonunion labor organizations. In most professional occupations, there is an association that provides information, holds meetings, and represents the occupation to the public. Workers join these organizations when they believe it benefits them. Economists join the American Economic Association. Convention managers join the Professional Convention Managers Association. Scientists join the American Association for the Advancement of Science, and so on. In all of these cases workers establish a traditional principal-agent relation with their organization. What is new is the pressure on these organizations to take on more of the functions of trade unions in the wake of union decline.

Labor analysts have not studied nonunion labor organizations to the same extent that they have studied trade unions, but there is no qualitative difference between modeling how a union operates on behalf of its members and how a nonunion labor organization operates on behalf of its members. In both cases, the economists' natural inclination is to treat the organization in terms of a maximizing model. Analysis of unions as optimizing organizations stretches back at least to the union maximand models of Dunlop (1944) and proceeds through the analysis of unions as responding to median members in Freeman and Medoff (1984). The key issue in maximand models of unions has been the relative importance of wages and employment as union goals in collective bargaining. By focusing on these two outcomes to the exclusion of others, the models ignore much of what unions do at workplaces. Median member models stress that senior immobile workers have a greater impact on outcomes than they would in nonunion markets, which respond to younger marginal workers. But, just as in median voter models in political science, median voter models of unions fail to allow for side bargains among groups, differences between active and nonactive members, and so on. Optimizing models of these kinds give analysts a framework in which to think about the factors that affect union decisions (Farber 1986) but have not succeeded beyond that. We see no reason to expect these models to be any more or less successful in accounting for the behavior of nonunion membership-based organizations than they have been of trade unions.

Nonmember-based organizations differ substantively from membership-based organizations and require a different framework for analysis. From the perspective of principal-agent theory, what is distinctive about NMOs is that the agents or activists select groups of workers as their principals—a reversal of the relation in the standard principal-agent model in which the principals select the agents. Legal services centers choose to defend workers in some areas on some issues. Antisweatshop activists make the well-being of workers in less-developed countries their cause. In neither case do the workers choose the lawyers or the activists to represent them. Because nonmember organizations have only recently attained some importance in the labor market, the analyses in this volume represent the first serious attempt to consider how they operate. The organizations have to please two quite different groups to survive. Because they have no members and thus no dues, NMOs have to raise resources from outside funders and thus must be responsive to those funders. Christine Jolls's analysis in chapter 4 gives a detailed discussion of this problem in the case of lawyers' groups who seek to aid workers. At the same time, the NMO must meet the potentially different needs of the workers it seeks to represent or service. In simplest form, we can think of the NMO as having to find the intersection of the two sets of interests in some space of actions, as shown in the Venn diagram of figure 1. Within that intersection, the NMO or its leadership presumably has freedom to exercise its own preferences about what is more important. Kimberly Ann Elliott and Richard B. Freeman's analysis of antisweatshop organizations—which must gain the support of Western consumers to pressure firms to improve conditions in developing countries and which must demand "reasonable changes" to help the workers they seek to

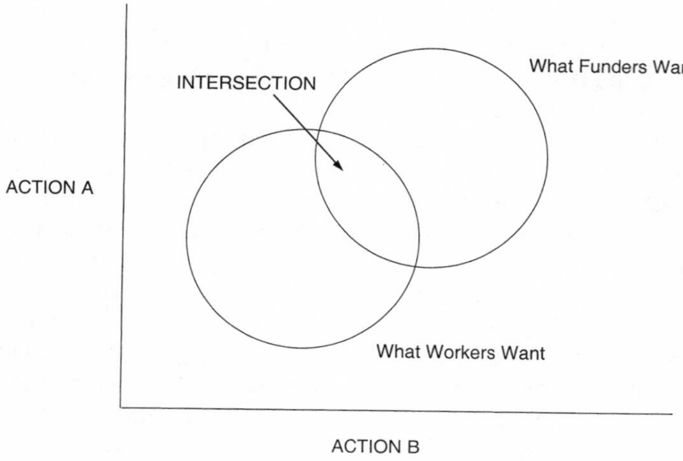

Fig. 1 Nonmembership-based organizations must seek intersection between funders' interests and workers' interest

represent—documents the way this process operates. They stress the entrepreneurial skills that activists must have to succeed.

A key question for this volume is the extent to which, if at all, the emerging labor institutions might substitute for declining unionism. This question has two parts: whether the new NMOs (or nonunion membership-based organizations) can provide services and representation of workers comparable to those of unions, and whether they can expand their reach to service as large a proportion of the work force that traditionally relied on unions as the worker-oriented institutions in the labor market. The studies in the volume answer both questions in the negative. The new institutions have a long way to go before they will be able to provide remotely comparable economic benefits to unions. Even in their weakened state, unions have major effects on wages and benefits, according to the analysis by Thomas C. Buchmeuller, John E. DiNardo, and Robert G. Valleta in chapter 7, which none of the new organizations studied in this book have come close to replicating, including the Working Today effort to provide selective group benefits studied by Joni Hersch in chapter 6. In addition, the new institutions have not managed to expand beyond small niches in the labor market. One of the most successful community based groups, the Industrial Areas Foundation discussed by Lisa M. Lynch in chapter 9, has succeeded in improving pay and training in San Antonio, Texas but has not been able to mimic that success broadly.

David Weil's analysis in chapter 1 provides some reasons for the negative answer to the question about whether the new institutions can substitute for unions. Weil presents a broad overview of the requisite activities any new institution will have to undertake to assist workers in exercising their rights. Whatever its organizational form—a trade union, a legal aid group, a narrowly focused membership organization, or a myriad of other possibilities—any agent for workers must deal with the standard "free-rider" problem. Activities that benefit workers in the totality, such as enforcing workplace rights, generate positive externalities so that the marginal benefit for the workplace as a whole is always greater than for any individual worker. Any labor organization must find ways to overcome this problem at the workplace. There is also the standard collective action problem. The marginal costs of exercising rights are likely to be lower for a group of workers than for a single individual. This combination implies that the outcome of individual action is likely to be inferior to the socially optimal level. But reaching the socially optimal level of group activity requires some mechanism or institution that aggregates worker preferences and reduces the marginal costs of exercising rights. Because the benefits of group activity require a significant number of persons to be involved, a key issue is how the institutions deal with the free-rider problem. Considering all of these requirements, Weil concludes that it is unlikely that a single nonunion institution can effectively implement worker rights, but he suggests that some mixture of groups could fill the gap left by the decline of unions. Alternatively, it is possible that union experiments with different forms of representing workers, such as the open-source unionism proposed by Freeman and Rogers (2002)—in which unions use the Internet to reduce the costs of servicing workers and form non-majority organizations inside firms—might evolve in ways that would fill the gap. But this volume did not explore that possibility.

The empirical parts of the book investigate the performance of some innovative alternative labor market organizations and initiatives in three parts. The first part deals with nonmembership activist organizations. The second section addresses how membership-based organizations attract members. The third section examines evolving union and related initiatives. The strategies and focus of these efforts are quite different, although all are initiatives that attempt to mobilize group action to solve workplace problems or improve workers' economic status.

Table 1 provides a broad overview of the institutions that the various chapters examine. The table delineates six characteristics of each of the labor institutions studied: the nature of the workers' problem that they try to address; the potential market failure that created the problem; whether the organization is membership based; its source of power and limits on that power; the funding source of the organization; and its success. We review briefly the studies in each area that underlie the summaries in the table.

Part I: Studies of Nonworker Organizations

Three chapters analyze the way NMOs operate in assisting workers. They examine the activities of human rights activists, living-wage cam-

Table 1 **A summary of labor institutions examined in this volume**

Institution or activity	Workers' problem	Market or government failure	Relation of association to constituency	Source and limits of influence	Funding sources	How successful?
Union	Economic and governance	Collective goods at workplace	Run by members	Extensive labor laws	Membership dues	Very good at raising pay/benefits but membership in decline
Professional associations	Information, advocacy in public	Status of profession in society	Run by members	May self-impose licensing	Member dues, for-profit activities	Too early to call but promising
Union-management partnerships	Economic (job growth, security)	Failure to reach mutually beneficial solutions to economic problems	Union representation on corporate boards	Laws require board members represent shareholders	Union and firm	Rare and not successful
National issues lawyers groups	Governance: enforcement of employment laws	Free riders; not attractive to private bar	Not membership	Has legal status to aid workers	Individual and foundation donors	Some successful discrimination lawsuits
Legal services centers	Governance: enforcement of employment laws	Low-wage constituency not attractive to the private bar	Not membership	Legal status to aid workers limited to certain types of cases	Government	Effective in processing unemployment claims
Human rights vigilantes	Economic and governance	Lack of information about working conditions	Not membership	Moral suasion	Unions, community groups, religious groups	High media visibility but little impact
Living-wage campaigns	Economic	Lower wages for publicly funded projects than desired	Not membership	Moral suasion	Unions, community groups	Limited impact on poverty or on employment
Training intermediaries	Economic	Free rider in training	Not membership	Moral suasion and firm self-interest	Foundations, government	Limited
Working Today	Economic	Benefits tied to employers	Not membership	Provision of group health benefits	Foundations	Limited

paigns, and lawyers' groups that assist workers in enforcing employment rights. The distinguishing feature of these initiatives and organizations is that the workers they represent do not run these organizations either directly or indirectly through elected leaders. Without a membership base, these organizations need alternative sources of funding, which oftentimes include financial support from unions or private donors. Some lawyers' groups, such as the American Civil Liberties Union (ACLU) and legal services centers, have a long history of helping workers with their legal problems. The antisweatshop initiatives of human rights activists and living-wage campaigns are more recent and aim to raise earnings and improve working conditions for low-wage workers in developing countries and in local U.S. communities, respectively. These two types of campaigns have much in common. Both mobilize community groups as well as student activists and political and religious groups. Both depend on unions for some financial support, and the unions look upon these campaigns both as ways to help nonunion workers and as an organizing tool.

While most of the institutions studied in this volume endeavor to help workers directly, the human rights vigilantes who run antisweatshop campaigns do not operate in the developing countries where they seek to improve conditions. They mobilize consumers in advanced countries to pressure firms for better treatment of workers. In chapter 2, Elliott and Freeman document that consumers care about labor standards and are willing to pay more for products made under better conditions and are unwilling to buy products made under certifiably bad conditions, such as child labor operating in horrific sweatshops. They note that human rights vigilantes have successfully raised public visibility of labor rights after such concerns had been dormant for years. These campaigns work because they gain media attention and involve churches and other morally concerned groups. The antisweatshop campaigns are among the few efforts that have mobilized student activists in recent years and almost the only area where unions have been instrumental in generating student activism.

Can consumer concern over labor standards be mobilized to improve worker conditions broadly? Based on the human rights campaigns, the efficacy of such consumer-driven movements is limited. Market pressures help drive such campaigns, yet, as Elliott and Freeman's survey data document, there is a limit to the price consumers will pay to purchase products made under good labor conditions. It is difficult to monitor whether firms comply with labor standards. In some cases, antisweatshop campaigns benefited from a series of circumstances that would be hard to predict or replicate. And even in the best of cases, the campaigns are limited to improving labor conditions for workers producing branded products for export to Western consumers. The campaigns have increased corporate codes of conduct in addressing labor standards, but Elliott and Freeman's assessment of whether targeted firms have changed their behavior is guarded. They conclude that to expand the number of workers who benefit from the antisweatshop campaigns beyond a very small number requires governmental actions and the rejuvenated International Labor Organization (ILO), which has received more resources to deal with labor standards issues, especially child labor, but which is dependent on the states, unions, and employer groups that constitute its membership.

A more direct approach than using consumer pressure to influence firms' treatment of workers is found in the living-wage referendum movement. Living-wage campaigns seek to raise the minimum wage that must be met by city contractors and/or those benefiting from municipal economic development programs. In chapter 3, Jared Bernstein reviews living-wage campaigns. Bernstein notes the rapid rise in living wage ordinances in the late 1990s/early 2000s, including ordinances in Baltimore, Boston, New York, and Los Angeles. Critics of such campaigns cite the potential for economic distortion and weaker local competitiveness, but Bernstein reports little evidence of adverse effects on employment, in part because the laws are targeted at small groups of workers in firms with municipal contracts.

A third source of nonmembership activism is lawyers' groups, many of which have helped workers with legal problems for decades. The United States has a substantial and expanding set of laws governing the workplace. But as Weil's analysis points out, however, in the absence of an agent to solve the public goods problem or to lower the costs to workers, laws are not likely to be optimally implemented and enforced. Unions have been active participants in enforcing employment laws, so the decline of unionism may further erode effective implementation and enforcement. Jolls notes in chapter 4 that hiring a private lawyer, the usual procedure of an aggrieved party who believes that someone has violated their legal rights, is less effective in the employment context for a number of reasons. Paying for a lawyer on an hourly basis is not financially feasible for lower-income workers, and contingent fee arrangements are generally not attractive to lawyers because damages in employment cases are typically small. Jolls describes two types of lawyers groups, national issues organizations and legal services centers, which help bridge the gap between the law "on the books" and the law "in action." National issues organizations focus on one or more broad-based issues and are primarily funded by private donations, and legal services organizations serve low-income individuals and are funded by the government. Jolls notes that given the funding distinction, it is not surprising that national issues organizations focus on a few high-profile, publicly-charged issues, such as discrimination, that attract private donations. In contrast, legal services centers focus on less controversial cases, such as unemployment benefits; handle a large number of cases; and are frequently explicitly restricted from handling discrimination suits. A key finding is that as a consequence of the funding structure, there is a gap with little provision of impact claims in mundane areas and day-to-day claims in high-profile areas. For example, low-wage workers are unlikely to have legal representation for a discrimination claim.

Part II: Studies of Membership-Based Initiatives

The two chapters in part II analyze the possibility that a membership organization—either union or nonunion—could represent white-collar workers, who increasingly dominate the economy but have traditionally been nonunion. Unions have had some success with white-collar workers in the public sector but represent few privately employed white-collar workers, especially in newer industries. Workers in newer, high-tech industries often have no experience with unions and see them as alien to their workplaces and employers. Factory workers may need unions, but programmers or engineers at IBM? The chapters in this section explore what attracts nonunion workers to join some type of representational membership organization, as well as examine their prospect of survival without union's legal rights to represent workers.

In chapter 5, Richard W. Hurd and John Bunge analyze a new survey of white-collar workers who experienced a union organizing campaign. The survey probes the attitudes of white-collar workers regarding the choice of a professional association versus unionization to represent their interests. Hurd and Bunge found a significant division among workers. Those favoring professional organizations feared that unions may create conflict at work or cause a loss of personal freedom and preferred an organization that developed a cooperative relationship with management. By contrast, union supporters were drawn to direct action and aggressive organizations that focus on terms and conditions of employment and workplace rights. At present, existing organizations have failed to meet the needs of these two groups. Unions have traditionally not appealed enough to the professional interests of employees who favor professional associations. Professional associations routinely eschew any form of union-like activity, although under pressure, even the American Medical Association has come to accept collective bargaining in its chapters that favor the union route. But for the most part, associations concentrate on issues such as licensing and professional opportunities rather than workplace concerns where the interests of workers and management may differ. Hurd and Bunge conclude that it is unlikely that unions will successfully expand coverage among white-collar workers unless they offer a substantially different set of services or adopt a substantially different strategic approach to better match the preferences and address the specific concerns of these workers.

In chapter 6, Hersch analyzes the organizational strategy of Working Today, a new organization that is striving to fill the lack of representation for professional and other white-collar workers. Working Today was founded to be a broadly based membership organization that represents all workers, with a special focus on independent workers. But its original design did not succeed, so the organization evolved. The evolution of Working Today demonstrates the challenge a new organization faces as it attempts to gain membership and, with membership, adequate funding for survival. In contrast to professional organizations considered by Hurd and Bunge, a broadly based organization lacks a natural constituency. Hersch models the organization in terms of generating revenues to fund its activities and building its membership base by offering public goods attractive to donors and private goods that attract individual membership. But Working Today largely failed to attract individual dues-paying members to support its public goods function of representing independent workers so that its financial survival depends on its serving as an intermediary for private selective benefits, especially group health insurance. Hersch's analysis of data on health insurance coverage suggests that, as most of the independent workers that would be attractive to insurers are already covered, an organization focused on provision of health insurance may reach a limited scale, which thereby limits the potential influence on the labor market at large.

Part III: New Union Opportunities and Initiatives

The chapters in part III examine potential opportunities to reinvigorate traditional unionism by considering the roles of nonwage benefits, union-management strategic partnerships, and expanded training opportunities.

Using several data sets covering three decades of union activity, Buchmueller, DiNardo, and Valletta examine the union effect on work hours and nonwage benefits in chapter 7. Their analysis demonstrates that for a worker with the attributes of a typical union member, a union job is associated with fewer hours worked, more vacation time, and higher health insurance and pension offer rates. While the union edge in hours worked per week and in benefit provision, especially health insurance, seems to have narrowed over time as union density has fallen, the union advantage remains substantial and offers members economic advantages far above those of any nonunion alternative. The ability of unions to form an actuarially attractive group stands in contrast to the attempt at benefits provision of an organization like Working Today.

There have been various forms of worker involvement in firm decision making, such as quality of work life and high-performance work systems. For the most part these programs provide some representation for workers at the worksite on day-to-day decisions but stop short of involving workers in the key strategic decisions such as downsizing, divesting divisions, or relocating operations. In chapter 8, Eileen Appelbaum and Larry W. Hunter examine two institutions that allow strategic participation for unions: negotiated union-management partnership decisions and union representation on corporate boards. Strategic partnerships allow some degree of union participation in decisions involving financial planning, corporate strategy, investments, technology, and production processes. Although cooperative arrangement between union and management seems to offer much to both parties, there are substantial barriers to strategic partnerships. Legal constraints limit union participation on corporate boards as corporate boards are required to represent shareholders, and shareholder interests will frequently be in conflict with the preferences of workers. Indeed, unions have good reason for distancing themselves from decisions that may have adverse consequences for their membership. Appelbaum and Hunter's survey of strategic partnerships indicates that employee involvement at the higher levels of corporate power are rare. Unlike the legally mandated works council or codetermination that exist in many European countries, in the United States such partnership agreements are not part of the legal landscape. Appelbaum and Hunter conclude by noting that the legal context is an essential component of the form and success of such partnerships.

In chapter 9, Lynch examines new community-based private-sector training initiatives. Because workers in unionized firms are more likely to receive training than other workers, the decline in unionization may lower the level of training in the economy. This creates a potential market failure for the provision of training. Nonunion training intermediaries need to be able to enforce long-term agreements between employers and workers, identify workers missed by traditional recruiting efforts, monitor training quality, and offer training beyond a single employer—that is, to exploit economies of scale. Without a proven track record, it can be difficult for training intermediaries to secure a reliable source of funding. Lynch provides an overview of a number of training intermediaries.

Conclusion

That all of the emerging labor institutions considered in this volume are struggling to develop strategies and tactics to survive and expand in the economic world is not surprising. We chose to study organizations in a formative or developmental stage to capture the process of adaptation and emergence in much the same way that analysts of industrial organization might study newly formed firms, knowing full well that 80 percent or more are unlikely to survive, or that evolutionary biologists might examine a set of mutations, knowing full well that few will pass the test of natural selection. This volume is just the first chapter in what may be a long story of innovations by nonmember organizations, by professional and other nonunion organizations, and by unions to find the best way to represent the interests of labor in an economic environment where traditional unionism is greatly weakened.

References

Dunlop, John T. 1944. *Wage determination under trade unions.* New York: Macmillan Company.

Farber, Henry. 1986. The analysis of union behavior. In *The handbook of labor economics.* Vol. 2, ed. Orley Ashenfelter and Richard Layard, 1039–89. Amsterdam: Elsevier Science.

Freeman, Richard B., and James Medoff. 1984. *What do unions do?* New York: Basic Books.

Freeman, Richard B., and Joel Rogers. 2002. Open source unionism: Beyond exclusive collective bargaining. *WorkingUSA: The Journal of Labor and Society* 6 (2): 3–4.

1

Individual Rights and Collective Agents
The Role of Old and New Workplace Institutions in the Regulation of Labor Markets

David Weil

1.1 Labor Market Institutions and the Regulation of Labor Markets

> The Committee recognizes that accomplishment of the purposes of this bill cannot be totally achieved without the fullest cooperation of affected employees.
> —Senate Report no. 91-1292, 91st Cong., 2d sess. (October 6, 1970), 10

So concluded members of the Senate in drafting the Occupational Safety and Health Act of 1970. Despite the fact that the new act created an extensive government enforcement system charged with improving workplace safety and health, the architects of the act recognized the centrality of workers to its implementation. The same might be said for a gamut of federal and state labor market regulation from the Fair Labor Standards Act of 1938 to the Family Medical Leave Act of 1993 to state workers compensation and unemployment benefit systems.

As representatives of individual employees, labor market institutions can affect the process of workplace regulation in two very different ways. First, they can affect the political process in passing legislation and, through executive agencies, in promulgating regulations—that is, the *enactment* of labor policies. Second, they can affect the way that those laws and regulations are enforced or administered—that is, the *implementation* of laws.

There is a significant literature on the role of interest groups in political processes that can inform the specific question of what alternative institu-

David Weil is associate professor of economics at Boston University School of Management and codirector of the Transparency Policy Project, Taubman Center for State and Local Government, John F. Kennedy School of Government, Harvard University.

tions might play the role of "employee lobbies" in the enactment of workplace policies. Although the specific constellation of factors that underlie political coalitions around employment issues differ from those underlying other public policy issues, the theoretical notions bounding the creation of such coalitions have parallels with those surrounding other areas of policy concern.[1] I, therefore, do not focus on the role for new labor market intermediaries in the realm of policy enactment here.

Implementation of workplace regulations arises either from the enforcement of standards created by that legislation or through the administration of programs created by legislation. For example, the federal Davis-Bacon Act that establishes floors for wages in the construction industry is implemented by enforcement actions that either directly or, through deterrence effects, indirectly raise the wages paid by construction companies to the "prevailing wage" set for that craft in a geographic market. Workers compensation legislation is implemented via administrative activities in two ways: through the incentive effect provided by experience rating of employers covered by the system on safety policies and by the filing of claims by workers injured on the job.

Implementation—whether through enforcement or administration—raises the question of the interaction between institutions created by labor policies to carry out laws and the activities of workplace based institutions that directly (e.g., unions) or indirectly (e.g., insurance companies) represent the interests of workers. To examine the need for alternative workplace institutions in this area of labor market activity requires one to establish what role institutions—regardless of form—play in the first place. It then requires one to examine the relative abilities of different types of institutions to play these roles.

This paper argues that there are two distinctive roles required for agents in the implementation of workplace policies. First, the agent must somehow help solve the public goods problem inherent in workplace regulation. Second, the agent must be able to reduce the marginal cost of exercising rights conferred to workers that are an important feature of most regulatory programs. One of the major costs in this regard is that of employer discrimination arising from exercise of those rights. Although a variety of institutions

1. For example, Stigler (1974) explains that the significant influence wielded by certain small interest groups arises from their ability to surmount the free-rider problem among supporters as a result of their potentially high payoff from political action and the ability of members of the coalition to sanction nonparticipants. In this view, an employment lobby representing individual workers faces a far greater problem of funding its political activities because of the more diffuse benefits conferred to individual workers arising from supporting the lobby's agenda and the difficulty of denying benefits or instituting sanctions because of nonparticipation. Unions address this free-rider problem by allocating a portion of dues revenues to political activities directed toward workplace issues (see Masters 1997 for a recent discussion). Whether other institutions can play a comparable role is discussed in Hersch (chap. 6 in this volume).

may be capable of stepping into the fray and serving as agents in the enactment of legislation, the roles required for implementation are more difficult to embody in a labor market agent. Laying out the theoretical requirements for such agents focuses attention on the features of "emerging labor market institutions" most important to the implementation of workplace policies.

This chapter begins with a discussion of federal labor regulations in the United States and the roles they establish for workers through the provision of individually based worker rights. It then presents a model concerning the decision by workers to exercise those rights. Based on insights from the model, it analyzes the requirements of workplace institutions in fulfilling those roles. The third section evaluates a variety of labor market institutions—beginning with labor unions as a benchmark—that potentially serve the role as agents. Based on this evaluation, the paper concludes with a discussion of how policies might be adapted to foster agents better able to serve the two central roles of labor market intermediaries in implementing labor regulations.

1.2 Individual Rights and the Need for Collective Agents

1.2.1 Federal Regulations and the Importance of Worker Rights

A complex web of laws and executive orders cover employment practices in U.S. workplaces. In most areas of workplace regulation, a division of the U.S. Department of Labor (e.g., the Wage and Hour Division; the Occupational Safety and Health Administration [OSHA]) acts as the enforcement agent for regulatory policies. The U.S. Department of Labor (DOL) exercises its authority either because of a legislative mandate providing it jurisdiction over all private sector workplaces or authority granted it arising from government's role as a major purchaser of services and products. The task of the DOL is to ascertain whether an employer is conducting human resource policies in a manner consistent with regulatory programs and then to change the behavior of those firms that are not. The majority of workplace regulations provide the DOL or other enforcement agents with a variety of civil and, in some cases, criminal sanctions to provide incentives to change behavior.

The behavioral model embodied in most federal labor policies is gaining employer adherence to standards primarily via the threat of inspection, compulsion, and fines. Adherence with regulations is secured either through the direct pressure arising from inspection activities (triggered either by the agency or covered workers) or through deterrence effects and the consequent voluntary decision to comply with labor policies. Thus, firms are assumed to act in accordance with the model of crime initially set out by Becker (1968) where crime (or here regulatory noncompliance) is a decreasing function of the return to crime or the avoidance of costs arising from regulatory compliance. Holding constant compliance costs, employers will choose not to comply with a labor regulation if it is easy to escape detection and/or because assessed penalties in the event of being detected are small.

The objectives of labor legislation and executive orders are therefore translated into practice via enforcement. There are three ways that enforcement can be undertaken under labor regulation: (1) the responsible government agency can initiate enforcement; (2) employees can initiate enforcement (via rights provided them); or (3) a mix of the previously mentioned, where employees trigger enforcement, bring government action, and/or use private rights through the courts. There is considerable divergence between the enforcement implied in statutes to actual enforcement as carried out in practice. For example, OSHA's inspection force has never exceeded 1,500 and currently hovers around 1,100. Resource limitations substantially lower the probability that a workplace will be inspected in a given year by the government. The annual probability of receiving an inspection for one of the 6.5 million establishments covered by OSHA is well below .001. Similarly, penalties under many statutes are relatively low. The ability of government agencies to fulfill their legislative mandates solely through enforcement is therefore limited. For this reason, the role of workers under workplace policies takes on great importance.

Federal workplace regulations provide employees with important roles directly affecting the implementation of those statutes. Much of workplace regulation dating back to the Fair Labor Standards Act (FLSA) of 1938 and going forward to the Family Medical Leave Act (FMLA) passed almost sixty years later provides workers with an opportunity to participate in one or more aspects of the regulatory process.[2] Most important of those rights is that of triggering regulatory activity itself. Although the right to trigger inspections dates back to some of the earliest state-level labor legislation (Common and Andrews 1936), regulations promulgated during the two most recent surges of workplace legislation or executive orders (in 1963–1974 and 1986–1993) have increased the number of regulations providing workers with a right to initiate civil actions under such laws as Title VII of the Civil Rights Act, the Americans with Disabilities Act (ADA), the Employee Polygraph Protection Act (PPA), and the Workers Adjustment and Retraining and Notification Act (WARN). This has resulted in an enormous increase in the number of cases filed under employment law, relative to other categories of litigation.[3]

2. Table 1A.1 provides a listing of the name, acronym, date of passage, and brief description of all of the regulations discussed in this paper.

3. This can be seen in the relative growth in five categories of employment related lawsuits filed in federal district courts between 1971 and 1991. The fastest-growing category in relative terms over the period has been litigation on employment law, which went in absolute terms from 4,331 cases filed in 1971 to 22,968 cases in 1991. As a result, employment law went from

Table 1.1 depicts a subset of these roles under federal workplace regulations: the right to initiate an agency action and the right to pursue private action in courts either as the first step in seeking to change employer behavior or after administrative remedies have been exhausted. Most federal legislation also establishes reporting/disclosure requirements that seek to inform employees of their rights, employer duties, or employer performance under the statute (these are depicted in the final two columns of table 1.1). In addition to these rights, many workplace statutes enumerate employee rights regarding participation in various stages of the regulatory process, such as by providing workers (or their designated representatives) with a right to accompany government officials during inspections (Occupational Safety and Health Act [OSHAct], Mine Safety and Health Act [MSHA] and to appeal decisions or participate in hearings arising from inspections (OSHA, MSHA, Contract Work Hours and Safety Standards Act [CWHSSA]).

There is little reason to believe that workers uniformly exercise rights granted them under labor policies. Studies in several different areas indicate that the propensity to exercise rights varies along systematic lines across different groups. A number of empirical studies have shown different propensities for individuals to litigate civil claims (see, for example, Hoyman and Stallworth 1981; Shavell 1987). Other studies have documented factors affecting workers' use of grievance procedures in union and nonunion workplaces (Peterson 1992; Feuille and Delaney 1992; Chachere and Feuille 1993). This literature suggests that factors related to the individual (sex, education, demographic background), the workplace environment (size, degree of conflict, management and union policies), and the specific grievance or civil problem involved affect under what circumstances individuals use their rights. Given limited government resources for enforcement, the conditions under which employees exercise their rights either to initiate suits or agency action fundamentally affect achievement of policy goals in the workplace. In a somewhat different vein, labor market programs, such as workers compensation and unemployment insurance, require that workers initiate the process leading to the issuance of benefits provided by those programs.

1.2.2 A Threshold Model of the Exercise of Individual Rights

The degree to which individual employees exercise rights granted them under labor regulations can be expected to depend on the perceived benefits versus the costs of exercising rights from the perspective of an individual worker. The benefits of exercising a right are a function of the

comprising about 6 percent of the 69,465 civil cases filed in federal district courts in 1971 to about 16 percent of the 146,790 civil cases filed in 1991. These figures are reported in Commission on the Future of Worker-Management Relations (1994, exhibit IV-3, 134).

Table 1.1 **Employee rights and reporting requirements under federal workplace regulations**

Labor statute or executive order[a]	Designated employee rights: Employee right to initiate agency action	Designated employee rights: Private right of action available to employee[a]	Designated employee rights: Private right of action, after exhaustion of administrative remedies	Reporting and disclosure requirements: Forms completed or filed with agency	Reporting and disclosure requirements: Payroll or other business data must be collected	Reporting and disclosure requirements: Notices must be posted in workplace	Reporting and disclosure requirements: Data on injuries and complaints reported
Labor standards							
FLSA	✓	✓			✓	✓	
Davis-Bacon Act	✓	✓		✓	✓	✓	
SCA					✓	✓	
Walsh-Healy Act					✓	✓	
CWHSSA		✓		✓	✓		
MSPA		✓	✓	✓	✓	✓	
Benefits							
ERISA		✓	✓	✓		✓	
COBRA		✓	✓				
Unemployment Compensation				✓	✓		
FMLA	✓	✓			✓	✓	

				Civil rights			
Title VII	✓	✓	✓	✓	✓	✓	✓
Equal Pay Act	✓	✓			✓	✓	✓
EO 11246				✓	✓	✓	
ADEA	✓	✓			✓	✓	✓
ADA	✓	✓	✓		✓	✓	✓
Rehabilitation Act						✓	✓
STAA							
				Occupational health and safety			
OSHA	✓			✓		✓	✓
MSHA	✓			✓		✓	✓
DFWA				✓		✓	✓
				Labor relations			
NLRA		✓				✓	
LMRDA		✓		✓			
RLA						✓	
				Hiring and separation decisions			
Veterans Re-employment Act		✓			✓		
IRCA		✓		✓		✓	
WARN		✓				✓	

[a]Full names of statutes, date of passage, and brief description provided in table 1A.1.

impact of labor legislation on the outcome of concern to the worker. For example, initiating an OSHA inspection potentially improves working conditions for the worker by diminishing or removing the risk of an injury or illness. The greater the level of perceived risk faced by the worker, the more likely they are to initiate an inspection or otherwise seek to affect redress of the problem. Similarly, the greater the divergence between the wages paid to workers and the wages that they are entitled to under the law (e.g., because of premium pay required for overtime), the more likely a worker is to exercise rights to initiate actions under the FLSA.

In order to ascertain the magnitude of these benefits, workers must acquire information on the *current* and *legally permissible* level of a regulated outcome. The costs of exercising rights are primarily a function of the costs of gathering this information. These are composed of costs associated with (1) obtaining information regarding the existence of basic rights as well as the standards to which employers are held accountable;[4] (2) gathering information on the current state of workplace conditions—a particular problem if the risks are complex as in the case of safety and health (Viscusi 1983; Viscusi and O'Connor 1984); and (3) learning about the specific details of how the law is administered (e.g., the procedures to initiate a complaint inspection). In addition to information-related costs, workers face significant costs arising from potential employer retaliation (the economic losses associated with retaliatory reassignment or, in the extreme, being fired)[5] as well as the potential cost of job loss arising from the chance that compliance will force a firm to reduce employment in the long run.

The decision facing a worker on whether to exercise a right is represented diagrammatically in figure 1.1. The horizontal axis, X_j represents the difference between current workplace conditions (e.g., exposure to a health risk; actual wage rate for hours of work) and the regulatory standard for that workplace outcome for workplace *j*. The value of X_j is defined where

$X_j < 0$ if the current workplace provides conditions above permissible levels (i.e., the firm goes beyond compliance required by the standard);

$X_j = 0$ if the current workplace provides conditions equal to the required levels (i.e., the firm is exactly in compliance with the law); and

4. This is a recurring problem under workplace regulation. For example, a survey of OSHA compliance officers by the U.S. GAO concluded that "many OSHA inspectors believe workers' participation [in OSHA] is limited by their lack of knowledge about their rights and lack of protection from employer reprisal" (U.S. GAO 1989). The decline in the take-up rate for unemployment insurance has been partly ascribed to the lack of information to workers about their access to unemployment benefits (Wandner and Skinner 2000). Freeman and Rogers (1999, chap. 6) also present survey evidence indicating pervasive worker misperceptions regarding their rights under employment and labor laws.

5. The costs of retaliation may be even more severe, such as in the well-known 1996 case of apparel workers in El Monte, California, held in virtual captivity by their employer who used physical intimidation to prevent the workers from leaving.

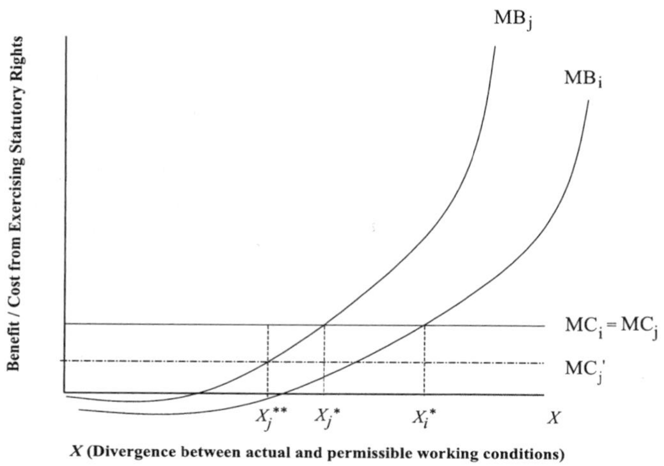

Fig. 1.1 Threshold model of employee exercise of rights

$X_j > 0$ if the current workplace provides conditions below permissible levels (i.e., the firm is out compliance).

This means that as X_j increases, a workplace falls further out of compliance with the regulatory requirement. In the case of health and safety regulations, this means that as X_j increases, worker exposure to risk increasingly goes beyond the risk levels if workplaces compiled with standards; for regulations related to compensation like FLSA or Davis-Bacon, this means that actual pay increasingly falls below that required under the statute. For a program like workers compensation, increases in X_j imply that the earnings received by the injured worker diverge more and more from those he or she is entitled by the program.

Given this definition of X_j, the figure presents two marginal-benefit functions. The lower function (MB_i) represents the marginal worker *i* in a workplace *j* who has the highest individual preference for compliance with the regulatory standard. As such, this function represents the worker who will first exercise his or her statutory right in the workplace. I assume that the marginal benefit of exercising a right that moves the firm into greater compliance with the standard is positive and increasing in X_j.

Because a violation of a workplace standard typically affects many workers and is often associated with violations of other standards that might not directly affect the worker triggering the inspection, employee exercise of workplace rights displays positive externalities. Because of this, the marginal benefit for the workplace as a whole is always higher than that of the marginal worker for any X_j. The upper marginal-benefit function in Figure 1.1 represents workers at the workplace as a whole (MB_j) and reflects the vertical aggregation of benefits for all affected workers for any given state X_j.[6]

Figure 1.1 first presents a simple case where the costs of exercising a right are invariant across the different levels of X_j and the same for an individual worker as they are for the workplace as a whole (the upper line, where $MC_I = MC_j$). If rights are vested at the individual level, worker *i* will choose to exercise the rights at the state of the workplace X_i^*), where $MB_i = MC_i$. Given that the decision is made by the marginal worker with the greatest preference for workplace conditions consonant with regulatory standards (i.e., the lowest tolerance for current conditions being out of compliance), X_i^* represents the level of noncompliance that will trigger the exercise of rights for that workplace when left to the decision of this "threshold" individual worker.

Given the public good character of the benefits ensuing from the exercise of rights, X_i^* is not optimal for the workplace as a whole because the marginal worker decides only on the basis of his or her individual preference. Accounting for all workers in the workplace, the optimal threshold in figure 1.1 is X_j^*, where $X_i^* > X_j^*$. That is, the exercise of right taken at the individual level leads to a "higher" threshold (i.e., current conditions being more out of compliance with standards) than the threshold that would prevail if the preferences of all workers were considered. Workplace rights, therefore, will be underutilized because the collective benefits arising from their action are not factored into the individual decision.

If the cost of exercising a right exhibits increasing returns to scale, such as because of efficiencies gained from collecting information at the workplace, or multiworkplace level, the divergence between threshold for an individual versus collective group of workers grow even further. Protections against discrimination for exercise of rights afforded by a method of collectively exercising rights may represent a second reason that the marginal cost of exercise may be far lower for a group of workers. In either case, this situation is depicted in figure 1.1 as MC_j', the lower dotted horizontal line, which is below the marginal-cost function faced by an individual. The collective threshold for exercise of rights now occurs at X_j^{**}, arising in an even larger gap from the individual threshold for exercising the right, X_i^*.

Thus, the problem arising from the structure of workplace regulations is that if left to the individual worker, the threshold for exercise of rights lies

6. The degree to which MB_i diverges from MB_j will differ across workplace regulations. For example, there are greater divergences between the functions for regulations like OSHA, FLSA, or policies dealing with discrimination where the risks or problems faced by one worker will likely be more pervasive and therefore affect many other workers as well. In contrast, under benefit programs like workers compensation or unemployment, the spillovers are likely much smaller because the program primarily confers benefits to the worker directly affected. The implications of these differences are discussed in section 1.3.

above the threshold optimal from the workplace—and societal—level. In order to close this gap, one must surmount the problems of (1) aggregating preferences across workers and (2) reducing the marginal cost of exercise of those rights.

1.2.3 Workplace Agents and the Exercise of Rights

A collective workplace agent can potentially solve the problem described previously. It can do so first by internalizing the positive externality to workers arising from a claim as a representative of all workers in the unit. A workplace agent can also gather and disseminate information, thereby lowering the cost of information acquisition faced by individuals. The specific elements required of such an agent are straightforward and flow from the threshold model in figure 1.1:

1. Interests aligned with workers—specifically an interest in representing the collective preferences of workers in regard to working conditions
2. A means of efficiently gathering and disseminating information on rights, administrative procedures, and the nature of workplace risks
3. A method of providing protection from employer discrimination against individual workers for their exercise of rights

The need for an agent to play these roles points to a conundrum embedded in many workplace regulations. Although most of the policies listed in table 1.1 create rights focused on the individual worker, social efficiency is enhanced where *individually based* rights are exercised via an agent operating in the *collective interest*.

The previous discussion also raises a related issue often overlooked in examining workplace regulation. One cannot detach the role of "command and control" regulatory systems from the operation of labor market institutions, even where labor market intermediaries are not explicitly set out in the legislation as the explicit agent for implementation. It is often assumed that under traditional regulatory structures, the government alone acts as the agent of enforcement. Yet as the review of labor regulations and the threshold model indicates, implementing workplace policies includes a role for workers and in that way for labor market intermediaries. The fact that an important avenue for enforcement of those laws is the exercise of individual rights belies a more complex interaction built into the structure of regulatory systems.

1.3 Alternative Labor Market Institutions

1.3.1 Unions and the Enforcement of Labor Policies

While a number of different arrangements can potentially satisfy the conditions for a workplace agent, labor unions potentially fulfill many of them through their basic agency functions.[7] Specifically, unions act as purveyors of workplace-based public goods regarding labor policies both by internalizing the benefits relating to worker exercise of rights across workers in the unit and by lowering the costs of information acquisition.

As the elected representative of workers, a union has incentives to act on behalf of the collective interests of members in the bargaining unit. This means that a union will not base perceptions of the benefit of pursuing a claim under laws based on the preferences of an individual worker at the margin but on inframarginal evaluations of those benefits. In facing this allocation problem, a union can vertically aggregate preferences for the "public goods" represented by workplace regulations, following the model of public goods seminally described in Samuelson (1955).[8]

Unions can efficiently gather and disseminate information on the existence of workplace laws and rights created by those laws. Unions provide this information formally through educational programs, in apprenticeship training, or through supplying educational materials. Informally, union leaders or staff can alert members of their rights when a problem or issue arises. Unions also provide information on the existence of specific underlying problems, particularly in the area of safety and health (see Viscusi 1983). This information may be collected and disseminated through formal programs or channels or informally via the union structure or fellow workers.

Unions also offer individual workers assistance in the actual exercise of their rights. This may result from the operation of committees established under collective bargaining, as is common in safety and health, or via the help of union staff who can trigger inspections, oversee pension fund investments, or assist members file unemployment claims. Most important, unions can substantially reduce the costs associated with potential employer discrimination by helping affected employees to use antidiscrimination provisions of the labor policies and providing this protection via collective bargaining agreements regulating dismissals. The formal protection

7. Williamson (1985, 254) points out, "[u]nions can both serve as a source of information regarding employee needs and preferences." In addition to Williamson, the role of unions in providing basic agency functions is discussed in Freeman and Medoff (1984), particularly in regard to personnel practices and benefits.

8. There might also be divergences in behavior arising from a number of sources. Median voter models of union behavior would predict that union leadership would tend to pursue policies reflective of more senior members of the unit which might not be synonymous with the public goods solution to benefit valuation. Alternatively, principal/agent divergences in interest may also lead away from optimal behaviors from the perspective of collective worker interests. For example, the union may have incentives to "overuse" certain rights for strategic reasons unrelated to the workplace regulation, for example, as a source of pressure in collective bargaining or strikes (U.S. GAO 2000). However, principal/agent divergences in behavior may be moderated both through electoral processes and by worker recourse via duty of fair representation claims that tend to induce unions to pursue activities consonant with the preferences of represented workers.

offered by a collective agreement provides security unavailable in the vast majority of nonunion workplaces, even where a grievance procedure exists (Feuille and Delaney 1992).

There might also be divergences in behavior between workers and unions arising from a number of sources. Median voter models of union behavior would predict that union leadership would tend to pursue policies reflective of more senior members of the unit that might not be synonymous with the public goods solution to benefit valuation. Alternatively, principal/agent divergences in interest may also lead away from optimal behaviors from the perspective of collective worker interests. For example, a union may have incentives to exercise certain rights for strategic reasons unrelated to the workplace regulation, for example, as a source of pressure in collective bargaining or strikes (U.S. General Accounting Office [GAO] 2000). Similarly, there might be cases where the political incentive of union leaders compels them to take adversarial positions toward management to enhance their position with respect to union members key to electoral success but precluding the union from achieving longer term solutions that might be welfare enhancing to workers (members and nonmembers) as a whole. For example, a union's corporate campaign that publicly exposes management's failure to adhere to the letter of the FMLA as part of a larger effort to increase collective bargaining strength might preclude the union and management from achieving more creative and flexible solutions regarding leave policies in the future.[9]

As such, some of the exercise of rights associated with unionization in table 1.2 might not be welfare enhancing to the extent that it pushes workers away from desirable resolution of their workplace problems. However, it should also be noted that systematic principal/agent divergences in behavior between unions and workers may be moderated through electoral processes and by worker recourse via duty of fair representation claims, both of which tend to induce unions to pursue activities more consonant with the preferences of represented workers.

In any event, union activity on behalf of the collective preferences of the workers in the bargaining unit can be expected to induce greater usage of rights. This leads to a testable empirical hypothesis: government labor market policies should be more fully implemented in unionized workplaces than in otherwise comparable nonunion workplaces. This hypothesis can be tested by examining empirical studies of labor market regulations that have measured union/nonunion differences in implementation.

Table 1.2 summarizes evidence of union impacts on both enforcement and compliance under a wide array of labor policies. It confirms the

9. This has been a recurring critique of corporate campaign tactics that rely on exposing management violations of various labor policies in the course of organizing or collective-bargaining efforts.

Table 1.2 **Impact of labor unions on enforcement and compliance with workplace regulations**

Labor statute or executive order	Union impact on enforcement	Union impact on employer compliance	Study
Fair Labor Standards Act—Overtime Provisions	Inclusion of premium pay for overtime standard in collective agreements	Increase the probability of compliance for unionized workers	Enforcement: Bureau of National Affairs ([BNA] 1997) Compliance: Ehrenberg and Schumann (1982); Trejo (1991)
ERISA	Increase in degree of scrutiny over eligible pension plans	Require more strict adherence to eligibility and financial management standards by employers	Enforcement: Langbert (1995) Compliance: Freeman (1985)
OSHA	Higher inspection probabilities; longer inspections; shorter abatement duration; higher penalties	Higher rates of compliance with specific OSHA standards	Enforcement: Weil (1991, 1992) Compliance: Weil (1996)
MSHA	Higher inspection probabilities; longer/more intense inspections; shorter abatement duration; higher penalties	n.a.	Weil (1990)
EO 11246	No impact on probability of receiving a federal contract compliance review	n.a.	Leonard (1985)
WARN	Increase in the probability of filing suit under WARN	No impact on the probability of providing advance notice to affected workers	Enforcement: U.S. GAO (1993); Ehrenberg and Jakubson (1990) Compliance: Addison and Blackburn (1994)
ADA	n.a.	Raise probability that firms comply with four core practices required by ADA	Stern and Balser (1996)
FMLA	Improved information to workers regarding rights and eligibility under FMLA	Increase probability that leave was fully paid by employer as provided	Budd and Brey (2000)
Workers Compensation	n.a.	Increase in probability of filings for benefits among eligible workers and benefit levels for given disability level	Butler and Worrall (1983); Hirsch, Macpherson, and DuMond (1997)
Unemployment Compensation	n.a.	Increase in the probability of filing for benefits among eligible workers	Blank and Card (1991); Budd and McCall (1997, 2004)

Note: n.a. = not available.

predicted presence of systematic differences between union versus non-union enforcement and compliance outcomes across diverse labor regulations and workplace policies. This includes regulations dating back to early labor legislation like the FLSA, where unions appreciably raise the probability of compliance with premium pay for overtime. Unions also increase an array of enforcement outcomes and compliance with health and safety standards under both OSHA and MSHA as well as provisions of the Employee Retirement and Income Security Act (ERISA). Unions also raise enforcement and compliance under some of the newest labor policies, such as WARN, ADA, and FMLA. Finally, unions substantially increase the probability that workers will receive benefits that they are eligible for under the two major workplace programs administered at the state level: unemployment insurance and workers compensation.[10] Thus, with the exception of their neutral impact on contract compliance reviews under Executive Order 11246, empirical studies of labor market enforcement indicate that unions act as agents that assist employee exercise of rights.

This review suggests that unions can address the major factors leading to a divergence between individual and collective exercise of rights under many different regulatory policies, albeit with potential principal/agent problems between members and unions that might diminish social welfare under certain circumstances. As a result, the role of unions as agents provides a useful benchmark to compare other potential parties that might play this role in the absence of union presence at the workplace.

How do other labor market intermediaries stack up in solving the problem posed by the individual versus collective exercise of rights? We evaluate six potential intermediaries in the following, each evaluated along the same dimensions developed in section 1.2. The following sections do not provide an exhaustive review of these mechanisms, many of which are discussed elsewhere in this volume. The intention instead is to examine each of the alternatives against the three dimensions described previously and indicate the relative strengths and weaknesses of each. This provides an analytic backdrop for the other papers that look into some of these mechanisms in greater depth.

1.3.2 National Issue Organizations and Legal Service Organizations

Christine Jolls (chap. 4 in this volume) describes the activities of national issue organizations that deal at least in part with employment law (e.g., American Civil Liberties Union; National Association for the Advancement of Colored People Legal Defense Fund; National Employment Law Project) and legal service organizations (primarily the organizations administered by the Legal Services Corporation, created by Congress in

10. This latter effect of unions as workplace agents is particularly important given the long-term decline in benefit recipiency under these programs (Wandner and Skinner 2000).

1974) as alternative institutions that assist employees exercise their rights. The role of national issue and legal service organizations lie either in terms of their impact on the public goods problem or in lowering the costs of exercise of rights (including the costs arising from employer discrimination).

Both types of organizations can act on the public goods aspect of the problem to the extent that they can serve as an agent to aggregate preferences for collective actions or lead workers to do so. One obvious mechanism for legal organizations to do so is by undertaking class action suits on behalf of groups of workers. Illustrative of this role are several recent cases of legal organizations doing so on behalf of agricultural workers and apparel workers in regard to violations arising under the FLSA.

What incentives and capacities do these organizations have to play this role? The evidence presented in Jolls suggests that the nature of funding for the two organizations creates incentives that lead both organizations away from the role of solving the workplace public goods problem. National interest organizations tend to focus on fundraising and involvement in high-profile litigation focused on setting larger legal precedent. Legal service organizations, in contrast, tend to focus on specific cases that arise from individuals coming to those organizations. Thus, national interest organizations focus on "high-profile, publicly charged issues . . . [working on] a few . . . influential cases," while legal service organizations "tend to work on many routine cases" (Jolls, chap. 4 in this volume).

The different character of the subject matter of legal activities suggests a fundamental agency problem in both organizations that may reduce their abilities to play a role analogous to labor unions in the workplace. National interest organizations act at least in part as agents of their principal sources of funding—private donors and foundations. Those parties seek to maximize their investment (donations or grants) in terms of public impact (or at least perceptions of public impact). This tends to push those organizations away from workplace-level interventions and toward cases involving major precedent and public controversy.

Legal service organizations, in contrast, are agents of their very different funding source, the U.S. Congress. Although Congress cannot be considered a principal with a single utility function, Jolls's evidence is consistent with a story that the long-term coalition necessary to sustain funding is one where the median congressional voter seeks to focus those organizations on the modest goal of lowering the cost faced by low-income individuals in pursuing civil claims. The median congressional voter, however, has historically rejected the notion that legal services should act as an agent for larger groupings of individuals.[11] In this view, legal service organizations

11. Jolls (chap. 4 in this volume) cites a number of examples of Congress curtailing class action activity by legal service attorneys. The median voter hypothesis advanced here could be more rigorously tested by examining changes in legal service activities over time given shifts in political coalitions in Congress.

might lower the marginal cost of exercise of rights, but only on an ad hoc basis, driven by the individual worker decision to approach legal services for assistance in the first place.

1.3.3 Other Public Interest Organizations

There are many other public interest groups that have been organized to deal with the workplace issues, with less focus on legal assistance than the organizations studied by Jolls. These include Committees on Safety and Health (COSH) groups, organized in a number of states and focused on safety and health; disabled workers groups focused on issues of workers compensation, the ADA, and, to a lesser extent, OSHA; and groups focused on workplace regulations affecting low-wage workers in specific industries (e.g., "sweatshop" problems in apparel; child labor problems in agriculture or retail). One activity of many of these groups is lobbying and participating in legislative and executive forums at the state and federal level. In this capacity, they attempt to affect either the enactment of laws and regulations or appropriations toward existing programs as opposed to the implementation issues of central interest here (see Hersch, chap. 6 in this volume, for discussion of the role of new labor market institutions on legislative enactment).

However, a second set of activities pursued by these groups is direct worker assistance. In the 1970s, for example, many COSH groups formed in states to provide information and assistance to workers under OSHA. The intention of many of these groups was to provide workers—in particular nonunion workers—with information regarding their rights under the newly passed act. A comparable group was formed for nonunion miners to assist them exercise rights under MSHA (McAteer 1985).

These groups tend to receive their donations from a mix of labor unions (a significant source of funding for COSH and disabled worker groups in particular), foundations, and individual workers or donors. The importance of labor unions as a funding source as well as small donors (often those with a personal connection to the issue) tends to lessen the agency problem discussed in regard to either national interest or legal service organizations. This potentially leads to better alignment between the objectives of the groups and those of the workers they intend to assist.[12]

The main difficulty facing these groups is that they operate outside of the workplace, although one of their intentions is to help solve the public

12. This is not to argue that the alignment between these organizations and workers is as close as found in the case of labor unions. For example, donors to COSH or disabled worker groups may be similarly interested in "large impacts," such as those funding national interest organizations, which may skew institutional activities in a similar manner. The importance of union funds may also lead these organizations to direct their resources toward certain nonunion workplaces of strategic interest to unions. Even more, union funding could lead COSH groups to devote their resources supplementing the activities of unions in already organized workplaces. There is some evidence of the latter behavior described in the following.

goods problem that exists within it. This limits their potential impact on the exercise of rights primarily to an informational role—that is, toward reducing the marginal costs of exercise of rights. However, even here their impact is modest: their lack of presence at the work site means that they can have limited impact on the threat of discrimination arising from exercise of rights, perhaps the highest cost facing workers. It is noteworthy that COSH groups in many states have concentrated much of their efforts over time in their work in conjunction with unions and unionized workplaces, where they take advantage of an established agent (comparable to the effects of workplace committees described in the following).[13]

The threshold problem presented by workers compensation and unemployment insurance is somewhat different than that posed by OSHA or MSHA. Here, the public goods aspects of providing information and assistance regarding benefits are somewhat less than in regulatory programs (that is, the benefits provided by the program look less like public goods). The threshold problem therefore arises more from the difference between the marginal costs of disseminating information to workers on a collective versus individual basis. The potential for employer discrimination is also much less for these benefit programs, in part because their financing (and, therefore, the potential costs to employers) is disconnected from the provision of benefits. As a result, the network of disabled worker organizations can potentially play a more fruitful role—outside of the workplace—in providing information on the availability of benefits and assistance in filing claims. Although alternative institutions potentially could assist workers in the area of unemployment insurance in a comparable way, there is an absence of a large network of such organizations in this realm.[14]

1.3.4 Mandated Workplace Committees

A number of U.S. states mandate that employers establish workplace safety and health committees. Mandated workplace committees potentially can play an important regulatory role because they can have better and more timely information about prevailing health and safety condi-

13. Indicative of this is the history of "New Directions" grants provided by OSHA in the 1970s and 1980s that provided financial assistance for promotion of private health and safety programs. The majority of these grants went either to unions or to joint COSH-union initiatives.

14. Differences in the presence of worker groups to assist disabled workers versus unemployed workers once again raises the economics of interest group formation discussed by Stigler (1974) and others. The longevity of the effects of workplace disability as opposed to the transient nature of unemployment creates greater incentives for the formation of sustainable organizations concerning the former issue and the difficulty of sustaining organizations (particularly over the course of business cycles) in the latter area. Thus, to the extent that workers groups have formed over the latter issue, they have been linked to industries facing periods of intense crisis (e.g., steel) or deep recessions. After crises pass (or industry restructuring occurs and workers find other employment) these groups tend to disband. See Hoerr (1988) for a discussion of these types of assistance groups in the steel industry.

tions. In addition, committees might be able to reach agreement with management about resolving particular workplace problems that are better tailored to underlying conditions than might an outside government regulator who must conform to more general standards or procedures (Rogers 1995).

Workplace committees conceivably fulfill the two roles for a workplace intermediary for implementing labor policies. First, by being mandated by the government (rather than voluntarily adopted by employers), the committee can serve as an agent of employees at the workplace. In this way, it has an intrinsic interest in vertically aggregating preferences for the public goods created by workplace regulations. Second, a well-functioning committee can provide information on worker rights, workplace conditions, and administrative procedures, thereby lowering MC_j. Finally, a workplace committee might also provide a protective shield for individual workers who might be more inclined to report problems before, during, or after inspections than they would in the absence of such committees. As a result, mandated committee structures potentially fulfill the major roles described previously.

The primary question in evaluating workplace committees concerns whether mandated committees function effectively. One major concern comes back to the agency problem: if workers view the committee primarily as a creature of the employer, the nature of the agency relation between the committee and workers is weakened, and it will be less effective in its public goods provision role as well as in lowering the perceived costs arising from discrimination. A second question concerns its capacities to undertake activities effectively (even if it functions independently of the employer). This will affect its ability to appreciably lower the marginal costs of exercising rights.

The experience of mandated health and safety committees in the state of Oregon provide one indication of the determinants of their effectiveness. Weil (1999) examines the impact of committee mandates on the union effect on OSHA enforcement. Comparing OSHA inspection outcomes for two years preceding and following implementation of committee mandates, he finds that mandated committees significantly increase the *differential* between union and nonunion enforcement, arising from considerable strengthening of enforcement activity in union workplaces and only modest increases in enforcement in nonunion workplaces. The only exception to this is in the case of large nonunion establishments where committees have more appreciable impacts on enforcement activity.

The results suggest that mandated committees do not represent a simple solution to the problem of finding alternative workplace institutions to help implement labor policies. Effectiveness in filling the roles laid out in figure 1.1 is a function of at least two factors. First, the regulations mandating committees in the first place must allow the establishment of independent workplace structures. Safety and health committee mandates vary enormously in terms of their delegated roles, authority, and the methods in which they are established (see Bernard 1995; Reilly, Paci, and Holl 1995; Rogers 1995; U.S. GAO 1992). Second, committee effectiveness is related to antecedent conditions in the workplace itself, in particular characteristics of workforce that affect committees' capacity to take on its activities as well as its ability to function independently. In addition to the size of the workplace, factors might include worker turnover, skill and education level, and factors affecting informal worker organization.

1.3.5 Third-Party Monitors

In recent years, the use of third-party monitors as regulatory agents has been discussed as a possible solution to limited government enforcement resources. Proposals for the use of third-party monitors (such as accounting firms) in the area of safety and health gained public attention and became the subject of criticism when it appeared as part of Vice President Al Gore's "Reinventing Government" proposals for the federal sector.

In more recent years, third-party monitors have been used as part of innovative efforts for enforcing the FLSA provisions on minimum wage and overtime in the U.S. apparel industry. In particular, the DOL has secured agreement by apparel manufacturers to use third parties to monitor aspects of compliance with the FLSA as part of larger settlement agreements with the DOL. The role of these monitors is to be able to conduct surprise inspections on behalf of the manufacturer among subcontractors used by the manufacturer. The results of the inspections can be used by the manufacturer to monitor cases where noncompliant contractors are violating the act, thereby exposing the manufacturer to civil penalties and, more importantly, supply disruptions (U.S. Department of Labor 1999).

Monitors can either be drawn from the private sector (accounting firms; for-profit enterprises specifically created for this function) or the not-for-profit sector (that is, independent organizations created to act as workplace monitors). In the case of monitors created under "Compliance Program Agreements" between the DOL and apparel manufacturers, their structure, funding, and activities are negotiable, although the DOL has "model provisions" that it encourages manufacturers to adopt (U.S. Department of Labor 1998).

The agency relations of third-party monitors are complex in that—at least on paper—they act as agents of government. However, in reality they are agents of other private parties who have an interest in allowing them to take on certain quasi-governmental activity. In the area of apparel, third-party monitors are usually the agents of manufacturers who use them to monitor their subcontractors in terms of compliance with minimum wage and overtime laws required by FLSA. Manufacturers have the incentive to agree to use such outside monitors to ensure that their sewing contractors comply with labor standards because of concern that noncompliance with laws can lead their goods to be embargoed by the DOL. Resulting delays in shipments to retailers can have costly consequences to the manufacturer (Weil 2002). As a result, the interests of third-party monitors, though agents of the manufacturer, are also aligned to some extent with those of the government.[15]

Third-party monitors, then, may help deal with the threshold gap depicted in figure 1.1 more in their capacity to supplement the enforcement activities of the DOL than in their potential role as an institutional agent for workers. Although the presence of a third-party monitor raises the probability that a given workplace will be inspected and that workers might have an opportunity to report problems, the threshold problem is much the same as under the traditional regulatory system. Monitors may, however, lower the marginal cost associated with worker exercise of rights, particularly if they provide a "shield" against discrimination if workers bring labor standards violations to their attention. The degree to which they play this role has, in large part, to do with the specific monitoring protocols negotiated between manufacturers, monitors, and the government. Examining how different types of protocols affect the exercise of rights and implementation of regulations presents an important area for future study.

1.3.6 Alternative Dispute Resolution Systems

On the surface, alternative dispute resolution (ADR) systems may not seem to fit the description of an emerging labor market institution in that ADR describes a *process* of resolving disputes arising under workplace regulation rather than being a workplace entity per se. It has been used in a variety of forums, but ADR is discussed here in its specific use as a means for resolving employment disputes arising under labor statutes through mediation, arbitration, or some combination of the two (for an overview of the use of ADR in this capacity and others, see Lipsky and Seeber 1998; Dunlop and Zack 1997, 2001).

Under ADR, an employee seeks recourse to a problem such as discrimination via an internal mediation or arbitration procedure rather than through the relevant agency or via the courts. Because these procedures are administered within the company and predominately rely, at least at initial stages, on mediation, disputes can in theory be resolved more rapidly.[16]

Two major Supreme Court decisions, the *Gilmer* decision of 1991 and

15. Where monitoring has been adopted out of strictly voluntary agreements and lacking the "teeth" of government sanctions, such as the right to embargo goods, the identification of third-party monitors with regulatory objectives will be far weaker. This raises one of the limitations of using third-party monitors in the international arena to police labor standards where there is no comparable government authority underlying the agreements. Third-party monitors in the international labor standards arena are discussed in Elliott and Freeman (2003).

16. Lipsky and Seeber (1998) report that 87 percent of ADR processes of the Fortune 1000 corporations that they sampled used mediation at least once in the prior three years.

the *Circuit City* decision in 2001 raise the stakes of ADR as a means of resolving such claims.[17] Both *Gilmer* and *Circuit City* extend the Federal Arbitration Act from its historic focus on commercial disputes to those involving employment contracts. Specifically, they support the right of an employer to require employees to sign prehire agreements compelling them to use company-sponsored dispute resolution (usually arbitration) for statutory disputes rather than using the administrative channels established in the legislation (as described in table 1.1). In effect, employees forgo their right to pursue such claims through administrative channels as a condition of employment.[18]

Not surprisingly, the *Gilmer* and *Circuit City* decisions led to increases in the use of ADR for employment disputes. The use of ADR under these circumstances is controversial, most notably because of doubts that employees will receive a fair hearing in company-sponsored arbitration or other ADR systems. In fact, many companies in the immediate wake of *Gilmer* adopted arbitration procedures that were decidedly tilted toward the employer in that companies unilaterally chose the arbitrator, established rules of procedure (including barring formal depositions or even written records of the arbitration), and held the right to unilaterally change those procedures.[19] In response to the employer bias of many post-*Gilmer* ADR systems, a number of the institutions drawn upon by companies to serve in arbitration proceedings (including the American Association of Arbitrators and the American Bar Association) created a "Due Process Protocol," which establishes that signatory associations and their members will only serve as arbitrators in systems that adhere to basic conditions of procedural fairness.[20]

If the "Due Process Protocol" is able to assure the fairness of such proceedings in nonunion workplaces, does establishing internal procedures for mediation and/or arbitration of statutory disputes provide a solution to the rights problem portrayed in figure 1.1? On one hand, ADR can be seen

17. *Gilmer v. Interstate/Johnson Lane Corp.* 500 U.S. 20, 111 S. Ct. 1647 (1991); *Circuit City Stores, Inc. v. Adams.* 532 U.S. 105 (2001).

18. In a more recent Supreme Court decision than *Circuit City, EEOC v. Waffle House, Ind.,* (534 U.S. 279 [2002]), the Supreme Court held that an individual employee's assent to a preemployment arbitration agreement did not preclude the Equal Employment Opportunity Commission (EEOC) from bringing its own enforcement actions against an employer, including seeking remedies for individual workers. Although the ruling does not overturn *Circuit City,* it does underscore an agency's continued interest and ability to seek its own actions on behalf of workers in enforcing statutes like the ADA.

19. See, for example, "Some Employees Lose Right to Sue for Bias at Work," *New York Times,* March 18, 1994, A1.

20. Among those conditions, the Due Process Protocol specifies that the arbitration system provide employees with a right to representation in proceedings and a right to participate in the selection of an arbitrator or mediator drawn from "a demographically diverse panel of trained mediators and arbitrators" (Dunlop and Zack 2001, 6). The Due Process Protocol has been adopted by a wide variety of institutions drawn on by companies for arbitration.

as a means of lowering the marginal cost of exercise of rights in that it makes (potentially) the cost for the disputant lower than under the traditional system where workers must press their own claims under various federal labor statutes. By lowering the costs of exercise, the gap depicted in figure 1.1 narrows.

On the other hand, the use of ADR by parties in nonunion workplaces presupposes that an employee comes forward with a claim. Yet the existence of an internal procedure (and the requirement to use that system via prehire agreement) does not inherently create an agent for those employees.[21] The fact that the procedure is governed by the employer rather than a third party (i.e., the government) may further dampen the extent to which workers collectively might pursue a claim involving more widespread violations of a statutory right.

As a result, ADR may be most beneficial in those cases where the divergence between individual and workplace marginal benefits is relatively small, such as in resolving disputes arising under workers compensation or very specific claims under statutes like FLSA or ERISA. But in many areas of workplace regulation—particularly regarding workplace discrimination that has motivated many nonunion companies to adopt internal arbitration systems[22]—ADR by itself does not solve the public goods problem. However, it remains to be seen if the growth of ADR potentially fueled by the *Circuit City* decision will induce existing institutions (e.g., labor unions, workers' rights groups, law firms) to serve a new role as third-party representatives within nonunion firms. If existing or new players move into this representation role, ADR processes may prove an important venue for the exercise of employment rights.

1.4 Concluding Thoughts and Implications

> It is easy for politicians, or reformers, or trade union officials to boast of the laws which they have secured for labor, and it is just as easy to overlook the details, or appropriations, or competent officials that are needed to make them enforceable.
>
> –Commons and Andrews 1936, 448

Can emerging labor market institutions play the role of collective agent in a workplace that draws heavily upon the exercise of individual rights for

21. Note that this argument also supports the use of ADR in cases where some form of worker representative is already present, such as in unionized workplaces. Here, ADR can lead to more speedy and cost-effective resolution of statutory disputes at the same time that workers' interests are protected through third-party representation.

22. The *Gilmer* case involved a case of age discrimination under Federal law; *Circuit City* involved a charge of discrimination because of sexual preference under state law; *Waffle House, Inc.* arose from a discrimination claim under the ADA.

implementation? Are there emerging labor market institutions that plausibly can take up this role where labor unions are not present?

Table 1.3 summarizes the analysis of the ability of the alternative workplace institutions surveyed previously to do so. An implication of the foregoing analysis is that it may be difficult for a single institution to play the varied roles required of a collective agent across a range of workplace regulations. In particular, absent a labor union, it is difficult to devise an institutional arrangement that effectively aligns its interests with those of the workforce and at the same time has the kind of access to the workplace necessary to act upon those interests. Nonetheless, table 1.3 suggests that a mixed approach, incorporating different institutions for different areas of regulation, might help to close the gap arising in implementation of workplace regulations. Posed in this way, the policy question shifts from a focus on the agent per se and to the functions that must be performed to assure that the objectives of workplace regulations are achieved. For example, one set of policy options revolves around reducing the marginal cost of exercise of rights. This might include finding new means of making workers aware of their statutory rights or reducing the perceived cost of exercise by improving protections against employer discrimination (e.g., administrative procedures that protect employees' identity in the case of triggering inspections). Recent efforts by OSHA to create an extensive "workers' page" on their website provides one example of interventions of this type. The page includes instructions on filing a complaint with OSHA (including downloadable complaint forms), information about statutory coverage, employee rights, and health and safety standards.[23]

Another range of policy options involves creating incentives to foster new workplace institutions that might provide some of the core functions of a collective agent. One approach would be to restructure aspects of regulatory systems to create incentives on the regulated parties themselves to fashion agents (such as private monitors) that provide at least some of the functions of collective agents. One example of this type of policy described previously is the DOL's apparel enforcement strategy that induces manufacturers to create third-party monitors to oversee the activities of subcontractors.

Alternatively, public policies might assist existing labor market institutions sharpen their abilities to undertake the central aspects as collective agents. Policy proposals in this vein include improving the access that public interest groups and other institutions have to employees at workplaces, thereby enhancing their potential role as third-party representatives in ADR systems. By improving employee access to potential outside representation, ADR systems (which will undoubtedly become even more

23. The "Workers' Page" can be found at http://www.osha.gov/as/opa/worker/index.html.

Table 1.3 **Evaluation of alternative labor market institutions in implementing labor market policies**

Labor market institution	Address the public goods problem?	Lower marginal cost of exercise of rights?	Protect against worker discrimination?	Comments on effectiveness of workplace institution
Labor unions (benchmark)	Yes	Yes	Yes	See table 1.2 for empirical results
National issue organizations	No	No	No	Agency problems limit role to precedent-setting cases
Legal service organizations	No	Partially	No	Agency problems limit role to individual advocacy
Other public-interest organizations (e.g., COSH/disabled workers advocacy organizations)	No	Yes	Partially	Largest impact in assisting workers in receiving benefits (e.g., workers compensation)
Mandated workplace committees	Yes/No	Yes	Yes/No	Effectiveness is function of nature of the mandate and antecedent conditions in the workplace (e.g., size, workforce turnover)
Third-party monitors (e.g., FLSA)	?	Yes	Partially	Monitors agency relationship with third party and government creates a role as supplementary enforcement resource
Alternative dispute resolution systems	No	Yes	?	Most effective where divergence of private and workplace benefits from exercise of rights is small

Note: ? = effect unclear.

prevalent in the wake of the *Circuit City* decision), will be better prepared to deal with systemic workplace problems. Developing a more robust set of institutions capable of representing nonunion workers in such company-based mediation and arbitration procedures may prove an important new means of improving the exercise of individual rights in nonunion workplaces.

Many of the emerging institutions discussed in subsequent chapters are beginning to play at least some of the central roles for labor market regulation discussed above. A central analytic question, then, is whether they can be expected to develop over time to prove effective and sustainable collective agents given their different institutional forms, incentives, and activities. A full answer to this question requires observing these institutions as they evolve over the next decade.

Commons and Andrews (1936) recognized at the dawn of the modern era of workplace regulation that enactment of labor regulations did not assure implementation. Along with guaranteeing that the agencies vested with enforcement or administrative authority receive adequate appropriations and are staffed with competent personnel, this essay underscores the need to develop complementary institutions in the labor market to assure full implementation. Creating and fostering the institutions capable of taking on these functions may prove to be one of the most challenging aspects of regulating the labor market in the twenty-first century.

Appendix

Table 1A.1 Major federal workplace regulations

Labor statute or executive order	Acronym	Date of passage	Description
Labor standards			
Fair Labor Standards Act	FLSA	1938	Establishes minimum wage, overtime pay, and child labor standards
Davis-Bacon Act	—	1931	Provides for payment of prevailing local wages and benefits to workers employed by contractors and subcontractors on federal contracts for construction, alteration, repair, painting, or decorating of public buildings or public works
Service Contract Act	SCA	1963	Provides for payment of prevailing local wages and fringe benefits and safety and health standards for employees of contractors and subcontractors providing services under federal contracts
Walsh-Healy Act	—	1936	Provides for labor standards, including wage and hour, for employees working on federal contracts for the manufacturing or furnishing of materials, supplies, articles, or equipment
Contract Work Hours and Safety Standards Act	CWHSSA	1962	Establishes standards for hours, overtime compensation, and safety for employees working on federal and federally funded contracts and subcontracts
Migrant and Seasonal Agricultural Workers Protection Act	MSPA	1983	Protects migrant and seasonal agricultural workers in their dealings with farm labor contractors, agricultural employers, associations, and providers of migrant housing
Benefits			
Employee Retirement and Income Security Act	ERISA	1974	Establishes uniform standards for employee pension and welfare benefit plans, including minimum participation, accrual and vesting requirements, fiduciary responsibilities, and reporting and disclosure
Consolidated Omnibus Budget Reconciliation Act	COBRA	1986	Provides for continued health care coverage under group health plans for qualified separated workers for up to 18 months

(*continued*)

Table 1A.1 (continued)

Labor statute or executive order	Acronym	Date of passage	Description
Unemployment Compensation provision of the Social Security Act	—	1935	Authorizes funding for state unemployment compensation administration and provides the general framework for the operation of state unemployment insurance programs
Family Medical Leave Act	FMLA	1993	Entitles employees to take up to 12 weeks of unpaid, job-protected leave each for specified family and medical reasons such as the birth or adoption of a child or an illness in the family
Civil rights			
Title VII of the Civil Rights Act	—	1964	Prohibits employment or membership discrimination by employers, employment agencies, and unions on the basis of race, color, religion, sex, or national origin; prohibits discrimination in employment against women affected by pregnancy, childbirth, or related medical condition
Equal Pay Act	—	1963	Prohibits discrimination on the basis of sex in the payment of wages
Executive Order 11246	EO 11246	1962	Prohibits discrimination against an employee or applicant for employment by federal contractors, and requires federal contractors to take affirmative action to ensure that employees and applicants for employment are treated without bias
Age Discrimination Employment Act	ADEA	1967	Prohibits employment discrimination on the basis of age against persons aged 40 years and older
Americans with Disabilities Act	ADA	1990	Prohibits employment discrimination against individuals with disabilities; requires employer to make "reasonable accommodations" for disabilities unless doing so would cause undue hardship to the employer
Rehabilitation Act (Section 503)	—	1973	Prohibits federal contractors and subcontractors from discriminating in employment on the basis of disability and requires them to take affirmative action to employ, and advance in employment, individuals with disabilities
Antiretaliatory provision—Surface Transportation Assistance Act	STAA	1978	Prohibits the discharge or discriminatory action against employees for filing complaints relating to a violation of a commercial motor vehicle safety rule or regulation or for refusing to operate a vehicle in violation of federal rules, or because of a fear of serious injury due to an unsafe condition

Occupational health and safety			
Occupational Safety and Health Act	OSHA	1970	Requires employers to furnish each employee with work and a workplace free from recognized hazards that can cause death or serious physical harm
Federal Mine Safety and Health Act	MSHA	1969	Requires mine operators to comply with health and safety standards and requirements established to protect miners
Drug Free Workplace Act	DFWA	1988	Requires recipients of federal grants and contracts to take certain steps to maintain a drug-free workplace
Labor relations			
National Labor Relations Act	NLRA	1935	Protects certain rights of workers, including the right to organize and bargain collectively through representation of their own choice
Labor-Management Reporting and Disclosure Act	LMRDA	1959	Requires the reporting and disclosure of certain financial and administrative practices of labor organizations and employers; establishes certain rights for members and imposes other requirements on labor organizations
Railway Labor Act	RLA	1926	Sets out the rights and responsibilities of management and workers in the rail and airline industries and provides for negotiation and mediation procedures to settle labor-management disputes
Hiring and separation decisions			
Employee Polygraph Protection Act	PPA	1988	Prohibits the use of lie detectors for preemployment screening or use during the course of employment
Veterans' Reemployment Rights Act	VRR	1940	Provides reemployment rights for persons returning from active duty, reserve training, or National Guard duty
Immigration Reform and Control Act (employment provisions)	IRCA	1986	Prohibits the hiring of illegal aliens and imposes certain duties on employers; protects employment rights of legal aliens; authorizes but limits the use of imported temporary agricultural workers
Workers Adjustment and Retraining Act	WARN	1988	Requires employers to provide 60 days' advance written notice of a layoff to individual affected employees, local governments, and other parties

Source: Adapted from U.S. GAO (1994), Table 2.1, Figure 2.1.

References

Addison, John, and McKinley Blackburn. 1994. The Worker Adjustment and Retraining Notification Act: Effects on notice provision. *Industrial and Labor Relations Review* 47 (4): 650–62.

Becker, Gary. 1968. Crime and punishment: An economic analysis. *Journal of Political Economy* 76:169–217.

Bernard, Elaine. 1995. Canada: Joint Committees on Occupational Safety and Health. In *Works councils: Consultation, representation, and cooperation in industrial relations,* ed. Joel Rogers and Wolfgang Streeck, 351–74. Chicago: University of Chicago Press.

Blank, Rebecca, and David Card. 1991. Recent trends in insured and uninsured employment: Is there an explanation? *Quarterly Journal of Economics* 106 (4): 1157–89.

Budd, John, and Angela Brey. 2000. Unions and family leave: Early experience under the Family Medical Leave Act. University of Minnesota, Industrial Relations Center. Unpublished manuscript.

Budd, John, and Brian McCall. 1997. The effect of unions on the receipt of unemployment insurance benefits. *Industrial and Labor Relations Review* 50 (3): 478–92.

———. 2004. Unions and unemployment insurance benefit receipt: Evidence from the Current Population Survey. *Industrial Relations* 43 (2): 339–55.

Bureau of National Affairs (BNA). 1997. *Basic patterns in union contracts.* 16th ed. Washington D.C.: Bureau of National Affairs.

Butler, Richard, and John Worrall. 1983. Workers' compensation: Benefit and injury claims rates in the seventies. *The Review of Economics and Statistics* 65: 580–89.

Chachere, Denise, and Peter Feuille. 1993. Grievance procedures and due process in nonunion workplaces. In *Proceedings of the 45th annual meeting of the Industrial Relations Research Association,* 446–55. Madison, Wisc.: IRRA.

Commission on the Future of Worker-Management Relations. 1994. *Fact finding report.* Washington, D.C.: U.S. Department of Labor.

Commons, John R., and John Andrews. 1936. *Principles of labor legislation.* 4th ed. New York: Augustus M. Kelley.

Dunlop, John T., and Arnold Zack. 1997. *Mediation and arbitration of employment law disputes.* San Francisco: Jossey Bass.

———. 2001. Mediation of statutory enforcement disputes. Harvard University, Department of Economics. Unpublished Manuscript.

Ehrenberg, Ronald, and George Jakubson. 1990. Why warn? Plant closing legislation. *Cato Review of Business and Government* 13 (2): 39–42.

Ehrenberg, Ronald, and Paul Schumann. 1982. *Longer hours or more jobs? An investigation of amending hours legislation to create employment.* Ithaca, N.Y.: ILR Press.

Elliott, Kimberly, and Richard Freeman. 2003. *Can labor standards improve under globalization?* Washington, D.C.: Institute for International Economics.

Feuille, Peter, and John Delaney. 1992. The individual pursuit of organizational justice: Grievance procedures in nonunion workplaces. *Research in Personnel and Human Resources Management* 10 (2): 187–232.

Freeman, Richard. 1985. Unions, pensions, and union pension funds. In *Pensions, labor and individual choice,* ed. David Wise, 89–121. Chicago: University of Chicago Press.

Freeman, Richard, and James Medoff. 1984. *What do unions do?* New York: Basic Books.

Freeman, Richard, and Joel Rogers. 1999. *What workers want.* Ithaca, N.Y.: ILR Press.

Hirsch, Barry, David Macpherson, and Michael DuMond. 1997. Workers' compensation recipiency in union and nonunion workplaces. *Industrial and Labor Relations Review* 50:213–36.

Hoerr, John. 1988. *And the wolf finally came: The decline of the American steel industry.* Pittsburgh, Pa.: University of Pittsburgh Press.

Hoyman, Michele, and Lamont Stallworth. 1981. Who files suits and why: An empirical portrait of the litigious worker. *University of Illinois Law Review* 198 (1): 115–59.

Langbert, Mitchell. 1995. Voice asymmetries in ERISA litigation. *Journal of Labor Research* 16:145–74.

Leonard, Jonathon. 1985. The effect of unions on the employment of blacks, Hispanics, and women. *Industrial and Labor Relations Review* 39 (1): 115–32.

Lipsky, David, and Ronald Seeber. 1998. The appropriate resolution of corporate disputes: A report on the growing use of ADR by U.S. corporations. Ithaca, N.Y.: Cornell/PERC Institute on Conflict Resolution.

Masters, Marick. 1997. *Unions at the crossroads: Strategic membership, financial, and political perspectives.* Westport, Conn.: Quorum.

McAteer, Davitt. 1985. *Miner's manual.* Washington, D.C.: Keystone Publishers.

Peterson, Richard. 1992. The union and nonunion grievance system. In *Research frontiers in industrial relations and human resources,* ed. David Lewin, Olivia Mitchell, and Peter Sherer, 131–62. Madison, Wisc.: IRRA.

Reilly, Barry, Pierella Paci, and Peter Holl. 1995. Unions, safety committees and workplace injuries. *British Journal of Industrial Relations* 33 (2): 275–88.

Rogers, Joel. 1995. United States: Lessons from abroad and home. In *Works councils: Consultation, representation, and cooperation in industrial relations,* eds. Joel Rogers and Wolfgang Streeck, 375–419. Chicago: University of Chicago Press.

Samuelson, Paul. 1955. Diagrammatic exposition of a theory of public expenditure. *Review of Economics and Statistics* 37:350–56.

Shavell, Steven. 1987. *Economic analysis of accident law.* Cambridge, Mass.: Harvard University Press.

Stern, Robert, and Deborah Balser. 1996. Regulations, social control, and institutional perspectives: Implementing the Americans with Disabilities Act. Cornell University, New York State School of Industrial and Labor Relations. Unpublished Manuscript.

Stigler, George. 1974. Free riders and collective action. *Bell Journal of Economics* 5:359–65.

Trejo, Stephen. 1991. The effects of overtime pay regulation on worker compensation. *American Economic Review* 81 (4): 719–40.

U.S. Department of Labor (DOL). 1998. Full hot goods compliance program agreement. DOL Form FCPA(AB).CP1. Washington, D.C.: U.S. Department of Labor, Wage and Hour Division.

———. 1999. Protecting America's garment workers: A monitoring guide. Washington, D.C.: U.S. Department of Labor.

U.S. General Accounting Office (GAO). 1989. *How well does OSHA protect workers from reprisals: Inspector opinions.* GAO/T-HRD-90-8. Washington, D.C.: GPO.

———. 1992. *Occupational safety and health: Worksite safety and health committees show promise.* GAO/HRD-92-68. Washington, D.C.: GPO.

———. 1993. *Dislocated workers: Worker Adjustment and Retraining Notification Act not meeting its goals.* GAO/HRD-93-18. Washington, D.C.: GPO.
———. 1994. *Workplace regulation: Information on selected employer and union experiences.* GAO/HEHS-94-138. Washington, D.C.: GPO.
———. 2000. *Worker Protection: OSHA Inspections at Establishments Experiencing Labor Unrest.* GAO/HEHS-00-144. Washington, D.C.: GPO.
Viscusi, W. Kip. 1983. *Risk by choice: Regulating health and safety in the workplace.* Cambridge, Mass.: Harvard University Press.
Viscusi, W. Kip, and Charles O'Connor. 1984. Adaptive responses to chemical labeling: Are workers Bayesian decision makers? *American Economic Review* 74 (5): 942–56.
Wandner, Stephen, and Andrew Skinner. 2000. Why are many jobless workers not applying for benefits? *Monthly Labor Review* 123 (June): 21–32.
Weil, David. 1990. Protecting the mine face: The United Mine Workers and the enforcement of the Mine Health and Safety Act. Boston University, School of Management. Unpublished Manuscript.
———. 1991. Enforcing OSHA: The role of labor unions. *Industrial Relations* 30 (1): 20–36.
———. 1992. Building safety: The role of construction unions in the enforcement of OSHA. *Journal of Labor Research* 13 (1): 121–32.
———. 1996. If OSHA is so bad, why is compliance so good? *The RAND Journal of Economics* 27 (3): 618–40.
———. 1999. Are mandated health and safety committees substitutes or supplements to labor unions? *Industrial and Labor Relations Review* 52 (April): 339–60.
———. 2002. Regulating noncompliance with labor standards: New tools for an old problem. *Challenge* 45 (1): 47–74.
Williamson, Oliver. 1985. *The economic institutions of capitalism.* New York: The Free Press.

I

Studies of Nonworker Organizations

2

White Hats or Don Quixotes? Human Rights Vigilantes in the Global Economy

Kimberly Ann Elliott and Richard B. Freeman

Labor standards in less-developed countries became a hot-button issue in discussions of trade and economic development in the 1990s. Standards rose to the top of the public agenda not because workers were unionizing in mass numbers, nor because management had turned over a moral leaf, nor because the International Labor Organization (ILO) had asserted itself in the global economy. Labor standards came to the fore because nongovernmental groups in advanced countries—the human rights vigilantes of our title—galvanized consumers to demand that multinational firms and their suppliers improve working conditions and pay living wages in developing countries.

How did human rights vigilantes bring labor standards to the center of public discourse? Will the antisweatshop activists create a permanent global movement for workers rights, or will public interest dissipate over time? Can concerned citizens in advanced countries pressure firms to improve the economic condition of workers in poorer countries, or will their activities inadvertently make things worse? Which appellation best characterizes the human rights vigilantes—white hats or Don Quixotes?

We analyze these questions in terms of a "market for standards" in

Kimberly Ann Elliott is a research fellow at the Institute for International Economics and the Center for Global Development, Washington, D.C. Richard B. Freeman is the Herbert Ascherman Professor of Economics at Harvard University, director of the labor studies program at the National Bureau of Economic Research, and a senior research fellow at the Centre for Economic Performance of the London School of Economics. The authors would like to thank Sumaira Chowdhury, who wrote up a detailed history of the Kathie Lee Gifford story, and Peter Siu, who developed our survey of student activists and interviewed them, as well as provided us with a detailed history of United Students Against Sweatshops. The views expressed herein are those of the authors and not necessarily those of the National Bureau of Economic Research or of the Institute for International Economics.

which consumers, stimulated by vigilante intermediaries, demand that corporations improve working conditions in supplier factories. Section 2.1 presents evidence that a consumer demand for minimum labor standards exists and explores the nature of that demand. Section 2.2 examines the incentives that exist for firms to respond to this demand and considers how industry structure influences the nature of the response. Section 2.3 introduces the human rights activists of our title and assesses their role as intermediaries who expose sweatshop abuses and trigger consumers to demand changes in corporate behavior. Section 2.4 examines the major antisweatshop campaigns of the 1990s and their achievements. Section 2.5 considers the arguments that antisweatshop campaigns risk doing more harm than good by raising costs and deterring investment in poor countries and assesses the limitations of activist consumer-based campaigns. Section 2.6 concludes with a summary of our conclusions as to when and how human rights vigilante efforts actually do good.

2.1 Consumer Demand for Labor Standards

> [I] had a hard time making up my mind how bad a company had to be before I could bring myself to give its products the old heave-ho.
> —Joe Queenan, *My Goodness*

> I still shop at those brand-name stores, but I feel really guilty about it.
> —Founding member of a New York City high school Student Committee Against Labor Exploitation, *Business Week,* September 11, 2000

The sine qua non of activist efforts to improve labor standards around the world is that consumers care about the conditions of the workers who make the items they consume. If consumers do not care or do not associate the conditions with their consumption, human rights vigilantes could not pressure firms to improve working conditions. The extent to which consumers care and their willingness to act on their concerns is, as the previous commentators indicate, uncertain. Indeed, many consumers, like the previously quoted high school student, would just as soon not know about poor conditions because that knowledge reduces the utility of their consumption. Activists inform consumers about the conditions of production in ways that resonate with moral concerns and develop campaigns to turn concern into improvements. From this perspective, the activists are entrepreneurs who identify latent market demands and find ways to meet those demands.

In this section we present survey evidence that consumers care about labor standards and will buy products made under better conditions in preference to those made under worse conditions. That many corporations respond to the activist-induced pressures, at least rhetorically, shows that they believe such a demand exists.

2.1.1 Survey Evidence

You are offered two identical t-shirts with your favorite logo. One was made in good conditions in some third world country. The other was made in a firetrap factory by people paid near starvation wages. Which t-shirt would you buy when the t-shirts cost the same? Which t-shirt would you buy when the shirt made under good conditions costs a bit more?

Surveys that ask questions of this form invariably find that the vast majority of people report they would choose the garment made under better conditions, even if it costs a bit more. Table 2.1 summarizes the results from surveys undertaken by Marymount University's Center for Ethical Concerns (1999); by the University of Maryland's Program on International Policy Attitudes; and by our project.

The Marymount surveys were conducted in 1995, 1996, and 1999. In each survey, three of four consumers said they would avoid shopping in a store if they knew the goods were produced under bad conditions, while not quite two of three say they would be more inclined to shop in stores combating sweatshops. The greater response to knowledge about bad conditions than good conditions suggests that consumers respond more to information that reduces their utility than to information that increases it—consistent with Kahneman and Tversky's (1979) prospect theory that shows people weigh potential losses more heavily than potential gains. An average 85 percent of respondents in the Marymount survey said they would pay $1 more for a $20 item if they could be assured that it was made under good conditions.

The 1999 Program on International Policy Attitudes (PIPA) survey presented arguments for and against making labor standards part of the trade agenda (University of Maryland [PIPA] 2000). By covering a spectrum of trade-related issues, this survey put attitudes toward labor standards into a broader context. The survey found that most Americans favor linking labor standards to trade. Roughly three of four respondents said they felt a moral obligation to try to help workers faced with poor conditions and approximately the same proportion reported that they would pay $5 more for a $20 garment if they knew it was not made in a sweatshop.[1] Most respondents found convincing arguments for minimum standards—that harsh conditions are immoral and that standards eliminate unfair advantage through exploitation—while far fewer were convinced by arguments against standards—that they reduce jobs in affected countries and impinge on national sovereignty.

1. Comparing the Marymount and PIPA surveys, we see that a higher premium on a $20 item, $5 versus $1, reduces the number of people who say they would buy the product made under good conditions. In this range, moreover, the demand would appear to be modestly inelastic. Total revenues would rise with the increase in price from $21 to $25, but, because purchasers would fall from 85 percent of persons to 75 percent, revenues would still be maximized at the $20 price.

Table 2.1 **Survey findings on consumers' expressed desire for labor standards**

	1995	1996	1999
Marymount University Center for Ethical Concerns			
Would avoid shopping at retailer that sold garments made in sweatshop (%)	78	79	75
More inclined to shop at stores working to prevent sweatshops (%)	66	63	65
Willing to pay $1 more for $20 garment guaranteed made in legitimate shop (%)	84	83	86
Most responsible for preventing sweatshops (%)			
Manufacturers	76	70	65
Retailers	7	10	11
Both	10	15	19
What would most help you avoid buying sweatshop clothes (%)			
Fair-labor label		56	
Sweatshop list		33	
University of Maryland Program on International Policy Attitudes			
Feel moral obligation to make effort to ensure that people in other countries producing goods we buy do not have to work in harsh or unsafe conditions (%)			74
Willing to pay $25 for $20 garment that is certified not made in sweatshop (%)			76
Find arguments for/against labor standards convincing (%)			
Standards will eliminate jobs			37
Standards interfere with national sovereignty			41
Low standards give unfair advantage			74
Low standards are immoral			83
United States should not import products in violation of labor standards (%)			
Products made by children (under force or without chance for school)			81
Made in unsafe/unhealthy places			77
Workers not allowed to unionize			42
Do not expect workers in foreign countries to make U.S. wages, but expect countries to permit wages to rise by allowing unions/stopping child labor (%)			82
Favor lowering barriers that limit clothing imports (%)			
Without hearing about costs of protection			36
After hearing costs of protection			53
NBER Survey			
Consumers who say they care about the condition of workers who make the clothing they buy (%)			
A lot			46
Somewhat			38
Only a little			8
Not at all/no response			8
Willing to pay more for an item if assured it was made under good working conditions (%)			81
Amount willing to pay for $10 item			$2.78
Amount willing to pay for $100 item			$14.99
At same price would choose alternative to t-shirt that students say is made under poor conditions (%)			84

Table 2.1 (continued)

	1995	1996	1999
Would buy t-shirt made under poor conditions at average discount of			$4.30
Would not buy t-shirt made under poor conditions at all (%)			65
Would pay more for t-shirt if came with assurance it was made under good conditions (%)			78
Amount would pay, including those who did not offer to pay more			$1.83

People also differentiated among labor standards. More were concerned about child labor and safe conditions than about the right to unionize. Most consumers did not expect workers in foreign countries to earn U.S. wages (82 percent) and just over half favored lowering trade barriers after being informed about the costs of protectionism. This compares to only 36 percent who favored lowering barriers to clothing imports absent the information. Two-thirds favored free trade as long as society recompensed workers whose livelihood was hurt by trade, say with adjustment assistance and training. Nearly 90 percent said that "free trade is an important goal for the United States, but it should be balanced with other goals, such as protecting workers, the environment, and human rights—even if this may mean slowing the growth of trade and the economy."

Most striking, the largest majority on any trade question (93 percent) agreed that "countries that are part of international trade agreements should be required to maintain minimum standards for working conditions." Thus, Americans support international labor standards in both their private consumption behavior and in the public sphere.

2.1.2 Our Survey

To illuminate further the consumer demand for labor standards, we surveyed a small number of randomly chosen persons in the United States in fall 1999.[2] The survey used a split-sample design that posed different questions to different respondents to see whether responses varied with the wording or presentation of questions. The results parallel those of the Marymount and PIPA surveys. Most respondents said that they cared about the treatment of the workers who made the clothing they bought and that they would be willing to pay more for an item if they knew it was made under good working conditions (see table 2.1). On average, consumers said that they were willing to pay 28 percent more on a $10 item and 15 percent more on a $100 item (including as zeros consumers who said that they were unwilling to pay extra for the assurance). Eighty-four percent of a different subsample said that they would purchase a different t-shirt rather than one

2. Springfield Telemarketing conducted the survey for us.

"with a nice logo" that local students said was made under poor labor conditions. Nearly two-thirds said that they would not buy the t-shirt made under poor conditions at any price.[3] The third who said they would buy it if the price was lowered wanted a mean discount of $4.30. On the other side, consumers said that they would pay an average of just $1.83 for knowing the product was made under good conditions (including 0s for persons who said they would not pay the extra amount or who refused to answer).[4] The greater response to the utility-reducing information about bad conditions than to the utility-increasing information about good conditions again fits with prospect theory.

At the heart of any economic analysis of consumer tastes is the demand curve—the relation between the number of consumers who would buy products at different prices. Our survey allows us to estimate the demand curve for labor standards, taking account of the potential difference in responsiveness to products made under good conditions and those made under bad conditions. We asked some respondents how much more they would be willing to pay for items made under good working conditions for items worth $10 and $100. We asked others if they would buy a $10 t-shirt made under poor conditions if its price was lowered to $9, $8, or $7, and how much they would pay for the t-shirt if it was made under good conditions.

Panels A–D of figure 2.1 show that both designs give qualitatively similar results: high elasticities of demand for products made under good conditions but low elasticities of demand for products made under bad conditions.[5] The willingness to pay for items made under good conditions has elasticities ranging from –3.7 to –4.9. The 20 percent to 30 percent of consumers who are unwilling to pay anything extra produce an immediate loss in revenue that these estimates indicate cannot be recovered from those willing to pay more. In addition, there is a sharp drop-off in purchases as the price of the item rises. By contrast, roughly two of three consumers say they would not buy the item made under bad conditions under any circumstance, and the demand for t-shirts produced under bad conditions is inelastic (–0.29) among the third who said they would buy them at a discount.

The implication is that firms can lose greatly from having their products identified as being made under bad conditions but have only limited space to raise prices for products made under good conditions—unless con-

3. We did not ask if they would take the good if we paid them.

4. Due to a coding problem, this estimate may be too low, but we believe only moderately so.

5. Some respondents refused to answer these questions and some gave inconsistent answers—saying, for instance, that they would buy the cheaper product no matter what and then saying they would pay extra for the product made under better conditions. We made the conservative assumption that anyone who refused to answer or who gave an inconsistent response would not pay a premium for a product made under good conditions or would buy the product under poor conditions. But had we deleted these observations, our results would be qualitatively the same.

A

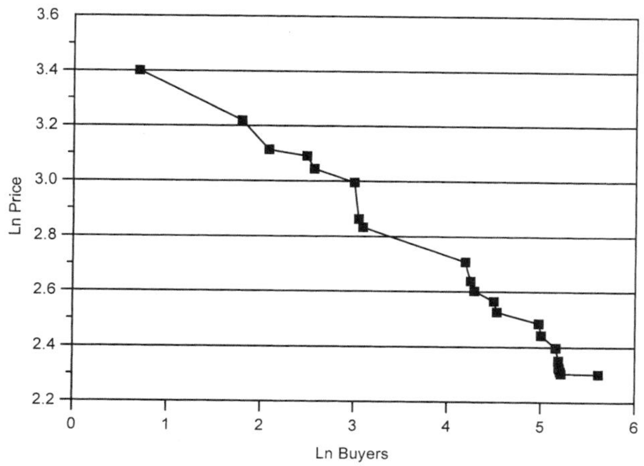

B

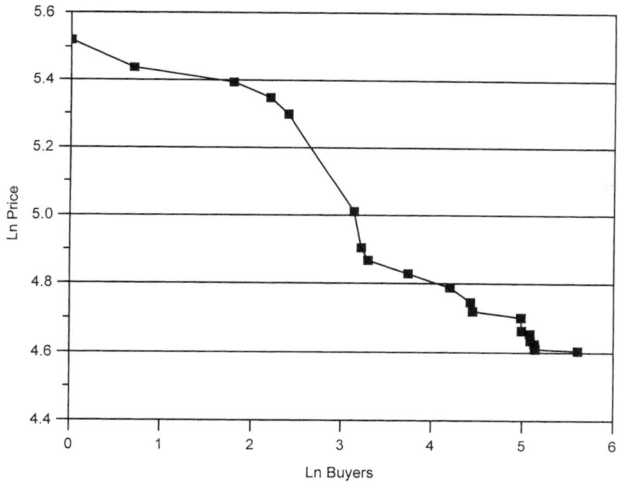

Fig. 2.1 Estimated demand curves for standards: *A*, $10 item made under good conditions; *B*, $100 item made under good conditions; *C*, Pay for $10 t-shirt under good conditions; *D*, Pay for $10 t-shirt under bad conditions

sumers see competing products as made under bad conditions.[6] The differential consumer response to information about good and bad conditions

6. Because we did not specify the conditions under which the alternative product was made, this is an inference from responses to the two sets of questions. The design that would provide a test of this inference would be to ask consumers to compare a product made under good conditions with one made under positively bad conditions (at varying prices) and a product made under good conditions with one made under unknown conditions. Our analysis compared bad conditions with unknown conditions and good conditions with unknown conditions.

C

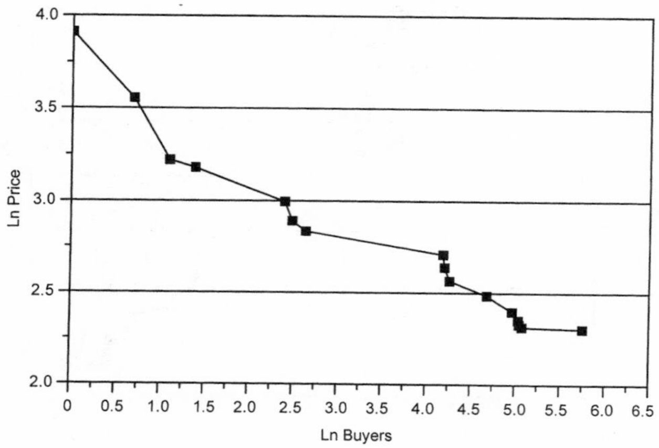

D

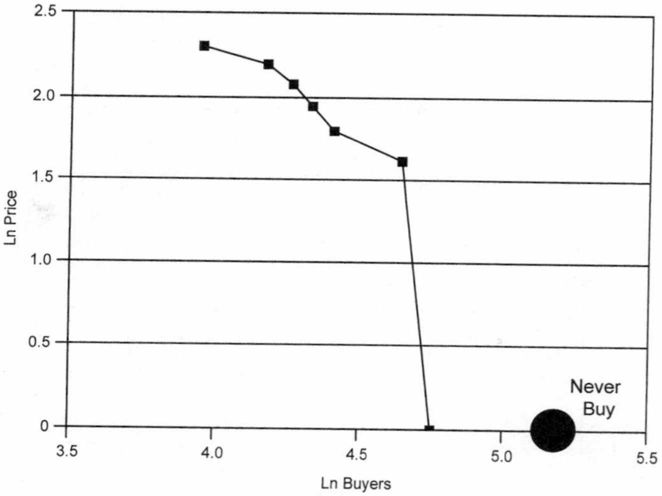

Fig. 2.1 (cont.)

helps explain, we argue later, the behavior of activists and firms in the market for standards.

2.1.3 Do Consumers Act as They Say?

Readers may question whether people will do what they say on a survey. Economists want to see behavior, not intentions. The best way to find out how many people would, in fact, pay extra for a product made under good conditions is to conduct a "Standards Experiment" by offering the product for sale alongside a similar product with no or negative information on working conditions and seeing what happens. Unfortunately, no one has done this systematically.[7] But experimental data and market behavior in other domains suggests that people care enough about the conditions of others to behave as they say they would in the surveys.

The "dictator's game" is perhaps the experimental economics game closest to the standards problem. Two players are given envelopes. One has $100 in it, while the other envelope has $0. The person with the $100 can simply keep the money and say "tough kazoo" to the person who got $0. The economically rational decision is to do just that. But behavior is different. Only about 20 percent of players keep all the money. The vast majority share some with their unlucky partner, albeit offering less than if the second player could veto the division (as in the "ultimatum game"). Another game that comes close to the standards problem is the "lost wallet game" (Charness, Haruvy, and Sonsino 2003). One person finds a wallet, which has more value to its owner than to the finder. The owner may or may not give a reward for finding the wallet. The greater the value of the wallet to the owner, relative to the finder, the more likely it is that the finder will return it, even though this will mean less money than if the finder kept the wallet. The implication is that people gain some utility from being "fair" to someone who values something more than themselves.[8] Thus, at least in laboratory situations, people behave in ways that lend believability to the responses from surveys on standards and purchasing behavior.

Going outside the laboratory, the fact that people contribute to charity and volunteer time for charitable activities shows that they sacrifice income for social goals. Charitable giving and volunteering is greater in the United States than in other advanced countries, presumably because the United States does not have a large welfare state. In the charitable sector, moreover, much giving and volunteering comes in response to requests from activists (Freeman 1997). Again, people behave as if they care for more than their own immediate consumption and thus could be expected to consider labor standards in their purchase of goods as they say they would in surveys.

Finally, the response of many companies to allegations of worker mistreatment also suggests that consumers act in accord with survey responses. If consumers did not care about conditions, firms would simply ignore the allegations as irrelevant to their bottom lines. Firm behavior is also consistent with the finding that consumer demand for good and bad conditions is asymmetric because, as we will document shortly, firms rarely address labor standards issues unless forced to do so by bad publicity. Inelastic consumer demand for goods produced under abusive conditions gives companies an

7. The few studies and "experiments" that shed some light on these questions are discussed in chapter 2 of Elliott and Freeman (2003).

8. The most famous experimental game, the "prisoner's dilemma," differs from the standards problem because it requires both persons to cooperate, but it shows the same thing: many people do not follow the pure maximizing strategy. The rational response in a fixed-period prisoner's dilemma game is to defect, but, in fact, people frequently choose to cooperate.

incentive to respond to negative publicity; elastic demand for "worker-friendly" products means that firms see little advantage in marketing their products on that basis unless it costs them little or nothing to do so.

2.2 Firms and the Market for Labor Standards

> Their image is everything. They live or die by their image. That gives you a certain power over them.
> —Charles Kernaghan, National Labor Committee, *The New York Times,* June 18, 1996

Some well-known firms have responded to activist campaigns alleging that they or their subcontractors mistreat workers. Levi's adopted the first code addressing sweatshop issues after allegations of abuse among its suppliers in Saipan. Wal-Mart followed after its products were linked to child labor in Bangladesh. Nike initially rejected responsibility for conditions in its supplier factories but then took steps to improve conditions in order to blunt unceasing criticism from activists. Alternatively, Reebok has tried to avoid being tarred by the same brush as Nike by creating a human rights award to honor activists fighting for democracy and against child labor and other abuses. Critics argue that Reebok is hypocritical and has done little to upgrade working conditions in its factories, but so far the strategy has worked because activists have not targeted Reebok as aggressively as they have Nike.

Allegations of sweatshop abuse generally arise in the apparel and footwear sectors, which are labor intensive, geographically mobile, and highly price competitive (International Labor Organization [ILO] 2000). Companies in these sectors focus on product design and marketing while contracting out most or all of the actual production. Large retailers with a prominent market presence, such as Wal-Mart and Gap, or firms with high brand name recognition and recognizable logos, such as Nike and Levi's, are the most vulnerable to activist campaigns because they sell their "image," which can be tarnished by campaigns. Indeed, Klein (1999) argues that these companies are the victims of their own success because they increasingly base their marketing not on the utility of the products they sell but on the "statement" the product makes about the person consuming it. In addition, many of the targeted firms market heavily to teenagers and young adults, where demand for branded clothing and footwear is often faddish. No one wants the statement they make by wearing Nike shoes or Gap jeans to be that they are indifferent to young women their age or younger slaving in a stifling factory for twelve hours a day. If it becomes gauche to wear a given label's apparel because it was made in a sweatshop, retailers could lose sales quickly. Nor does it matter to the corporation whether the motivation is genuine concern for the workers who make the product or simply the desire to be cool with one's friends. In either case, "Brand image, the source of so much corporate wealth, is also, it turns out, the corporate Achilles' heel" (Klein 1999, 343).

The apparel industry has also moved to "lean retailing," which affects the response to antisweatshop campaigns. Going lean means holding low inventories of existing products and using information technology to tailor items to market preferences as quickly as possible (Weil 2000). This makes potential supply disruptions, say because of revelations of child labor in a contract facility, especially costly to firms. The premium on speed and the advantages of the North American Free Trade Agreement and other hemispheric trade preferences have led U.S. apparel firms to source more production in Mexico, the Caribbean, and Central America, which also makes it easier for activists to uncover abuses.

Offsetting the incentives to act preemptively are the costs of enforcing higher labor standards, which the consumer surveys suggest will be difficult to fully pass on. In addition to any direct costs of improving working conditions, the U.S. retailer must also pay for monitoring compliance throughout its supply chain. That means monitoring thousands of contractors around the world, who may, in turn, subcontract jobs to thousands more, including home workers in some cases. Figure 2.2 shows the chain of production for infant and children's apparel between one U.S. retailer, JC Penney, and workers in one country, the Philippines. Through this chain, JC Penney contracts with over 2,000 suppliers in more than eighty countries. And this is not unusual. Nordstrom has over 50,000 contractors and subcontractors, while the National Labor Committee estimates that Wal-Mart has used 1,000 factories just in China and that Disney licenses products in over 30,000 factories around the world.

2.2.1 The Firm's Response to Campaigns

Given an antisweatshop campaign, how will a profit-maximizing retailer or marketer respond?[9] Absent a campaign, we assume that the firm cares nothing about labor standards and leaves it to the contractor to balance the costs of improved work conditions against the potential productivity gains. This gives the starting level of standards, S0. An activist campaign forces firms to reassess the costs of supplying standards against the potential loss of consumer demand. Increasing standards means that the firm will require contractors to abide by a code of higher minimum standards and monitor compliance.

Figure 2.3 shows how a campaign can change the price that consumers will pay for a product and the cost per unit of a product after raising standards to different levels. Absent a campaign to inform consumers about

9. With suitable interpretation of variables, votes rather than prices, for instance, the same model applies to the potential catalytic effect of activists on governments.

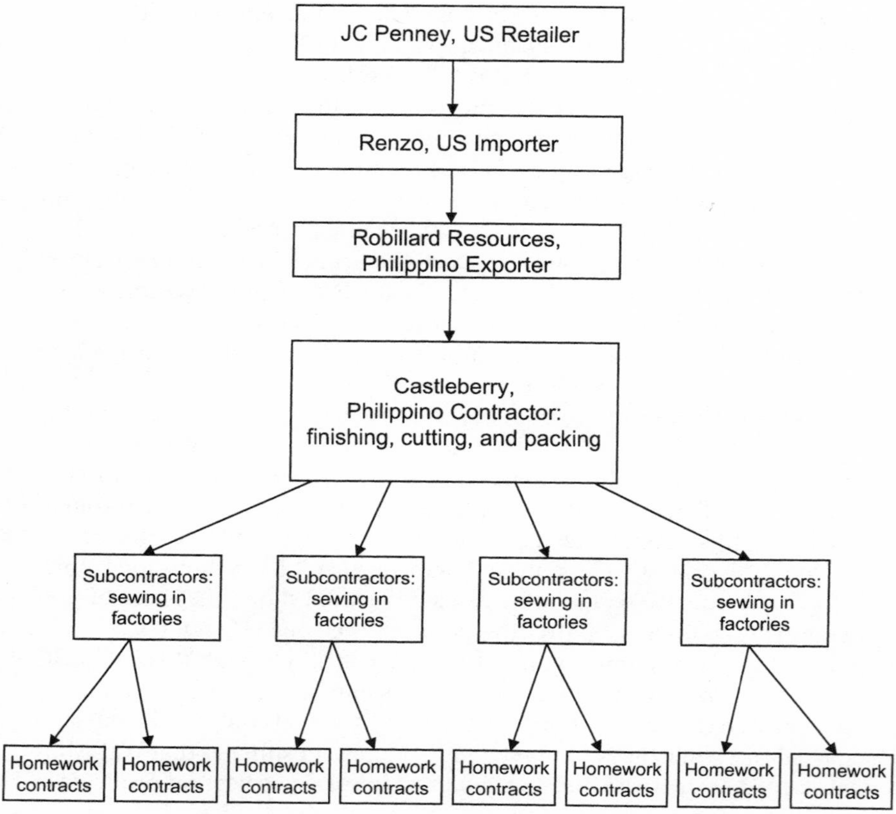

Fig. 2.2 The chain of production for a typical U.S. retailer

conditions, the firm charges P0 while producing at base level standards, S0. A campaign that fails to engage consumers, such as unsuccessful efforts against Disney in Haiti, leaves the price unchanged. By contrast, a successful campaign reduces the price the firm gets for producing under bad conditions and raises the price if they produce under good conditions. On the basis of our survey results, we assume that the slope of the price curve is kinked around the level of standards, S*, that consumers would accept. Firms suffer large reductions in price for below-S* standards but gain only modestly from above-S* standards.

Given the new price curve that the campaign has produced, the firm will assess the benefits and costs of raising standards. In the figure, the cost curve starts at 0 and then rises linearly. The firm maximizes profits by picking the level of standards where the price received for the good, inclusive of standards, most exceeds the cost of standards. With cost curve C1, the costs of improving standards are so high they cannot be recovered, so the

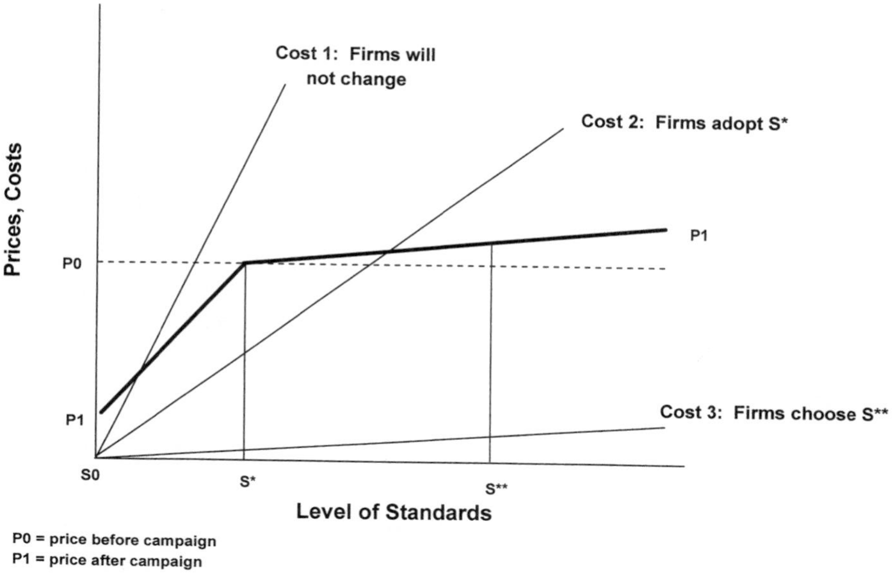

Fig. 2.3 Incentives to improve standards

firm will not raise standards. In this situation the activist campaign has failed in two ways. It has failed to raise standards, and it has probably reduced the employment or earnings of workers in contract facilities because the firm will reduce orders because it makes less money.

With cost curve C2, by contrast, the maximum profit occurs at the kink point.[10] The campaign has attained its goal, S*, by presenting the firm with a stark choice: fail to meet S* and suffer price cuts to sell the same amount (or alternatively, suffer reductions in sales at the same price) or enforce higher standards throughout their supply chain with only modest possible gains in price.

Finally, with cost curve C3, the firm will produce standards in excess of the kink point. Here the marginal cost of standards is so modest that the firm can potentially make more money by producing high standards than it did before the campaign. For example, a firm that improved health and safety among its suppliers, as Nike and Reebok did by moving to water-based adhesives in shoe production, might publicize this in its advertisements, potentially gaining extra sales while also lowering injury rates and improving worker effort or morale.

The diagram directs attention to three determinants of the success of activist campaigns: the cost of producing the standards; the level of

10. Beyond that point the marginal increase in price is less than the marginal increase in cost while before that point the marginal increase in price exceeds the marginal cost.

standards at which the price curve changes shape; and the twist in the price schedule when consumer concerns are stimulated. The asymmetry in demand reflected in the price schedule explains why activists emphasize transparency of information while firms try to control information about conditions as tightly as possible. Information about bad conditions is highly costly, while information about good conditions raises revenues only modestly. This means that full disclosure of the location of plants and independent monitoring of compliance with standards become issues of conflict. If consumers responded more to information about good conditions, activists and firms would have common ground on which to work.

But the activists also face a dilemma in their campaigns. On one side, to rouse interest, activists must highlight the evils of low labor standards and stress how far current standards are from S* or some higher value the activists seek. On the other side, they need business and governments to improve conditions, which requires some compromise with these groups. If activists are too moderate or compromise too readily, they will not gain the support of consumers. But if their demands are too radical, they will alienate business and government. By being either too "soft" or too "hard," activists can fail, because in either case firms will get greater profit from maintaining standards than from working with suppliers to upgrade them.

In sum, consumer demand for labor standards represents concerns that can readily show up in the marketplace. But because consumers have no direct information about the conditions of work, their demand for standards is a latent one that would typically remain beneath the surface but for the work of the human rights vigilantes. The vigilante activists are catalytic agents, stimulating consumers through their campaigns and pressuring firms to improve conditions. Without them, there would be no antisweatshop movement.

2.3 Who Are the Vigilantes?

> The rights and interests of the laboring man will be protected and cared for not by the labor agitators, but by the Christian men to whom God in his infinite wisdom has given the control of the property interests of the country.
>
> —George F. Baer, President, Anthracite Coal Trust, 1902

> Clothing bearing our university logos ought to be produced under healthy, safe and fair working conditions.
>
> —United Students Against Sweatshops (USAS), College Clothes From the Concrete Prison, 1999, 1

Human rights vigilantes are self-appointed advocates, motivated by moral concerns, rather than elected representatives of workers, employers, or consumers. They are a varied group, with differing expertise and modes of operation. In a 1999 directory of U.S. antisweatshop organizations, Global Exchange listed forty different groups involved in antisweatshop campaigns in the United States. Web search yielded several additional groups, including some outside the clothing area (coffee farmers, rug makers), as well as groups outside the United States. A more extensive search would undoubtedly yield many more.

Appendix A lists 40 U.S.-based groups identified from these sources. Most are small rather than mass membership organizations, and most are relatively new. Slightly more than half were formed in the 1990s and nearly 80 percent have existed only since 1980. Most groups concentrate on a particular group of workers, either geographically, ethnically, or by industry or company. Some groups started as antiapartheid campaigners while several formed to protest human rights abuses and American policy toward repressive regimes in Central American. For these groups, antisweatshop campaigns are the next phase in their fight for peace and social justice.

The groups constitute an ecology with varying orientations from moderate to militant. Some have a religious base—the Interfaith Center for Corporate Responsibility, which was a key actor in the efforts to reduce foreign investment in South Africa, and the New York State Labor-Religion Coalition are cases in point. Others, such as the National Labor Committee (NLC) and the USAS, have an activist-left orientation. Yet others, such as Verité, an organization that monitors conditions of subcontractors for firms, or Co-op America, are apolitical do-gooders. As the groups vary along many dimensions, the classification in appendix A is by no means perfect.

These organizations also play a variety of roles in the "market for standards." Some, like Corporate Watch or Jeff Ballinger's Press for Change, focus on providing information about abuses. Some seek out other key players to negotiate standards, and a few provide monitoring services. Some groups are vertically integrated, like Social Accountability International, which negotiated a standard with various stakeholders and created an agency to oversee enforcement.

Morton Winston (forthcoming) of the College of New Jersey and Amnesty International has categorized the groups into "confronters"—who take a confrontational and adversarial approach to corporations in the belief that only the threat of reduced profits will induce them to improve conditions—and "engagers"—who seek to persuade firms to do "the right thing." While the two groups often appear to be at loggerheads, both are, in fact, necessary for the market for standards to function. Confronters keep consumers riled up with their exposés and gain support by generating strong campaigns. But they cannot readily compromise with firms and, therefore, find it difficult to point consumers to acceptable alternatives. Engagers broker agreements with firms but risk losing credibility by compromising with "the enemy." Without the confronters, firms, governments, and international agencies could easily ignore moderate desires for improved standards. Without the moderates, firms, governments, and agencies would declare it impossible to meet militant demands and would reject them out of hand.

Thus, we have a classic mixed-strategy-type game. In equilibrium, there should be an evolutionarily stable strategy division of activists between the two groups. When the marginal return to confrontation is higher, more activists should adopt a confrontation strategy; when the marginal return to engagement is higher, more activists should adopt that strategy until the marginal returns from each are equated. In the current phase of the movement, however, Winston (forthcoming) points to the risk of a backlash among corporations if confronters refuse to recognize progress, relentlessly criticize corporations that inevitably fall short, and "ensure that no good deed goes unpunished." Fear of becoming a target can then deter a company from taking even the first steps toward adopting a code or allowing external monitoring.

Among confronters, the NLC has been highly effective due to the skills of Charles Kernaghan and to luck in the form of the Kathie Lee Gifford case, which we summarize shortly. Global Exchange has also generated considerable media attention with its campaigns in favor of "fair trade" and against unfettered globalization more broadly. In terms of providing "muscle" for campaigns, church and student groups are the most important. Religious groups link antisweatshop activities to congregations while the USAS (2001) has spurred students around the country to protest poor labor standards related to college-licensed products. Student activism in fact took center stage in the antisweatshop movement in the 1990s, as USAS successfully pressured companies to make public the names and locations of subcontractors and spearheaded the Worker Rights Consortium.

2.3.1 The Student Activists

The growth of antisweatshop activism among students has been sudden and sharp—an example of the spurt phenomenon that often characterizes social movements (Freeman 1999). In 1995 there was no student antisweatshop movement in the United States. The first Union Summer of the American Federation of Labor-Congress of Industrial Organization (AFL-CIO) in 1996 generated some student interest, but it was the Union of Needletrades, Industrial, and Textile Employees (UNITE) that did the most to catalyze student antisweatshop activity. In 1995, UNITE hired a young bachelor's graduate, Ginny Coughlin, to coordinate their antisweatshop activity. Two years later, the union hired eleven summer interns, all of whom had been active in a campaign against Guess jeans, to work on antisweatshop activities. One intern, Tico Almeida, returned to his campus, Duke, and initiated an antisweatshop campaign. When Duke agreed to demands that the university insist that its licensees produce items under safe working conditions with freedom to organize and independent monitoring, *The New York Times* carried the story (March 8, 1998, A16). In spring 1998, at a conference in New York, fifty students involved in university-based antisweatshop campaigns started USAS. Their major demand was that the Collegiate Licensing Company, the licensing agent for some 160 universities, implement stronger codes of conduct for its suppliers. By 2000, USAS had chapters on nearly 140 campuses, ranging from highly elite universities with a tradition of student protest to small liberal arts schools.

What kinds of students become involved in antisweatshop activities? How much time and effort do they give to anti-sweatshop campaigning? What motivates their efforts? To answer these questions we surveyed nearly 100 USAS members in summer 1999.[11] Forty-two percent of our sample classified themselves as leaders, and 31 percent viewed themselves as critical people in their campus antisweatshop activities. Nearly three-fourths said they had helped initiate or participate in their local campus campaign. In terms of demographics, the sample is divided nearly evenly between men (53 percent) and women (47 percent) and is dominated by whites (84 percent) and nonblack minorities (15 percent). Seventy-five percent of the activists are social science majors (some joint majors), usually sociology or political science; 18 percent were humanities majors, and the remaining 7 percent were science or mathematics majors.

Panel A of table 2.2 shows the family background of student activists. Many come from relatively well-to-do families: 36 percent report their family income as exceeding $100,000—more than twice the 16 percent of all first-year college students with that family income, while just 8 percent report a family income of less than $40,000, compared to 35 percent of first-year college students. The parents of activists are more progressive than most Americans, and many parents are themselves activists. As a result of this concordance of attitudes, the activist students receive considerable support from their parents. In fact, among parents, the proportion who support student activists exceeded the proportion critical of their activity by a greater margin than that existing among professors or friends of the students not involved in the antisweatshop movement. These student activists are not Lewis Feuer's (1969) generation rebelling against their parents. Rather, they are the product of a generational transmission of political attitudes and activity. (For another perspective on student activism, see Duncan and Steward 1995.)

Panel B of table 2.2 shows that the students have a history of activism.

11. We distributed forty-five surveys at the USAS National Organizing Conference in July and sent e-mails to an additional 140 activists listed on the USAS listserver or suggested by respondents. We obtained thirty-nine responses from persons at the conference and fifty-five from those sent the e-mail instrument, giving ninety-four responses and an overall response rate of slightly over 50 percent.

Table 2.2 **Characteristics of student antisweatshop activists**

	Quantity
A. Family background	
Family income (%)[a]	
> 100,000	36
75–100,000	22
40–75,000	34
< 40,000	8
Political attitudes of parents (%)	
Progressive	40
Nonpartisan	27
Conservative	34
Involved in activism in college	29
Involved in activism after college	25
Attitude of others to involvement (%)	
Parents	
Supportive	58
Critical	11
Professors	
Supportive	67
Critical	24
Uninvolved friends	
Supportive	37
Critical	7
B. Orientation toward social activism	
Involved in activism before (%)	
High school	52
College	84
Ever member of trade union (%)	31
Involved in Union Summer (%)	9
View self as politically committed activist rather than apolitical do-gooder (%)	90
% Rating happiness as 9–10 on 10 point scale	
All As	48
Living wage agreed to by corporations and labor	81
Collegiate licensing companies agree to full disclosure of factory locations	69
U.S. unions increase share of work force	68
United States cancels debt to third-world countries	74
C. Allocation of time	
Hours per week on antisweatshop activities	6.2
Hours per week on other extracurricular activities	10.3
Hours per week studying	14.3
Held job (%)	40
Hours if held job	10.8
If not involved, would spend time on (%)	
Another cause	47
Arts/athletics	36
Socializing	30
Schoolwork	27
Sleep	13

Table 2.2 (continued)

	Quantity
D. Net effect of antisweatshop efforts	
Net effect on (minus sign indicates negative; %)	
Grades	–16
Romantic life	3
Friendships	46
Self-confidence	76
Communication and leadership skills	83

Source: Tabulated from Survey of Student Activists.

[a]For comparison, in the UCLA/ACE Freshman Survey, the proportion in these categories was Family Income: > 100,000 = 16 percent; 75–100,000 = 12 percent; 40–75,000 = 36 percent; < 40,000 = 35 percent.

Over half were involved in campaigns in high school, and 84 percent had done activist work prior to their involvement with USAS. Nearly one-third had been members of trade unions, and 9 percent had been involved in Union Summer. The vast majority viewed themselves as politically committed activists rather than as apolitical do-gooders. Indicative of their values, the activists said that raising the well-being of third-world workers and greater unionization in the United States would make them happier than getting all As in their classes.

Panel C of table 2.2 shows the time students gave to the antisweatshop campaign, to other extracurricular activities, and to their studies. The activist students spend about six hours a week on antisweatshop work, with a small number giving over twenty hours a week to the campaign. In addition, the activists spend thirteen hours on other extracurricular activities so that their total time spent on nonacademic pursuits exceeds the time spent studying. Forty percent hold jobs and work around eleven hours per week. Nearly half say that if they were not involved in the antisweatshop movement, they would devote the time to another cause. The final panel of table 2.2 shows that students see the main cost of activism as lower grades, but they see little effect on their romantic life and believe that their activism has increased their self-confidence and communication and leadership skills.

Table 2.3 compares the attitudes of student activists to those of first-year college students in the University of California, Los Angeles/American Council on Education (UCLA/ACE 1998) Annual American Freshman Survey on identical questions.[12] The activists are more "liberal" than freshmen on most issues: they have a more open view toward sex, are less

12. The questions were identical because we asked the activists questions from the American Freshman survey regarding attitudes and goals.

Table 2.3 **Activists compared to college freshmen overall**

	Activists (%)	College freshmen overall (%)
Agree strongly or somewhat		
Sex OK if people really like each other	81	42
Racial discrimination no longer a problem	1	20
Prohibit racist/sexist speech	38	64
Wealthy should pay more taxes	93	63
Disobey laws that violate values	74	37
Individual can do little to change society	9	33
Deems essential or very important		
Becoming authority in field	52	63
Raising family	46	73
Being very well-off financially	6	75
Influencing political structure	84	17
Being community leader	70	31

Sources: Tabulated from Survey of Student Activists; ACE/UCLA (1998) survey of college freshmen.

likely to believe that race discrimination is a thing of the past, and are more likely to believe that the wealthy should pay more taxes. At the same time, they are more tolerant of views with which they disagree—only 38 percent believe that colleges should prohibit racist or sexist speech compared to 64 percent of all freshmen. The activists are also more favorable to disobeying laws when the laws contravene their convictions and more likely to believe that individual actions can change society. Finally, the activists are markedly less interested in being well-off financially or in raising a family than the freshmen and more interested in influencing political outcomes and becoming community leaders. In short, their attitudes show that they are indeed "listening to a different drummer" than other college students.[13]

2.4 What Activists Produce: Campaigns

> Look, I don't have time to be some kind of major political activist every time I go to the mall. Just tell me what kind of shoes are okay to buy, okay?
>
> —Teenage girl, St. Mary's Secondary School, Pickering, Ontario

Human rights vigilantes produce campaigns for labor standards in the global economy. In so doing, they hope to stimulate the concerns reflected in this young woman's statement and help her find "okay shoes." Their targets are simultaneously consumers like her and the corporations that sell shoes to her. The tools they use in their campaigns are the same as those

13. For analysis of the student activists of the civil rights era, see McAdam (1986, 1989, 1993) and Soule (1997). For further discussion of student activists, see Van Dyke (1998).

used by other international advocacy networks to pressure targeted actors to change: information politics, symbolic politics, accountability politics, and leverage politics (Keck and Sikkink 1998, 16–25). Most antisweatshop campaigns explicitly combine elements of the first three. Over time, the cumulative effect of many campaigns allows activists to leverage their influence with governments and international institutions, such as the ILO, which have greater resources to act against sweatshop abuses.

The first challenge facing an antisweatshop campaign is to obtain accurate, credible information about labor conditions in factories producing brand name goods. Getting such information is difficult, given the long production chains that often link manufacturers or retailers to workers in less-developed countries (see figure 2.2; Verité). In addition, managers of export processing zones and unsympathetic authoritarian governments often restrict access to facilities, making information gathering in some cases even more difficult (Klein 1999, 203–4, 212–13).

The second challenge is to package the information in a way that strikes a moral chord among consumers and generates enough publicity to put labor conditions on the public agenda. This is also no easy task. Human rights vigilantes do not have large public relations (PR) budgets nor automatic access to major media. In a world plagued by catastrophes, wars, and multiple injustices, they compete for attention with other compelling issues as well as with the weekly entertainment, sports, and scandal reports. Often this means that the campaigns need to personalize the message through a spokesperson who becomes the symbol of exploitation or through the closeness between the consumer and the product, as with college-logo products. The type of abuse highlighted also matters, with child labor and unsafe working conditions attracting more sympathy than restrictions on union activities.

A campaign that succeeds in the first two tasks must then get firms or governments to undertake corrective policies. The typical firm's first response to a campaign is to claim ignorance; then it will announce it has developed a code to prevent such occurrences in the future. In most cases, however, the firm resists independent monitoring of code compliance, which might force it to expend real resources. This is the point where activists turn to accountability politics, using the firm's own promises to pressure them to follow words with deeds. Writing about the corporate responsibility movement, William Greider commented, "An enduring truth, a wise friend once explained to me, is that important social change nearly always begins in hypocrisy" (Greider 2000, 1). Thus, antisweatshop campaigns usually must generate several rounds of publicity and pressure to have any hope of producing a change in behavior.

At this writing, the antisweatshop activists have exposed bad conditions in some factories and elicited promises of reform but have shied away from pointing consumers to shoes and sweatshirts that are "okay." Activists are cautious here for two reasons. First, a campaign that reduces sales will harm the very workers the campaigns are designed to help, so activists generally eschew calls for consumers to boycott products. Second, if activists endorse a given product, and someone finds that somewhere in the world the firm or one of its subcontractor's workers is abusing workers (highly likely given the long supply chains), the activists risk losing their credibility.

2.4.1 The 1990's Antisweatshop Campaigns

Sweatshops have characterized apparel production since industrial revolution days, and so too have campaigns to improve labor conditions in the industry. Many economists point out that low-wage, labor-intensive production of items like apparel is often a taking-off point for development in poor agrarian countries with abundant labor and little capital. But low wages alone do not a sweatshop make. Though much debate focuses on wages, there are other practices, such as forced labor or safety conditions or denial of legally mandated benefits, that campaigns also address.

Many of the issues are the same, but a major difference between antisweatshop campaigns at the turn of the twenty-first century and those at the turn of the twentieth century is that sweatshops then were largely local, whereas today they are found mostly in poor developing countries.[14] This means that U.S.-based activists cannot lobby the U.S. government to directly improve labor standards. Instead, they must target U.S.-based corporations who operate or source in developing countries or pressure the world trading community to demand changes in less-developed countries. This strategy, as well as many of today's human rights vigilantes, have roots in the antiapartheid campaign (see appendix B). Antiapartheid activists first pressured firms through the Sullivan Principles and then, when progress lagged, turned to pressing governments to impose economic sanctions on the apartheid regime. It is perhaps no coincidence that antisweatshop campaigns gathered steam in the 1990s after apartheid was formally buried.

Table 2.4 summarizes the 1990s antisweatshop campaigns. They begin in 1992 when Levi Strauss adopted the first known code of conduct addressing sweatshop abuses in response to a U.S. Department of Labor investigation into illegal wage and other practices at supplier factories in the U.S. territory of Saipan (Varley 1998, 12). This code included criteria for source country selection as well as terms of engagement for suppliers. A year later, Levi's announced that it would withdraw from China because the human rights situation was unacceptable, but Levi's never completed the withdrawal and, in April 1998, reversed course and announced it was expanding operations in China.

14. But sweatshops are also coming back in the United States; Weil (2000) and Duong (2000).

Table 2.4 **Timeline of antisweatshop activities**

	Event
1990	Charles Kernaghan becomes the director of NLC, founded in 1981 to oppose Reagan administration policies in Central America.
1992	Levi Strauss develops first code of conduct for suppliers following U.S. Department of Labor (DOL) suit against contractors in Saipan over wages, conditions; a year later, Levi's announces plans to withdraw from China because of human rights situation there.
1992	Senator Tom Harkin (D-IA) introduces a bill to bar imports of goods produced using child labor; he reintroduces in each Congress until 1997 when he substitutes legislation calling for beefed up enforcement of existing law barring imports of goods produced with forced labor, including bonded or other forced child labor.
1993	Wal-Mart publishes "Standards for Vendor Partners" after revelations regarding child labor use by suppliers in Bangladesh are televised.
August 1993	Clinton administration negotiates side agreements on labor and environment to accompany the North American Free Trade Agreement.
March 1995	Criticized for "de-linking" human rights from most-favored nation trade status for China in 1994, Clinton administration releases "model business principles" to encourage multinational corporations (MNCs) to adopt voluntary codes of conduct in operations around the world.
August 1995	The U.S. Department of Labor closes down sweatshop in El Monte, California after discovering immigrant Thai workers being forced to work in slave-like conditions; the incident gives momentum to Secretary Robert Reich's campaign to combat sweatshops in the U.S.
December 1995	Under pressure from NLC and the People of Faith Network over working conditions in El Salvador, The Gap agrees to independent monitoring of contractor facility.
Spring 1996	NLC's Kernaghan reveals Wal-Mart clothing endorsed by television personality Kathie Lee Gifford (KLG) is produced under exploitative conditions, including child labor; Gifford vows to remedy situation; the second scandal involving Gifford-endorsed clothing produced in American sweatshops in New York leads to collaboration with Labor Secretary Reich on his "No Sweat" campaign.
August 1996	President Clinton and Secretary Reich announce creation of Apparel Industry Partnership, bringing together retailer/importers, unions, and NGOs to address the sweatshop issue.
March 1997	Management in a Phillips-Van Heusen (PVH) contract facility in Guatemala recognizes a union, a first in that country's apparel export sector.
April 1997	The AIP report outlines "Workplace Code of Conduct" and "Principles of Monitoring."
August 1997	Duke University students form a group called Students Against Sweatshops; in subsequent months, the movement grows on campuses across the country, eventually becoming United Students Against Sweatshops (USAS).
October 1997	The Council on Economic Priorities, following consultations with companies and NGOs, releases a plan for "social audit" dealing with worker rights and creates an agency to accredit compliance monitors.
April 1998	Levi Strauss announces its return to China, arguing that the human rights situation has improved sufficiently "that the overall environment now is such that the risks to our reputation are minimal" (*Financial Times,* 8 April 1998).

(*continued*)

Table 2.4 (continued)

	Event
Spring 1998	Under pressure from the student group, Duke University releases a code of conduct for suppliers of apparel licensed by Duke to display the university name or logo; the code calls for independent monitoring of compliance, through the AIP if appropriate, and requires suppliers to disclose names and addresses of all contractors and plants involved in production of Duke-licensed apparel.
Summer 1998	UNITE commits interns and resources to helping establish USAS on a national basis.
August 1998	A joint NLC-USAS delegation visits Central America to meet workers and NGOs.
November 1998	The AIP agrees on the creation of a Fair Labor Association and accreditation of independent monitors to monitor compliance with the code.
December 1998	PVH closes unionized plant in Guatemala, saying it lost a major contract and has excess capacity; production will continue at nonunion plants elsewhere in Guatemala.
January 1999	UN Secretary General Kofi Annan, at World Economic Forum in Davos, Switzerland, announces new "Global Compact" calling on the business community to respect basic principles on human rights, worker rights, and protection of the environment but with no means for monitoring of compliance. NGOs followed a year later with a "Citizens' Compact" that rejects "partnership" between the UN and the business community and calls on the UN to make the principles mandatory with provisions for monitoring.
Early 1999	USAS criticizes universities for signing on to the FLA model for monitoring without consulting them; students hold sit-ins to demand a stronger code at Duke, Georgetown, Wisconsin, North Carolina, and, for 226 hours, Arizona. In April, USAS releases detailed report on inadequacies of the FLA code and monitoring process and gives universities until October 15 to seek improvements.
October 7, 1999	Under pressure from USAS and universities, Nike discloses the locations of 41 factories producing licensed apparel for Duke, North Carolina, Georgetown, Michigan, and Arizona.
October 19, 1999	After rejection by the FLA of their suggestions and passage of the 6-month deadline with no other action by universities, USAS announces the alternative Worker Rights Consortium and calls on universities to withdraw from the FLA. Brown University is the first to respond, announcing that it will join the WRC but also remain in the FLA; others, including Phil Knight alma mater University of Oregon, follow.
December 1999	Liz Claiborne agrees to independent monitoring at a supplier facility in El Salvador; the report is published in full on the International Labor Rights Fund website (see appendix A).
December 9, 1999	The Philadelphia City Council calls on area colleges and universities to join the WRC.
Spring 2000	Nike retaliates against Brown and the University of Oregon for joining the WRC and terminates the contract to provide hockey products in one case and ends personal and corporate philanthropic relations in the other.

Shortly after Levi's announced its code, a television broadcast showing children in a Bangladesh factory sewing Wal-Mart label garments led that retailer to develop "Standards for Vendor Partners." But Wal-Mart also soon found itself back in the spotlight. In Spring 1996, the NLC's Kernaghan revealed that clothing endorsed by television personality Kathie Lee Gifford and sold at Wal-Mart was made under exploitative conditions in Honduras. Kernaghan had a powerful symbol for this campaign in fifteen-year old Wendy Diaz, a Honduran orphan who had worked long hours at low wages at the plant since she was thirteen to support herself and three younger brothers. Her story struck a particular chord because the Kathie Lee labels advertised her commitment to children and pledged a share of the profits to children's causes. Gifford initially denied the allegations, then condemned the sweatshop practices and pledged to ensure that her clothing line was never again made under such conditions. After other Gifford-endorsed clothing was discovered being manufactured in a New York City sweatshop that ignored labor laws, Secretary of Labor Robert Reich enlisted her into his "No Sweat" campaign to combat sweatshops in the United States.

Around the same time, activists pressured Gap to allow independent monitoring by a local nongovernmental organization (NGO) of a contract facility in El Salvador. Under similar pressure in 1997, Phillips-Van Heusen (PVH), whose chief executive officer (CEO) sits on the board of Human Rights Watch, recognized a union at a joint venture facility in Guatemala, a first in that country's apparel export sector (Varley 1998, 141–49). With the sweatshop issue in the headlines, President Clinton joined with Reich, Gifford, and others in August 1996 to create the Apparel Industry Partnership (AIP) to combat sweatshop practices internationally. Although many multinational corporations and U.S. retailers sourcing abroad had responded to activist pressure and bad publicity by adopting corporate codes of conduct, the codes varied widely in the issues they addressed and did not seriously address issues of compliance. The AIP brought together apparel manufacturers and importer-retailers, unions, and NGOs in an effort to develop an industry-wide code and a credible monitoring mechanism to verify compliance.

When the AIP released its draft code and principles for monitoring in April 1997, antisweatshop activists had divergent views on its value. Global Exchange's Medea Benjamin (1998) blasted it as a "lousy agreement," primarily because it did not include a living wage. Jay Mazur, the president of UNITE and an AIP member, called the code "unprecedented" and "a step in the right direction" (Mazur 1997). Continuing negotiations on implementation quickly bogged down, however. In November 1998, the AIP unveiled plans to create a Fair Labor Association (FLA) to oversee implementation and monitoring of the code. Both UNITE and the other union member, the Retail, Wholesale and Department Store Union, as well as the Interfaith Center for Corporate Responsibility rejected the FLA as too weak and left the organization. These groups complained that the code failed to require payment of a living wage, had weak language with respect to union rights in nondemocratic countries, and had an inadequate monitoring and verification mechanism.

Nearly two years later, the FLA still had no union representatives, though Lenore Miller of the Retail, Wholesale and Department Store Union was serving on the newly formed NGO Advisory Council in her personal capacity. As of the end of 2003, thirteen companies had been accepted for FLA participation, including such large importer-retailers as Nike, Reebok, Liz Claiborne, Eddie Bauer, and adidas-Salomon, and the FLA had certified twelve auditors, including NGOs in Guatemala and Bangladesh, operating in sixteen of the top twenty countries supplying apparel and footwear to the U.S. market (www.fairlabor.org; accessed April 1, 2004). By mid-2001, more than 150 universities had also affiliated with the FLA, and their pressure on licensees to certify compliance with minimum labor standards led to nearly 1,000 suppliers of college-logo apparel applying for participation in FLA monitoring. Seven years after the AIP was launched, the FLA finally released its first monitoring reports in the summer of 2003.

The student activists in USAS, however, view the FLA as ineffective and condemned their universities for joining. In mid-2000, they created the Worker Rights Consortium (WRC), with a stronger code and alternative "verification model." The USAS pressured universities to join the WRC instead of the FLA, and, by June 2001, more than eighty universities had signed on, though some, such as Brown University and the University of Michigan, affiliated with the FLA as well. In early 2001, the WRC conducted its first investigation of alleged code violations at a Mexican factory supplying Nike and Reebok. While finding that further actions were needed, it praised the companies and factory management for taking "significant constructive steps" to remediate the problems found in the investigation (Worker Rights Consortium [WRC]).

In a separate effort, the Council on Economic Priorities (CEP), which has for many years provided information on the social and environmental policies of companies, developed SA 8000 in consultation with corporations, unions, and NGOs, including representatives from developing countries. The CEP also established an agency, Social Accountability International (SAI) to accredit auditors of the SA 8000 standard. As of mid-2003, SAI had accredited 9 auditors who had in turn certified more than 300 manufacturers or business service organizations, 49 of them in China, as in compliance with SA 8000. At least one of the plants in China was decertified, however, after an NLC report alleging a variety of violations was confirmed by SAI auditors (Roberts and Bernstein 2000). The organization also has ten retailer "members," including Avon, Toys R Us, and Dole Foods, who are expected to encourage their suppliers to seek certification.

Another organization, Verité, established in 1995, provides firms with independent monitoring of working conditions through human rights inspections of factories worldwide, particularly in China and Asia. Though hired by firms, Verité retains the right to publish the results of its inspections if the firm does not rectify problems in six months (Rothstein 1996). The Ethical Trade Initiative is a European effort that combines elements of the FLA and SAI, though it does not plan to create its own monitoring mechanism. Rugmark is another European initiative that a U.S. group has replicated here, to label handmade carpets as child labor free.[15]

Arguments over codes of conduct among activists and between them and firms have highlighted three key issues in using workplace codes to improve labor conditions: what goes into the code, the disclosure of plants covered by the code, and who monitors the code. The most divisive issue regarding the content of codes is whether to include a living wage: SA 8000 and the WRC do; the FLA does not. The idea of a living wage resonates with many people, but it is difficult to define and many corporations oppose it, which could deter broad acceptance of codes that include this provision. The WRC has said that, while a living wage is crucial to their code, universities are not required to implement that provision pending research on how to measure it. A second area of disagreement has been over how to ensure freedom of association in countries such as China where the state restricts this right.

Regardless of content, codes can gain broad public support only if they have a credible monitoring mechanism. For outside NGOs or any other independent organization to monitor adherence to codes, there must be transparency in the names and locations of subcontractors. Initially, major manufacturers refused to identify their subcontractors, claiming it was a trade secret. The failure of the FLA to require such disclosure contributed to the decision by USAS to develop the WRC as an alternative. The students' persistence on the disclosure issue was rewarded in fall 1999 when several firms agreed to make this information public, including Nike, which released a list of forty-one plants producing licensed apparel for Duke, North Carolina, Georgetown, Michigan, and Arizona (www.nikebiz.com/labor/disclosure.shtml; accessed January 1, 2001).

Equally divisive is the issue of who does the monitoring. Firms prefer monitors from the business community, such as PricewaterhouseCoopers (PwC) and Ernst and Young, whom they pay and with whom they often do

15. This is a model not addressed here, in which activists try to organize alternative markets by linking consumers in rich countries to producers in poor countries who are paid premium prices for products such as coffee, tea, bananas, or local handicrafts. In addition to its work with the FLA, the International Labor Rights Fund was involved in creating the U.S. Rugmark program; other groups are listed in the appendix.

other business. Activists prefer monitors from local NGOs because they believe workers will feel more comfortable talking to them and, therefore, are more likely to be honest in discussing problems at the plant. They are suspicious of business monitors and are fearful of Potemkin Village audits of the kind that Andrew Young performed for Nike in 1997 with a whirlwind tour of factories that concluded all was well. Such skepticism appeared justified when the Transnational Resource and Action Center posted on its Corporate Watch website (www.corpwatch.org) a leaked Ernst and Young audit that concluded that Nike violated a number of Vietnamese labor laws. A recent report by O'Rourke (2000) identified a number of problems with company-arranged audits by PwC, especially in the areas of freedom of association and health and safety. O'Rourke concluded that PwC's methodology was flawed, biased toward management, and that the auditors themselves were inadequately trained.

The FLA and SAI address these problems by requiring that companies use an auditor that has been certified by them as qualified to do independent verification of compliance. Both organizations require monitors to consult with local NGOs and encourage NGOs to apply for accreditation, but critics argue that the accreditation procedures are too expensive or too complex for most NGOs to master. In an interesting variation, the FLA allows agents to be accredited to monitor particular parts of the code without being expert in all of them. Although the FLA does not explicitly encourage member companies to use teams of monitors with expertise in different areas, this provision at least envisions such a possibility.

But USAS objects to the fact that the traditional accounting firms can be certified under these programs and believes that the FLA approach leaves too much control in the hands of the corporations.[16] Realizing that even the best monitoring system cannot certify with 100 percent certainty that even one factory is in compliance with a code 365 days a year, the WRC rejects the typical monitoring and certification model because it conveys a "good housekeeping seal of approval," even when problems remain in some areas. Their verification model enforces compliance through complete disclosure of plant locations and information on conditions in them, backed by a system of local NGOs prepared to receive worker complaints.

Indicative of the depth of these conflicts, in spring 2000 Nike ended licensing agreements with Brown and the University of Michigan and cut off personal and corporate contributions to CEO Phil Knight's alma mater, the University of Oregon, after these universities joined the WRC. Nike objected to the unwillingness of USAS to include corporations in the negotiation of WRC principles and procedures and also criticized the "ambiguous living wage" provision and "gotcha monitoring" (www.nikebiz.com/media/n_uofo.shtml; accessed September 1, 2000).

16. Thus far, none of the six auditors accredited by FLA is one of the traditional accounting firms, though two are established quality certification firms.

2.4.2 Assessing the Effectiveness of the Campaigns

In their analysis of transnational advocacy, Keck and Sikkink (1998, 25) identify five levels of potential effectiveness:

- "[I]ssue creation and agenda-setting"
- "[I]nfluence on discursive positions of states and international organizations"
- "[I]nfluence on institutional procedures"
- "[I]nfluence on policy change in 'target actors'" (states, international organizations, corporations, or other private sector actors)
- "[I]nfluence on state [or corporate] behavior"

Examining selected antisweatshop campaigns from this perspective shows that activists have succeeded in getting the sweatshop issue on the agenda of corporations, governments, and international organizations and have influenced the discursive position of states, international organizations, and firms as well. Most major visible retail marketers have adopted corporate codes of conducts addressing various labor standards.[17]

But the effects on behavior are weaker. Table 2.5 provides a summary of various campaigns, together with a crude measure of their achievements, using a 1 (little or no effect) to 5 (very effective) scale. We have given low scores even to relatively successful campaigns in part because some targeted firms backed off from their early responses or were subsequently found to have done less than they promised. For instance, Kernaghans's revelations about Kathie Lee apparel raised questions about Wal-Mart's earlier commitment to enforcing its code of conduct. Subsequent allegations about Wal-Mart contractors in China, Saipan, and elsewhere suggest changes in behavior remain elusive. Phillips-Van Heusen canceled its contract with the unionized plant in Guatemala, forcing its closure. Phillips-Van Heusen claimed it did so because it lost a major contract and had excess capacity, but critics questioned the significance of the business lost and wondered why PVH could not have reduced capacity at a nonunionized plant. Independent monitoring at Gap facility in El Salvador continues and Liz Claiborne, a member of the FLA, also signed an agreement for independent monitoring of a supplier there. Levi Strauss expanded its operations in China despite a worsening human rights environment and initially resisted joining the FLA or allowing any external monitoring at its facilities. In 1998, however, Levi's approached Oxfam about establishing a

17. An ILO report (1998) on corporate codes and social labels surveyed 200, while the Investor Responsibility Research Center (Varley 1998) collected 121 codes from a survey of the S&P 500 companies and eighty retailers. Activists recognize that their main success has been in putting labor standards on the world policy agenda. In our survey of USAS activists, 94 percent rated their campaign as very or somewhat successful in increasing public awareness and 90 percent rated their campaign as very/somewhat successful in increasing student activism.

Table 2.5 **Assessment of selected antisweatshop campaigns**

Company or campaign	Influence on procedures	Influence on behavior	Assessment[a]	Comments
Disney	None: Disney has a code but refused to respond to NLC campaign on Haiti (except by allowing one licensee to withdraw).	None detected.	–1–0	Young children are difficult to mobilize and parents are reluctant to say no.
Levi Strauss	Levi Strauss was an early promoter-of code; Levi Strauss traditionally opposed independent monitoring but recently joined ETI in Europe.	In 1993, Levi Strauss announced withdrawal from China because of human rights abuses; it later stopped sourcing in Burma.	3	Levi Strauss has always promoted itself as caring about workers in the US and abroad, but sales are down, and profits are under pressure in recent years; they froze withdrawal from China in 1996, announced expansion in 1998, and closed plants in the U.S. and Western Europe.
Liz Claiborne, Inc.[b]	Liz Claiborne, Inc. accepted independent NGO monitoring at a contract facility in El Salvator.	Shortfalls were identified and publicly reported; there is need to verify remediation.	2–3	Experiment was not independently replicated but monitoring now by FLA
Nike[b]	Nike became much more open; though criticized, Nike hired the Andrew Young group to monitor facilities in East Asia; the locations of factories producing licensed university apparel were revealed.	Like Reebok, Nike is eliminating toxic solvents from the production process; it has improved ventilation in factories and raised wages above the official minimum wage after the Asian financial crisis.	2–3	There has been criticism of the Young report (nothing on wages); Corpwatch releases leaked Ernst & Young audit showing violations of Vietnamese law, but concludes the plant in compliance with the Nike code of conduct.
Phillips-Van Heusen[b]	PVH asked Human Rights Watch to investigate complaints at a Guatemalan facility.	Following the Human Rights Watch report, PVH recognized union in Guatemala maquila.	1–2	CEO Klatsky is on board of HRW and has direct ownership stake in the facility. The plant is shut after the union is recognized.

Reebok[b]	Reebok adopted the code early; Reebok recently elicited and published a NGO report on factories producing 2/3 of Reebok footwear in Indonesia.	The report also included steps taken by contractors to address health and safety problems identified in the NGO report; Reebok raised wages above the official minimum wage after the Asian financial crisis; like Nike, Reebok is eliminating toxic solvents from the production process	3	The Reebok letter accompanying the NGO report says it is too expensive to replicate elsewhere, though it hopes to apply lessons; critics target the failure to independently inspect all factories producing for Reebok and for not doing enough on wages.
Starbucks	In 1995, following picketing/leafleting at stores by the U.S./Guatemala Labor Education Project, Starbucks announces a code of conduct for coffee pickers in Guatemala and elsewhere. In 2000, Starbucks preempts planned protests at stores in Washington, DC and elsewhere by announcing it will buy and sell Fair Trade Coffee.	Starbucks announced an action plan to assist small-scale coffee producers in improving quality and expanding overseas markets but takes no steps to monitor code implementation. As of Fall 2000, Fair Trade coffee beans are available in Starbucks stores and online.	2–3	Starbucks promotes itself as a socially conscious company, provides benefits to part-time employees, and donates profits to charity (largest direct corporate contributor to CARE according to promotional material in store).
Wal-Mart and Kathie Lee	Wal-Mart adopted the code early, and KLG agreed to ensure independent monitoring to enforce the code in facilities supplying KLG-label clothing. Publicity contributed-to the creation of AIP but, while KLG joined, Wal-Mart did not.	None detected?	1	Independent monitoring has not occurred, and allegations about facilities in China and elsewhere continue; Wal-Mart is also a defendant in the Saipan sweatshop case.

[a]From 1 for negative outcome to 5 for very successful.
[b]Member of FLA.

pilot monitoring program in its Dominican Republic operations and subsequently joined the Ethical Trade Initiative in Europe (Oxfam 1998–1999).

In contrast to these partial or sometimes temporary successes is the failed NLC campaign against Disney and its licensees in Haiti. With its focus on children and family values, Disney looked like a good follow-on to the Kathie Lee campaign. Instead, Disney was perhaps the NLC's biggest failure. Although Disney sent its own investigators to check out the facilities in Haiti and reportedly pressured them to make some improvements (see www.cleanclothes.org), one Disney subcontractor in Haiti withdrew, causing the shutdown of the plant. Disney alternated between flatly denying the allegations and simply not responding. Although Kernaghan staged protests outside a Disney store in New York, consumers did not respond, and the pressure did not force any substantial change in Disney's operations (*Los Angeles Times,* July 25, 1996). One possible reason this campaign failed is that children are the ultimate consumer, and many parents cannot say no when their child desperately wants the latest Disney product that all their friends have. Another possible explanation is that it was difficult to embarrass Disney CEO Michael Eisner as a hypocrite because he lacks visible links to human rights and charitable causes that other targets have had.[18]

The narrow membership of the FLA and SAI, difficulties in getting the FLA monitoring system up and going, the split between the FLA and WRC, and the development of SA 8000 in competition with both highlight two weaknesses of the antisweatshop campaigns. The limited membership of the umbrella groups, combined with Nike's reaction to the WRC and Disney's stonewalling of Kernaghan, suggest that most firms still view the activists as a minor rather than serious threat. The proliferating number of groups risk consumer confusion and frustration, which could further exacerbate the problem of generating enough demand to force changes in corporate behavior (Freeman 1998; Liubicic 1998).[19]

Could these divisions be reduced and the various participants in the antisweatshop activity advance under a common banner? The example of environmental groups interested in promoting sustainable forestry suggests that under some circumstances different activists and firms can coalesce around a common standard overseen by a single accreditation agency. In 1993 environmental groups, forest companies, and retailers negotiated a code and developed the Forest Stewardship Council (FSC) for certifying compliance (see appendix C). Some environmentalists have criticized the

18. Bruce Klatsky of PVH demonstrates a strong personal commitment to human rights through his work with Human Rights Watch, and Kathie Lee Gifford demonstrated concern for the well-being of children through her charitable contributions to children's causes.

19. For an alternative view of the benefits of "open standards" and competition among monitoring agencies, see Sabel, O'Rourke, and Fung (2000).

FSC for cooperating too closely with industry groups, but large American timber companies formed the rival Sustainable Forestry Initiative because they regard FSC standards as too stringent. Nevertheless, the FSC has succeeded in getting commitments from major retailers selling more than 20 percent of the lumber products used in home repair and remodeling in the United States and an even higher share in Europe. "Industry executives say the movement is quickly reaching critical mass, and could soon make it a liability for wood products producers not to have the FSC imprimatur" (*Wall Street Journal,* September 26, 2000, 1).

However, there are important differences between consumer desire for clothing made outside of sweatshops and the desire for sustainable forestry. Self-interest among firms operated as an important motivator in sustaining the FSC campaign in ways that it has not in the antisweatshop area. Several wood products retailers identified a competitive advantage in being "green" and thus were willing to make commitments to buy FSC-certified products.[20] Individual consumers also often see gains to themselves from environmental improvements, whereas the beneficiaries from improvements in sweatshops are the workers in those factories. The sustainable forestry campaign also suggests that vigilante pressure works better when there are a relatively small fixed number of market leaders whose actions can be readily monitored. Sweatshop activists have focused on major firms, but the wide supply chain in apparel makes it hard to pin down key decision makers. Moreover, in both forestry and apparel, a successful campaign can disadvantage small suppliers. In the forestry case, this presumably creates no new environmental problem, but in the sweatshop case, success may displace home workers or others in the informal sector who cannot enter the formal economy for cultural, child rearing, or other reasons.[21]

The antisweatshop activists also have a more difficult task than antiapartheid activists in an earlier era. In contrast to ending apartheid, success in eradicating sweatshop exploitation is more difficult to measure: exactly what defines a sweatshop, and what does it mean to clean them up? Success is measured in incremental steps and requires constant vigilance to guard against backsliding. The antiapartheid activists had strong union and nongovernmental groups in less-developed countries with which to work and the African National Congress (ANC) to press for changes on the ground.

20. Of course, given the paucity of such products in the market today, there is little cost attached to the promise, and the true test will come when more final consumers have the choice before them.

21. Concerns about the effects of codes on homeworkers were raised by Southern NGOs in a workshop organized by NGOs participating in the Ethical Trade Initiative in the United Kingdom (CAFOD 1998). Concerns have also been raised about the impact of the agreement to create stitching centers for the production of soccer balls in Sialkot, Pakistan. Shifting production from homes to centralized locations facilities monitoring of the agreement to end child labor but makes it difficult for some adult women to earn income because they cannot leave home (see the Clean Clothes Campaign website at www.cleanclothes.org).

Indeed, in contrast to the antisweatshop activists, who are leading the worldwide campaign against sweatshops, antiapartheid activists played a more secondary role, supporting the ANC in its efforts to overturn the minority apartheid regime in South Africa.

2.5 Risks and Limitations of the Activist Consumer-Based Model

> Bad jobs at bad wages are better than no jobs at all.
> —Paul Krugman[22]

> Empleo sí, pero con dignidad.
> —Nicaraguan María Elena Cuadra, Movement of Working and Unemployed Women[23]

Most developing country governments, multinational corporations, and trade economists, and many development experts argue that antisweatshop campaigns are likely to do more harm than good.[24] How valid are their concerns? How much good can even the most successful activist-initiated, consumer-based campaign do in improving labor standards in poor countries?

2.5.1 The Risk That Doing Good Will Do Harm

The argument that antisweatshop campaigns risk harm to workers in less-developed countries begins with the fact that sweatshop jobs are better than jobs in rural agriculture or the informal sector, particularly for the young women who make up the bulk of the sweatshop workforce. Studies of wages and employment show that foreign-owned and export-oriented factories in developing countries typically offer higher pay and better conditions than those of domestic firms producing for the local market (Varley 1998). Wages in footwear and apparel may be at the bottom of manufacturing, but they are generally higher than the minimum wage level in many developing countries and better than conditions in agriculture (U.S. Department of Labor 2000). While there are situations where workers are misled by employer promises, subject to forced labor, or paid less than they are promised, workers choose sweatshop jobs because those jobs are the best alternatives available to them.

22. See http://web.mit.edu/krugman/www/. "A policy of good jobs in principle, but no jobs in practice, might assuage our consciences, but it is no favor to its alleged beneficiaries."

23. See Lynda Yanz (2000, 6).

24. For example, Columbia University Professor Jagdish Bhagwati argued in *Financial Times* (May 2, 2000) that "[A] minuscule minority of students who are captive to unions such as the apparel industry's UNITE, have used the language of 'social responsibility' towards the poor countries, to advance an agenda, both illegitimate and narrow, that will in fact harm the very countries and workers they claim to assist." Bhagwati also served on the steering committee of the Academic Consortium on International Trade, which in September 2000 delivered a letter from academic economists to the presidents of universities targeted by USAS expressing similar, though less virulent, concerns.

Critics of human rights vigilantes fear that the campaigns will discourage exports from less-developed countries and reduce foreign investment in those countries, which would lower the demand for labor and reduce worker well-being. Some believe that the activists are motivated by protectionism or are misguided followers of those who are. The evidence in earlier sections rejects this assertion. The human rights groups, students, and church groups who make up the activist community do not compete with low-paid workers in developing countries. If they succeed in their campaigns, they will raise the prices of the goods they consume rather than raise trade barriers. The USAS, which has close ties to the apparel union UNITE, has opposed firms shifting production of college-logo clothing to U.S. factories as a means of improving standards (Moore 2000, 10). The NLC's Kernaghan has also criticized firms that "cut and run" rather than clean up and monitor a substandard facility.

But motivation aside, antisweatshop campaigns could still have adverse effects on developing-country workers. Even if antisweatshop campaigns do not call for consumer boycotts of targeted goods, negative publicity could deter trade and investment and reduce the number of jobs available in countries with already high levels of unemployment and underemployment. Or campaigns could have the perverse effect of pushing production out of the formal sector into areas of the economy with even lower standards and less visibility. Demands for living wages in antisweatshop campaigns run the greatest risk of backfiring, because such demands could price workers in less-developed countries out of some markets. This is particularly the case if the living-wage target is determined by outside activists with strong ideological stances rather than by local NGOs or unions who can better weigh the danger to jobs of large imposed increases in wages. In terms of our analysis, an "excessive living wage" would place the cost curve for making improvements far above the price line so that firms would fight this demand or close shop.

To date, however, the danger that antisweatshop campaigns will harm workers in less-developed countries has been more rhetoric than reality. One reason is that the activists are aware of the dangers and try to avoid them. Indeed, the wide range of groups in the activist community almost guarantees that if some group pushes demands that are counterproductive, another group will modify them or take corrective action.

Campaigns against child labor provide an example of this. The ILO's International Program on the Elimination of Child Labor works to replace child labor with better opportunities. In two cases, involving the Bangladesh garment industry and Pakistani-produced soccer balls, external pressure led to joint initiatives involving industry, government, and the ILO that required the provision of educational alternatives for displaced child workers and turned a potential harm into a positive outcome. In Bangladesh, more than 12,000 children were moved from work to school, and their share of the workforce in the garment sector has fallen from an estimated 30 percent to just 5 percent five years later (ILO 2000, 55). In Pakistan, thousands more children also have better opportunities as a result of outside intervention and assistance. Similarly, consumers buying Rugmark-labeled, child-free carpets pay a premium that, in addition to paying the costs of certification, goes to build schools for affected children. In the absence of ready alternatives, NLC campaigns that target child labor concentrate on increasing the pay for children rather than on getting firms to produce goods child free.

Activist debates over living wages also give considerable attention to the dangers of unintended adverse consequences. A 1999 antisweatshop symposium at the University of Wisconsin warned that campaigns

> may produce serious negative feedback loops. These could include the following: Firms may concentrate their production of college apparel in high-wage countries, moving more of their other operations to the lower-wage economies. . . . Firms could maintain production in the low-wage economies, but create small high-wage enclaves within them (which would have) little positive effect on the rest of the local labor market. Setting the wage too high relative to local market conditions could create difficulties for monitoring. This is because a strong incentive would be created to circumvent the wage mandate. For example, workers could sell a share of their high-wage jobs under the table to their relatives or friends; so that, in fact, multiple workers are employed at a single "living wage" job.

The conclusion was that any campaign had to take account of local market conditions and base its decision on "What would be the wage bargained for by workers if they were allowed to organize and bargain collectively in a free, democratic environment?"[25]

Fears that antisweatshop campaigns could reduce foreign investment and jobs in less advanced countries seem in any case beside the point in a world where the overwhelming trend is toward expansion of manufacturing, particularly apparel and shoes, into less-developed countries. The income gaps between those countries and advanced countries are so great that it is difficult to imagine a scenario where antisweatshop activism could reverse this trend, even if, contrary to the evidence, the activists wanted to accomplish as much. The danger is much more that firms will shift their operations from less-developed countries with higher and more expensive standards to similar countries with lower and less-expensive labor standards. As an example, in the banana industry, lower-cost labor in Ecuador—

25. See http://www.lafollette.wisc.edu/livingwage/Final_Report/report.htm. A considered defense of a living wage can also be found in a student dissent to the May 2000 University of Michigan task force report on labor standards "The Final Report of the Advisory Committee on Labor Standards and Human Rights," University of Michigan, May 2000. Available on the University of Michigan website at http://www.umich.edu/~newsinfo/BG/humright.html.

in part the result of low unionization rates—threatens workers in Colombia. But such threats are likely with or without activist campaigns.

2.5.2 Limits of the Market for Standards

Assume that human rights vigilantes ran a completely successful antisweatshop campaign, inducing all their targets to have verifiable codes of conduct and avoiding adverse unintended consequences. By itself, how much would this raise living standards in the targeted countries? Sadly, not by much. Consumers appear to care largely about the ways in which the things they personally consume are produced so that virtually all campaigns focus on standards in export sectors in less-developed countries rather than in sectors with the worst labor conditions or on conditions in less-developed countries more broadly.[26] In total, exports by low-income countries of apparel and footwear are only 2 percent of world exports, 14 percent of total low-income country exports, and 3 percent of their gross domestic product (GDP).

Moreover, because the major stick behind the campaigns is the threat to corporate reputations or brand names, activist campaigns target well-known firms rather than producers of generic and unbranded products, who may produce goods under poorer conditions than better-known firms. The high-end retailer/marketer who uses a relatively smaller number of more stable suppliers is also more likely to be able to enforce compliance with standards. Lower-end retailers, such as Wal-Mart, who are more interested in price than quality or design, often use middleman buyers to locate suppliers, making it hard to enforce their codes of conduct. The college-apparel market targeted by USAS is smaller yet.

In short, human rights vigilantes cannot greatly improve living standards in poor countries under any realistic scenario—only sustained economic growth can do that—though they may be able to bring some modest gain in well-being to some workers.

2.5.3 What About the Workers?

> In the end the only ones who can stand up for workers' rights are workers themselves.
>
> —Medea Benjamin[27]

Antisweatshop campaigns in advanced countries would be unnecessary if workers in less-developed countries were free to defend their own well-being by forming trade unions or other such organizations. At best, activists in advanced countries interceding for workers is a second-best

26. Most child labor, for example, occurs in agriculture, construction, and domestic services, where antisweatshop campaigns cannot readily reach.

27. See Benjamin (2000).

alternative to workers defending their own rights, negotiating with management-appropriate standards, and jointly monitoring implementation. In industries with high labor turnover, external monitors cannot readily inform workers about codes of conduct nor provide the day-to-day scrutiny of facilities that workers can (Frost 2000; Bernard 1997).

More broadly, Keck and Sikkink (1998) find that having allies within the targeted country is a factor in many of the successful cases of transnational advocacy that they studied. Vocal support for economic sanctions by black leaders in South Africa, even though they were the ones expected to suffer the most economic pain, was an important factor in the success of the antiapartheid campaign.

In contrast, antisweatshop campaigns have made little or no headway in pressing for freedom of association in less-advanced countries, which would give exploited workers a voice. The WRC, the FLA, and SA 8000 codes include respect for freedom of association and collective bargaining rights, but implementation of these codes is difficult absent major changes in the developing countries themselves. Even corporations concerned with standards typically leave union rights out of their codes of conduct (ILO 1998; Varley 1998) Business is typically antiunion because unions will alter authority relations within firms and shift revenues from owners to workers (ILO 2000, 61–63). The government of many less-developed countries, including China, oppose freedom of association because unions are an independent source of power on a political scene otherwise dominated by a single party or narrow elite. These attitudes make unionization extraordinarily difficult to attain, even in countries that nominally accept the freedom of association standard of the ILO. At the same time, activists are likely to have trouble arousing consumer concern over the freedom to unionize, according to the PIPA poll in table 2.1.

Campaigns where unionism was a key issue, as with the PVH plant in Guatemala, have not been sustained for long. By shifting orders to a nonunion firm, multinationals can readily undo the effects of successful organization or they can accede to other demands but not to demands for organization. At the Gap's Mandarin factory in El Salvador, the main source of contention was the unwillingness of management to allow formation of a union and the firing of union organizers. After the campaign publicized violations in the company's code of conduct, the Gap worked to improve conditions and even guaranteed a minimum number of orders, offsetting lost orders from elsewhere that resulted from negative publicity (Varley 1998, 302). In addition, the Gap allowed independent monitoring, but there is still no union in that plant at the time of this writing.

In fact, although some human rights vigilante groups, such as the NLC and USAS, have close ties to trade unions, there are serious tensions between the vigilante groups and unions (Compa 2000). The antisweatshop NGOs are not elected by workers. They are accountable to consumers, funders, and other Western supporters. Some trade unionists fear that the vigilantes' demands for corporate codes of conduct and independent monitoring will inadvertently serve as a weak substitute for unions. On the other side, the NGOs feel that they can accomplish something, while it is unrealistic to expect free and independent unions to operate in many third world countries.

In a September 1998 workshop organized by the British-based NGO Labour Rights Network (the NGO representatives to the Ethical Trade Initiative), representatives from developing countries stressed the importance of involving local NGOs and unions from the beginning in antisweatshop campaigns to ensure that they address *local* priorities and interests. They agreed that while

> Codes could be useful as a means of exerting leverage on management, the key issue was workers' own level of organisation and ability to carry out collective bargaining. . . . The ideal combination is for NGOs to play a supporting role by providing training and services and campaigning for the respect of trade union rights, and encouraging more traditional unions to take up previously unrepresented groups and gender issues.[28]

Of the other human rights vigilante groups, USAS has been particularly attuned to the need to gain support from workers groups on the ground. The WRC eschews the usual monitoring agencies and emphasizes the need to engage and strengthen local workers' organizations and NGOs by providing financial and technical assistance.

2.6 Conclusion: When Does Doing Good Do Good?

> Not to sound Pollyannish, but I believe there is a basic decency in the American people that these companies don't understand. We have to try to tap this decency. When we do that, we get a tremendous response.
> —Charles Kernaghan, *The New York Times,* June 18, 1996

The goal of antisweatshop campaigns is to improve conditions for workers in less-developed countries. But they cannot do this directly. Their effectiveness depends on catalyzing other economic agents: firms, governments, international agencies, and the sweatshop workers themselves. To what extent and under what conditions have campaigns succeeded?

A priori, there are a range of possible outcomes from antisweatshop campaigns: (1) the campaigns could make things worse by generating negative publicity that causes sales or prices to drop for the products of sweatshop workers; (2) the campaigns could have no effect at all if firms do not view the threat of a consumer backlash as credible; (3) the campaigns could

28. A conference report from the workshop is available from the Catholic Agency for Overseas Development (CAFOD) at http://www.cafod.org.uk/policyviews.htm.

catalyze firms to improve standards when the consumer threat is credible relative to the cost of improvements; or (4) the campaigns could catalyze firms, governments, and international agencies to undertake broader sustainable improvements.

Our analysis rejects the first possible outcome and indicates that the activists have had at least limited success in catalyzing consumers and firms to change their behavior to improve sweatshop conditions. Activist campaigns have succeeded in getting most major, visible retailers and marketers to develop their own corporate codes of conduct addressing various labor standards. They have induced some, such as the Gap and Nike, to improve labor conditions in their overseas factories at some expense. The April 2000 Starbucks agreement to market Fair Trade–certified coffee, which gives farmers a premium over the prevailing market price, would never have been done had not human rights vigilantes developed a social climate where such actions are seen as being in the corporate interest. Similarly, the fact that Nike and Reebok eliminated toxic chemicals in the production of athletic footwear is, at least in part, a response to activist pressures. And while many activists attack the FLA because it is much weaker than they would like, its creation, and that of SA8000, are also a product of their campaigns. Some campaigns have indeed shifted the price curve facing firms so that the firms have chosen the "improved standards" solution (see figure 2.3). So far, however, the successes are ad hoc and often temporary.

The limited direct effects of campaigns are not the end of the story, however. The antisweatshop activists have gotten sweatshop issues on the international agenda and, together with unions and other groups protesting the policies of the World Trade Organization (WTO), have convinced key governments and international agencies that they must deal with labor standards to maintain support for liberal trade policies. This pressure has contributed to a variety of efforts by agents with more reach and power than the activists to empower workers and better enforce labor standards.

On the government side, the insistence of the Clinton administration that new multilateral trade negotiations address labor standards issues is a response to activist and U.S. union pressures. Without these pressures, new "fast-track" trade negotiating authority likely would have been approved by Congress without attention to this issue (Elliott 2000). Congress also would not have raised the U.S. contribution to the ILO campaign to eliminate child labor from $2.1 million in 1995 to $45 million in 2001 (*Congressional Record* 2000). While the United States cannot dictate the place of labor standards in the next round of world trade negotiations—China and other less-advanced countries are adamantly opposed—the fact that the debate is not *whether* but *how* to strengthen enforcement of core labor standards (as defined by the ILO, World Summit for Social Development, and others) is an important outcome from a decade of activism.

On the international agency front, activists have put labor rights on the world agenda in a big way. In 1999, United Nations (UN) Secretary General Kofi Annan unveiled a new "Global Compact," calling on the business community to respect nine core principles in the areas of human rights, worker rights, and environmental protection. The Organization for Economic Cooperation and Development recently added language on worker rights to its guidelines for multinational corporations, and the World Bank has a child labor program and is focusing more attention on gender discrimination issues. Maybe with a bit more pressure, the International Monetary Fund will endorse transparency in labor markets as it does in capital markets, and the World Bank will drop its ambivalence about the role of unions in development.

The major beneficiary of activist pressures to strengthen enforcement of standards is the ILO. As a result of the desire of employers and key governments to divert pressures to incorporate labor standards in the WTO and other trade agreements, the ILO is receiving both more attention and more resources to deal with "core" labor standards, especially child labor. Yes, the 2000–2001 $56 million budget for the ILO's Program to Eliminate Child Poverty is minuscule in comparison with the revenues and expenditures of almost any multinational firm. The ILO also does not have anything like the financial resources to push its child labor program that the IMF or World Bank have to push their programs of financial reforms or economic rectitude. But this is a huge increase over previous budgets, with much of the increase funded by the United States. In addition, the ILO codified the consensus definition of "core" labor standards in its 1998 "Declaration on Fundamental Principles and Rights at Work."

The best example of how activism has galvanized the ILO and produced a better outcome for workers than activists could have attained by themselves is in the child labor area. In the mid-1990s, activists exposed the use of child labor in the Bangladeshi garment industry and in the soccer ball industry in Pakistan and pressured producers and retailers to address the problem. The initial industry response in Bangladesh was to throw the children out on the street, and it was only after the ILO and United Nations Children's Fund (UNICEF) intervened that a constructive solution was found. Manufacturers in Bangladesh and Pakistan agreed not simply to stop employing children but to cooperate with and assist in the funding of programs to put them in schools or other rehabilitative training and to allow the ILO to monitor the results.

Finally, the upsurge of labor activism in some poor Asian countries, notably Cambodia and Indonesia, shows how external pressure and support, in these cases from activists, governments, and the ILO, can empower workers (Spaeth 2000). In a bilateral trade negotiation with Cambodia, the United States responded to activist and union pressure to promote labor standards by using its market power as a carrot rather than a stick. As part of a bilateral textile trade agreement, U.S. negotiators offered to expand Cambodia's export quota by 14 percent if "working conditions in the Cambodia textile and apparel sector substantially comply with [local] labor law and standards."[29] In the first review in December 1999, U.S. officials concluded that "substantial compliance" had not been achieved but, in recognition of the progress that had been made, they offered a 5 percent quota increase to be implemented when Cambodia completed an agreement with the ILO, creating an independent monitoring program (United States Trade Representative [USTR] press release, May 18, 2000). The ILO agreed to the plan after gaining a commitment from U.S. officials to fund a parallel program to provide technical assistance and training to the Cambodian labor ministry, and the quota increase was granted in May 2000. In response to worker protests following conclusion of the bilateral agreement, the secretary-general of the Cambodia Garment Manufacturers Association complained, "All the attention gives the workers the comfort level that they are calling the shots" (*Financial Times,* April 7, 2000, 5). In this case, activist pressure contributed to empowerment of the 15 to 20 percent of Cambodian workers in the apparel sector, at least some increased access to the U.S. market, and increased bureaucratic capacity to enforce labor standards for all workers.

Despite signs of movement, activists have been least successful in moving the core labor standard of freedom of association and the right to collective bargaining from rhetoric to reality. These "enabling rights" would allow sweatshop workers to decide for themselves what issues to pursue, trade-offs to make, and battles to conduct with their employers and would probably do more for improving labor standards than anything else. The activists are a key voice directing attention to violations of the rights of workers who seek to exercise their rights overseas, but they ultimately must rely on workers and institutions in those countries to take the lead, much as the African National Congress and Congress of South African Trade Unions (COSATU) did in South Africa.[30]

Still, these cases show that activist pressure can catalyze more powerful actors on the world scene and contribute to improvements in whole sectors rather than single plants. Such agreements are likely to be more sustainable than standard antisweatshop campaigns because the ILO and Western governments provide financial and technical assistance and because the ILO monitors implementation.

Finally, while antisweatshop campaigns do risk reducing the flow of resources to less-developed countries, they can also increase those flows. At the consumer level, this can occur when consumers pay for improvements

29. The text of the bilateral agreement may be found on the Department of Commerce's Market Access and Compliance website at http://www.mac.doc.gov.

30. See the NLC's campaign to help workers at the Mil Colores workers plant in Nicaragua.

in labor standards through higher prices or when the campaigns squeeze oligopolistic profits on branded goods. In some sectors, such as soccer balls, which are overwhelmingly sourced in Pakistan, or in cases where campaigns cover the bulk of firms in a sector, they have the potential to improve the terms of trade for the less-developed country (Brown, Deardorff, and Stern 1993). At the national or international level this can occur through an increase in expenditures in technical assistance or funding of programs, for instance, to move children from work to school. But to have a bigger effect, the antisweatshop activists would have to tackle issues that go beyond poor labor conditions in particular factories or in particular products—such as debt relief and reduction of trade barriers to developing countries—that they have thus far not put at the front of their agenda.

In sum, by putting labor rights and the living standards of workers in poor countries on the agenda of powerful economic agents and governments and international agencies, human rights vigilantes have catalyzed something that has the potential for improving the well-being of workers in poorer countries. There is nothing in economic analysis, however, that guarantees a positive result nor that guarantees the bad outcomes that critics of the activists fear. It depends on the smarts of the activists and their campaigns.

Appendix A

Transnational Labor Rights Activist Organizations

	Specialization	Year formed	Orientation
American Friends Service Comm (http://www.afsc.org/)	General	1917	Religious
Asian Immigrant Women Advocates (http://www.corpwatch.org/feature/hitech/aiwa.html)	U.S. Asians	1983	Ethnic
Asian Law Caucus (http://www.asianlawcaucus.org/)	U.S. Asians	1972	Ethnic
As You Sow Foundation (http://www.asyousow.org/index40.htm)	Shareholder activism	1992	Do-gooder
Bangor Clean Clothes Campaign (http://www.bairnet.org/organizations/pica/cleanclo.htm)	Code of conduct	1997	Do-gooder
Campaign for Labor Rights (http://www.summersault.com/~agj/clr/)	General	1995	Activist-left
Coalition for Justice in Maquiladoras (http://www.coalitionforjustice.net)	Mexico	1989	Do-gooder
CISPES (http://www.cispes.org/)	El Salvador	1980	Activist-left
Co-Op America (http://www.coopamerica.org/)	General	1982	Do-gooder
Fair Labor Association (http://www.fairlabor.org)	Code/monitoring	1998	Do-gooder
Fair Trade Federation (http://fairtradefederation.org)	Codes/labels	1996	Do-gooder
Free the Children USA (http://www.freethechildren.org/main/index.html)	Children	1995	Do-gooder
Global Exchange (http://www.globalexchange.org/)	General	1988	Activist-left
Global Kids (http://www.globalkidsinc.org/)	Children	1989	Do-gooder
Human Rights Watch (http://www.hrw.org/)	General	1978	Do-gooder
Human Rights for Workers (http://www.senser.com/)	General	1996	Do-gooder
Interfaith Center for Corporate Responsibility (http://www.icer.org)	Shareholder activism	1971	Religious
International Labor Rights Fund (http://www.laborrights.org/)	General	1986	Do-gooder
La Mujer Obrera (http://mujerobrera.org)	El Paso	Unknown	Activist-left
Labor Defense Network	Sweatshops	1997	Do-gooder
National Consumer League, Child Labor Coalition (http://www.natlconsumersleague.org/)	Children	1989	Do-gooder

	Specialization	Year formed	Orientation
National Labor Committee (http://www.nlcnet.org/)	General	1981	Activist-left
NY State Labor-Religion Coalition (http://www.labor-religion.org/)	Codes	1980	Religious
Nicaragua Network Education Fund (http://summersault.com/~agi/nicanet/index.html)	Nicaragua	1980	Activist-left
Press for Change (http://www.nikeworkers.org/)	Nike	Unknown	Activist-left
Resource Center of the Americas (http://www.Americas.org/)	Latin America	1991	Do-gooder
Rugmark Foundation USA (http://www.rugmark.org/)	Child labor/carpets	1995	Do-gooder
Social Accountability International (http://sa-intl.org)	Code/monitoring	1997	Do-gooder
STITCH (http://stitchonline.org)	Guatamala	1992	Activist-left
Support Committee for Maquiladora Workers (http://enchantedwebsites.com/maquiladora/index.html)	Mexico	Unknown	Do-gooder
Sweatshop Watch (http://www.sweatshopwatch.org/)	General (mainly U.S.)	1995	Do-gooder
Transnational Resource and Action Center (Corporate Watch) (http://www.corpwatch.org/)	General	1996	Activist-left
Transfair America (http://www.transfairusa.org/)	Coffee; Starbucks	1996	Do-gooder
UNITE (union) (http://www.uniteunion.org/)	Apparel	1994	Activist-left
U.S./Guatemala Labor Education (Now U.S. Labor Education in the Americas Project) (http://usleap.org/)	Central America	1987	Activist-left
USAS (http://www.umich.edu/~sole/usas/)	College apparel	1997	Activist-left
Verité (http://www.verite.org/)	China, Asia	1995	Do-gooder
Vietnam Labor Watch (http://www.saigon.com/~nike/)	Nike, Vietnam	1996	Do-gooder
Witness for Peace (http://www.witnessforpeace.org/)	Central America	1983	Activist-left
Witness Rights Alert (http://www.oddcast.com/witness/)	Human rights groups	1992	Do-gooder

Sources: Global Exchange (1999), a directory of U.S. antisweatshop organizations; Internet search.

Appendix B
Precedents in the Antiapartheid Campaign

An early attempt to use grassroots pressure to influence corporate policies in foreign countries was the antiapartheid campaign of the 1970s and 1980s.[31] Seeking to pressure the minority white government to reform, antiapartheid activists first tried to convince foreign investors to withdraw from South Africa. When that failed, the Reverend Leon Sullivan developed a code of conduct to encourage corporations in South Africa to treat black workers equally and to set an example by promoting them to management positions. To induce companies to either withdraw from South Africa or accept the Sullivan Principles, activists used threats of boycotts, shareholder pressure by church organizations, and protests by college students calling on their universities to cleanse their endowments of investments in companies operating in South Africa. The Sullivan Principles were adopted by hundreds of companies and improved conditions for black workers in some facilities. But the ultimate goal remained the end of apartheid and the principles had little impact on the white regime's commitment to or ability to sustain it.

As unrest and violence escalated in the mid-1980s, increasing numbers of foreign investors withdrew from South Africa, but this was largely due to the deteriorating economic and political situation in South Africa rather than to pressure from antiapartheid activists. In particular, the decision by Chase Manhattan not to rollover loans to South Africa in mid-1985, following the government's declaration of a state of emergency, appears to have been driven by an assessment of the risks involved in investing in South Africa, not activist pressures in the United States. That decision in turn triggered a financial crisis in South Africa.

Frustrated by the intransigence of the white regime, American activists turned their attention to the U.S. Congress. Civil disobedience by protestors over the course of many months in front of the South African embassy in Washington raised the profile of the issue and contributed to passage of legislation imposing economic sanctions against South Africa in 1986. In 1987, Sullivan gave up on his code and called for additional sanctions, including mandatory corporate withdrawal from South Africa. Although economic sanctions did not cause the financial crisis, public pressure and sanctions complicated its resolution and contributed to the realization in South Africa that fundamental political reforms would be needed to achieve sustainable growth (Hufbauer, Schott, and Elliott, forthcoming). After more than two decades of sustained activism with limited success, the financial crisis coupled with the end of the cold war contributed to rapidly accelerating reforms and the fall of the white minority regime in 1994.

31. For an excellent history of the antiapartheid movement, see Massie (1997).

Besides providing precedent and people, the antiapartheid story contains potential lessons for the antisweatshop activists. First, it underscores the fact that corporations typically respond only to external pressures that tangibly affect their bottom line. Most multinationals in South Africa were willing to adopt the Sullivan Principles because it was a relatively inexpensive way to protect their reputation while maintaining profitable operations. The accelerated pace of withdrawal in the mid-1980s was largely due either to conditions in South Africa that increased risk or reduced profitability, such as the financial crisis, or to government actions that had similar effects, such as the denial of credits for taxes paid in South Africa.

Second, perhaps the most important roles that the antiapartheid activists played were in terms of symbolic and leverage politics. Antiapartheid activists *within* South Africa supported and gained politically from sanctions. The support of external activists bolstered the ANC and their allies psychologically and, when the white regime finally came to the table, sanctions gave the ANC leverage in negotiating the terms of the transition. In addition, by influencing the American and Commonwealth governments, the activists contributed to the sense of isolation and growing hopelessness about the future among whites in South Africa.

Appendix C

Environmental Labeling and the Forest Stewardship Council

The FSC is an independent nonprofit NGO that accredits certifying organizations who, in turn, monitor member companies and certify forest products as being in compliance with the FSC's code of ten principles for sustainable forestry. It was founded in October 1993 when the WWF joined with the Rainforest Alliance (a New York-based NGO with its own certification scheme) and representatives of forest companies and retailers, including B&Q (Britain's largest home improvement retail chain), to negotiate a code and procedures for certifying compliance.[32] The organization is transparent and democratic, with a governing body composed of three separate "chambers" with representatives of social, environmental, and economic interests. Although more radical environmental groups criticized the FSC for having corporations as members, several of the most prominent environmental activist groups joined, including Greenpeace International, the Sierra Club, and various chapters of Friends of the Earth. With their support and that of a few large retailers, FSC quickly became the market leader in forest product certification. It created a standard code,

32. A description of the FSC may be found at http://www.panda.org/forests4life/certify_fsc.cfm (accessed June 9, 2000). See also the FSC homepage at http://www.fscoax.org.

established credibility through independent monitoring, and provided consumers with readily available information by creating an easily recognized logo to mark certified products.[33]

In its first seven years, the FSC accredited nine "certification bodies" in six countries, has seven applications pending, and has certified nearly 20 million hectares in thirty-three countries, including 1.8 million hectares in the United States. To keep up the pressure on the demand side, NGOs convinced Ikea, the world's largest furniture retailer with 1999 sales of $8.5 billion, and Home Depot, the largest do-it-yourself company with 1997 sales of $24 billion, to phase out wood products from old-growth forests that have not been certified.[34] In 1998, under pressure from its customers, the largest forestry company in British Columbia, MacMillan Bloedel, announced that it would no longer clear-cut old-growth forests in coastal British Columbia. The following spring, two other British Columbian forestry companies followed suit (Hoberg 1999). In addition, there are a number of national initiatives to form "forest and trade networks," which have evolved from "buyers' clubs" with the aim of "span[ning] the industry from forest owner to architect, manufacturer to retailer," to promote FSC certification (http://www.panda.org/tradefair2000/network.htm; accessed June 9, 2000). As of June 2000, there were networks in North America, Australia, the Nordic countries, and eight other European countries involving more than 500 member companies.

The FSC example shows that activist-inspired, consumer-based campaigns can contribute to changes in market behavior, but it also underscores the limitations to such campaigns. First, as the WWF concedes, the area of certified forest is "modest," and the supply of certified products is "limited." The 20 million certified hectares compares to an average 11.3 million hectares lost each year to deforestation out of a total 3.5 billion hectares of global forest cover. Only around 3 million hectares are certified in tropical forests areas of the developing world, where deforestation is of the most concern.[35] Second, the market impact of certification is difficult to assess because there are no data on the volume or share of wood products

33. The World Wildlife Fund (WWF) is now trying to replicate the FSC's success with a Marine Stewardship Council to certify fish products as having been sustainably harvested (see http://www.msc.org).

34. Ikea asked its suppliers of *solid* wood products to ensure that none of their wood came from uncertified old-growth forests by September 2000. A second phase will extend the same requirement to suppliers of other wood products, including paper, cardboard, and furniture made with particleboard, but no target date has been set. See Greenpeace, November 24, 1999 (available at http://www.greenpeace.org/%7Eforests/reports/Re-Source/ikeaarticle.html; accessed June 8, 2000). Ikea sales are from their website, http://www.ikea.com; accessed June 8, 2000; Home Depot sales are from *Journal of Commerce* (November 12, 1993, A9).

35. The FSC website (http://www.fscoax.org) has a list of certified areas; see also Food and Agriculture Organization of the United Nations' ([FAO] 2000) annual report for 1999. Recognizing the lagging progress in developing countries, the WWF joined the World Bank in an alliance to promote sustainable forestry management globally, with a target of 200 certified hectares by 2005, evenly divided between temperate and tropical forests.

from certified forests. Third, FSC credibility depends on the ability to verify the chain of custody, which is most easily done when there are relatively small numbers of large buyers and sellers. Small forest owners complain that certification is too expensive and the standards inappropriate for them. Fourth, the impact of certification is limited because slash and burn agriculture and the use of wood for fuel are much greater threats to forests in many countries.

References

Benjamin, Medea. 1998. A Critique of Fair Labor Association (FLA). Available at [http://www.citinv.it/associazioni/CNMS/archivio/strategie/doc_globalexchange.html].

———. 2000. Interview. *Human Rights Dialogue* 2 (4): 7.

Bernard, Elaine. 1997. Ensuring that monitoring is not co-opted. *New Solutions* 7 (4): 10–12.

Brown, Drusilla, Alan V. Deardorff, and Robert M. Stern. 1996. International labor standards and trade: A theoretical analysis. In *Fair trade and harmonization: Prerequisites for free trade?* ed. Jagdish N. Bhagwati and Robert E. Hudec, 227–80. Cambridge, Mass.: MIT Press.

Catholic Agency for Overseas Development (CAFOD). 1998. Views from the South. Conference Report on Ethical Trade. Available at [http://www.cafod.org.uk/policyviews.htm].

Charness, Gary, Ernan Haruvy, and Doron Sonsino. 2003. Social distance and reciprocity: The internet vs. the laboratory. Available at [http://www.ssrn.com/abstract/312141].

Compa, Lance. 2000. NGO-Labor union tensions on the ground. *Human Rights Dialogue* 2 (4): 12–14.

Congressional Record. 2000. Conference report on H.R. 4577, Departments of Labor, Health and Human Services, and Education, and related agencies. 106th Cong., 2d sess. Vol. 146, pt. 155: H 12128.

Duncan, Lauren E., and Abigail Steward. 1995. Still bringing the Vietnam War home: Sources of contemporary student activism. *Personality and Social Psychology Bulletin* 21 (September): 914–24.

Duong, Trinh. 2000. Codes of conduct don't work: A view from the factory floor. *Human Rights Dialogue* 2 (4): 5.

Elliott, Kimberly Ann. 2000. (Mis)managing diversity: Worker rights and US trade policy. *International Negotiation* 5:97–127.

Elliott, Kimberly Ann, and Richard B. Freeman. 2003. *Can labor standards improve under globalization?* Washington, D.C.: Institute for International Economics.

Feuer, Lewis S. 1969. *The conflict of generations: The character and significance of student movements.* New York: Basic Books.

Food and Agriculture Organization of the United Nations (FAO). 2000. *State of the world's forests 1999.* Rome: FAO.

Freeman, Richard. 1997. Working for nothing: The supply of volunteer labor. *Journal of Labor Economics* 15 (2): 265–95.

———. 1998. What Role for Labor Standards in the Global Economy? Paper presented at conference, United Nations Expert Meeting on Policy Perspectives on International Economics and Social Justice. 13 November, Pocantico, N.Y.

———. 1999. Spurts in union growth: Defining moments and social processes. In *The Defining moment: The Great Depression and the American economy in the twentieth century,* ed. Michael D. Bordo, Claudia Goldin, and Eugene N. White. Chicago: University of Chicago Press.

Frost, Stephen. 2000. Factory rules versus codes of conduct. *Human Rights Dialogue* 2 (4): 4.

Global Exchange. 1999. A directory of US anti-sweatshop organizations. Available at [http://www.globalexchange.org/campaigns/sweatshops/links.html].

Greider, William. 2000. Waking up the global elite. *The Nation*. Available at [http://www.thenation.com/doc.mhtml?i/20001002&s/greider].

Hoberg, George. 1999. The coming revolution in regulating our forests. *Policy Options* 20:53–56.

Hufbauer, Gary Clyde, Jeffrey J. Schott, and Kimberly Ann Elliott. Forthcoming. *Economic sanctions reconsidered,* 3rd ed. Washington, D.C.: Institute for International Economics.

International Labor Organization (ILO). 1998. *Overview of global developments and office activities concerning codes of conduct, social labeling and other private sector initiatives addressing labour issues.* Report to the Governing Body of the Working Party on the Social Dimension of the Liberalization of International Trade. Geneva, Switzerland: ILO.

———. 2000. *Labour practices in the footwear, leather, textiles and clothing industries.* Report for discussion at the Tripartite Meeting on Labour Practices in the Footwear, Leather, Textiles and Clothing Industries. 16–20 October, Geneva, Switzerland: International Labor Office.

Kahneman, Daniel, and Amos Tversky. 1979. Prospect theory: An analysis of decision under risk. *Econometrica* 47 (2): 263–91.

Keck, Margaret E., and Kathryn Sikkink. 1998. *Activists beyond borders: Advocacy networks in international politics.* Ithaca, N.Y.: Cornell University Press.

Klein, Naomi. 1999. *No logo: Taking aim at the brand bullies.* New York: Picador USA.

Liubicic, Robert J. 1998. Corporate codes of conduct and product labeling schemes: The limits and possibilities of promoting international labor rights through private initiatives. *Law and Policy in International Business* 30 (1): 112–58.

Marymount University Center for Ethical Concerns. 1999. The consumer and sweatshops. Available at [http://www.marymount.edu/news/garmentstudy/overview.html].

Massie, Robert Kinloch. 1997. *Loosing the bonds: The United States and South Africa in the Apartheid years.* New York: Doubleday.

Mazur, Jay. 1997. Interview by Charles Krause. *NewsHour,* PBS. April 14.

McAdam, Doug. 1986. Recruitment to high risk activism: The case of Freedom Summer. *American Journal of Sociology* 92 (July): 64–90.

———. 1989. The biographical consequences of activism. *American Sociological Review* 54 (October): 744–60.

———. 1993. Specifying the relationship between social ties and activism. *American Journal of Sociology* 99 (November): 640–67.

Moore, David. 2000. Speaking with a unified voice: Student consumers make targeted change. *Human Rights Dialogue* 2 (4): 10–11.

O'Rourke, Dara. 2000. Monitoring the monitors: A critique of Price Waterhouse Coopers (PWC) labor monitoring. Available at [http://web.mit.edu/dorourke/www].

Oxfam. 1998–99. Levi's works with Oxfam on updated codes of conduct. *Oxfam Campaigner* 30 (Winter). Available at [http://www.oxfam.org.uk/campaign/campaigner].

Queenan, Joe. 2000. *My goodness: A cynic's short-lived search for sainthood.* New York: Hyperion Press.

Roberts, Dexter, and Aaron Bernstein. 2000. Inside a Chinese sweatshop: A life of fines and beating. *Business Week Online.* Available at [http://www.businessweek.com/2000/00_40/b3701119.htm].

Sabel, Charles, Dara O'Rourke, and Archon Fung. 2000. Ratcheting labor standards. World Bank Social Protection Discussion Paper no. 11. Washington, D.C.: World Bank.

Soule, Sarah. 1997. The student divestment movement in the United States and the shantytown: Diffusion of a protest tactic. *Social Forces March* 75 (3): 855–83.

Spaeth, Anthony. 2000. Hell no, we won't sew. *Time,* July.

United Students Against Sweatshops (USAS). 1999. College clothes from the concrete prison. USAS. Mimeograph.

———. 2001. Sweatshop-free campus campaign organizer's manual. USAS. Mimeograph.

University of California, Los Angeles/American Council on Education (UCLA/ACE). 1998. *Annual American Freshman Survey.* Los Angeles: UCLA Press.

University of Maryland, Program on International Policy Attitudes (PIPA). 2000. *Americans on globalization: A study of public attitudes.* Available at [http://www.pipa.org/OnlineReports/Globalization/global_rep.html].

U.S. Department of Labor, Bureau of International Labor Affairs. 2000. *Wages, benefits, poverty line, and meeting workers' needs in the apparel and footwear industries of selected countries.* Washington, D.C.: U.S. Department of Labor.

Van Dyke, Nella. 1998. Hotbeds of activism: Locations of student protest. *Social Problems* 45 (2): 205–20.

Varley, Pamela, ed. 1998. *The sweatshop quandary: Corporate responsibility on the global frontier.* Washington, D.C.: Investor Responsibility Research Center.

Verité. Dynamics of the global assembly line. Available at [http://www.verite.org/dynamics_verite.html].

Weil, David. 2000. Everything old is new again: Regulating labor standards in the U.S. apparel industry. *Proceedings of the 52nd annual meeting of the Industrial Relations Research Association,* 146–155. Madison, Wisc.: IRRA.

Winston, Morton. Forthcoming. NGO strategies for promoting global corporate social responsibility. In *Justice in the world economy: Globalization, agents, and the pursuit of social good,* ed. Robin Hodess. New York: Carnegie Council on Ethics and International Affairs.

Worker Rights Consortium (WRC) home page. Available at [http://workersrights.org].

Yanz, Lynda. 2000. Constructing codes from the ground up. *Human Rights Dialogue* 2 (4): 6.

3

The Living Wage Movement
What Is It, Why Is It, and What's Known about Its Impact?

Jared Bernstein

3.1 Introduction

Although living wage movements have appeared throughout this century (Glickman 1997) the contemporary movement is centered on a specific policy: passing a local ordinance to raise the wage floor for a specified group of workers covered by the ordinance.

Since the mid-1990s, such ordinances have proliferated. According to a recent review by Brenner (2003b), more than 100 cities, counties, or other entities had enacted living wage laws by the end of 2002. The community-organizing group Association of Community Organizations for Reform Now (ACORN), prominent living wage advocates, reports that as of mid-2003 there are seventy-two ongoing living wage campaigns. University students have also mobilized recently on behalf of low-wage workers, calling for ordinances to raise the pay of support staff.

Each of these ordinances is unique. Thus, the first part of the paper suggests a typology for the different ordinances currently in place based on coverage, wage levels, and other requirements. The second section will address the arguments for and against living wages, examining the motivations behind the campaigns, such as the increase in wage and income inequality, the increase in privatization of public services, and the increase in the use of tax abatements to increase local economic activity.

This section then turns to the arguments of those who oppose living wages. These arguments typically stress negative employment effects

Jared Bernstein is a senior economist at the Economic Policy Institute. The author thanks Mark Brenner, Chauna Brocht, David Fairris, Richard Freeman, Jen Kern, Stephanie Luce, Paul Sonn, and anonymous reviewers for helpful comments. The text does not necessarily represent their views. Yulia Fungard provided helpful research assistance.

engendered by intervening in the locality's wage structure and the potential for service cuts, tax increases, and reduced competitiveness of the contracting process. In an important recent development for the movement, in numerous localities antiliving wage activists are attempting to pass preemptive legislation prohibiting living wages. Utah, for example, has such a law, prohibiting any locality within the state from adopting a living wage ordinance.

The next section examines the evidence on the impact of current ordinances. While many of the impact studies are prospective—they forecast the effect of an ordinance based on assumptions about coverage and costs—there now exists a small academic literature on the impact of passed ordinances, including two pre/post studies with controls. There are also a number of administrative reports from cities that have adopted living wage ordinances, and while such reports tend not to invoke counterfactuals, they do offer useful "on the ground" reports on impacts from the perspective of those who help implement the programs.

A key question of this overview is whether the living wage movement is an effective policy tool for raising the living standards of the working poor. The answer that I offer, after a fairly exhaustive review of the evidence, is that the movement is beset by a paradox. By keeping the coverage of the ordinances quite limited in terms of the number of workers whose wages are lifted by the policy, living wage campaigns are quite effective at quelling officials' concerns regarding economic problems caused by the wage mandate, and, according to the available evidence, limited coverage appears not to generate significant inefficiencies. At the same time, limited coverage constrains the ability of the policy to reach many low-wage workers.

I explore this trade-off in greater detail and examine alternative policies that have emerged in recent debates around living wages. One innovative approach with the potential to meet both the goals of the movement and concerns of those who oppose living wages is combining a living wage with a local Earned Income Tax Credit (EITC), an approach that currently exists in two U.S. localities (Montgomery County, Maryland and Denver, Colorado).

3.2 What are Living Wage Ordinances?

A living wage ordinance is legislation that establishes a wage floor above that of the prevailing minimum wage for workers covered by the ordinance.

There are something on the order of 100 living wage ordinances in place, and no two are the same. Table 3.1 provides a sample of existing ordinances. Their differences can be understood in the following framework: who is covered on the employer and employee side, and what is the nature of the coverage (e.g., what is the wage level, are fringe benefits included, are there local hiring restrictions)?

Table 3.1 **A sampling of active living wage ordinances**

City and year enacted	Wages and benefits	Employers covered	Miscellaneous provisions
Alexandria, VA: 2000	$10.89 index annually to the poverty line for a family of four with cost for health insurance (7/03)	City employees, contracts, and subcontracts and other firms who benefit from over $75,000	
Arlington, VA: 2003	$10.98; index annually (7/03)	Service contractors; contracts over $100,000 for services provided on county-owned or county-controlled property	
Baltimore, MD: 1994	$6.10 in 1996 to $8.70 (8/03) later	Service contractors; construction contracts over $5,000; includes subcontractors	Must pay employees biweekly
Berkeley, CA and Marina: June 2000, amend. October 2000	$10.76 with health; $12.55 without (8/03)	City, contracts, financial assistance recipients, and leaseholders of city land	
Boston, MA: 1997	$10.96 (8/03); adjusted annually by the higher of the federal poverty line for a family of 4, CPI or 110% of the federal minimum wage	Contracts and subcontracts over $25,000, subsidies (grant, loan, tax incentive, bond financing) for-profits with over 25 employees and nonprofits with over 100 employees; leaseholders or renters of beneficiaries; exemptions for hardship	
Buffalo, NY: 1999	1999: $8.08 with health; $9.08 without health (8/03); [2000: $6.22, 2001: $7.15, 2002: $8.08 with health; $1.00 more each year without health]	City service contracts and subcontracts over $50,000	
Burlington, VT: 2001	$11.67 with health; $13.49 without (7/03); annual adjustment to a state-issued "basic needs budget" for a single earner (a concept and formula introduced by the Vermont Livable Wage campaign)	City, service contractors, or businesses with grants from the city of at least $15,000	Companies have to provide at least 12 compensated days off per year for employees who fall under the law. (Vermont Livable Wage Campaign)

(*continued*)

Table 3.1 (continued)

City and year enacted	Wages and benefits	Employers covered	Miscellaneous provisions
Cambridge, MA: 1999	$10.68, increased later to $11.48 (8/03) adjusted annually by CPI	City, contract or subcontracts over 10,000, and firms that benefit from at least $10,000 annually	
Central Arkansas Library System, 2001	$8.75, $9.00 starting July 1, 2002, plus full health benefits and retirement benefits, indexed for inflation	All Central Arkansas Library System employees	
Chicago, IL: 1998	$7.60 increased to $9.05 in 2002, annual indexing was added in 2002	Service contracts with over 25 employees; includes subcontractors; exemptions for nonprofits, home and health care workers, security guards, parking attendants, day laborers, cashiers, elevator operators, custodial workers and clerical workers	n.a.
Cincinnati, OH: November 2002	$8.70 with health; $10.20 without, adjusted annually	City itself, city service contractor with a contract worth at least $20,000	
Cleveland, OH: June 2000	$8.20, increased to $9.20 Oct. 2002 (indexed accordingly thereafter on annual basis)	Contracts and subsidies over 75,000 with at least 20 employees (profit) and 50 employees for nonprofit with a wage ratio greater than 5:1, subcontractors, leaseholders, or tenants of recipients of assistance	
Denver, CO: February 2000	100% of poverty line for a family of four, updated annually	City employees, contractors, subcontractors with a contract of $2,000 or more engaged in the work of a parking lot attendant, security guard, clerical support worker, or child care workers on city owned or leased property	
Detroit, MI: 1998	100% of poverty line for a family of four with health benefits; 125% of poverty line without benefits	Service contracts or subsidies (federal grant programs, revenue bond financing, planning assistance, tax increment financing, tax credits) over $50,000; includes subcontractors and leaseholders	Must attempt to hire city residents for new jobs

Hartford, CT: September 1999	110% of poverty level for a family of 4, with health benefits that requires employees to pay no more than 3% of annual wages (or equivalent)	Contracts over $50,000 in the following categories: food service, security services, custodial/maintenance, clerical/office, transportation, and parking services	
Jersey City, NJ: 1996	$7.50	City contractors employing clerical, food service, janitorial workers, or security guards	Employer has to provide health benefits and vacation to full-time workers.
Los Angeles County, CA: 1999	$8.32 with health benefits; $9.46 without health benefits	Contractors $25,000	Prohibits the use of part-time employees on county contracts without justifiable cause and prohibits the use of county funds to inhibit employee organization; provides that its provisions may be expressly superseded by a collective-bargaining agreement
Madison, WI: 1999	100% of poverty line for a family of four in 1999; 105% of poverty line in 2000; 110% of poverty line in 2001	Certain contracts over $5,000 and certain subsidies over $100,000; categories: food preparation, security, custodial, clerical, transportation and parking services	The ordinance also allows that the terms of a collective-bargaining agreement may supersede the requirements of the living wage ordinance.
Miami-Dade County, FL: 1999	$9.00 with health; $10.30 without	County workers, service contractors ($100,000), and airport licensees; categories: food preparation and/or distribution; security services; routine maintenance services such as custodial, cleaning, refuse removal, repair, refinishing, and recycling; clerical or other nonsupervisory office work, whether temporary or permanent; transportation and parking services including airport and seaport services; printing and reproduction services; and, landscaping, lawn, and/or agricultural services	The ordinance establishes a Living Wage Commission to enhance compliance and review the effectiveness of the law.

(*continued*)

Table 3.1 (continued)

City and year enacted	Wages and benefits	Employers covered	Miscellaneous provisions
Milwaukee City, WI: 1995	$6.05 adjusted annually by federal poverty line for a family of three. The current living wage is $7.06 (as of 9/02).	Service contracts; excludes contracts that involve the purchase of goods; includes subcontractors	n.a.
Milwaukee County, WI: 1997	$6.25; adjusted by union pay scales	County workers, categories: janitors, parking lot attendants, and unarmed security guards	n.a.
Milwaukee Public Schools; 1996	$7.70		Direct employees and contractors
Milwaukee School Board, WI: 1996	$7.70	School board workers	n.a.
Minneapolis, MN: 1997	110% of poverty line for a family of 4, currently $9.57	Subsidies over $100,000 in one year	60% of new jobs will go to city residents.
Missoula, MT: 2001	100% or more of the lowest wage of full time employees of the City of Missoula, currently $8.80, and provide health benefits	Recipients of city economic development assistance	The ordinance also requires the recipients to comply with the Fair Labor Standards Act.
Monroe County, MI: October 2001	$8.70 with health; $10.20 without; indexed annually	County itself, county contractors (greater than $10,000 per year)	
Montgomery County, MD: June 2002	$10.50	County contracts over $50,000 and at least 10 employees	The measure also includes a "nonpenalty" clause that encourages nonprofits that contract with the county to pay a living wage by insuring that the bidding process does not unfairly undercut them.

New York City, NY: November 2002	$8.60 with health; $10.10 without; The wage rate will rise in two steps until it reaches $10.00 an hour in July of 2006.	City service contractors, principally health care workers	
Oakland, CA: 1998	$8.00 with health benefits; $9.25 without benefits; adjusted yearly by regional CPI, bringing the current wage requirements to $9.58 and $11.02; 12 days paid leave	Service contracts over $25,000 or subsidies over $100,000; includes subcontractors	The ordinance also allows for the terms of a collective-bargaining agreement to provide that said agreement may supersede the requirements of the living wage ordinance.
Pima County, AZ: 2002	$9.00 with health; $8.00 without, adjusted by CPI	Categories: facility building, maintenance, refuse collection and recycling, temporary employee services, janitorial and custodial services, landscape maintenance and weed control, pest control, security, and moving services	
Port of Oakland, CA: 2002	$9.58 with health; $11.02 without	1,500 low wage workers at Oakland's Airport and Seaport, including baggage handlers, security guards, drivers and food service workers	
Portland, OR: 1996	$6.75 in 1996; $7.00 in 1997, $7.50 in 1998 and $8.00 in 1999 through the year 2000.	Service contracts; categories: janitors, parking lot attendants, temporary clerical services and security workers	n.a.
Prince George's County, MD: 2003	$10.50, adjusted by CPI	County service contractors ($50,000) who employ 10 or more workers	
San Francisco, CA: 2000	$9 without health; $10 next year, followed by 2.5 percent raises for three more years, an additional $1.25 without health, 12 paid days off and 10 unpaid days for family emergencies. The current rate is $10.25 (8/03).	City service contractors, including nonprofit agencies and leaseholders at San Francisco International Airport	

(*continued*)

Table 3.1 (continued)

City and year enacted	Wages and benefits	Employers covered	Miscellaneous provisions
San Jose, CA: 1998	$10.10 with health; $11.35 without (8/03)	City service contracts worth at least $20,000; direct financial grants from the city valued at $100,000 or more in a year; categories: automotive repair and maintenance, food service, janitorial, landscaping, laundry, office/clerical; parking lot management, pest control, property maintenance, recreation, security shuttle services, street sweeping, and towing	
Santa Fe, NM: 2003	$8.50 (6/03); the wage will rise $1.00 every two years until it reaches $10.50 in 2008, when it will be indexed to inflation.	Any business in the city with at least 25 employees	
Stanford University; 2002	$10.10 with health; $11.35 without.	Major university contractors with nonunionized employees	
Toledo, OH: 2000	110% of the federal poverty level for a family of 4, currently $9.57 with health; 130% of the poverty level, currently $11.31, without health	City contracts over $10,000 (and more the 25 employees) and recipients of city subsidies over $100,000 (with more than 50 employees), tenants	
Tucson, AZ: 1999	$8.77 with health; $9.87 without (8/03), adjusted to CPI	City contractors; categories: facility and building maintenance, refuse collection and recycling, temporary employee services, janitorial and custodial, landscape maintenance and weed control, pest control, security, moving services	60% of workforce must be city residents.
Ypsilanti Township, MI: 1999	$8.50 with health; $10.00 without (8/03)	City service contracts or financial assistance over $10,000 ($20,000 for nonprofits)	

Note: n.a. = not applicable.

3.2.1 Coverage: Employers and Workers

Luce (2003) points out that seventy-four existing ordinances cover employers who contract with the city to provide a service. The next largest group covers businesses that receive some type of subsidy under the rubric of economic development assistance, such as a tax abatement, a below-market-cost loan, or the below-cost provision of a city service or good (e.g., as when a city agrees to pay for new infrastructure to facilitate a new factory or office building).[1] On the employee side, coverage can be specific to industry, occupation, or part-time or full-time status.

Ordinances can be quite specific about who is covered. For example, in Los Angeles, nonsupervisory workers who work for a service contractor are covered, but if such a worker provides *goods* under the city contract, they would not be covered. Thus, a security guard who works for a firm contracted to provide services to the city (e.g., cleaning or busing services) would be covered, while a guard who worked for a firm providing the city with goods (e.g., building supplies) would not be covered. In Portland, occupational coverage is very specific as only janitors, security guards, and parking attendants are covered by the ordinance. Turning again to Los Angeles, there is a distinction made between workers employed by those firms who contract with the city, and those working for firms who receive a subsidy. Any worker meeting the industry or occupational criteria is covered in the former case. But in the latter case, the ordinance language covers only a worker who "expends at least half of his or her time on the funded [i.e., subsidized] project" (http://www.laane.org/lw/docs-lacitylwordinance.pdf).

As a result of bargaining during the political process, certain exemptions from coverage usually find their way into most of the ordinances. For example, contracts and subsidies below a certain dollar value may be exempted. A glance at table 3.1 shows the range of these values in different localities. In Arlington County, Virginia the threshold in $100,000; in Cincinnati, it is $20,000. In Boston, the original law stated that direct service contracts with the city must be fore over $100,000 for the living wage ordinance to be applied (for subcontractors, the limit was $25,000), but advocates later successfully campaigned to lower the direct contractors' cutoff to $25,000 in order to increase coverage. The Oakland, California law requires coverage for workers on service contracts of at least $25,000 and development assistance of $100,000 or more (including the tenants and leaseholders of the subsidy recipient). In Chicago and other cities, nonprofits that contract with the city are exempted; in other cities, they are included, though there often exists a threshold here as well in order to exempt smaller providers.

1. As shown in table 3.1, a single ordinance can cover both service contracts and subsidized businesses.

As noted previously, hours worked can also be a coverage criterion. In Jersey City, all workers under service contracts are covered by the living wage, but only full-time workers are required to receive vacation and health benefits. In Milwaukee, on the other hand, the ordinance has very specific language to cover all workers, including part-time and temporary workers.

One relatively new application of the living wage model is in the university setting (ACORN reports three such policies currently active). Perhaps the more renowned example is Harvard University, where student supporters staged an aggressive campaign in support of low-wage workers employed directly or indirectly (through subcontractors) by the university. The ordinance covers security guards, custodians, and dining services. A significant motivation for the campaign was the observation that outsourcing of jobs previously held in house was leading to lower campus-wide wages in these occupations. Thus, along with initial pay raises, the ordinance includes a "wages and benefits parity policy" requiring that outsourced jobs provide wages and benefits comparable to in-house unionized workers performing the same work. The use of living wage laws to address such concerns as outsourcing is not uncommon and is examined further in the following.

A key point, one that will surface throughout this review, is the specific and generally quite narrow nature of the coverage of living wage ordinances. However, a recent trend in the movement is to push for laws closer in spirit to the minimum wage but for substate areas. The only active such policy is in Santa Fe, New Mexico, passed in February 2003: a minimum wage of $8.50 that applies to any establishment with at least twenty-five employees. New Orleans also passed a city-wide minimum wage, but its implementation was prohibited by the state's supreme court, based on jurisdictional issues (more on this issue in the following).

In this review, I choose not to focus on these city-level minimum wage laws. Their coverage, structure, and likely impact are very different than the much more dominant model covering service contracts and subsidized businesses. The evolution of these local minimum wage laws are worth tracking, and I speak to their relevance to the living wage movement in the conclusion of this report, but they are quite a different policy from the one discussed thus far.

3.2.2 Wages and Benefits

The wage levels also differ between contracts, as do the provision and extent of fringe benefits. Also, some ordinances call for indexing of the wage.

The living wage level, as well as the extent of benefits, is derived by the campaign organizers and community activists who introduce and develop the ordinance. The name "living wage" implies a wage level that would enable its recipient to meet their basic consumption needs. However, a comparison of recent work on family budgets—the dollar amount needed by families of a specific type in a given locality—and prevailing living wage levels shows that living wages are pegged below the wage needed to meet a family budget. For example, Bernstein, Brocht, and Spade-Aguilar (2000) show that a single parent with two children living in Baltimore in 1998 would need $30,100 to meet her basic needs. Assuming year-round full-time work, this implies a living wage level of $14.48, significantly higher than the actual living wage in Baltimore of $7.10.

In this sense the living wage is somewhat of a misnomer. In many cases, the level is derived with reference to the U.S. poverty line for a given family size, usually a family of four, which was $18,392 in 2002. This value, divided by full-time, full-year hours of work (usually 2,080) comes to just under $9, and it serves as a basis for the wage level in various ordinances. Living wage levels in Baltimore, Los Angeles, Chicago, Detroit, and many other smaller cities are close to this level, though many are higher. In 1998, for example, the city of San Jose passed an ordinance requiring service contractors (with contracts of at least $20,000) to pay a living wage of $9.50 an hour with health benefits or $10.75 if the company does not provide benefits, and these values were recently raised to $10.10 and $11.35. This last model, with a lower wage tier when fringe benefits (typically health insurance and/or vacation days) are provided, is also quite common.

More than half of current ordinances include cost-of-living adjustments. Milwaukee's ordinance, which is derived from the poverty line for a family of three (divided by 2,080) calls for the level to be updated annually when the government releases the new poverty lines (which are updated by the growth of consumer prices). Other ordinances are explicitly tied to the consumer price index (CPI). Finally, in a departure from the poverty-line derivation, the Harvard ordinance, as noted previously, includes a compensation parity clause for workers subcontracted by the university.

3.2.3 Enforcement and Other Miscellaneous Provisions

Other than coverage and compensation, some ordinances have provisions relating to labor relations, hiring practices, and enforcement.

Owens (1997) points out that labor activists involved in living wage campaigns often try to include provisions that lower barriers to labor organizing and "help to promote a more labor-friendly environment." In San Jose, for example, the ordinance calls for proposed contracts to undergo a so-called "third-tier review," where proposals must be examined by the city with regard to good labor practices. Also, the city department that awards the contract must provide the request for proposals to the local American Federation of Labor-Congress of Industrial Organization (AFL-CIO) labor council, ostensibly for the council's review and input as to whether the employer has a history conducive to maintaining "labor peace." The Minneapolis ordinance states that "other things being equal and to the extent legally possible," it will give preferential treatment to firms that engage in "responsible labor relations," defined as neutrality towards organizing, voluntary recognition based on card checks, and binding arbitration of the first contract.

Other ordinances try to insure that those hired under the covered contact or subsidy will come from the local community. In Minneapolis, recipients of contracts or subsidies of at least $100,000 are required to set a goal that 60 percent of new jobs created will be held by city residents. Other provisions call for retention guarantees and the prohibition of privatization of services currently performed by city employees.

Finally, the issue of enforcement is surfacing as a crucial component to the success of the ordinance. While most ordinances include at least some language regarding enforcement and penalties for noncompliance, some laws include no reporting requirements or staff to monitor compliance (Luce 1998). For ordinances lacking enforcement provisions, violations are only identified through complaints by workers, who may not be aware of the law or be willing to risk filing a complaint. Additionally, preliminary findings suggest that that some of the existing enforcement provisions are inadequate to ensure compliance. For example, although the Baltimore ordinance requires contractors to submit payroll information to the Wage Commission, the limited staff has been unable to monitor all contacts; in fact, there are no central data on contracts nor is staff able to ensure that payroll data are submitted by all contractors (Niedt et al. 1999). Luce (1998) reports that the only violations sited by the Wage Commission to date were uncovered when activists helped workers file a complaint charging that bus companies did not increase wages as scheduled by the ordinance.

The Boston ordinance is unique in that it formalizes activist involvement in enforcement through a "city assistance advisory committee," which includes one AFL-CIO member, one ACORN member, and five mayoral appointees (Spain and Wiley 1998). However, there was also strong opposition by some members of the business community to the degree of these reporting requirements.

What is one to make of this rich array of ordinances? In the sense of a central goal of the movement—to lift the living standards of low-income workers under city contracts or working for firms with business subsidies—such diverse coverage criteria is hard to rationalize. Why should your employer or sector matter? Why should a low-income worker under a small contract be exempt while the same worker on a large contract is covered? Why cover workers on service contracts but not those on manufacturing contracts?

While the rationale for these coverage differences is hard to square with the goals of the movement, they do provide a degree of flexibility that is valued by city councils, community activists, and perhaps even the business community. Pragmatic political concerns often generate compromises regarding coverage. Also, this flexibility avoids the "one-size-fits-all" model of, for example, the federal minimum wage, where regional differences are not taken into account. For example, the San Jose living wage is relatively high compared to other ordinances around the nation, but community organizers there pushed for this level based on the very-high cost of housing in the Silicon Valley area, and the fact, due to the high housing costs, many of the covered workers had to travel long distances to get to work. In other cases, workers in certain occupations, such as those who work in the school system (as in Milwaukee) might be seen as particularly deserving by influential parties and thus might be strategically highlighted in the campaign and ultimately in the ordinance.

Flexibility also carries political risks for all sides. If the organizing environment is fertile for activists, they can push for more progressive ordinances, such as those that include indexing requirements. Conversely, even if an ordinance were to pass in an environment dominated by opposing interests, it may be watered down to the point where it has no bite at all, either in terms of coverage, wage level, or enforcement mechanisms. Another potential downside is that of unintended consequences. Some of the ordinances described previously create obvious "kink points" regarding coverage. For example, depending on the extent to which employers or contractors respond to the increase in the wage floor (an issue discussed in the following), one could imagine the dollar value of contract offers "bunching" right below the eligibility cutoff point. Freeman (2000) suggests a more fluid approach to thresholds, with a graduated schedule of living wage levels as a function of firm revenues or size.

3.3 Living Wage Campaigns

Arguably, social and economic policy over the past few decades have titled toward less intervention in markets.[2] Policies and institutions intending to sway the "invisible hand" have generally been viewed with much suspicion, even by traditional Democratic allies. Why, then, have living wage campaigns been so successful in getting city councils or similar bodies (e.g., university presidents) to pass ordinances? The explanation derives from the logic of the campaigns' core message, the strategy of the organizers, the nature of their coalitions, and the small magnitude of the ordinances.

3.3.1 The Motivations behind the Living Wage Movement

A primary motivation for living wage campaigns is the difficult economic circumstances facing low-income working families. Over the 1980s and mid-1990s, the hourly wages of low-wage workers fell 18 percent in

2. See Kuttner (1997).

real terms. The tight labor market of the latter 1990s reversed this trend (a minimum wage increase in 1996 also helped), but even so, wage levels for most low-wage jobs remain well below the levels needed to meet basic needs, as noted previously.[3]

Another motivation for the movement comes from the trend toward privatization of services formerly provided by public-sector workers. A 1998 survey found that more than half of state governments had increased the number of functions performed under private contracts over the prior five years, and many others said they planned to increase privatization in the following five years (Chiand Jasper 1998). The largest amount of privatization occurred in transportation agencies, followed by administration and general services, corrections, and social services. At the municipal level, waste management is the most likely service to be privatized. One survey of 516 towns in Illinois found that almost every city in the survey contracts for at least one service, and 53 percent contract for at least ten services. Again, the highest levels of privatization were in waste management, with 92.6 percent of municipalities using private commercial solid waste services and 87.7 percent using private residential solid waste services (Moore 1998).

Living wage advocates and public-sector unions have stressed concerns about the effects of privatization on job losses and decreases in wages among public-sector workers. A study by the Chicago Institute on Urban Poverty compared the wages and benefits of Chicago employees to contractual employees for ten job titles representing parking attendants, guards, and custodial workers. They found that privatization led to compensation losses for entry-level workers ranging from 25 percent to 46 percent for the various job titles. For senior-level workers in the same job categories, two job titles experienced moderate increases in wages and benefits of 4 percent to 7 percent, while the other eight categories experienced losses of 9 percent to 46 percent. Because government agencies disproportionately hire (and advance) female minority workers, these changes have meant the loss of relatively high quality jobs for these workers (Jackson 1997).

In a similar spirit, living wage advocates are also motivated by the proliferation of economic development incentives such as tax subsidies, loans, publicly provided services, or goods to private-sector firms to influence their mobility (i.e., to get them or keep them). The motivation for attaching living wage provisions to these incentive agreements is as stated on the ACORN web cite: to ensure that "private businesses that benefit from public money . . . pay their workers a living wage."

3. These statistics, derived from the CPS outgoing rotation groups (ORG) files, are for the 18–64-year-old wage and salary workforce. They can be found in the DataZone section of the Economic Policy Institute (EPI) website available at http://www.epinet.org. For a description of their construction, see Mishel, Bernstein, and Boushey 1999.

Embedded in this quote is an important economic insight into the movement's motivation. Much living wage advocacy literature, either implicitly or explicitly, claims that both contractors and subsidy recipients are receiving some degree of economic rents from the city. The ordinance is designed to reclaim some portion of those rents and redistribute them among low-wage workers. If, in fact, the higher wages are paid out of redistributed rents, we would not expect to observe market inefficiencies, such as employment or price adjustments (i.e., higher contract costs passed through to the city), resulting from the ordinances.

These developments have provided fertile ground for organizers. According to living wage organizers, living wage campaigns provide a channel through which low-wage urban workers and those who sympathize with them can actively pursue social justice. They challenge city councils, who in many cases have recently privatized a public service or granted a sizable subsidy to an entrepreneur, to make sure the local workforce is not economically undermined by these policies. In this regard, campaigns have pressured local governments to require subsidized firms to keep public records of the number and quality of the jobs they create.[4]

3.3.2 The Coalitions

One of the most interesting aspects of the living wage movement is the nature of the coalitions that have organized and supported the campaigns. Community organizers and labor, political, and religious groups have been the at the core of the coalitions, but like the ordinances themselves, the coalitions have been extremely diverse.

The alliance between labor and national community organizing groups, such as ACORN or the Industrial Areas Foundation, has been instrumental in the movement's success (Zabin and Martin 1999). For labor unions, their stated support for the living wage movement is to promote "economic justice" and join forces with low-wage workers in typically unorganized sectors. But as numerous analysts have pointed out (discussed in the review of the impact literature), unions, especially those representing public-sector workers, are also motivated by the desire to reduce competitive pressures engendered by outsourcing their tasks to lower-wage contractors in the private sector. From the perspective of community organizers, labor often brings clout, money, and political strength.

Zabin and Martin (1999) provide a case study of a highly successful activist coalition in Los Angeles, led by the Los Angeles Alliance for a New Economy (LAANE). They note that LAANE, which was created by the Hotel Employees and Restaurant Employees Union (HERE), embraced the living wage as way to raise wages and organizing potential of low-wage workers in their industries. The broad coalition they built included His-

4. LeRoy and Slocum (1999) stress the importance of these reporting requirements.

panic neighborhood groups, Communities for a Better Environment, a tenants' union, and religious organizations (Clergy and Laity for Economic Justice (CLUE) grew out of these efforts).[5]

In their discussion of LAANE's successful Los Angeles campaign, Zabin and Martin (1999) stress another point that is often made is this context—the living wage campaign as a union organizing tool: "LAANE organized workers who would be affected by the ordinance, incorporating them into the campaign in mobilizations and as spokespeople in city council hearing. This was not just a campaign tactic, but rather an integral element of their central objective of building support for union organizing" (13).

To this end, LAANE incorporated some of the language noted by Owens (1997) designed to facilitate organizing. For example, an enforcement provision in the ordinance "allows a third party to inform and educate affected workers about their rights under the living wage law" (15). Organizers from HERE and Service Employees International Union (SEIU) used this clause to gain access to workers at the Los Angeles International Airport (LAX) for a large-scale unionization drive.

That said, it should be noted that beyond this anecdotal evidence, there is as yet little evidence that the living wage movement is having an identifiable impact on strengthening the labor movement, a point I return to in the conclusion.

Most successful campaigns seem to pursue a very similar strategy to that of LAANE, with labor, community, and religious groups working together, often in consultation with sympathetic economists and lawyers offering technical support.[6] Legal support has become more important, as cities and states have begun trying to raise legal objections to living wage ordinances or pass legislation to prohibit them. For example, officials of the city of Alexandria, Virginia argued that under state law (the so-called "Dillon Rule") localities were prohibited from legislating activities, such as a wage mandate, not expressly granted to them in the state constitution, an argument ultimately rejected by the city council.

Those who actively oppose living wage movements generally represent two related camps: affected employers (writ broadly to include contractors and subsidy recipients) and some members of local government (e.g., city councilors) and their "clients": tax payers and other citizens who could potentially face greater tax liabilities or reduced services. In the first case, employers who oppose living wage campaigns typically do so on the grounds

5. Luce (2000) describes a similarly diverse coalition in a successful Cambridge, Massachusetts campaign, including community groups, a carpenters local, and the National Lawyers Guild.

6. Research by Martin (2001) lends statistical support to this combination. He ran city-level logistic regressions on the probability of a successful campaign, finding that the interaction of the presence of ACORN and union density was a significant positive predictor, while direct effects of each variable were not significant.

of labor costs. As in the minimum wage debate, such employers argue (in so many words) that they are currently paying what the market will bear, as determined by supply, demand, and the marginal product of their low-wage workforce. A mandated increase in wages will force them to pay above the market wage, compromising their ability to remain competitive, and they will be forced to cut employment and/or leave the market.

Leaving the market, in this case, means either not bidding for the contract or relocating to a city without a living wage ordinance, and this is one concern of local officials. Those city officials who oppose living wage ordinances typically do so based on the arguments that the ordinance will (1) hurt the city's ability to compete for jobs with other localities and (2) increase the cost of contracts and thus force them to raise taxes or lower services.

The campaigns and their opponents continue to devote considerable resources to making their cases. A particularly notable example of a living wage battle, also involving LAANE, occurred in Santa Monica, California from 2000–2002 in the context of an ordinance designed to introduce a $10.50 living wage ($12.25 without health care benefits) to all firms within the so-called "coastal zone" of the city. This is a beachfront area wherein the city restricts growth, thus reducing competitive pressures for the resident businesses and arguably generating some rents for them. After the ordinance was introduced, the local business community, aided by national groups like the National Restaurant Association, fought back especially hard, spending, according to LAANE, over $1 million to stop the ordinance.[7] They introduced legislation, deceptively entitled "The Living Wage Initiative," which would have prohibited such ordinances in the area. This was defeated and the city council passed the law in 2001. The opposition responded with another million-dollar campaign to repeal the ordinance, and this time they were successful.

In this case, millions were spent on defeating a proposal that a representative from the restaurant industry described as their industry's "bogey man."[8] In their successful efforts to urge voters to repeal the living wage, the industry engaged in election practices that led to a "commission of inquiry." The commission found various fraudulent election practices and called for ballot reforms against such tactics as "dishonest slate mailers."[9] I discuss this case in some detail not simply from prurient interest but to show that even though most of these ordinances are small in an economic sense—the Santa Monica ordinance was projected to reach 2,000 workers

7. This information is from the LAANE website available at http://www.laane.org.

8. See Tanner (2002).

9. See http://www.democracydistorted.com/DemocracyDistorted_ExecutiveSummary.pdf. The inquiry claimed that opposition groups sent out mailers that falsely claimed that the Democratic party, prochoice leaders, and educators opposed the ordinance. The Santa Monica city council agreed to consider the inquiry's recommendations.

and cost less than 5 percent of gross receipts (Pollin and Brenner 2000)—the stakes are high and engender heated debates and actions on both sides.

Much of this debate has occurred in a context lacking solid information about the actual impact of living wage ordinances, largely because such information did not exist. But there is now a growing literature on impacts that has the potential to provide a bit more light to this heated debate. I turn to that work in the next section.

3.4 What's Known about the Impact of Living Wages?

Most of the impact studies of living wages have been prospective. The most thorough of these studies, some of which are reviewed in the following, take the available information on city contracts that would be covered by the ordinance, use input/output assumptions to generate the employment counts based on the dollar value of the contracts, and use microdata on jobs in the relevant occupations and industries to figure out how many workers will be affected and how much the ordinance will cost, a technique pioneered by Pollin and Luce (1998).

There is, however, a small body of work looking at the actual outcomes of ordinances that have been passed and at least partially implemented, including a before/after study using original survey data. In addition, there are now several reports from city agencies that have adopted living wages. While such reports differ from economic analyses in that they tend to ignore counterfactuals, the fact that these officials are "on the ground" where the increases take place renders them useful to gauging living wage impacts.

3.4.1 Prospective Studies

Most of the impact studies of living wages have been prospective. The most thorough of these studies take the available information on city contracts that would be covered by the ordinance, use input/output assumptions to generate the employment counts based on the dollar value of the contracts, and use microdata on jobs in the relevant occupations and industries to figure out how many workers will be affected and how much the ordinance will cost. Some of the studies add indirect costs associated with wage spillovers predicted to occur in affected firms.[10] The most common outcome measures from these studies are the number of workers affected and the potential increase in labor costs to contractors or subsidized businesses.

Given the many possible reactions to the introduction of a living wage, uncertainties about the relevant elasticities, and limited data on what are often small geographical areas, any prospective study is of limited use.

10. See, for example, Pollin and Luce (1998) and Reich, Hall, and Jacobs (2003).

However, this is a relatively young movement, and actual impact studies are only now being produced (they are reviewed next). Still, these studies make a few key points that are worth noting. In addition, the two pre/post actual-impact studies and the administrative impact reports mentioned in the following come up with findings that are broadly similar to those predicted by the highest-quality prospective studies.

As Brenner (2003b) shows in a review of some of the best prospective studies, the predicted numbers of affected workers under contractor/subsidy models is small relative to the city's labor force (never more than 1 percent).[11] Similarly, costs relative to some aggregate for firm or for cities, either revenue or city contract costs, range from 0.3 percent to 4.6 percent. The determinant factors driving these employment and cost results are the level of the living wage relative to the minimum wage in the area, the coverage of the ordinance, and the wage structure in the affected industries. Regarding this latter point, prospective studies on business subsidies to manufacturers tend to yield much lower cost projections (and affect fewer workers) than low-wage service contract ordinances, such as those covering custodial or food service workers. Thus, a key insight from these studies is that the "bite" from the ordinance is partly a function of where it meets the wage structure of affected industries.

Despite the fact that these studies yield estimates of costs and affected numbers of workers that are small relative to some aggregate, the ordinances could still lead to less than optimal outcomes. Even small changes can generate undesirable responses, such as layoffs or less-competitive bidding, especially for firms operating within narrow cost margins. And the fact that an ordinance generates costs that are small relative to the city's budget does not preclude a specific business or contractor from facing a hefty increase, especially in low-wage industries where the living wage is much higher than the prevailing wage. In fact, Brenner (2003b) finds that the average living wage in the eight prospective studies cities he reviews is 76 percent above the prevailing minimum wage.[12] Even a very steep labor demand curve (i.e., a highly inelastic labor demand response to wage changes) could yield significant employment losses when hit with such a large shock to wages.

The question is, do such effects actually occur? The prospective studies by advocates tend to say no; those by opponents predict otherwise. For example, in their debate over the impact of the Santa Monica, California living wage ordinance, supporters of the proposal argued that based on assumptions regarding other absorption mechanisms (higher prices, more

11. Brenner's (2003b) review of these studies (in his table 2) includes Pollin, Luce and Brenner's (1999) study of the New Orleans city-level minimum wage, which was, of course, predicted to cover a much larger share of the workforce—close to 10 percent.

12. This average excludes New Orleans, a city-wide minimum wage (which was pegged at 19 percent above the minimum [Brenner 2003b, table 2]).

efficient production through efficiency wage effects, and lower profits) "it is not likely that the ordinance will induce significant layoffs."[13] The same study argued that most of the benefits from the increase go to low-income families who need the extra income, that is, the policy is at least decently targeted (Pollin and Brenner 2000). Opposing researchers argued that the Santa Monica ordinance would affect far more workers than claimed by the supporters' study and thus be much more costly with greater worker dislocations. This study also argued that the benefits of the higher wage were poorly targeted, with more than half going to families in the top half of the income scale (Sander, Williams, and Doherty 2002).

Such disagreements are inevitable and should by no means undermine interest or support in prospective studies, which are commonly used to forecast policy impacts. Evidence presented in the following suggests that the prospective studies do a fairly good job in two areas: estimating coverage and estimating the characteristics of affected workers. That said, there are very significant uncertainties in assessing the impact of living wage ordinances. Specifically, it is difficult to know how firms will respond. The true employment elasticities are unknown, and while the minimum wage literature suggests they are "small," as noted previously, the magnitude of the wage increases could be large enough to generate significant layoffs. Assumptions about efficiency wage effects are also questionable. It's certainly possible that firms will absorb higher costs through, for example, lower turnover, but whether they actually will do so is wholly an empirical question. With these caveats in mind, we now turn to the precious few studies that examine actual impacts.

3.4.2 Actual Impact Studies

These impact studies can usefully be divided with reference to their methods. I first discuss a set of studies by David Neumark (both alone [2002] and with coauthor Scott Adams [2001a,b] that use secondary data analysis—the Current Population Survey (CPS)—to measure the wage, income, and employment impacts of living wage laws. Next, I examine two studies using primary data sources. These two controlled studies provide particularly useful information on living wage outcomes. Finally, I present information from a set of administrative reports.

3.4.3 Secondary Analysis

The economist David Neumark has done the most econometrically rigorous analysis of the impact of living wages based on secondary data sources, specifically. Neumark's questions focus mainly on the impact of ordinances on jobs and income (along with poverty status), though in one paper he asks whether living wages are in part a tool of public-sector

13. Pollin and Brenner (2000, 5).

unions to reduce wage competition. Some of these papers also make a useful distinction between living wage ordinances that apply solely to contractors and those that apply to firms receiving subsidies.

The results from these papers tend to find significant wage and income gains from living wage laws and, in some models, significant job displacement effects as well. In fact, on the basis of his results suggesting that living wages led to lower urban poverty rates, Neumark, who had earlier been critical of living wage laws based on their inefficiencies as observed in his analysis, told *Business Week* (2000) that "I'm no longer ready to dismiss these policies out of hand." Neumark also finds support for the notion that municipal unions are using living wage ordinances to protect their jobs by raising the costs of contracting out jobs they currently perform.

These authors have quickly amassed a considerable body of literature on the topic of living wage impacts. In every report, their models run off of a cross-sectional time series panel of metropolitan areas derived from the CPS. The identification of a living wage effect—a regression-adjusted difference-in-difference estimator—derives from the variation in wage and employment outcomes between cities that have passed ordinances and those that have not.

There are three central concerns regarding this work: (1) the inappropriate use of CPS data for research on this issue; (2) the magnitude of the results, which appear too high given the size of the interventions; and (3) measurement error, particularly regarding the classification of potentially covered workers and a lack of attention to whether the business-subsidy ordinances actually reached any workers in "treatment" Metropolitan statistical areas (MSAs).

On the first point, because the CPS does not identify living wage workers, Neumark and Adams (2001a,b) are unable to examine the wage and employment outcomes for those directly affected by the policy. Thus, they have to aggregate to the MSA level and hope they can pick up a signal from the ordinances, which they acknowledge affect less than 1 percent of the bottom quartile of the workforce. They also have to assume that workers who live in the city also work there because they are deriving city-level wages from the reports of households who live there but do not necessarily work there.

However, putting aside the residence critique, the lack of a living wage coverage variable in the CPS is not necessarily fatal. If the ordinances raise the market wage for an occupation—if uncovered firms have to raise wages to the living wage level in order to attract and keep workers—this would boost the signal from the intervention. Also, Bartik (2002) notes that the ordinances could cause "large changes in social norms" (27), pressuring noncovered employers to pay "fairer wages." This too could boost the signal-to-noise ratio such that city-level observations could reveal a living wage effect.

The fact that so few workers tend to be covered by existing ordinances, as well as implementation problems discussed in greater detail in the following, works against the notion that uncovered firms would respond to the ordinances and brings into question the magnitude of some of the results. Papers such as that of Neumark and Adams (2001a,b) find wage and (dis)employment elasticities that are far larger than others in the literature on low-wage labor markets.

For example, some of their reported wage elasticities translate into wage gains for all workers in the bottom decile—not simply those directly affected—in an affected MSA of 3–7 percent, employment elasticities that lead to 6 percent employment reductions, along with 8 percent poverty-reduction effects.[14] It is worth reiterating that Adams and Neumark find these effects to reach all workers in the bottom decile, not simply those affected by the ordinance (evidence presented in the following shows much larger wage gains among affected workers).

The extent of these spillovers from a very small number of affected workers to much larger numbers of low-wage workers is a hallmark of this research. While literature on "threat effects" certainly show that intervening forces, such as unions or international trade agreements, can have measurable impacts on jobs and wages that go beyond the directly affected group, the threat needs to be of a magnitude that could plausibly cause the spillovers. This would seem not to be the case regarding living wages, and thus the scope of Neumark's results is hard to believe. Bartik (2002) notes that Neumark and Adam's employment elasticity (the decline in employment with respect to the wage increase) is about twice that in survey literature; their antipoverty elasticity is also about twice what would be expected given literature on the impact of minimum wage increases on poverty. As Bartik writes "This is difficult to believe because the living wage covers far fewer workers" (27).[15]

Brenner, Wicks-Lim, and Pollin (2002) examine Neumark's work on this issue especially carefully and uncover a number of significant problems. Essentially, by rerunning the same models with the same CPS data, they show that results such as those cited previously derive from choices made by Neumark and Adams regarding who is identified as potentially covered by the ordinance, despite that fact that the vast majority of these laws are not covering any workers.

Their critique focuses largely on ordinances tied to business subsidies because laws of this type are more likely to reach statistical significance in the Neumark papers (see, for example, Adams and Neumark [2003] where

14. These effects are derived in Bartik (2002) using the coefficients from various Neumark and Adams's (2001a) regressions and the magnitude of living relative to minimum wages as presented in their 2001 paper.

15. Bartik (2002) also notes that it's hard to square the large disemployment effects with the large poverty-reduction effects.

"contractor only" cases prove to have an insignificant effect on wages and employment). When constructing their coverage variable, Adams and Neumark assume that because any private firm can receive a subsidy from the city, all private-sector workers are potentially covered.[16] This creates an erroneous measure that when corrected leads to insignificant results.

In order to determine who was truly covered by ordinances tied to business subsidies, Brenner, Wicks-Lim, and Pollin (2002) conducted interviews with living wage administrators in the cities classified by Neumark and Adams (2001a) as having business assistance provisions. Based on these interviews, they found that with the exception of San Antonio, none of the 'business assistance' cities Neumark and Adams examine had actually applied this provision of their living wage ordinance to any private-sector businesses over the period covered by the Neumark and Adams paper they examined. Bartik (2002, 27) is also "skeptical" that business subsidies reach enough workers to generate the Neumark and Adams results.

Adams and Neumark (2003) respond to this claim by citing some of their own follow-up calls to city administrators. They agree that "in the initial period there was some uncertainty as administrators worked out procedures for implementing living wage laws," but argue that this "does not imply the laws were ineffective in this period, and city administrators suggested otherwise" (20). However, while Neumark and Adams appear to have been asking whether city agencies were implementing and monitoring the programs (and finding that this was the case in the three cities they checked), Brenner, Wicks-Lim, and Pollin (2002) argue that his team was examining not simply whether the ordinances were up and running but whether there were actually any firms in the city to which the law applied. That is, Brenner, Wicks-Lim, and Pollin asked whether the coverage requirements of the law engendered actual coverage for any firms in the city. Among the cities in Neumark and Adam's (2001a,b) most recent work, they found only one city where this was the case. This approach appears to speak more to the issue of whether Neumark and Adam's coverage variable was too broadly specified.

In sum, and despite their academic rigor, there are reasons to view Neumark and Adam's results as nonrobust. There are serious measurement concerns both regarding the use of CPS data for this analysis and the extent to which they correctly identify coverage on a key identifying variable.[17] The author's argue, however, that these issues are not derailing the

16. In footnote 31 of Adams and Neumark (2003), the authors respond to Brenner, Wicks-Lim, and Pollin (2002) that this coverage variable was merely used this definition as a "specification check." It does, however, appear to be critical to their results.

17. Another econometric concern which has been raised in various critiques (Brenner, Wicks-Lim, and Pollin [2002] and DiNardo, unpublished comments at American Social Science Association [ASSA] presentation by Neumark) regarding the fact that Neumark and Adams (2001a,b), by restricting their sample to the bottom wage decile, are selecting on the

analysis, and their defense is not unreasonable. However, all parties agree that these ordinances affect very small shares of the workforce, and thus the large magnitude of the effects—specifically, the notion that the wage and employment impacts reach workers throughout the bottom decile—in tandem with some of the more controversial aspects of the work, will leave many objective readers unconvinced that such analysis is the best way to learn about the impacts of living wages.

More direct evidence comes from two sources: reports from cities that have implemented living wage ordinances and two pre/post implementation studies based on original survey data.

3.4.4 Primary Analysis

There are two recent high-quality analyses of the impact of living wage ordinances on wages, employment, and contracts that compare outcomes before and after an increase using survey data of covered and uncovered firms: David Fairris's (2003) analysis of the Los Angeles ordinance and Mark Brenner's (2003a) analysis of Boston's ordinance.

The Los Angeles ordinance was passed in 1997, and it has broader coverage than most, if not all, other ordinances in the nation. The threshold level over which service contracts are covered—$25,000—is low relative to most other contract models, and the ordinance also covers companies that receive subsidies of at least $1 million (or $100,000 annually for several years) as well as companies that have a lease or license with the city, such as shops at the airport (see table 3.1). Fairris (2003) notes that at the time of his survey—2002—about 7,000 low-wage workers were covered. The wage is two-tiered; at the time of the study, it was $9.52 without a fringe "benefit credit" and $8.27 with the employer's $1.25 contribution to the workers' health benefits.

In order to examine differences-in-differences, Fairris (2003) needed survey data from covered and uncovered establishments. For the former, he conducts an original survey of living wage employers identified from the city's records, asking establishments about the period before and after the ordinance went into effect. His sampling methodology—a two-stage stratified cluster approach—was designed to capture covered workers in all the relevant occupations. For the control, Fairris uses data from a different survey of Los Angeles establishments. While the use of different data sources is an acknowledged limitation of the study, engendering potential biases based on differences in sampling, subject matter, and timing, Fairris provides some convincing analyses that the extent of this bias is not severe

dependent variable. This, in essence, tends to create an automatic correlation between dependent and independent variables and biases results toward significance. While Brenner, Wicks-Lim, and Pollin (2003) argue that this is a fundamental problem driving the results, Adams and Neumark (2003) disagree.

and does not undermine the results.[18] The surveys enable Fairris to investigate the impact of the introduction of the ordinance and compare results before and after the mandate over affected and unaffected firms.

He finds a significant wage effect from the ordinance, leading to a 35 percent increase among affected low-wage workers in "living wage establishments" compared to an 11 percent increase in the control group, yielding a significant difference-in-difference, which remains intact after controlling for various firm-specific factors, including firm size, union coverage, and industry. A second interesting finding regarding compensation is that there is no effect of living wages on the offering of health coverage. Fairris (2003) suggests this may be due to the fact that firms with city contracts were already (prior to the passage of the ordinance) offering more health coverage than other firms.

Finally, Fairris (2003) usefully examines a set of what he calls "indirect effects of the living wage" differences in turnover, absenteeism, training, and overtime between affected and unaffected firms. These measures are potentially helpful in understanding how firms absorb the increase in labor costs resulting from the wage mandate as living wage advocates frequently raise efficiency wage effects as an absorption mechanism. His difference-in-difference estimates reveal what appear to be very large turnover reduction effects, with affected establishments posting turnover rates that were one-third to one-half that of unaffected establishments.

However, the levels of turnover, data on which were only gathered postincrease, are so much higher in the living wage settings (close to three times that of the control establishments) that one suspects that these firms with city contracts may be operating under a different turnover regime that is not successfully differenced out by Fairris's (2003) method.[19] He does, however, show that the lower turnover rates in affected firms is fully a function of their higher wages relative to the unaffected firms, a result that supports the efficiency wage explanation. The other results suggest the living wages reduce absenteeism but also may reduce the provision of job training compared to non–living wage firms. Fairris argues that this latter result may support the notion that "wage mandates such as living wages prevent workers from striking a deal with employers that reduces wages temporarily in exchange for job training" (21).

Because the survey of unaffected firms did not ask about employment levels, Fairris (2003) is unable to do a controlled analysis of this key variable.

18. Fairris (2003) notes, for example, that as the living wage survey had the official endorsement of the government, it had a much higher response rate than the other survey: 68 percent versus 23 percent. However, in one important verification test, he shows that wage levels paid to low-wage workers are statistically indistinguishable between the two surveys controlling for the presence of the living wage itself (14–15).

19. There are also significant measurement differences in turnover between the two surveys, discussed in detail by Fairris (2003, 16–17).

In his living wage survey, however, he does ask about changes in staffing levels and whether such changes were attributable to the ordinance. These results show that 18 percent of affected employers claimed that the living wage ordinance led them to reduce employment. These job losses amounted to 1.6 percent of the workforce of all firms covered by the ordinance, and 2.6 percent of firms were forced to raise wages. Given the average wage increase among affected workers noted, Fairris derives a disemployment elasticity of –0.1 percent. However, without controls, it is impossible to know if these layoffs were truly a living wage effect or were a function of some broader economic phenomenon. Thankfully, another pre/post study, Mark Brenner's (2003a) investigation of the Boston ordinance, examines the employment question with a controlled design.

The Boston ordinance was also passed in 1997 but was not implemented until the next year. It was expanded considerably in 2001, with broader coverage and higher wage levels implemented in 2002. In mid-2002, it was set at $10.54, 56 percent higher than the Massachusetts minimum wage of $6.75. In 2001, Brenner (2003a) surveyed the universe of firms subject to the living wage law, that is, the 140 firms holding service contracts with the city that met the criteria for coverage by the ordinance. While his response rate was just above half, he shows that the responders do not appear to differ on observables from the nonresponders.

The variation that enables Brenner (2003a) to conduct his study comes from the fact that 25 percent of the contractors he surveyed were forced to raise wages by the law (which turns out to be only around thirteen firms). His control group is not a random group of Boston firms with similar workers that were not subject to the ordinance; it is contractor firms that paid wages above the mandated levels and were thus unaffected. Thus, the research question here is really "among firms that contract with the city, how does the introduction of a living wage affect those contractors who must raise wages (or fringes) to comply compared to contractors who do not have to do so?" In a sense, Brenner examines what happens within a fairly narrow economic group (Boston city contractors) when the playing field (concerning labor costs) is leveled by a wage mandate.

His difference-in-difference results show that while employment increased among both affected and unaffected contractors after the implementation of the living wage, the increase was only slightly greater among unaffected firms (those that did not have to raise wages), and the difference (in difference) was not great enough to reach statistical significance. Affected firms increased employment by an average twenty-one jobs (11 percent) over the period, while unaffected firms grew by an average of twenty-seven jobs (17 percent). Interestingly, the increase in full-time equivalents (FTEs) was the same—twenty-two FTEs—for both groups, so the difference-in-difference in employment growth by this measure was zero. In fact, one of the two statistically significant findings in this comparison is a decrease in the use of part-time workers by firms that had to raise wages compared to those that did not.

Other results show significant wage compression among affected firms relative to the controls, an expected result because the affected firms had to essentially truncate the lower tail of their premandate wage distribution. Unlike Fairris (2003), Brenner's (2003a) statistical results show no significant changes in turnover or absenteeism between the two groups, although he does report that 25 percent of affected firms report "greater employee effort" and "greater employee morale" after the wage increase.

While both the Fairris (2003) and Brenner (2003a) studies have acknowledged limitations, they are well designed and provide much needed direct information on the impact of these two living wage ordinances. Both studies directly survey affected firms and add controls to identify a living wage effect. Both find large wage effects, and Brenner finds insignificant disemployment effects both for raw job counts and for FTE's (he finds a significant decline in the relative use of part-time workers by affected firms). On the other hand, some of the affected employers in the Fairris study report that the living wage led to layoffs, though he is unable to measure this effect relative to unaffected firms. They present mixed evidence for "efficiency wage effects" with Fairris's study showing fairly strong effects and Brenner's showing none relative to unaffected firms despite some claims of greater effort among affected workers by firms that had to raise wages to comply with the ordinance.

Neumark and Adam's studies are of a very different ilk, using a national microdata set to search for living wage effects. Surprisingly, given the known small magnitude of the numbers of workers directly affected by living wages, they find large (relative to the literature on such effects) wage, employment, and poverty-reduction impacts not just for covered workers but also for the whole bottom tail of the MSA wage distribution. I argue that the limitations of secondary data analysis along with measurement error of a key indicator variable cast doubt on these results.

At this stage, it's fair to say that the policy does quite clearly appear to lift the wages of affected workers with somewhat ambiguous results as to the employment effects. Much more work in the spirit of Brenner (2003a) and Fairris (2003) is needed to answer this important question. Additional survey-based studies will also help to determine the impact of different attributes of the ordinances because no two policies are identical. Given the nature of these mandates, there are rich opportunities here for quasi-experimental designs, a relatively rare but highly valuable occurrence in our field.

3.4.5 Administrative Reports

Another useful source of information on living wage impacts comes from reports by city administrators overseeing the implementation and running of the program. Various towns, cities, and counties (though by no means all of those that have adopted the policy) have produced reports that document the status of the policy and in some cases present some evaluation of impacts, particularly on city budgets, contracting costs and activities, and business climate. Many of the reports also give the numbers of affected workers, a valuable administrative check on the reach of these ordinances.

These reports have the advantage of reflecting information by some of the people who are "closest to the ground" regarding the implementation and impact of the laws. They lack, however, the academic rigor of the studies cited previously; in particular, they do not formally consider counterfactuals (though administrators do sometimes discuss impacts with reference to earlier periods, and most consider the impact of the business cycle). Still, these are clearly useful data on actual impacts.

The city/county studies are summarized in a review paper by Andrew Elmore (2003), who writes that these reports "suggest that localities after implementation of a living wage law tend to experience modest contract price increases for a small proportion of contracts" (7), leading to overall increases in contract costs to the city that were usually less than 1 percent. These values confirm the work cited earlier from the prospective studies claiming that the increase in city budgets from living wage ordinances are not expected to be large. Elmore does, however, note a few larger increases in individual contracts due to the ordinances, including a 31 percent increase in a security contract in Hartford (the only contract covered there), a 22 percent increase in a janitorial contract in Warren, Michigan, and increases of 10 percent in about 5 percent of the city contracts in Berkeley, California.

Again, the magnitude of these increases are driven by coverage. Among the reports that give the numbers of directly affected workers are the following:[20]

- 41 workers in Corvallis, Oregon
- 54 workers in Hartford, Connecticut
- 54 workers in Hayward, California
- 338 in Minneapolis, Minnesota
- 106 in Pasadena, California
- 55 in San Jose, California
- 75 in Ventura County, California

The fact that these budgetary increases are small relative to the total budgets of the localities does not, of course, imply that they are trivial or nonproblematic. For example, such costs could be passed along to tax payers in greater tax liabilities or service reductions. While both would pre-

20. These values are taken from the actual reports, not from Elmore's (2003) review.

sumably be marginal, they could still be viewed with displeasure by residents, especially those who opposed the ordinance. Or contractors might decide to no longer bid with the city, thus reducing the competitiveness of the process with negative cost results for the city. The determinant question is the extent to which these increases are absorbed by the contractors or passed through.

As Elmore (2003) reports, contractors appeared to absorb at least some portion (in some cases, all) of the increase, and there was little evidence of any diminution of competitiveness in the bidding process. Regarding pass-through, he followed up with some of the administrators and asked them why they thought this occurred.[21] Some (e.g., Pasadena) reported that the city "negotiated with contractors for a substantial absorption of contract costs," which turned out to amount to about half of the increased labor costs. An Ypsilanti town supervisor found that the cost of the ordinance there was held down by an increase in the numbers of bidders. Her explanation, reported by Elmore (2003, 11), is that "now that the wage standard is equal, the ability to compete is based on factors other than wages, so you've got to be tighter and provide less of a profit margin," a view that gives some support to the "redistribution of rents" argument by living wage advocates. Note that Brenner (2003a) also reports that 38 percent of affected firms in his study report taking lower profits as the primary means by which they have adjusted to the Boston living wage law. Of course, here's where the lack of a counterfactual is evident—there could be other economic reasons why bids increased.

While the above all relates to service contracts, Elmore (2003) also reviews the impact of private-sector subsidy-based living wage ordinances, and here the results are more mixed. He reviews nine cities with subsidy-based living wage ordinances and reports that only one—Oakland—reported a decline in the number and size of economic development projects. However, the example of Oakland may reveal an important impact of this dimension of the policy.

When cities provide subsidies to manufacturing firms and such subsidies include living wage provisions, the wage structure in such firms makes it unlikely that the ordinance will have much bite, a point also made by Bartik (2002). Elmore's study suggests that this explains most of the results from the city surveys and his discussions with administrators. But when the subsidies apply to retailers, as was the case in Oakland, the number of affected workers could potentially be considerably higher. The impact of the ordinance then becomes a greater consideration in the retailer's decision whether to accept the subsidy. He cites two national retailers that abandoned projects in Oakland, in part due to the living wage ordinance.

Elmore (2003) argues that while "a living wage law may deter retailers

21. It would be useful to do so with contractors as well.

from pursuing economic subsidies . . . attracting national retailers through a subsidy program may not be a wise public policy approach" (15). This is perhaps true, but one can easily imagine cases where a locality, say one with very weak employment growth, would benefit considerably from attracting retailers. At any rate, living wage advocates need to be mindful of this potential cost when they attach the wage mandate to retailer subsidies.

Two final impact studies are worth noting. Reynolds and Vortcamp (2000) examine the impact of the Detroit living wage on nonprofits. This group is of special interest because they presumably have no pricing markups and thus cannot absorb the increase through lower profits (I return briefly to this topic under "Emerging Issues" in the following). They can also have low pay scales for some workers and thus face relatively high coverage (though Reynolds and Vortcamp find that only a few hundred Detroit nonprofit workers were directly affected by the ordinance). As seen in table 3.1, these realities have led some cities to exempt nonprofits from the ordinance.

Like the city reports discussed previously, Reynolds and Vortcamp's (2000) study does not involve any counterfactuals. They do, however, present survey results wherein they asked employer respondents in the nonprofit sector how their establishments were affected by the law. While most respondents reported that the impact of the law has been "minor" or "minimal," 32 percent reported an impact of "significant" or "major." Reynolds and Vortcamp report that "at most" 25 percent face "significant financial problems in implementing the living wage requirements" (2). They note that these firms generally absorbed the increase by cutting hours of some staff and "cuts in supplies for client events."[22] At the same time, they report the "several hundred" low-wage non-profit employees experienced wage gains that ranged from 10 to 74 percent.

A final important impact study is Reich, Hall, and Jacobs's (2003) analysis of a particularly broad ordinance (in terms of coverage, wages, and other mandates, such as training standards) implemented at the San Francisco International Airport in 2000. While the authors find the expected increase in wages (they note that the wage of affected entry-level workers rose by an average of 33 percent), what's most notable about their findings are the efficiency wage effects. They report that turnover fell by an average of 34 percent among firms covered by the ordinance and that the decline in turnover rates increase with wages. To cite a particularly relevant occupation in our post-9/11 world, they report that turnover among airport security screeners, whose average wage rose by 55 percent after the living wage went into effect, fell from 94.7 percent per year to 18.7 percent fifteen

22. Reynolds and Vortcamp (2000) report that rather than be exempt from the law, these firms said they would rather the city pass-though the extra resources they need in higher contract levels. Some advocates have suggested that "full pass-through" for nonprofits be part of living wage legislation.

months later.[23] While Fairris (2003) finds a negative relation between living wages and training, Reich, Hall, and Jacobs report increased training as mandated by the ordinance itself. Finally, while they argue that employment levels were not affected by the ordinance, they do not offer the controls that would enable them to test this assertion relative to unaffected firms.

The impact studies thus reveal somewhat of a "mixed bag." As the low-coverage/low-impact arguments suggest, the ordinances have not thus far led to far-reaching disruptions of employment or contract costs. Relative to the size of the low-wage labor market, the wages of a small number of workers have gotten a significant lift. There are over 100 of these ordinances, and as living wage expert Robert Pollin (2002) has quipped, if the enacted ordinances were leading to significant problems, we'd be hearing about it.[24] Yet, while minor, disemployment effects do show up in some of the work, and, perhaps more importantly, Elmore (2003) reports that the Oakland living wage probably played a role in discouraging two national retailers from locating there. This one case does not imply that such firms will invariably make this choice or that localities will necessarily decide that such a tradeoff is unacceptable, but it is a finding of which advocates and policymakers should take note. On the other hand, as reported in a newspaper story about a new ordinance in Lawrence, Kansas, a site-selection consultant stated, "'I don't think that [living wage] knocks you out of the running' in attracting new businesses."[25] Clearly, we need to learn more about the impact of living wages on such incentives.

3.5 Can Living Wage Ordinances Help Raise the Living Standards of Low-Income Working Families?

This key question is by no means a simple one. Its answer depends on the extent of coverage, targeting, the reaction of firms to higher labor costs, the impact of the ordinance of contracting, the interaction of the wage increase with other social programs, the indirect effect of the ordinances (e.g., the extent of wage spillover), and myriad other factors. Two other relevant summary evaluation questions are (1) if ordinances themselves are of limited value, do they have other effects which affected groups might view as desirable, such as reducing private-sector outsourcing of publicly provided services or strengthening union power, both of which have the potential to raise living standards among affect workers but which could have other economic implications as well, such as raising the costs of providing

23. The authors report that Federal Aviation Authority (FAA) data show that lower screener turnover is associated with "higher rates of detection of security breaches" (10).

24. Quoted in *Time Magazine,* April 2002.

25. See "City Approves Living Wage," *Lawrence Journal-World* (Lawrence, Kansas), October 22, 2003.

services in living wage cities relative to those without the policy? and (2) do better policies exist that conflict with the passage of living wage ordinances, that is, policies which are substitutes, not complements?

Regarding targeting, questions have been raised as to whether the beneficiaries of the higher-wage mandate are appropriate targets for such a policy. While they surely earn low wages, this does not necessarily imply low family incomes. Some critics of living wage ordinances have been especially critical of this aspect of the policy (Sander, Williams, and Doherty 2002).

While not much empirical work has been done on this question regarding living wages, a good deal has been done on minimum wages. In my own work with various coauthors, I've consistently found that most of the benefits, about 60 percent, of a minimum wage increase flow to working families in the bottom 40 percent of the income scale, whose average income is about $27,000 in 2002 dollars (Bernstein and Schmitt 1998). Other authors, such as Burkhauser, Couch, and Glenn (1996) get worse targeting results for the minimum wage, but this is largely due to measurement choices, such as including nonworking families and placing greater emphasis on the extent of benefits that flow to families below the poverty line, whereas Bernstein and Schmitt argue that an assessment of targeting need not be limited to the officially poor. At any rate, this research shows some positive correlation between low earnings and low incomes, though one that is not very high.

The most detailed work on living wages and family incomes is in Pollin and Brenner's (2000) prospective study of the Santa Monica ordinance. They use both CPS data and their own survey results from the specific area affected by the proposed ordinance. Their CPS results examine the characteristics and incomes of Los Angeles families with earnings between the California minimum wage of $5.75 and the proposed living wage of $10.75. They find that a large majority of these workers are adults, with median incomes in the $30,000 range and mean incomes of around $44,000 (1999 dollars). Their more localized survey of low-wage workers in the affected area show much lower incomes for low-wage workers, with median income of about $20,000 and mean income of about $31,000. Clearly, all these income values are well above the poverty line, but, as Pollin and Brenner (2000) argue, they are below the amount that family budget experts have estimated are needed to meet basic needs for safe, affordable housing; health and child care; food; taxes; and miscellaneous expenses in California (see California Budget Project 1999; Bernstein, Brocht, and Spade-Aguilar 2000).

Thus, the targeting question is well taken, and the results can be viewed as somewhat ambiguous. For those who believe the policy should reach only the working poor, the policy is poorly targeted by family income. For those who believe this benchmark is too restrictive and that lower-middle-income families should benefit from the policy, targeting concerns will be significantly mitigated. Most of the beneficiaries are likely to reside in families with incomes above the poverty line but below the levels needed to consistently meet their basic needs.

Another potentially important type of "leakage" that relates to the targeting question asks about the extent to which higher mandated wages will displace the lowest-skilled workers who will be replaced by those with higher skill levels. This issue has not been examined directly by the previously mentioned pre/post studies, although anecdotal data in Neidt et al. (1999) reveal that such displacements did not occur in their study of the Baltimore ordinance. Also, the significantly lower turnover levels associated with the Los Angeles ordinance in Fairris's (2003) study may mitigate against this effect if, in fact, workers in place when the ordinance is implemented stay with the firm longer than would otherwise have been the case.

Pollin and Brenner's prospective study (2000) also investigates this issue by looking at the age and education composition of low-wage occupations. They argue that over time, the Santa Monica ordinance could potentially displace 10–20 percent of high school dropouts to be placed by high school graduates and those with some college. They consider this a modest effect, but others may view this as a problem for the policy.

There is also the question as to whether income gains to low-wage workers through mandated wage hikes will be offset by cuts in means-tested benefits such as food stamps or the EITC as well as higher payroll and income taxes. Tolley, Bernstein, and Lesage (1996) originally examined this possibility in their prospective review of the Chicago, Illinois living wage, arguing that these tax and transfer policies would "claw-back" as much as 75 percent of the benefits from the living wage. Later work by Baiman, Persky, and Brunick (2002) estimated the net gain from the wage increase to be closer to 50 percent, but this is still quite significant leakage. Pollin and Brenner (2000) also find this effect to be significant in their Santa Monica analysis, such that for every dollar increase in the living wage, disposable income increases by $0.57, while the rest is transferred back to the federal and state government.[26]

Freeman (2000) notes that such transfers should be distinguished from the usual leaks in such programs wherein resources are essentially wasted. These transfers revert to state and local governments and thus do not generate inefficiencies typically associated with leakages. They do, however, create a potential wedge between the pre- and posttransfer incomes of living wage beneficiaries. More research is needed in the case of actual ordinances to determine the extent of the wedge.

Can the living wage movement help low-wage workers by raising their levels of union coverage? Can it improve the quality of low-wage employment by slowing the rate of privatization or the subsidization of poverty-

26. This figure comes from Freeman's (2000) review of Pollin and Brenner (2000). He averages the results for the two cases presented by the authors.

level jobs? Certainly this is the hope of many organizers, and many who have observed and studied the movement raise this possibility. While there's some evidence in favor of the latter point, as of now, there's little evidence of such spillovers regarding union coverage.

Luce (2000) points out that while central labor councils commonly partner with living wage advocates, their involvement in a living wage campaign is not a guarantee that either they or their affiliated local unions will always support the issue or make political choices favorable to the campaign. She cites a few examples where, for political expediency, unions backed candidates who were on record against the ordinance. Second, simply putting labor-friendly language into ordinances is not enough to generate new membership, particularly when those affected by the ordinance are few and far between. Third, living wage campaigns and union organizing drives typically take place on very different time frames. A living wage campaign can take years, involving much coalition building, community education, frequent meeting with key actors, and so on. Union organizers tend to work on much shorter time frames.

Nissen (2000) essentially agrees, questioning, on the basis of his involvement with the (successful) Miami campaign, whether meaningful complementarities between living wage campaigns and the labor movement can emerge. He argues that the goal of a campaign—an ordinance—is modest relative to social and organizational needs, for example, a revived labor movement. At least in the Miami case, no broad-based coalition emerged with roots into all aspects of the low-income community, and this, Nissen argues, diminishes both the lasting impact of the campaigns and their effectiveness and status as a true social movement.

Reynolds (2001) disagrees somewhat, pointing out that while many campaigns might be characterized this way, others have made lasting contributions, either birthing or significantly strengthening existing coalition-based institutions, such as LAANE, a group very active in various living wage campaigns along with other extensive labor/community organizing.

At this point, it is unknowable whether this relatively new labor market institution can make a significant difference in the economic lives of more than a small number of the low-income workers. One can certainly conclude that the ordinances in their current format do not reach enough workers to the direct effect of lifting the living standards of significant numbers of low-wage workers. In fact, their low coverage rates are the primarily selling point by advocates who support them.

From the perspective of raising living standards, for the movement to morph into an important institution with the potential to reach many more workers, at least one of two things must occur: coverage must expand or indirect effects must become more dominant. Regarding coverage, recent campaigns to introduce policies more in the spirit of minimum wages, such as in Santa Monica, California, New Orleans, and Santa Fe, may signal that the movement is turning in that direction, although only one of these (Santa Fe) is actually on the books. Of course, with greater coverage comes greater potential for economic distortions. Regarding indirect effects, the potential of living wage campaigns to serve as organizing tools for unions remains a goal of the movement, though research suggests it has not of yet made significant inroads here. One area where there may be some indirect benefits to public-sector workers is in discouraging outsourcing of their tasks. Elmore's (2003) study of city administrators' reports (and his follow-up conversations with some of them) suggest that ordinances may be playing this role and thus preserving jobs that could be lost through low-wage outsourcing. Other more recent ordinances, such as that of Harvard University, also have this as an explicit goal, using pay-parity rules to discourage such outsourcing.

Are there other policies which could help low-wage low-income workers more that conflict with the passage of living wage ordinances? Certainly, many make the case that the EITC is a far more efficient way to raise the incomes of low-income families (Turner and Barnow 2003). Given that eligibility for the EITC is based on family income and not wages, there can be no argument that the tax credit is more target efficient. However, living wage advocates argue that the two policies are complementary, not competitors.

In fact, it is difficult to see why the existence of the EITC would, or should, deter any policymaker from considering the living wage. Clearly, the wage mandate is about adding something extra to the incomes of low-income working families, and the fact that a generous and well-targeted federal tax credit exists is not particularly relevant, if not a non sequitur. Advocates correctly note that even considering the leakage from means-tested programs such as the EITC noted above, many living wage families need the extra resources, and combining the two makes sense from their perspective.

However, in at least one case (Montgomery County, Maryland) forces that opposed and ultimately defeated a living wage ordinance supported and passed a local EITC, that is, an add-on to the federal credit for county residents worth 16 percent of the family's federal credit. This alternative, of course, does yield new and better-targeted benefits to low-income working families. Simulations by Turner and Barnow (2003) compare the targeting of an equally costly living wage and local EITC and find that while about 25 percent of poor families reached by the wage mandate are poor, 44 percent of those reached by the local EITC are in poverty. The local tax credit is also almost certain to reach many more workers than the living wage.[27]

27. The Montgomery County add-on went to over 12,000 workers in 2000, far more residents than would have been affected by the living wage (note the affected worker counts from the city reports shown previously or the fact that Fairris reports 7,000 covered by the Los Angeles ordinance). See http://www.montgomerycountymd.gov/mc/news/press/00-33.html for information on the Maryland county EITC.

Still, there are other considerations to be made when comparing the living wage to the local EITC. Regarding efficiency concerns, along with better targeting, supporters of this alternative point out that it is less likely to have a negative impact on jobs, contracts, or the business climate. On the other hand, this alternative represents a direct cost to local tax payers, whereas other sources exist through which the cost of the living wage may be absorbed, specifically lower profits, efficiency wage effects, and higher contract prices (this latter possibility would, like the local EITC, be passed through to tax payers in some form). Bernstein (2002) points out that while the EITC is a fine way to help low-income workers, it does have the potential to lower market wages in low-wage jobs, thus partially serving a subsidy from taxpayers to low-wage employers. Also, the EITC does little for workers without children. Finally, adding a local EITC in place of a living wage does not accomplish the stated goal of advocates noted previously from the ACORN website to ensure that "private businesses that benefit from public money . . . pay their workers a living wage" (http://www.livingwagecampaign.org/).

Given these dual concerns, combining the two policies may be a useful innovation with the potential to better meet both the goals of the movement and address concerns regarding targeting and inefficiencies. In fact, Montgomery County later passed a living wage law and Denver, Colorado also has both a local EITC and a living wage. The local EITC, an innovation favored by some opponents of living wages, adds a smaller amount of income (relative to the living wage) to a broad group of low-income working poor families. The living wage adds more income to a much smaller group of beneficiaries, but it addresses the movements goals of rent redistribution, social justice, and a higher pretax or "market" wage for covered workers.[28]

3.6 Emerging Issues

As the movement matures, a few issues are emerging. First, as noted previously, opponents are mounting legal challenges, either arguing that current law prohibits local governments from enacting such mandates or trying to pass such legislation. Although the validity of these efforts is far

28. The local EITCs are likely to add between $400–$600 to the incomes of recipients in those cities, while the living wage could add closer to $1,500. The former range is based on my estimates given the local EITC percents of the federal credit. The latter takes Fairris's $1.70 estimate of the wage benefit from the Los Angeles ordinance multiplied by 1,800—the number of hours worked by low-wage workers in Los Angeles according to Pollin and Brenner (2000). That yields about $3,000, half of which I assume "leaks" out in taxes and loss of means-tested benefits. While these are, of course, very rough estimates, it is very likely the case that living wage recipients receive considerably more income from the wage mandate than from the local EITC.

from clear at this point, it does appear that language in some state constitutions could be construed to prohibit localities from implementing living wage policies. That is, these states prohibit localities from assuming powers that they are not expressly granted by the state. In other states, localities have the same regulatory power as the state itself.

However, even when state law appears to prohibit local mandates, this is often a matter of interpretation. That is, state constitutions are unlikely to contain language expressly forbidding localities from enacting ordinances. They may, however, disallow any laws that assume more regulatory power than the state intended to grant them or that raise the costs of doing business. In the latter case, campaigns have countered with "efficiency wage" arguments, which point out that efficiency gains resulting from higher wages (e.g., less turnover, fewer vacancies, greater effort) absorb the higher labor costs, implying that contractors will not necessarily have to raise costs to the city as a result of the ordinance.

Numerous states have, however, responded to the living wage movement by adopting preemption language.[29] In some states, the language in these laws are broadly preemptive, prohibiting localities from enacting any wage mandates. For example, Utah's preemption prohibits not living wage requirements for contractors or subsidy recipients but also city-wide minimum wage increases. Others are more narrowly construed to prohibit only city-wide minimum wage increases.

A second emerging issue involves the coverage of nonprofits. It is not uncommon for nonprofits, who may be philosophically disposed to support living wage campaigns, to argue that due to their status they should be exempt. Some campaign organizers view this as a problem, both because it can lead to opposition by traditional supporters and because low-wage employees at nonprofits arguably need the raise as much as other covered workers. These organizers have argued that in cases where this dynamic develops, the ordinance should contain "full pass-through," meaning that any higher labor costs are reflected in an increase in the nonprofit's contract with the city (the economic assumption here is that such firms have no rents to redistribute). Of course, this validates opponents' objection regarding higher costs to the city.

A final emerging issue relates to implementation. It is widely believed that in many cities, living wage ordinances are not appropriately implemented such that not all covered workers are receiving the higher wages mandated by the law. Sander and Lokey (1998) attribute the low numbers of covered workers in Los Angeles to lax implementation. Luce (2000) notes that in most cases the monitoring of the ordinances has been left up to the city. While this does not necessarily imply lax enforcement, it is

29. These include Louisiana, Oregon, Colorado, Missouri, Arizona, and Utah.

certainly worrisome from the perspective of living wage advocates, particularly in cases where the campaign was met with resistance from city officials. Most organizers thus argue that the groups who campaigned for the ordinance should play some role in its implementation, and some ordinances include language and resources to this effect.

3.7 Conclusion

Living wage ordinances face a paradox. By remaining limited in their coverage, their advocates have been able to convince city officials and, by proxy, taxpayers that they will accomplish their stated goals of raising the economic fortunes of affected workers without leading to economic distortions in the form of significant layoffs, tax hikes, or reduced competition for contracts. The evidence presented previously is somewhat mixed on these points—supporters and opponents can both point to studies that support their cause. But while the research remains limited at this point, there is little evidence of very significant problems. The ordinances appear to provide a sizable wage lift to workers, many of whom, while not poor, have income levels that are low enough to warrant concern. And while some employment losses are reported, they appear to be marginal. Similarly, city administrators widely report that major disruptions to the contracting process or to costs have not occurred.

But the marginal coverage of the policy limits its effectiveness to raise the living standards of more than a few thousand workers. While no national total of affected workers (those who have received wage hikes due to the policy) is knowable and is a quickly moving target, a rough count would be unlikely surpass 100,000 and may well be closer to half that level. In a low-wage labor market of roughly 30 million (Mishel, Bernstein, and Boushey 2002), this gives a sense of the limitations of the movement and the nature of the paradox it faces.[30]

With this in mind, there is still a lot to say for the living wage movement. It has been extremely successful in a climate not particularly conducive to interventions intended to guide the "invisible hand." Again, limited coverage surely plays a role here as city councils are surely more willing to take risks with small programs than large ones.[31] But it is also the case that the coalitions are generally very strategic, taking considerable time to build

30. This is the number of persons earning less than the poverty-level-wage in 2000, defined as the poverty line for a family of four divided by full-time full-year work: 2080 hours or $8.46 (data from the CPS earnings files).

31. As an anonymous reviewer of an earlier draft of this paper pointed out, part of the movement's success may stem from the fact that "state governments are soft targets—budget constraints are squishy, there are concentrated beneficiaries, and diffuse claimants [taxpayers]."

broad movements comprising labor, activists, and religious actors. Given the long-term negative trend that has beset low-wage workers in tandem with more privatization and subsidies, the campaigns' message of economic justice is difficult for elected officials to dismiss.

As with any new policy, especially one as diverse as this, important questions remain. Given the nature of the paradox noted previously, two questions stand out. First, to what extent can coverage be expanded without generating unacceptable inefficiencies? Taken together, much—not all—of the literature on minimum and living wages suggests that given the indeterminacy of wages and the myriad other factors that determine employment elasticities, quite modest wage increases with broad coverage (as in minimum wage increases) and much less modest increases with very limited coverage (living wages) can be absorbed without significant displacements or distortions. If, in fact, the next stage of the living wage movement is toward expanding coverage, as in city-level minimum wages, research will be needed to gauge the impact on the relevant outcome variables.

Second, even if coverage remains limited, there is the question of spillovers from the living wage movement to larger existing institutions, specifically the labor movement. There is some evidence that living wages dampen localities' incentives to outsource publicly provided services, and such effects should continue to be monitored. But a larger question is the extent to which living wage campaigns can serve as organizing tools for unions. Thus far, this appears not to be the case, but there is almost no systematic research on this important question.

At this point, the living wage is one of the better-known policies designed to "take wages out of the market" and to address the difficulties faced by low-wage workers in the new economy. And, as I have stressed, the living wage movement is a juggernaut; unless the landscape changes quickly, the number of ordinances is only like to grow, perhaps at an even faster rate. Getting the hard data needed to learn more about the movement's impacts can only help us advance our knowledge about this important new policy.

References

Adams, Scott, and David Neumark. 2003. Living wage effects: New and improved evidence. NBER Working Paper no. 9702. Cambridge, Mass.: National Bureau of Economic Research, May.

Baiman, Ron, Joseph Persky, and Nicholas Brunick. 2002. *A step in the right direction: An analysis of forecasted costs and benefits of the Chicago living wage ordinance.* Chicago: University of Illinois, Chicago, Center for Economic Development, College of Urban Planning and Public Affairs.

Bartik, Timothy J. 2002. Thinking about local living wage requirements. Upjohn Institute Staff Working Paper no. 02-76. Kalamazoo, Mich.: Upjohn Institute.

Bernstein, Jared. 2002. Two cheers for the EITC. *The American Prospect* 11 (15).

Bernstein, Jared, Chauna Brocht, and Maggie Spade-Aguilar. 2000. *How much is enough? Basic family budgets for working families.* Washington, D.C.: Economic Policy Institute.

Bernstein, Jared, and John Schmitt. 1998. *Making work pay: The impact of the 1996–97 minimum wage increase.* Washington, D.C.: Economic Policy Institute.

Brenner, Mark D. 2003a. The economic impact of the Boston living wage ordinance. University of California, Riverside, Institute for Labor and Employment. Unpublished manuscript.

Brenner, Mark D. 2003b. The economic impact of living wage ordinances. University of Massachusetts, Amherst, Political Economy Research Institute. Unpublished manuscript.

Brenner, Mark, Jeannette Wicks-Lim, and Robert Pollin. 2002. Measuring the impact of living wage laws: A critical appraisal of David Neumark's "How living wage laws affect low-wage workers and low-income families." PERI Working Paper no. 43. Amherst, Mass.: Political Economy Research Institute.

Burkhauser, Richard V., Kenneth A. Couch, and Andrew J. Glenn. 1996. Public policies for the working poor: The Earned Income Tax Credit versus minimum wage legislation. In *Research in labor economics,* ed. Sol Polacheck, 65–110. Greenwich, Conn.: JAI Press.

Business Week. 2000. What's so bad about a living wage?: Paying above the minimum seems to do more good than harm. September 4.

California Budget Project. 1999. *Making ends meet: How much does it cost to raise a family in California?* Sacramento, Calif.: California Budget Project.

Chi, Keon S., and Cindy Jasper. 1998. Private practices: A review of privatization in state government. Lexington, Ky.: Council of State Governments.

Elmore, Andrew. 2003. *Contract costs and economic development in living wage localities: A report from cities and counties on the impact of living wage laws on local programs.* New York: Brennan Center for Justice.

Fairris, David. 2003. The impact of living wages on employers: A control group analysis of the Los Angeles ordinance. Paper prepared for the Living Wage Research Conference. 11–12 April, Riverside, Calif.

Freeman, Richard. 2000. Report on "Economic analysis of Santa Monica Living Wage" study. Available at [http://www.santa-monica.org/cityclerk/council/freeman.htm].

Glickman, Lawrence. 1997. *A living wage: American workers and the making of consumer society.* Ithaca, N.Y.: Cornell University Press.

Jackson, Cynthia. 1997. Strategies for managing tension between public employment and private service delivery. *Public Productivity and Management Review* 21 (1).

Kuttner, Robert. 1997. *Everything for sale: The virtues and limits of markets.* New York: Alfred A. Knopf.

LeRoy, Greg, and Tyson Slocum. 1999. *Economic development in Minnesota: High subsidies, low wages, absent standards.* Washington, D.C.: Good Jobs First.

Luce, Stephanie. 1998. Living wage campaigns: Parts I and II. *Against the Current* 13 (4–5).

———. 2000. Building political power and community coalitions: The role of central labor councils in the living wage movement. University of Massachusetts, Labor Center. Mimeograph.

———. 2003. Fighting for a living wage: The politics of implementation. University of Massachusetts, Department of Economics. Unpublished manuscript.

Martin, Isaac. 2001. Dawn of the living wage: The diffusion of a redistributive municipal policy. *Urban Affairs Review* 36 (4).

Mishel, Lawrence, Jared Bernstein, and Heather Boushey. 2002. *The state of working America, 2002–03.* Ithaca, N.Y.: Cornell University Press.

Moore, Adrian. 1998. *Privatization 1998.* Los Angeles: Reason Public Policy Institute.

National Priorities Project. 1998. *Working hard, earning less.* Northampton, Mass.: National Priorities Project.

Neumark, David. 2002. *How living wage laws affect low-wage workers and low-income families.* San Francisco: Public Policy Institute of California.

Neumark, David, and Scott Adams. 2001a. Detecting effects of living wage laws. PPIC Working Paper. San Francisco: Public Policy Institute of California.

Neumark, David, and Scott Adams. 2001b. Do living wage ordinances reduce urban poverty? PPIC Working Paper. San Francisco: Public Policy Institute of California.

Niedt, Christopher, Greg Ruiters, Dana Wise, and Erica Schoenberger. 1999. The effects of the living wage in Baltimore. Johns Hopkins University, Department of Geography and Environmental Engineering, Working Paper no. 119.

Nissen, Bruce. 2000. Living wage campaigns from a "social movement" perspective: The Miami case. *Labor Studies Journal* 25 (3).

Owens, Christine. 1997. A living wage! *NFG Reports* 4 (1).

Pollin, Robert. 2002. How much is a living wage? Inside the movement to boost minimum pay: It may ease poverty, but does it also cause job cutbacks? *Time*, April 8.

Pollin, Robert, and Mark D. Brenner. 2000. Economic analysis of "Santa Monica Living Wage Proposal. Research Report no. 2. Amherst, Mass.: Political Economy Research Institute.

Pollin, Robert, and Stephanie Luce. 1998. *The living wage: Building a fair economy.* New York: The New Press.

Pollin, Robert, Stephanie Luce, and Mark Brenner. 1999. Economic analysis of the New Orleans minimum wage proposal. Available at [http://www.umass.edu/peri/research.html].

Reich, Michael, Peter Hall, and Ken Jacobs. 2003. *Living wages and economic performance: The San Francisco airport model.* Berkeley, Calif.: University of California, Berkeley, Institute of Industrial Relations.

Reynolds, David. 2001. Living wage campaigns as social movements: Experiences from nine cities. *Labor Studies Journal* 26 (2): 31–65.

Reynolds, David, and Jean Vortcamp. 2000. *The impact of Detroit's living wage law on nonprofit organizations.* Detroit, Mich.: Wayne State University, Center for Urban Studies and Labor Studies Center, College of Urban, Labor and Metropolitan Affairs.

Sander, Richard H., E. Douglass Williams, and Joseph Doherty. 2002. *The economic and distributional consequences of the Santa Monica Minimum Wage Ordinance.* Washington, D.C.: Employment Policies Institute.

Sander, Richard, and Sean Lokey. 1998. The Los Angeles living wage: The first eighteen months. University of California, Los Angeles and Fair Housing Institute. Mimeograph.

Spain, Selena, and Jean Wiley. 1998. The living wage ordinance: A first step in reducing poverty. *Clearinghouse Review* (September–October): 252–67.

Tanner, Jane. 2002. Living-wage movement. *CQ Researcher* 12 (33): 771–78.
Tolley, George, Peter Bernstein, and Michael Lesage. 1996. Economic analysis of the living wage ordinance. Chicago: RCF Economic and Financial Consulting.
Turner, Mark D., and Burt S. Barnow. 2003. *Living wage and Earned Income Tax Credit: A comparative analysis.* Washington, D.C.: Employment Policies Institute.
Zabin, Carol, and Isaac Martin. 1999. Living wage campaigns in the economic policy arena: Four case studies from California. Berkeley, Calif.: University of California, Berkeley, Center for Labor Research and Education, Institute of Industrial Relations, June.

4 The Role and Functioning of Public-Interest Legal Organizations in the Enforcement of the Employment Laws

Christine Jolls

4.1 Introduction

Today's American legal system affords a significant array of protections to employees. Although most workers in this country do not enjoy a general right to be dismissed only for cause—a right characteristic of many European countries (Issacharoff 1996, 1806–7) and now of one American state, Montana (Mont. Code Ann. Secs. 39-2-901 to 39-2-915)—they benefit from a host of specific prohibitions on arbitrary or inappropriate behavior by employers. Examples include prohibitions on discriminatory behavior (on the basis of race, sex, religion, national origin, age, or disability) and on behavior that interferes with other personal rights of employees. Employers are also under certain affirmative obligations to employees, including the obligation to provide a safe workplace and the obligation (indirectly, through experience-rated insurance premiums) to fund unemployment benefits for employees who are out of work.[1]

There is, however, a critical and oft-emphasized distinction between the law "on the books" and the law "in action," as the Legal Realist movement

Christine Jolls is professor of law at Harvard Law School, and a research associate at the National Bureau of Economic Research. The research in her chapter was performed over the period from 1999 to 2001 and reflects facts and sources as they existed at that time. Sam Bagenstos and Margo Schlanger offered extremely helpful comments on and reactions to this work. Thanks go as well to Amanda Rocque for outstanding research assistance, and to participants in the May 1999 and August 2000 Emerging Labor Market Institutions conferences for helpful suggestions. Special thanks to Kip Viscusi and David Weil, the commentators on this chapter at the August 2000 session, for their help. Finally, financial support from the John M. Olin Center for Law, Economics, and Business at Harvard Law School is gratefully acknowledged.

1. For an overview of legal obligations on employers, see Willborn, Schwab, and Burton (1998).

famously taught long ago (Pound 1910). What ultimately matters for many, if not most, purposes is how the law actually operates, not what protections it ostensibly provides. The law "in action" includes not only how courts apply the law as written (the original emphasis of the Realists) but also how well the law is enforced by the institutions and parties affected by it (Llewellyn 1930, 435n3).

The distinction between law "on the books" and law "in action" is clearly important in the employment law context, where employees are ordinarily not in a strong position to enforce their rights. Indeed, Roscoe Pound (1910, 35), the father of the "on the books"–"in action" distinction, wrote almost a century ago that "our copious labor legislation for the most part fails of effect because of defective administration." The significant decline in union membership in recent decades, from its high in the middle of the twentieth century, can only have exacerbated the problem.

The goal of the present chapter is to examine some of the distinctive public-interest legal organizations that exist to help to enforce the employment laws. The chapter focuses on two broad categories of such organizations: "national issue organizations" (for instance, the NAACP Legal Defense and Education Fund), which are defined here as organizations that focus on one or more broad-based issues and are funded predominantly by private donations; and legal services organizations, which serve exclusively low-income individuals and are funded primarily by the government. The focus, as just indicated, is on "enforcement" (or "implementation") of existing laws, not "enactment" of new laws, to use the dichotomy drawn by David Weil (chap. 1 in this volume).

Many different mechanisms exist for "enforcing" the employment laws. The mechanisms include, most obviously, providing conventional legal representation to employees whose rights may have been violated, but they also include providing information to workers about what rights the law gives them, facilitating the enforcement of these rights through means other than filing lawsuits, and providing research and support assistance to attorneys providing direct representation to clients. There are a number of examples of entities providing these latter sorts of services; the Workplace Project of Long Island, for instance, offers informational courses for workers (Trubek 1998, 806) and facilitates enforcement of employment laws through means other than litigation (Gordon 1995, 430–37), and the Migrant Legal Action Program offers research and support assistance to attorneys who provide direct representation to migrant workers.[2] Many legal websites also offer employment law information to workers.[3] For reasons

2. See http://buscapique.com/latinuse/buscafile/wash/mlap.htm; accessed July 11, 2000.

3. See, for example, http://www.nwjustice.org/law_center/employment.html; accessed September 21, 1999. This is the website of the Northwest Justice Project, which offers, among other things, a downloadable document on "Your Rights and Responsibilities as an Employee."

of scope, however, this chapter focuses on the more conventional activity of direct legal representation of employee interests.

It is interesting to note in this connection that Charles Tilly and other theorists of social movement apparently have not viewed such litigation or representation activity as a central component of social movement, as it is not necessarily "outsider" behavior. I agree, by contrast, with Paul Burstein (1991, 1203–5, 1222), who, after making this observation about Tilly and other theorists, argues that litigation is an important element of social movement. This importance justifies the emphasis I give it here.

Section 4.2 below lays the groundwork for the examination of the role of public-interest legal organizations in representing employees by describing why the usual mechanism for protecting legal rights—retention of a private lawyer by the aggrieved party—is of limited effectiveness in the employment context. Section 4.3 overviews some of the key features of national issue organizations and legal services centers (the organizations on which this chapter focuses). Section 4.4 provides institutional detail on how the two types of organizations are funded. Finally, section 4.5 develops the chapter's primary analytic point, which is the way in which funding sources exert a significant and often problematic influence on the sort of employment law litigation in which an organization engages—a species of the general point about the influence of funding sources on public-interest legal organizations (Komesar and Weisbrod 1978, 96–97). As discussed below, national issue organizations, funded largely through donations, do primarily high-level, high-impact work in areas with a significant public profile, such as discrimination; by contrast, legal services centers, supported by the government, work primarily at low levels and in areas, such as unemployment benefits, that lack the public profile of areas such as discrimination. This distinction between the two types of organizations is not absolute (there are some exceptions), and also there are other types of public-interest legal organizations that do some work in the employment arena, but still the overall pattern of activity seems to be what the distinction between national issue organizations and legal services centers suggests.

As a result of this pattern of activity, neither national issue or organizations nor legal services centers succeeds very well in meeting the full set of needs of employees for enforcement of the employment laws. For both types of organizations, a very important component of the organizational objective function is attracting or maintaining funding from either large private donors (such as foundations) or the government, and this focus on receiving such forms of funding detracts from the organizations' ability to serve the full range of their constituencies' needs (see also Weil [chap. 1 in this volume]). My conclusion here complements Weil's suggestion that reliance on either unions or small individual donors with a personal connection to the issues in question provides "better alignment between the objectives of the groups and those of the workers they intend to assist" (Weil [chap. 1 in this volume]).

A final terminological point is important here. Lawyers commonly distinguish between "employment law" and "labor law," where the former is the body of (largely substantive) rules protecting workers regardless of union status, while the latter is the body of (often procedural) rules governing the formation and conduct of unions and their relationships with employers. This chapter follows that terminological distinction; thus its focus on organizations involved in enforcing "the employment laws" means a focus on organizations that work on employment law, not labor law, issues.

4.2 The Limited Efficacy of Private Legal Representation in the Employment Law Context

In most of the economy, the primary institution that operates to protect parties' legal rights is the private bar; an aggrieved party retains (and pays for) a lawyer who works to vindicate the client's rights. Perhaps not surprisingly, this approach seems to work less well in the employment context than in many other contexts. This is so for several reasons.

First, individual employees will quite often lack the funds to hire a lawyer on an hourly basis, the usual arrangement for large commercial clients. In this respect the problem is parallel to the one that arises in the personal injury context, where individual victims often cannot afford to hire lawyers on an hourly basis while defendant corporations can.

In the personal injury context the solution is representation of victims on a contingent-fee basis, where the lawyer is compensated by receipt of a share of any winnings garnered by the accident victim. But employees generally do not have as great an opportunity to hire lawyers on a contingent-fee basis as do victims of personal injuries. The reason is that employees' damages are ordinarily far lower than those of personal injury victims. It is true that some employment law claims sound in tort (like personal injury claims) and thus can produce verdicts for millions of dollars; in *Wilson v. Monarch,* 939 F.2d 1138 (5th Cir. 1991), for instance, an employee netted a $3.1 million verdict on a tort claim for emotional distress. However, a large number of employment claims—most prominently, discrimination claims brought under federal law—do not fall into this potential-seven-figure-verdict category. Until 1991, employees in such cases were limited to reinstatement together with limited amounts of lost wages (see, for example, Selmi 1998, 1427–28), and even now monetary relief beyond what was available under the old regime is capped at amounts ranging from $50,000 to $300,000, depending on the size of the offending employer (see 42 U.S.C. sec. 1981a[b][3]). (State claims, however, are not subject to these caps.) Also consistent with the idea that limited damages pose a barrier to private representation in the employment area is the fact that age discrimination plaintiffs are generally viewed as having the easiest time finding legal representation, and their damages are generally higher than those of other employment discrimination plaintiffs (Rutherglen 1995, 505–9).

A further dimension of the problem of relying exclusively on privately hired attorneys to bring employment law claims is that the potential damages of the employee will frequently be highly correlated with the employee's earnings. Thus employees who earn low to modest wages—and thus are particularly unable to hire hourly fee attorneys—will also tend to be particularly unattractive to contingent-fee practitioners.

A third reason for the limited efficacy of privately retained counsel in the employment law context is that, while some employment laws do provide for the recovery of attorney fees, that right is limited in important respects and often does not provide private attorneys with sufficient compensation to ensure that taking an employment case is worthwhile. To begin, it is primarily antidiscrimination laws, as distinguished from other employment laws, that provide for the recovery of attorney fees at all; other sorts of laws may not contain such provisions.[4] Moreover, even those laws that do authorize the recovery of attorney fees authorize recovery only if the employee is the prevailing party in the case.[5] In addition, if a party prevails but only to a limited extent, attorney fees are accordingly limited.[6] A final, and critical, point is that even if fees are recoverable, there is no upward adjustment to account for the risk that the employee's attorney would end up not prevailing.[7] The lack of an upward adjustment means that on an expected basis attorney fee awards under the employment law statutes that permit them at all are systematically undercompensatory relative to the attorney's performance of work on a regular hourly fee basis.

For all of these reasons, the "ordinary" approach of privately retained legal counsel is a very incomplete strategy for the enforcement of the employment laws. As Lewis Maltby (1998, 56) has written, "The economic hurdles facing an employee who seeks justice in court are staggering." An intriguing question, not addressed here because it would go too far afield

4. Examples of laws that authorize the recovery of attorney fees under certain circumstances include Title VII of the Civil Rights Act of 1964, see 42 U.S.C. sec. 2000e-5(k), and the Americans with Disabilities Act of 1990, see 42 U.S.C. sec. 12205.

5. See, for example, 42 U.S.C. sec. 2000e-5(k) (Title VII attorney fee provision); 42 U.S.C. sec. 12205 (disability discrimination attorney fee provision).

6. See *Farrar v. Hobby,* 506 U.S. 103, 114–16 (1992). *Farrar* involved an action under 42 U.S.C. sec. 1983 outside of the employment law context. However, the Supreme Court has made clear that its interpretations of fee-shifting provisions apply to such provisions in general, including those in employment statutes. See, for example, *Buckhannon Board and Care Home, Inc. v. West Virginia Department of Health and Human Resources,* 121 S. Ct. 1835, 1839 n.4 (2001). Numerous courts of appeals have applied *Farrar* to the fee-shifting provisions under employment statutes. See, for example, *Pino v. Locascio,* 101 F.3d 235, 237–39 (2d Cir. 1996); *Brandau v. State of Kansas,* 168 F.3d 1179, 1181–83 (10th Cir. 1999).

7. See *City of Burlington v. Dague,* 505 U.S. 557, 561–67 (1992). *City of Burlington* involved a statute permitting attorney fees in environmental cases, but the Court made clear that its reasoning applied to other fee-shifting provisions—including those in employment statutes—as well.

from the central topic of this chapter, is why "prepaid legal services" (programs under which individuals make advance payments, in the nature of insurance premiums, for future legal services) have had relatively little effect in achieving legal representation for employees.

The point here is of course not that representation by privately retained counsel in employment law matters is never available. One institution of particular importance in providing such representation is the "private public-interest law firm." Firms in this category are private law firms that are supported by ordinary legal fees but that may represent certain clients for reduced fees based on the client's level of need. As Louise Trubek (1996, 436) writes, "Social justice law firms serve diverse social classes by using sliding-scale fee schedules based on income." In the employment law context, the paying clients may be unions and the subsidized clients may be individual employees. In addition, class action suits brought by private counsel may play a role in vindicating employees' rights in some contexts.

Nonetheless, notwithstanding the existence of a role for private counsel on the employee side, it remains the case that alternative institutional arrangements, and in particular the public-interest legal organizations discussed in this chapter, have an important role to play in the enforcement of the employment laws. In addition to the points about retention of private counsel described above, there is the overarching fact that, as described by Weil (chap. 1 in this volume) and Burton Weisbrod (1978, 20–21), enforcing many aspects of employment (or other laws) involves a significant public good component—a fact that suggests the need to rely at least in part on various sorts of public entities for enforcement.

An obvious question to ask in light of the comment just made concerns the potential role of the government in the enforcement of the employment laws. Often, of course, the government has a role to play when the private market fails to provide a particular good or service. However, for a variety of reasons that have been explored in the existing literature, the government is limited in its ability to provide direct legal representation for employees, both as a matter of theory and as an empirical matter (Handler 1978a, 259–68; Selmi 1998, 1427–38, 1447–49). Thus, there remains an important role for the public-interest legal organizations discussed in this chapter to play.

Along with the government, unions are an institution that obviously can help to overcome public-good problems. Consistent with this suggestion, union counsel can and do play a role in enforcing the employment laws in addition to their work in labor law arenas. Examples of such union counsel include the American Federation of Labor-Congress of Industrial Organization (AFL-CIO) General Counsel's Office and the legal counsel of the American Federation of State, County, and Municipal Employees (AFSCME), each of which has been involved in a number of important employment law cases.[8] Professor Catherine Fisk (2001) goes so far as to describe union initiatives in the employment law area as "major efforts to enforce employment law in nonunion workplaces." The role of such union counsel thus complements the role of the public-interest legal organizations emphasized here.

4.3 National Issue Organizations and Legal Services Centers—In General

The present section describes two leading types of public-interest legal organizations involved in the employment law area. The first is national issue organizations; as noted above, these are national entities that focus on a particular set of issues or topics (related at least in part to employment law) and are funded largely or exclusively by sources other than the government. The second is legal services centers; these provide legal representation to low-income individuals at government expense. The present section presents introductory information on the two types of organizations, and the following section discusses in more detail how the organizations are funded. The goal of these two sections together is to paint a descriptive picture of the two types of organizations, similar in spirit to—but with different emphases than—the portrait offered of public-interest legal organizations in general (not with specific reference to the employment law area) offered more than twenty years ago by Joel Handler, Betsy Ginsberg, and Arthur Snow (1978).

This section relies heavily on Internet presence to describe and identify organizations. In this respect it differs from earlier work (for instance, O'Connor and Epstein 1989; Sturm 1993a), which relied significantly on mass-mailed surveys to gather information. The advantage of relying on the Internet is the likely greater accuracy, on average, of information as compared to what is reported by a particular individual in response to a survey. The obvious limit of the present methodology, of course, is that entities with an Internet presence will receive disproportionate coverage.

4.3.1 National Issue Organizations

Table 4.1 provides a list of entities that qualify as national issue organizations according to the above definition. Note that an organization need

8. For the AFL-CIO, see, for example, Brief of the American Federation of Labor and Congress of Industrial Organizations as Amicus Curiae in Support of Petitioners, *Christensen v. Harris County,* No. 98-1167, United States Supreme Court, 1999 WL 1114682 (amicus brief in employment law case involving the Fair Labor Standards Act); for AFSCME, see, for example, Brief of the American Federation of Labor and Congress of Industrial Organizations as Amicus Curiae in Support of Petitioners, *Sutton v. United Air Lines,* No. 97-1943, United States Supreme Court, 1999 WL 86514 (amicus brief in employment law case involving the Americans with Disabilities Act).

Table 4.1 **National issue organizations (devoted at least in part to employment law issues)**

AARP Foundation Litigation[a]
American Civil Liberties Union[b]
Anti-Defamation League[c]
Asian American Legal Defense and Education Fund[d]
Asian Law Caucus[e]
Bazelon Center for Mental Health Law[f]
Disability Rights Education and Defense Fund[g]
Equal Rights Advocates[h]
Guild Law Center for Economic and Social Justice[i]
Lambda Legal Defense and Education Fund[j]
Lawyers' Committee for Civil Rights Under Law[k]
Legal Action Center[l]
Mexican-American Legal Defense and Education Fund[m]
NAACP Legal Defense and Education Fund[n]
National Employment Law Project[o]
National Partnership for Women and Families[p]
National Senior Citizens Law Center[q]
National Women's Law Center[r]
NOW Legal Defense and Education Fund[s]
Puerto Rican Legal Defense and Education Fund[t]

[a]See http://www.aarp.org/litigation/ for a mission statement describing employment law as well as other areas of litigation; accessed August 31, 2001.

[b]See http://www.aclu.org/issues/immigrant/workrights.html for employment law litigation activities of the American Civil Liberties Union's Immigrant Rights Project; accessed July 6, 2000. The American Civil Liberties Union also brought a prominent employment discrimination suit, *Shahar v. Bowers,* against the state of Georgia. See http://www.aclu.org/issues/gay/aboutgl.html; accessed July 6, 2000.

[c]See Civil Rights Report, ADL in the Courts: Litigation Docket 1999, at 35–36, 40–43, for information about employment law litigation activities. The report is available at http://www.adl.org/frames/front_civil_rights.html; accessed July 13, 2000.

[d]See 1998 annual report, Asian American Legal Defense and Education Fund, at 5–7, for a description of employment law litigation activities.

[e]See http://www.peggybrowningfund.org/alc.html for a description of the Asian Law Caucus's Employment/Labor Project; accessed July 10, 2000.

[f]See, for example, 1998–1999 annual report, Bazelon Center for Mental Health Law, at 5, for information about a prominent recent employment discrimination suit brought by the Bazelon Center.

[g]See, for example, http://www.dredf.org/sandiego.html for information about the employment discrimination suit brought by the Disability Rights Education and Defense Fund and others against the City of San Diego; accessed September 1, 1999.

[h]See http://www.equalrights.org/legal/amicusbr.htm for information about current litigation activity, a substantial portion of which is in the employment law area; accessed July 10, 2000.

[i]See http://sugarlaw.org/projects/plantclosings/plantclosingsproject.htm for information about the Plant Closings Project and its litigation activity under the Worker Adjustment and Retraining Notification (WARN) Act; accessed July 11, 2000.

[j]See 1998 annual report, Lambda Legal Defense and Education Fund, at 8–9, 11, for information about employment law litigation activities.

[k]See http://www.lawyerscomm.org/projects/employ.html for information about the Lawyers' Committee's Employment Discrimination Project; accessed July 6, 2000.

Table 4.1 (continued)

[l]See Lopez (1998, 446) for a statement of the organization's focus on employment discrimination.

[m]See 1998–1999 annual report, Mexican-American Legal Defense and Education Fund, at 6–7, for information about employment law litigation activities.

[n]See 1998 annual report, NAACP Legal Defense and Education Fund, at 10–11, for information about employment law litigation activities.

[o]See, for example, http://www.nelp.org/contingent.htm for information about the Contingent Worker Project and accompanying litigation activities; accessed July 6, 2000.

[p]See 1997–1998 annual report, National Partnership for Women and Families, at 5, 7, for information about employment law litigation activities.

[q]See http://www.nsclc.org/about.html for a listing of pension rights and age and disability discrimination as focus areas, and for the statement that "NSCLC has a long tradition of national advocacy through impact litigation"; accessed July 7, 2000.

[r]See http://www.afl.org/mem.nwlc.html for a general description of the organization's role in litigating women's rights in areas including employment; accessed July 11, 2000.

[s]See 1998 annual report, NOW Legal Defense and Education Fund, at 2–3, for information about employment law litigation activities.

[t]See http://guthrie.hunter.cuny.edu/centro/archives/aids/prldef.html, which notes that the Puerto Rican Legal Defense and Education Fund has brought lawsuits across the country in a range of areas including equal employment rights, and listing project areas including employment rights; accessed July 10, 2000.

not be exclusively devoted to employment law issues to meet the definition; indeed, most of the entities listed divide their time between employment and other issues, including housing, education, and consumer rights. An organization also need not be exclusively devoted to litigation, as opposed to other forms of public advocacy, to meet the definition. As long as litigation—meaning representation of clients in lawsuits, negotiating settlements, filing amicus briefs, and so forth—is an important component of the entity's activity, the entity qualifies as a national issue organization.[9] As already noted, funding information is presented in section 4.4 below.

The organizations in table 4.1 vary significantly in the proportion of their time devoted to employment law issues, both as a fraction of the organization's overall activity and in absolute terms. In terms of the fraction of an organization's overall activity, the National Employment Law Project is exclusively devoted to employment law issues, while a relatively small proportion of the overall activities of the Bazelon Center appears to involve such issues. (Note that, as discussed more fully in section 4.5 below, the National Employment Law Project was previously a government-funded "support center" for local legal services centers.) Similarly, in terms

9. One example of a national entity that works on employment law issues but does not engage in any litigation is the Pension Rights Center, which is active in public advocacy but provides referrals for individuals seeking legal representation. See http://www.aoa.dhhs.gov/aoa/dir/210.html; accessed July 11, 2000. Another example is the National Employee Rights Institute, which provides information and referrals to workers but does not engage in significant litigation itself. See http://www.nerinet.org/; accessed July 12, 2000.

of the absolute level of employment law work, the activities of the NAACP Legal Defense and Education Fund, with close to two dozen staff attorneys,[10] are surely substantially greater in magnitude than those of the Equal Rights Advocates, with four staff attorneys.[11] If, however, employment law involvement is relatively rare or quite sporadic, then I do not include the organization in table 4.1.[12]

Omitted from table 4.1 are organizations that do not have staffs of their own lawyers but rather provide coordinating services to their attorney membership, which engages in employment law litigation. These organizations are not providing direct client representation as I conceive of it. The most prominent example of such an organization in the employment area is the National Employment Lawyers Association, which coordinates writing of amicus briefs by its members but does not employ the attorneys who write the briefs.[13]

As discussed in section 4.5 below, in addition to the organizations listed in table 4.1 there are entities that look similar to these organizations but seem to predominantly (although not necessarily exclusively) operate on a more regional or local level; examples (all listed in table 4.3 below) include the Asian Pacific American Legal Center of Southern California, the Center for Law in the Public Interest, the Employment Law Center of the Legal Aid Society of San Francisco, Gay & Lesbian Advocates & Defenders, the Northwest Women's Law Center, Public Advocates, Inc., and the Public Justice Center.

4.3.2 Legal Services Centers

A second leading type of public-interest legal organization involved in the enforcement of the employment laws is legal services centers. These centers arose in the 1960s as part of the federal government's War on Poverty (Bellow 1980, 337–38). Since 1974 the centers have been administered through the Legal Services Corporation, an arm of the federal government that makes grants of funds to local centers around the country.[14]

10. See 1998 annual report, NAACP Legal Defense and Education Fund, at 2.

11. See http://www.equalrights.org/about/director.htm; accessed July 12, 2000.

12. For instance, table 4.1 does not include People for the American Way (PFAW); PFAW has been involved in employment law litigation on a few occasions, but such litigation does not appear to be a regular staple of its activity. See http://www.pfaw.org/courts; accessed July 7, 2000. Similarly, the National Center for Lesbian Rights focuses on a range of discrimination and civil rights issues but does not appear to work on employment law matters and thus is not listed in table 4.1. See http://www.nclrights.org/cases.html; accessed July 10, 2000. The same is true of Trial Lawyers for Public Justice. See http://www.tlpj.org/tlpjf/caseup.htm; accessed July 11, 2000.

13. See *The Employee Advocate,* Spring 2000, at 6, 10. For a general description of the National Employment Lawyers Association, see http://www.nela.org/; accessed July 12, 2000.

14. See http://www.lsc.gov/welcome/wel_who.htm; accessed July 14, 2000.

Legal services centers provide legal representation free of charge across a range of areas to low-income clients who cannot afford ordinary private lawyers.[15] The eligibility cutoff established at the federal level is at 125 percent of the federal poverty guidelines, and local centers may, if they choose, limit their services to persons even closer to the poverty line (Spar 1996, 2). As examples of the income cutoff levels, Alaska Legal Services sets the cutoff for a family of three at $21,700, while Gulfcoast Legal Services of Florida sets it at $17,063.[16] As a result of the cutoffs, legal services centers cover only a distinct subset of the population of individuals who may be unable to retain a private lawyer for representation on an employment law matter. As Justice Denise Johnson (Johnson 1998, 480–81) of the Vermont Supreme Court has noted, "It is not just the poor who cannot afford justice in today's society. Courts across the country have experienced an explosion in pro se litigation [where the client is not represented by an attorney], and many people representing themselves are of modest income levels and would not be eligible for publicly funded legal services."

Legal services centers perform limited work in the employment law area (Gordon 1995, 422); indeed, many potential clients may be entirely unaware of their ability to get help with employment law matters from legal services entities. The Legal Services Corporation compiles aggregate statistics on the types of cases handled by legal services centers. Nationwide, income maintenance claims, which include claims for unemployment benefits as well as other types of public benefits,[17] comprise about one-sixth of the overall caseload of legal services centers.[18] Other employment cases are a few percent of the overall caseload.[19]

A few of the local legal services centers provide detailed quantitative breakdowns of their activities by subject matter. Atlanta Legal Aid, for example, reports an annual caseload for 1997 of 11,552 total cases, of which 241 involved unemployment benefits, 74 involved discrimination claims, and 185 involved other employment claims.[20] The Maryland Legal Aid Bureau reports an annual caseload for 1998 of 33,048 total cases, of which 2,256 (7 percent) involved income maintenance and 743 (2 percent) involved employment matters other than unemployment benefits claims.[21]

15. See, for example, the description of the activities of the Legal Services Program for Pasadena and San Gabriel-Pomona Valley, at http://www.firms.findlaw.com/LASP/; accessed September 12, 1999.

16. For the Alaska Legal Services Corporation, see http://www.ptialaska.net/~aklegal/; accessed September 21, 1999; for Gulfcoast Legal Services, see http://www.gulfcoastlegal.org/guidelines.htm; accessed September 21, 1999.

17. See, for example, http://www.gulfcoastlegal.org/priorities.htm; accessed September 21, 1999.

18. See, for example, 1997 annual report, Legal Services Corporation, at 4.

19. See, for example, source in footnote 18.

20. See http://www.law.emory.edu/PI/ALAS/97cases.html; accessed September 21, 1999.

21. See http://www.mdlab.org/Statistics.html; accessed September 21, 1999.

The Legal Aid Society of Nebraska reports a 1997 annual caseload of 4,762 cases, of which 286 involved income maintenance and 19 involved employment matters other than unemployment benefits claims.[22] Many other centers, however, do not even have an "employment" category apart from the income maintenance category.[23]

4.4 Funding of National Issue Organizations and Legal Services Centers

The previous section described national issue organizations and legal services centers involved in employment law representation. This section examines the manner in which these organizations are funded.

4.4.1 National Issue Organizations

As already noted, and as discussed more fully below, legal services centers get a substantial amount of funding from the government. National issue organizations, by contrast, typically get little or no government funding. Neither the NAACP Legal Defense and Education Fund nor the Lambda Legal Defense and Education Fund, for example, appears to have gotten any government support in 1998, according to their annual reports for that year; the NOW Legal Defense and Education Fund received a government grant for $394,682, approximately 10 percent of its total revenue.[24] Some national issue organizations, such as the American Civil Liberties Union, categorically refuse to accept any government funding on principle;[25] presumably these organizations fear that such funding would compromise their ability to bring aggressive, broad-based challenges, particularly when those challenges involve the government in any way. The history of legal services funding, discussed in section 4.5 below, provides a good deal of support for these concerns about the consequences of accepting government funding.

The primary sources of funding for national issue organizations are generally individual contributions and foundation grants; other sources include attorneys' fees and donation of private attorneys' time.[26] Often con-

22. See http://www.las.omaha.org/1997Rep.htm; accessed September 21, 1999.

23. See, for example, case types listed at http://www.mlan.net/lacm/Whattemplace.html; accessed September 22, 1999.

24. For the NAACP Legal Defense and Education Fund, see 1998 annual report, NAACP Legal Defense and Education Fund, at 25–27 (listing institutional donors at length, and describing how to make individual contributions, but making no mention of government funding); for the Lambda Legal Defense and Education Fund, see 1998 annual report, Lambda Legal Defense and Education Fund, at 31 (dividing donors into "foundations" and "individuals," while making no mention of government funding); for the NOW Legal Defense and Education Fund, see 1998 annual report, NOW Legal Defense and Education Fund, at 17 (listing government grant of $394,682).

25. See http://www.aclu.org/library/pbp1.html; accessed July 6, 2000.

26. The NAACP Legal Defense and Education Fund, for example, lists attorney fees and costs as the source of $1,116,878 in revenue, just under 10 percent of the total intake, in its 1998

tributions by the government or by corporations are grouped with foundation grants in the reporting of financial information,[27] so the category of foundation support as discussed here includes those additional sources of funding. As noted above, however, government funding appears limited, and the same is generally true of corporate contributions, to the extent one can tell from the information that is publicly reported.[28]

Across the two major categories of funding for national issue organizations—individual contributions and contributions from foundations—the organizations vary considerably in the proportion of funding that comes from each source. For example, according to figures from annual reports, in 1998 the Mexican American Legal Defense and Education Fund got 33 percent of its funding from individual contributors and 47 percent from foundations,[29] while the Lambda Legal Defense and Education Fund got 69 percent of its funding from individual contributors and only 8 percent from foundations.[30] (It should be noted that such differences conceivably could result from variations in how organizations categorize different contributions. Unfortunately, none of the national issue organizations' annual reports provide a great deal of detail about how they compute the various figures. On the other hand, the fact that the organizations' financial reports are audited presumably suggests at least some commonality of practice across them. Still, this caveat should be borne in mind in interpreting the figures given here.)

An interesting normative dimension of the differences in sources of funds is that some types of national issue organizations may have greater access to foundation funds than others. A striking feature of data I compiled for four national issue organizations—the NOW Legal Defense and Education Fund, the Lambda Legal Defense and Education Fund, the Mexican American Legal Defense and Education Fund, and the National Partnership for Women and Families—over a several-year period is that, as already suggested above, the Lambda Legal Defense and Education

annual report. See 1998 annual report, NAACP Legal Defense and Education Fund, at 24. For the Lambda Legal Defense and Education Fund, donated legal services were the source of $961,962 in revenue, approximately 20 percent of the total intake, according to its 1998 annual report. See 1998 annual report, Lambda Legal Defense and Education Fund, at 31.

27. The NOW Legal Defense and Education Fund, for example, grouped contributions from foundations and government in a single category in 1996. See 1996 annual report, NOW Legal Defense and Education Fund, at 17. For the NAACP Legal Defense and Education Fund, the category of "institutional donors" includes both foundations and corporations in the 1998 annual report. See 1998 annual report, NAACP Legal Defense and Education Fund, at 25–26.

28. For instance, the NOW Legal Defense and Education Fund currently groups contributions from foundations and corporations in a single category, but until 1996 it separated them out. In 1996 corporate contributions were $61,350, compared to $1,281,298 from foundations and government. See 1996 annual report, NOW Legal Defense and Education Fund, at 17.

29. See 1998–1999 annual report, Mexican-American Legal Defense and Education Fund, at 24.

30. See 1998 annual report, Lambda Legal Defense and Education Fund, at 31.

Fund gets far less of its funding from foundations than any of the other national issue organizations just mentioned. Foundations may be more likely to contribute to more "conventional" civil rights organizations than to organizations such as Lambda's. (Lambda's central focus is facilitating and protecting civil rights for lesbians, gay men, and bisexual individuals.) The funding pattern described here is consistent with Felix Lopez's (Lopez 1998, 453) observation about the difficulty of attracting foundation support for representation in employment law matters of ex-offenders, people in recovery, and people with AIDS.

4.4.2 Legal Services Organizations

The fundamental contrast between national issue organizations and legal services centers in terms of their funding is that while the former get little to no government funding, the latter get a substantial (albeit decreasing) fraction of their funding from government sources. The following analysis presents more detailed information on the funding of legal services centers and how it differs from the funding of national issue organizations.

Table 4.2 shows both the absolute dollar amounts and the percentage of funding for legal services centers from a range of sources for the years 1980 to 1998. The second column of the table gives the amount of funding from the Legal Services Corporation;[31] the third column gives the amount of funding from other federal government sources (for instance, social services grants);[32] the fourth column gives the amount of funding from state and local government sources; the fifth column gives the amount of funding from Interest on Lawyers Trust Accounts (IOLTA);[33] and the sixth column gives the amount of funding from other sources. The nature of these "other sources," to the extent it can be discerned from publicly available information, is discussed later in this section.

The percentage figures in table 4.2 make clear that the percentage of funding for legal services centers that comes from a government source of one type or another is very large—just under 75 percent in 1998, and 98 percent in 1980. The composition of the government support has changed somewhat over time, however; the role of state and local governments has grown, while the role of the federal government has shrunk (from 97 percent of total funds in 1980 to 58 percent of total funds in 1998).

31. Actually this figure is approximate, as the dollar amount in the second column of table 4.2 is the congressional appropriation to the Legal Services Corporation; most, but not all, of this amount ultimately flows to legal services centers in the form of grants.

32. For instance, Legal Services of New Jersey lists federal funding from a Social Services Block Grant, Department of Human Services and Community Affairs, as well as from the Legal Services Corporation. See http://www.lsnj.org/glance.htm; accessed September 22, 1999.

33. "Under these [IOLTA] programs, certain client funds held by an attorney in connection with his practice of law are deposited in bank accounts. The interest income generated by the funds is paid to foundations that finance legal services for low-income individuals." *Phillips v. Washington Legal Foundation,* 524 U.S. 156, 160 (1998).

Table 4.2 **Funding for legal services centers 1980–1998: Dollar and percentage figures**

Year	Legal Services Corporation	Other federal	State and local	Interest on Lawyers Trust Accounts (IOLTA)	Other	Total
1980	$300,000,000 (88.85%)	$27,167,000 (8.05%)	$3,557,000 (1.05%)	$0 (0.00%)	$6,938,000 (2.05%)	$337,662,000 (100%)
1981	$321,300,000 (86.97%)	$26,478,927 (7.17%)	$6,258,655 (1.69%)	$0 (0.00%)	$15,405,921 (4.17%)	$369,443,503 (100%)
1982	$241,000,000 (82.82%)	$27,500,000 (9.45%)	$6,500,000 (2.23%)	$0 (0.00%)	$16,000,000 (5.50%)	$291,000,000 (100%)
1983	$241,000,000 (82.26%)	$25,490,293 (8.70%)	$9,522,332 (3.25%)	$1,500,000 (0.51%)	$15,443,426 (5.27%)	$292,956,051 (100%)
1984	$275,000,000 (81.19%)	$23,166,872 (6.84%)	$16,082,836 (4.75%)	$1,273,842 (0.38%)	$23,168,566 (6.84%)	$338,692,116 (100%)
1985	$305,000,000 (78.92%)	$24,718,960 (6.40%)	$20,067,745 (5.19%)	$2,656,146 (0.69%)	$34,007,507 (8.80%)	$386,450,358 (100%)
1986	$292,363,000 (76.26%)	$25,399,966 (6.63%)	$23,730,987 (6.19%)	$15,029,328 (3.92%)	$26,834,413 (7.00%)	$383,357,694 (100%)
1987	$305,500,000 (71.63%)	$25,412,407 (5.96%)	$30,913,128 (7.25%)	$28,664,710 (6.72%)	$36,026,378 (8.45%)	$426,516,623 (100%)
1988	$305,500,000 (70.28%)	$27,678,482 (6.37%)	$33,755,106 (7.76%)	$29,951,205 (6.89%)	$37,834,710 (8.70%)	$434,719,503 (100%)
1989	$308,555,000 (67.42%)	$28,132,139 (6.15%)	$42,968,230 (9.39%)	$35,994,959 (7.87%)	$42,007,908 (9.18%)	$457,658,236 (100%)
1990	$361,525,000 (66.29%)	$28,473,066 (5.22%)	$50,180,646 (9.20%)	$55,005,222 (10.09%)	$50,201,397 (9.20%)	$545,385,331 (100%)
1991	$328,182,000 (62.09%)	$29,512,709 (5.58%)	$52,023,260 (9.84%)	$73,918,224 (13.98%)	$44,936,714 (8.50%)	$528,572,907 (100%)

(continued)

Table 4.2 (continued)

Year	Legal Services Corporation	Other federal	State and local	Interest on Lawyers Trust Accounts (IOLTA)	Other	Total
1992	$350,000,000 (59.46%)	$31,434,331 (5.34%)	$58,737,676 (9.98%)	$87,948,080 (14.94%)	$60,517,386 (10.28%)	$588,637,473 (100%)
1993	$357,000,000 (59.22%)	$32,182,415 (5.34%)	$70,041,391 (11.62%)	$75,879,344 (12.59%)	$67,737,581 (11.24%)	$602,840,731 (100%)
1994	$400,000,000 (62.22%)	$34,605,425 (5.38%)	$75,139,727 (11.69%)	$64,882,679 (10.09%)	$68,216,677 (10.61%)	$642,844,508 (100%)
1995	$400,000,000 (61.21%)	$40,000,658 (6.12%)	$75,497,133 (11.55%)	$60,194,149 (9.21%)	$77,821,214 (11.91%)	$653,513,154 (100%)
1996	$278,000,000 (57.08%)	$28,740,312 (5.90%)	$68,191,385 (14.00%)	$53,312,540 (10.95%)	$58,799,129 (12.07%)	$487,043,366 (100%)
1997	$283,000,000 (55.30%)	$27,814,679 (5.44%)	$79,884,074 (15.61%)	$57,452,515 (11.23%)	$63,609,910 (12.43%)	$511,761,178 (100%)
1998	$283,000,000 (51.85%)	$35,996,269 (6.60%)	$87,720,710 (16.07%)	$63,457,108 (11.63%)	$75,594,473 (13.85%)	$545,768,560 (100%)

Sources: Legal Services Corporation websites: http://www.lsc.gov/sfb99app.html and http://www.lsc.gov/sfb99nlf.html; both accessed September 12, 1999.

In terms of nongovernmental funding, the Legal Services Corporation data reported in table 4.2 distinguishes between IOLTA funds and funds from other private sources. In fact, IOLTA funds may bear important similarities to government funds in terms of the pressures and restrictions (detailed more fully in section 4.5 below) that accompany the funding. Entities that receive Legal Services Corporation funds are forbidden, for example, to bring class action lawsuits or to engage in lobbying activity (Udell 1998b, 338); some state laws impose similar restrictions on the use of IOLTA funds (Udell 1998a, 908n42). Also of interest for present purposes, at least one state, Washington, prohibits the use of IOLTA funds for bringing employment discrimination suits (Udell 1998a, 908n42). It should also be noted that as of the time of this chapter's preparation the legal status of IOLTA funds remains up in the air following a 1998 Supreme Court decision involving a federal constitutional challenge to the collection of such funds (Resnick and Bazelon 1998, 299).

The remaining funding category for legal services centers reflected in the Legal Services Corporation data is funding from "other" sources.[34] The 1997 annual report of the Legal Services Corporation shows a breakdown of this category between private grants ($20,747,857) and sources other than private grants ($42,862,053).[35] Information from local legal services centers provides some further detail about the sources of this set of funds. Often the funds come from state bar foundations that wish to support the provision of legal services to low-income citizens.[36] Other foundations, as well as private individuals, may contribute as well, although in these instances the fraction of support provided by such actors, as compared to government sources, is far smaller than in the case of national issue organizations.[37] United Way campaigns are also another source of funding.[38]

It should be noted in conclusion that entities that receive funds from the Legal Services Corporation are currently prohibited from collecting attorneys' fees from opposing parties (Udell 1998b, 338). Thus, while some em-

34. Officially the Legal Services Corporation calls this category "private and other." See http://www.lsc.gov/sfb99nlf.html; accessed September 21, 1999.

35. See 1997 annual report, Legal Services Corporation, at 7.

36. For instance, the New Orleans Legal Assistance Corporation reports $160,250 in funding from the Louisiana Bar Foundation and $20,746 in funding from "other foundations." See http://www.nolac.org/humanresources.html; accessed September 21, 1999. Likewise, Gulfcoast Legal Services lists as one of its funding sources the Florida Bar Foundation. See http://www.gulfcoastlegal.org/; accessed September 21, 1999. Legal Services Agency of Western Carolina, too, lists state bar foundation support. See http://www.greenwood.net/~lsawc/about_us.htm; accessed September 22, 1999.

37. For example, Northwestern Legal Services lists, as its sole source of private monetary support, a single foundation, but then goes on to note that this foundation donated $300. See http://www.nwls.org/funding.htm; accessed September 21, 1999. Similarly, Pine Tree Legal Assistance lists the Gene R. Cohen Charitable Foundation, the Stephen and Tabitha King Foundation, and individual donors as contributors, but notes that 85 percent of funding comes from governmental sources and IOLTA. See http://www.ptla.org/funding.htm; accessed September 22, 1999.

38. See, for example, http://www.lsnj.org/glance.html; accessed September 22, 1999.

ployment laws provide for the recovery of attorneys' fees from employers under certain circumstances (as described more fully in section 4.2 above), entities that receive funds from the Legal Services Corporation are not presently eligible for this source of private funding. By contrast, as noted above, recovery of attorneys' fees can be a meaningful source of funding for national issue organizations.[39] The Supreme Court, in *Legal Services Corporation v. Velazquez*, 121 S. Ct. 1043 (2001), struck down a different aspect of Congress's limitations on the activities of entities that receive Legal Services Corporation funds, but the case did not involve the restriction on recovery of attorney's fees or any of the other restrictions discussed in this chapter.

4.5 The Relationship between Funding Sources and the Nature of Legal Work Performed by National Issue Organizations and Legal Services Centers

The previous two sections described national issue organizations and legal services centers and their respective sources of funding. This section looks more closely at the relationship between funding sources and the nature of employment law representation provided by each type of entity.

The basic thesis advanced here is that the different funding sources of national issue organizations and legal services centers produce systematic differences in the nature of the employment law work they perform. In particular, national issue organizations, which depend for support largely on private donations from individuals and foundations, tend to focus on high-profile, publicly charged issues such as discrimination and tend to work on a few important or influential cases rather than a large number of more day-to-day claims; legal services centers, which depend for support largely on government sources, focus heavily on less controversial topics such as unemployment benefits and tend to work on many routine cases rather than a few attention-getting ones. The distinction is not hard and fast (and some counterexamples are discussed below, including the legal services "support centers" that used to play an important role), but it does capture a general difference between the two types of entities. Moreover, the distinction is an unsurprising consequence of the sorts of incentives created by the distinctive patterns of funding for the two types of entities.

As a result of the link between funding sources and activities, neither national issue organizations nor legal services centers succeed very well in meeting the full set of employees' needs for legal representation. The objective function of these organizations is tilted (understandably) toward maintaining the funding they need, and the natural result of this dependence is distortion in the activities that they perform.

39. See, for example, 1998 annual report, NAACP Legal Defense and Education Fund, at 24 (reporting $1,116,878 in recovered fees and costs).

4.5.1 The Relationship between Funding and the Subject Matter of Legal Work

Subject Matter of Work by National Issue Organizations and Legal Services Centers

Even the brief descriptions in section 4.3 above suggest important differences in the subject matter of the employment law work on which national issue organizations and legal services centers focus. National issue organizations are disproportionately devoted to issues involving discrimination; fourteen of the nineteen organizations listed in table 4.1 are exclusively or virtually exclusively devoted to discrimination issues (as their titles suggest), and an additional two organizations, the Lawyers' Committee for Civil Rights Under Law and the National Partnership for Women and Families, give heavy emphasis to such issues. Furthermore, the American Civil Liberties Union devotes a substantial amount of attention to discrimination issues; it also focuses heavily on other similarly high-profile civil liberties issues. The only national issue organizations that do not devote most of their energies to discrimination or other high-profile civil liberties issues are the Guild Law Center for Economic and Social Justice, which focuses on plant closings, and the National Employment Law Project, which works on a range of employment law topics including unemployment, benefits, wrongful discharge, and discrimination.[40] It also bears noting that the Guild Law Center for Economic and Social Justice, while national, is tiny, with only three lawyers on its staff.[41] The National Employment Law Project, however, is a key national player that has litigated major cases and submitted Supreme Court amicus briefs on employment law issues that have lower public profiles than discrimination claims; the Project is thus the major exception to the general pattern described in this chapter.[42]

40. See table 4.1, footnotes i and o, which describe the Guild Law Center for Economic and Social Justice and the National Employment Law Project. Other national entities that, like these two, focus on the plight of low-income individuals, and that thus might be more likely to be concerned with more mundane legal topics than the rest of the national issue organizations, include the National Center on Poverty Law and the Center for Law and Social Policy. However, with respect to the National Center on Poverty Law, it does not appear active in the employment area, as least insofar as is revealed by the case reports on its website. See http://www.povertylaw.org/; accessed July 7, 2000. The Center for Law and Social Policy apparently worked in the employment law area in the past; Settle and Weisbrod (1978, 228n23) describe occupational safety and health litigation by the organization in the 1970s. However, the current website for the Center for Law and Social Policy does not reveal any employment law work. See http://www.clasp.org/faq2.htm; accessed July 10, 2000.

41. See http://www.sugarlaw.org/about/staff.htm; accessed July 17, 2000.

42. Recent cases involving the National Employment Law Project include *Ansoumana v. Gristede's Operating Corp.*, 201 F.R.D. 81 (S.D.N.Y. 2001), a large-scale class action brought under the Fair Labor Standards Act, and *Auer v. Robbins,* 519 U.S. 452 (1997), a Supreme Court case involving the Fair Labor Standards Act in which the Project submitted an amicus brief.

By contrast, legal services centers focus heavily within the employment area on unemployment benefits claims, as noted in section 4.3 above. Indeed, help in getting clients unemployment benefits that have been denied to them is a service that is routinely provided by most legal services centers.[43] In contrast, wage claims and discrimination claims, while handled by some centers, are very far from universal in their coverage. For wage claims, the centers most likely to handle them seem to be those that focus on serving migrant workers and seasonal farmworkers.[44] Discrimination claims are handled by such centers as Gulfcoast Legal Services, Inc.[45] (which, in a fairly unusual practice, explicitly lists discrimination as one of its "priorities"), Atlanta Legal Aid,[46] Client Centered Legal Services of Southwest Virginia,[47] Legal Services of Northern Virginia,[48] and the Knoxville Legal Aid Society.[49] Other centers, by contrast, seem to focus exclusively or almost exclusively on unemployment benefit claims in their work in the employment area. At Legal Services of Eastern Missouri, for example, "[e]mployment cases usually involve the loss or denial of unemployment benefits."[50] And at the Legal Services Agency of Western Carolina, while unemployment benefits claims are "routinely *accepted* for representation," other "employment problems" are "routinely *rejected* for representation."[51] Some centers explicitly provide that discrimination claims are not handled.[52]

Sometimes only new resources allow a center to branch out and handle additional types of employment law claims. For instance, the New Orleans Legal Assistance Corporation reports in its 1998 annual report of handling wage and discrimination claims for the first time in twenty years due to the assistance of a Skadden Fellow (a recent elite law school graduate whose salary is paid by the law firm of Skadden, Arps, Slate, Meagher & Flom).[53]

43. For instance, Legal Services Agency of Western Carolina states on its website that unemployment benefits claims are "routinely accepted for representation." See http://www.greenwood.ned/~lsawc/case_acceptance.htm; accessed September 22, 1999. Likewise, Philadelphia Legal Assistance lists unemployment benefits claims as a service area. See http://www.philalegal.org/info.htm; accessed September 22, 1999.

44. For instance, Migrant Legal Services, a unit of Southern Minnesota Regional Legal Services, states that it handles wage matters. See http://www.mnlegalservices.org/about/mls.shtml; accessed July 11, 2000. So does Farmworker Legal Services, a division of Legal Services of Southeastern Michigan. See http://www.mlan.net/fwls/flsenglish.htm; accessed July 11, 2000.

45. See http://www.gulfcoastlegal.org/priorites.htm; accessed September 21, 1999.

46. See http://www.law.emory.edu/PI/ALAS/97cases.html; accessed September 21, 1999.

47. See http://www.iceman.naxs.com/ccls.info.htm; accessed September 21, 1999.

48. See http://www.members.aol.com/lsnvmain/programs.htm; accessed September 21, 1999.

49. See http://www.korrnet.org/klas/problems.htm; accessed September 21, 1999.

50. See http://www.lsem.org/services.htm; accessed September 21, 1999.

51. See http://www.greenwood.ned/~lsawc/case_acceptance.htm; accessed September 22, 1999.

52. Palmetto Legal Services of South Carolina is an example. See http://www.netside.com/~legalpal/priority.htm; accessed September 29, 1999.

53. See http://www.nolac.org/humanresources.htm; accessed September 21, 1999.

Thus, legal services centers focus on unemployment benefits claims and typically handle areas such as discrimination only sporadically, if at all. In this connection, it is interesting to note that, as mentioned briefly above, the National Employment Law Project, the only national issue organization to devote attention to the unemployment area, also used to be funded by the Legal Services Corporation[54] and in fact served as a national legal services "support center," authoring publications to assist local legal services centers on employment law matters (see, for instance, National Employment Law Project 1975). Legal services support centers are discussed more fully below.

The Role of Funding

The subject matter differences between national issue organizations and legal services centers seem unsurprising in light of their different funding sources. If an entity wishes to raise significant amounts of money from foundations and particularly private individuals, the entity is likely to have far more success if the entity's issues are high profile and publicly visible. As Karen Paget (1990, 123) notes, appeals to private individuals in particular need to be "as sharply ideological and urgent as possible." A plea for funds to help fight discrimination in the workplace seems likely to attract far more foundation, and particularly far more individual, support than a plea for funds to ensure the integrity of the unemployment benefits system.

At the same time, government funders may be more hesitant to fund relatively controversial types of legal claims than relatively mundane types, such as claims for unemployment benefits. An illustration here is the fact that, as noted above, the state of Washington has a law prohibiting the use of IOLTA funds (similar in certain respects to government funds) for bringing employment discrimination claims (Udell 1998a, 908n42). Alan Houseman, director of the Center for Law and Social Policy, offers a similar argument in response to the idea that government funds for legal services should have flowed to entities like the NAACP Legal Defense and Education Fund rather than to the sorts of entities that received them; he says that had entities similar to the NAACP Legal Defense and Education Fund applied for funds, "they would have sought funds for national civil rights and constitutional rights litigation," and "[f]unding such entities for civil rights and constitutional litigation would have created a political fight" (Houseman 1995, 1681).

A further point related to funding sources and the subject matter of legal work is that the congressional prohibition on recovery of attorneys' fees by any entity receiving any Legal Services Corporation funds, noted

54. See, for example, Legal Services Corporation Authorizes Temporary Program Funding, PR Newswire, December 30, 1988 (available on Lexis).

above, makes employment discrimination cases even less attractive for such entities.

In all, then, there are important subject matter differences between the work of national issue organizations and that of legal services centers, and these differences seem to mesh up with the differences in funding sources.

4.5.2 The Relationship between Funding and the Nature or Type of Legal Work

If the differences in subject matter were the only salient differences between national issue organizations and legal services centers, then there might be relatively little cause for interest or concern. For if national issue organizations raised money largely from private donors and then worked on high-profile issues, while legal services centers got funded largely by the government and then worked on more mundane issues, but both types of legal issues were fully covered, it might not matter that there were differences between national issue organizations and legal services centers. The difficulty, however, is that, as detailed in this subsection, the two types of legal issues are generally not being covered in the same way. Instead, the nature or type of work is quite different across national issue organizations and legal services centers, and again the difference traces directly to the difference in funding sources.

Nature or Type of Work by National Issue Organizations and Legal Services Centers

By and large, national issue organizations and legal services centers pursue cases at very different levels of the judicial system and have very different goals in their legal representation. A brief introductory point is in order here: Although this section will often use the term "impact" to refer to the sort of representation in which national issue organizations engage, it does so without meaning to embrace in an uncritical fashion the oft-drawn distinction between "impact" or "law reform" work, on the one hand, and individual client representation, on the other (Handler 1978b, 26–27). Marc Feldman (1995, 1537–38) nicely recaps the distinction:

> Service cases, undertaken for individual clients, . . . respond to the immediate problems of specific clients who present themselves at a program's offices seeking assistance. . . . Impact cases, on the other hand, are viewed as significant and special. These rare cases seek to advance the interests of a number of . . . persons by "reforming" some widespread practice or abuse.

However, the distinction between impact work and client service work is problematic on a number of grounds, perhaps particularly when used normatively to suggest the superiority of impact work (Trubek 1995, 1133–34; White 1987–88, 535–38). But for my descriptive purposes it is useful to distinguish in a rough way between work done to affect large numbers of individuals and work focused on meeting the individual needs of a particular client. Yet a third category is "implementation" work, or ensuring that legal victories in the courts are translated into real results "on the ground" (Sturm 1993b, 727). But this category is probably less pressing in the employment area than in the area of prison and other institutional reform work—the area in which the implementation model is often discussed (see, for instance, Sturm 1993a, 10, 15–16, 33–37).

National issue organizations typically focus their energies on a small number of impact-type cases, often at the appellate level of the judicial system. This emphasis is illustrated most starkly in the way in which these organizations explicitly discourage any impression that they are a resource for representing everyday claimants; for example, the website for the Western Regional Office of the NAACP Legal Defense and Education Fund contains this stern statement:

> The [office] handles civil rights impact litigation. It does not offer direct services or legal advice. . . . [It] takes cases that it feels will have a significant impact on a large community of people. Often these are class action cases. . . .
>
> Attorneys are not available to speak with people in person or on the phone to offer legal advice. [The office] is able to accept requests for assistance only in writing. [The office] is unable to handle most of the cases that people bring to its attention. . . . It usually takes 30–45 days to receive a response.[55]

Other national issue organizations, such as Equal Rights Advocates, do accept phone calls from individuals seeking legal advice, but even there the organization will provide legal representation (as distinguished from information or referral to another lawyer) only in "compelling, precedent-setting cases."[56]

By contrast, the primary emphasis for legal services centers is on serving large numbers of clients. The lead-off message in the Legal Services Corporation's 1997 annual report, for example, is that "269 programs served some 2 million clients in 1997, closing 1.5 million cases, an increase over 1996."[57] The report goes on to praise the fact that "[m]any programs . . . increased their efficiency by adopting advanced telephone intake systems that facilitated access to their services over a large geographical area."[58] As Gary Bellow (1980, 340) wrote more than two decades ago, speaking of legal services, there is "an almost exclusive focus, publicly and administratively, on 'access' and how it is to be realized"; "graphs and tables" sup-

55. See http://www.ldfla.org/rfa.html; accessed September 3, 1999.
56. See http://www.equalrights.org/legal/index.htm; accessed July 10, 2000.
57. See 1997 annual report, Legal Services Corporation, at 2.
58. See source in footnote 57.

plant "examples of practices changed and wrongs righted." While the NAACP Legal Defense and Education Fund brags in its annual report that it "has been involved in more cases before the U.S. Supreme Court than any organization except the U.S. Department of Justice,[59] the claim to fame of the New Orleans Legal Assistance Corporation is that "[i]n 1998, [it] completed work on 6058 cases affecting 19,264 persons in total" with "completed cases averag[ing] about 300 per attorney."[60] In sharp contrast to the NAACP Legal Defense and Education Fund's emphasis on its role in the highest court in America, Daniel Greenberg describes a legal services colleague who famously proclaimed that he (or she) had "the power to drag [an adversary] through the lowest courts in America."[61] It is hard to imagine a more striking difference in emphasis between the two types of organizations.

The difference is not, of course, absolute. While it is clear that "there is relatively little impact work compared to service actually being done" by legal services centers (Bellow and Charn 1995, 1645), it is also clear that at least a few centers do work on impact litigation. More likely than local centers to be involved with such litigation have been national or state-level "support centers" (previously called "backup centers"), which work together with local centers (Dooley and Houseman 1984, chap. 1, 12; chap. 2, 12–14; chap. 3, 49). These support centers were initially funded at least in part by Legal Services Corporation funds (Spar 1996, 2). Although the role of these centers has been greatly cut back in recent years (Houseman 1998, 370), at least some of the centers appear to remain active, perhaps relying on alternative funding sources. For instance, the Ohio State Legal Services Association State Support Center provides assistance, including direct representation of clients or co-counsel representation (presumably with the local center), to the eighteen local centers in Ohio and lists as one of its areas of coverage employment law, and in particular unemployment benefits.[62] It may be that this sort of entity is more inclined than the local centers to take on unemployment benefits cases at higher levels of the judicial system.

Also in Ohio is Advocates for Basic Legal Equality (ABLE), whose self-professed focus is "impact work."[63] True to this characterization, ABLE has brought a number of fairly high-profile discrimination suits in the employment area, including suits against government actors.[64] These are

59. See 1998 annual report, NAACP Legal Defense and Education Fund, at 2.

60. See http://www.nolac.org/humanresources.htm; accessed September 21, 1999.

61. See Proceedings of the Judicial Conference of the Second Judicial Circuit of the United States, 178 F.R.D. 210, 287 (1997).

62. See http://www.iwaynet.net/~oslsa/page2.html; accessed September 21, 1999.

63. See http://home.earthlink.net/~hn80/about.html; accessed September 22, 1999.

64. ABLE cases include *Brown v. Winkle,* a discrimination suit brought against the Toledo fire department that ABLE describes as yielding a consent decree providing relief to minor-

cases similar to those brought by national issue organizations. But does ABLE bring impact suits in more mundane areas such as unemployment benefits? It does not in the particular area of unemployment benefits; the cases it mentions in that area are highly fact specific and narrow, in stark contrast to the discrimination cases noted just above.[65] But ABLE does mention a Fair Labor Standards Act case involving overtime that it felt "could have an impact on the rest of the [landscape services] industry in eastern Ohio."[66] It also mentions a class action under the Fair Labor Standards Act, but this case had to be transferred to a non-legal-services attorney after the imposition of congressional restrictions that prohibited centers receiving Legal Services Corporation funds from representing parties in class actions.[67] Thus ABLE appears to do some work (probably less in recent years as the congressional restrictions have grown) of an impact nature in areas of employment law not emphasized by national issue organizations, such as the Fair Labor Standards Act; like the National Employment Law Project, discussed above, it is an exception to the general pattern of behavior and funding of public-interest legal organizations.

A number of other legal services centers have traditionally (although perhaps less so in recent years assuming they continue to receive Legal Services Corporation funds) engaged in some impact work, including in the employment law area. For instance, Community Legal Services of Philadelphia litigated a major employment discrimination case in the 1970s (Carr and Hirschel 1998, 320n3).

Nonetheless, it seems clear that impact work is not a staple of most legal services entities. This is particularly true for the local centers (as distinguished from the support centers, which, again, have been cut back in recent years). As Gary Bellow and Jeanne Charn (1995, 1647) wrote fairly recently, 'Many programs have abandoned any systematically oriented activities, treating the collective problems that plague the populations they serve as beyond their responsibility and competence." Feldman (1995, 1535, 1539) is similar. "Service work," he says, rather than impact or law reform work, "constitutes the bulk of" legal services centers' effort. He con-

ity employees, and *Gonzales v. Felker,* a discrimination suit brought against the Toledo police department that ABLE states yielded a consent decree providing relief to minority employees. See http://home.earthlink.net/~hn80/report.html; accessed September 22, 1999.

65. ABLE's unemployment benefits cases have involved issues such as the claim that being fired for a single offense violates company disciplinary procedure and the claim that a particular employer's work policy was too vague. See http://www.home.earthlink.net/~hn80/report .html; accessed September 22, 1999.

66. The case was *Llamas v. Mentor Landscape & Supply Co.* See http://www.home.earth link.net/~hn80/report.html; accessed September 22, 1999.

67. The case was *Villareal v. Wiers Farms*. See http://www.home.earthlink.net/~hn80/report .html; accessed September 22, 1999. Udell (1998b, 338) notes the congressional restrictions pertaining to representing parties in class actions. A related phenomenon is the spinning off of part of a legal services center into a new entity to handle the cases barred by the congressional restrictions; this is discussed further at the end of section 4.5.

tinues: "Currently, a [legal services] program spends the vast majority of its legal resources on cases in which the horizon of ambition is defined, even at its maximum, by the individual client. The goal of the legal work is . . . service to individual clients." Moreover, the congressional restrictions on Legal Services Corporation funds increase the degree to which this focus on individual client service exists, as, by banning class actions by entities that receive any financial support from the Legal Services Corporation (Udell 1998b, 338), they cut off a significant avenue through which impact work may get done.

One response to the foregoing discussion is that perhaps there is relatively little large-scale, impact-type work to be done in less high-profile areas of employment law such as unemployment benefits; thus, the argument would run, we see little of such work because there is simply little potential for it. (By contrast, it is clear that there is a large amount of service work for individual clients in high-profile areas such as discrimination.) The point about large-scale work in less high-profile areas of employment law seems hard to address in a definitive way, but the conjecture nonetheless seems wrong. Procedures relating to employment benefits, for instance, can be and occasionally have been challenged on due process grounds in major class actions, such as *White v. Evans,* 324 Md. 321 (1991); it is not at all clear why—apart from the lack of adequate sources of legal representation—these actions should not be more common. Similarly, reemployment participation requirements for unemployment benefits (Emsellem and Halas 1995–96, 298) may raise general legal issues that could benefit from impact-type litigation. Thus, there seem to be plausible areas of impact work that are not being well covered by existing public-interest legal organizations.

The Role of Funding

Once again, funding sources provide a clear explanation for the difference in the activities of national issue organizations and legal services centers. For national issue organizations, which, as noted, get most of their funds from private donations, it seems quite logical that raising money for high-impact work is easier than raising money to represent a large number of individuals in everyday, run-of-the-mill cases. Recall in this connection the NAACP Legal Defense and Education Fund's proud reference in its annual report to its dominant role in Supreme Court litigation. As Neil Komesar and Burton Weisbrod (1978, 97) have suggested, "the incentives provided by funding decisions" push toward "sexy" or "test" cases rather than "efforts to enforce previous . . . case determinations."

By contrast, the history of legal services centers makes painfully clear the quite different pressures that come with government funding. There is some dispute about how much impact work got done in the early days of legal services. Feldman (1995, 1579–81) contends that impact work never figured importantly in the mission of legal services, while Fox (1998, 305), Houseman (1995, 1669, 1677–78, 1685–86), Johnson (1974, 192–94), and Handler, Ginsberg, and Snow (1978, 45–46) all suggest that legal services in its founding years devoted meaningful focus to the impact model. However, what is clear is that at least a substantial fraction of centers, even early on in time, focused on representing a large number of individual clients rather than on bringing high-impact cases (Bellow 1980, 338). This may have been in part because the centers adopted the existing model of "legal aid" societies, which had a similar focus (Feldman 1995, 1562).[68] Some authors also link the predominant focus on day-to-day, routine representation to legal services' dependence on the support of the organized bar, which may have been threatened by a more aggressive embrace of impact work by legal services centers (Feldman 1995, 1578), although other authors (Bellow and Charn 1995, 1644) take a contrasting view.

But it seems clear that an important influence in the focus of legal services centers on individual client service was their dependence on government funding, for whenever these centers went beyond the client service model they seemed to encounter controversy. Johnson (1974, 193) describes some early incidents in the history. By 1975 Congress had acted to restrict legal services centers from participating in school desegregation litigation, a classic form of impact litigation (Parker 1994, 1211n323). Similarly, welfare policy was one of the areas in which legal services lawyers were most active in doing impact work, but again this led quickly to controversy (Melnick 1994, 75, 80–82). Houseman (1995, 1687) succinctly summarizes some of the key episodes:

> [T]he [legal services] program has been beset with the congressional and executive interference from the outset. It began in 1967 with the effort by Senator Murphy to ban suits against the government, and it continued throughout the history of the program: vetoes by governors over controversial programs; efforts to dismantle the program, first by Howard Phillips in 1973 and then again by President Reagan and his initial board of appointees in 1981–1984; and congressional restrictions on . . . what kind of advocacy was permitted.

The legal services program found itself in "deep political trouble" shortly after its founding, and this trouble culminated in the removal of legal services from the "politics" of the Office of Economic Opportunity, the center of the War on Poverty, and its instatement in the separate Legal Services Corporation in the 1970s (Bellow 1980, 340).

With the creation of the Legal Services Corporation came, as Bellow

68. Prior to the availability of federal government funding for legal services, the needs of low-income clients were met by private legal aid societies supported by charitable contributions and some municipal funding, as well as by individual lawyers on a voluntary basis (Bellow 1980, 337).

(1980, 340) has noted, "an almost exclusive focus, publicly and administratively, on 'access' and how it is to be realized." "The immediate goal now [was] . . . 'minimum access'—defined as 2 lawyers per 10,000 poor people in the United States."

As Houseman (1995, 1687) describes, however, the 1970s reform did not ultimately quell controversy over the legal services program. Following the changes he notes, Congress in the mid-1990s ordered a major restructuring of the program. Substantial new restrictions were imposed on all entities receiving Legal Services Corporation funds (Udell 1998b, 337). Prompting these reforms was the sense "the program was founded for the purpose of handling the routine, day-to-day problems of poor people and that what had evolved was major impact litigation, which had politicized the entire program" (Forger 1998, 335). As the Legal Services Corporation reported in its 1996 annual report:

> Congress determined that federally funded programs should focus on individual cases, while efforts to address the broader problems of the client community should be left to entities that do not receive federal funds. Certain kinds of advocacy that have always been recognized as important tools for attorneys to employ on behalf of their clients, such as class actions and most legislative advocacy, would no longer be permitted for legal service attorneys, even if non-federal funds were used for the purpose.[69]

The House Budget Committee was more direct: "Too often, . . . lawyers funded through federal LSC grants have focused on political causes and class action lawsuits rather than helping poor Americans solve their legal problems" (Spar 1996, 1).

The pressures against impact-type work imposed by government funding have not gone uncriticized. In Congress, Senator Kennedy decried the effect those pressures were having:

> I personally do not think Washington should be deciding what legal issues local attorneys may raise on their client's behalf; I do not think Washington should be deciding what forums they can raise them in; and I most emphatically do not think we have any business telling a lawyer that the touchstone of whether or not to represent a client should be a measure of how controversial or how popular the issue. (Udell 1998a, 901)

But Senator Kennedy's lament did not ultimately carry the day, either in 1974, when it was first made, or in the subsequent controversies.

As a final note, it is interesting to observe the striking parallel between the argument here and Michael Selmi's (1998, 1404, 1439) claim that direct government entities have a similarly narrow, circumscribed, cautious, bu-

69. See http://www.lsc.gov/anrep.html; accessed September 21, 1999.

reaucratized focus in their work in the employment law area. Selmi studies the Equal Employment Opportunity Commission and the Department of Justice and concludes that these entities "concentrate [their] efforts on small, routine cases" with the primary goal of "process[ing] and dismiss[ing] claims" and the goal of remaining "politically uncontroversial" (1404, 1439, 1447–49). The similarities to the picture painted above of legal services work in the employment area are hard to overlook.

4.5.3 Other Organizations: Funding and Nature of Employment Law Work

The discussion thus far has focused on two types of entities that provide legal representation in the employment law context: national issue organizations and legal services centers. The claim that has been advanced is that the work of these two types of entities produces a pattern of coverage of (1) impact claims for high-profile, publicly charged issues, and (2) day-to-day claims for mundane issues such as unemployment benefits. This pattern leaves uncovered the two remaining categories: impact claims in mundane areas and day-to-day claims in high-profile, publicly charged areas. These gaps in coverage are a natural consequence of the distortion of organizations' objective functions as a result of funding pressures.

Do other public-interest legal organizations fill the void left by national issue organizations and legal services centers? That is the question examined briefly in this section. The analysis first looks at an important set of organizations that are similar to national issue organizations but appear to operate predominantly at the regional or local level. It next looks at the network of government-funded disability discrimination ("protection and advocacy") centers, which do case-by-case work in a variety of areas including employment discrimination, and thus represent an exception to the general dichotomy drawn in this chapter. For reasons of space, this discussion only scratches the surface; an important question for future work is what can be learned from the alternative models described here, particularly the model used in the disability discrimination context.

"Regional Issue Organizations"

Table 4.3 contains a list of organizations that are similar to national issue organizations but seem to operate primarily (although not necessarily exclusively) on a more regional or local level (although it is sometimes difficult to draw a sharp line between work on a rational level and work on a regional or local level). Like the entities listed in table 4.1 above, the entities in table 4.3 focus on a particular set of issues or topics related at least in part to employment law, and they appear to be funded largely or exclusively by sources other than the government. (Sometimes publicly available information did not disclose sources of funding, but in no case was there any indication of a significant role for government funding. For five

Table 4.3 **"Regional issue organizations" (devoted at least in part to employment law issues)**

American Civil Liberties Union—State Affiliates[a]
Asian Pacific American Legal Center of Southern California[b]
Center for Law in the Public Interest (Southern California)[c]
Employment Law Center of the Legal Aid Society of San Francisco[d]
Gay & Lesbian Advocates & Defenders (New England)[e]
Lawyers' Committee for Civil Rights Under Law—Local Affiliates[f]
Northwest Women's Law Center (Seattle)[g]
Public Advocates (Western States)[h]
The Public Justice Center (Maryland)[i]
Washington Lawyers' Committee for Civil Rights and Urban Affairs[j]

[a]See, for example, http://www.aclu-mass.org/docket/docket99.2000.html, which lists employment law cases including *Monahan v. Dept. of State Police, Narrett v. Framingham State College,* and *Pereira v. Carlisle;* accessed July 5, 2001. For the statement that ACLU entities are not supported by government funding, see http://www.aclu-mass.org/issuebriefs/guardian ACLU.html; accessed July 5, 2001. For links to all of the ACLU state affiliates, see http://www.aclu.org/community/community.html; accessed July 5, 2001.

[b]See http://www.safenetwork.net/rd/sn000348.htm, which lists employment as one of several areas of activity; accessed July 10, 2000.

[c]See http://www.afj.org/mem/clpi.html, which lists employment discrimination as one of several areas of activity; accessed July 12, 2000. Barker (1997, 56) describes the funding sources for the Center for Law in the Public Interest as being various grants, including grants from the Ford Foundation.

[d]See, for example, Slind-Flor (1998), who describes a case brought by the Employment Law Center that produced a groundbreaking ruling on genetic and medical privacy in the workplace.

[e]See http://www.glad.org/docket.html for information about employment law litigation activities; accessed September 19, 2001.

[f]See the "local committees" link at http://www.lawyerscomm.org/ for a description of the functions of local affiliates; accessed September 3, 2001.

[g]See http://www.nwwlc.org/issues_employmentdiscrimination.shtml for "Employment Discrimination: Impact Litigation," a description of employment discrimination litigation activities of the Northwest Women's Law Center; accessed July 10, 2000. According to http://www.nwwlc.org/main/content/lawcenter/annualreport.shtml, sources of funding for the organization are special events, individual contributions, grants, seminars, and others; accessed October 15, 2001.

[h]See Center for Public Interest Law (1995, 19), which describes employment as an area of concentration for Public Advocates. Arriola and Wolinsky (1983, 1219–21) describe a specific employment class action brought by Public Advocates. In terms of funding, Fried (1998, 9) refers to Public Advocates as an "independent nonprofit," in explicit contrast to the Legal Aid Society of Alameda County, a legal services center. Barker (1997, 56) makes reference to Ford Foundation funding for Public Advocates.

[i]See http://www.publicjustice.org/reports.html for a link to "Cases and Projects List," which summarizes employment law cases such as *Talavera v. Hill & Sanders Ford* (a discrimination suit) and *Heath v. Perdue Farms, Fox v. Tyson Foods, Inc.,* and *Trotter v. Perdue Farms, Inc.* (all suits involving wage and hour issues; accessed July 11, 2000.

[j]See http://www.washlaw.org/default.htm, which lists employment law as one of several areas of activity; accessed July 3, 2001.

organizations, the Asian Pacific American Legal Center of Southern California, Gay & Lesbian Advocates & Defenders, the Lawyers' Committee for Civil Rights Under Law (local affiliate centers), The Public Justice Center, and the Washington Lawyers' Committee for Civil Rights and Urban Affairs, there was neither an indication of government funding nor any reason to suspect government funding. For the Employment Law Center of the Legal Aid Society of San Francisco, there was no indication of government funding, but the organization might receive such funding because it is part of a legal aid organization. At the same time, this organization clearly receives substantial foundation funding.[70] Other entities listed in the table provided more information about their funding, as detailed in the footnotes accompanying these entities.)

In addition to the entities listed in table 4.3, "legal services spin-offs"—entities spun off from legal services centers in the wake of the congressional restrictions on Legal Services Corporation funds and the resulting difficulty of impact work for such centers—may look similar to "regional issue organizations." Carr and Hirschel (1998) offer a detailed case study of one such spun-off entity. Some spun-off entities may well be doing impact work in the employment area, but it is interesting to note that Community Legal Services of Philadelphia, which did impact work in the employment area when it was funded by the Legal Services Corporation, is now, since being spun off, focusing its attention away from litigation as a model (Carr and Hirschel 1998, 330–31).

Like the national issue organizations listed in table 4.1, the organizations listed in table 4.3 generally focus on issues involving discrimination and other high-profile civil liberties matters, as is apparent from the descriptions given in the footnotes just above. The closest thing to an exception to this pattern is The Public Justice Center, which seems to do substantial work in the wage and hour area, as the description given above shows. But even that organization (like the National Employment Law Project, the primary outlier among the national issue organizations in table 4.1), also works on employment discrimination issues.

Also like the organizations in table 4.1, the organizations in table 4.3 are involved across-the-board in impact litigation. For instance, the Asian Pacific American Legal Center of Southern California has "spearheaded several lawsuits which have had a strong impact in the legal community,"[71] and the Northwest Women's Law Center "brings public impact cases throughout the Northwest."[72] Some of these organizations may also do

70. In 1998, for instance, the Employment Law Center received a $107,000 grant from the Rosenberg Foundation. See Foundation Center, Grants List 1/98–4/98. (This information is available in the Foundation Grants Index database on Westlaw.)

71. See http://www.safenetwork.net/rd/sn000348.htm; accessed July 10, 2000.

72. See http://www.nwwlc.org/main/content/lawcenter/; accessed July 17, 2000. Similarly, the Center for Law in the Public Interest brought an employment discrimination suit against

some individual representation; for instance, The Public Justice Center seems to engage in some such activity.[73] But other organizations on table 4.3 appear to be limited to impact work in their representation activities.[74]

Day-to-Day Representation in Discrimination Cases: The Case of Disability

The "regional issue organizations" just discussed fit neatly into the dichotomy drawn in this chapter between national issue organizations and legal services centers, as the regional organizations are so similar to the national issue organizations. Less easy to fit comfortably within the dichotomy are the state centers across the country serving the needs of disabled individuals, including disabled employees.[75] These centers are funded by the government (at least to a significant degree) and focus at least in significant part on day-to-day representation of individual clients[76]—so in those respects they are like legal services centers—but their primary focus in the employment area is, not surprisingly, discrimination[77]—so in that respect they are like national (and regional) issue organizations.

The example of disability centers, while important and interesting, does not disrupt in a fundamental way the more general idea that for many types of discrimination claims, legal representation on day-to-day matters seems likely to be severely limited. Lynn Kelly (1998, 725) notes that "there is almost no representation of low wage workers with discrimination claims." At the same time, the disability example similarly does not alter the suggestion above that legal representation for impact work in relatively mun-

the Los Angeles fire department forcing the department to hire more black and Hispanic employees (Barker 1997, 56), and Public Advocates also engages in class action activity (Center for Public Interest Law 1995, 19). Also listed in table 4.3 is The Public Justice Center, whose "Cases and Projects List" summarizes *Trotter v. Perdue Farms, Inc.*, a nationwide class action wage and hour lawsuit. See http://www.publicjustice.org/reports.html; accessed July 11, 2000.

73. For example, *Talavera v. Hill & Sanders Ford,* on the organization's "Cases and Projects List," appears to be a fairly fact-specific discrimination case. See http://www.publicjustice.org/reports.html; accessed July 11, 2000.

74. For instance, the Northwest Women's Law Center describes its services as a combination of "impact litigation" and "self help" for individuals through information packets and a telephone hotline (but not legal representation). See http://www.nwwlc.org/main/content/lawcenter; accessed July 17, 2000.

75. See 2000 annual report, National Association for Protection and Advocacy Systems, at 1–3 (overviewing activities of state centers).

76. The various government programs, including Protection and Advocacy for Persons with Developmental Disabilities (PADD), Protection and Advocacy for Individuals with Mental Illness (PAIMI), and Protection and Advocacy for Individual Rights (PAIR), are described at http://www.protectionandadvocacy.com/brochur1.htm; accessed July 14, 2000. The 2000 annual report of the National Association for Protection and Advocacy Systems, at 5, shows the large number of clients represented by the state centers.

77. For instance, Protection & Advocacy, Inc., of California lists employment discrimination, but not any other employment problems, as a service area. See http://www.pai~ca.org/pubs/500801.html; accessed July 14, 2000. The same is true of the Disability Law Center of Massachusetts. See http://www.dlc-ma.org/programs.html; accessed September 2, 1999.

dane areas of employment law such as unemployment benefits is highly inadequate and incomplete.

4.6 Conclusion

It bears emphasis that this chapter has not attempted to provide anything approaching a comprehensive normative assessment of how a range of legal institutions should, in an ideal world, function to enforce the employment laws. Projects of that broader and necessarily rather speculative sort have been undertaken in other contexts; for instance, Susan Sturm (1993a) has offered a broad set of recommendations for improving the enforcement of laws in another context involving even more vulnerable beneficiaries—the prisoners' rights context—and Houseman (1995) has recently undertaken a similar project for legal advocacy for low-income individuals in general. Joel Handler (1978a, 283–84) offers some brief remarks on the question of optimal institutional design in the specific context of employment discrimination law (although not employment law generally), prescribing a broad division of roles among government, private, and public-interest actors. The emphasis of the present inquiry, by contrast, has been on highlighting two central types of public-interest legal organizations involved in the enforcement of the employment laws and on assessing some of their features and functions.

This work also has not attempted to model in a comprehensive way the objective function of public-interest legal organizations working in the employment law area. Previous work on public-interest legal organizations in general (not specifically in the employment law area) has catalogued various of the objectives they may pursue (Komesar and Weisbrod 1978, 81–89, 96–99). The discussion here has focused more specifically on a particular and apparently distorting feature of the objective function of public-interest legal organizations working in the employment law area—the emphasis on attracting and maintaining funding from either large private donors, such as foundations, or the government. My conclusion about the apparently distorting nature of funding of public-interest legal organizations in the employment law area meshes with the more general conclusion reached by Neil Komesar and Burton Weisbrod (1978, 96–97) about funding-based distortions in public-interest legal organizations in a range of areas.

Future work might look at types of legal institutions other than those considered here—for instance, pro bono models, law school clinical programs, social justice law firms, and client nonprofits. As Louise Trubek (1998, 805) notes, some large law firms have set up community law offices as part of their pro bono efforts, and Lawrence Fox (1998, 315) describes the Litigation Assistance Partnership Project, an American Bar Association initiative that matches legal services centers needing help on major cases with private law firms seeking pro bono work. A broader inquiry into these additional types of institutions, and their potential role in enforcing the employment laws, would also have to face the fundamental question of whether more aggressive litigation of employment law claims would in the end help employees—a question whose answer depends on the degree to which the courts are likely to rule in favor rather than against employees' claims.

References

This section lists books, book chapters, academic articles on the internet, and articles in regularly published periodicals referenced in the chapter. For court decisions, publications by public-interest legal organizations, and internet sources apart from sources for academic articles, complete bibliographic information appears in the footnotes.

Arriola, Anita P., and Sidney M. Wolinsky. 1983. Public interest practice in practice: The law and reality. *Hastings Law Journal* 34:1207–29.
Barker, Emily. 1997. Doing good, doing well. *American Lawyer* 19 (June): 53–60.
Bellow, Gary. 1980. Legal aid in the United States. *Clearinghouse Review* 14:337–45.
Bellow, Gary, and Jeanne Charn. 1995. Paths not yet taken: Some comments on Feldman's critique of legal services practice. *Georgetown Law Journal* 83:1633–68.
Burstein, Paul. 1991. Legal mobilization as a social movement tactic: The struggle for equal employment opportunity. *American Journal of Sociology* 96:1201–25.
Carr, Catherine C., and Alison E. Hirschel. 1998. The transformation of Community Legal Services, Inc., of Philadelphia: One program's experience since the federal restrictions. *Yale Law and Policy Review* 17:319–35.
Center for Public Interest Law. 1995. Public interest organizations. *California Regulatory Law Reporter* 15 (1): 16–20.
Dooley, John A., and Alan W. Houseman. 1984. *Legal services history.*
Emsellem, Maurice, and Monica Halas. 1995–96. Representation of claimants at unemployment compensation proceedings: Identifying models and proposed solutions. *University of Michigan Journal of Law Reform* 29:289–332.
Feldman, Marc. 1995. Political lessons: Legal services for the poor. *Georgetown Law Journal* 83:1529–1632.
Fisk, Catherine. 2001. Union lawyers and employment law. Abstract available at http://papers.ssrn.com/sol3/papers.cfm?abstract_id=271150.
Forger, Alexander D. 1998. The future of legal services. *Fordham Urban Law Journal* 25:333–43.
Fox, Lawrence J. 1998. Legal services and the organized bar: A reminiscence and a renewed call for cooperation. *Yale Law and Policy Review* 17:305–17.
Fried, Rinat. 1998. The LSC investigates its offspring. *The Recorder* (April 2): 9.
Gordon, Jennifer. 1995. We make the road by walking: Immigrant workers, the workplace project, and the struggle for social change. *Harvard Civil Rights-Civil Liberties Law Review* 30:407–50.
Handler, Joel F. 1978a. Public interest law and employment discrimination. In

Public interest law: An economic and institutional analysis, ed. Burton A. Weisbrod, 251–84. Berkeley: University of California Press.
———. 1978b. *Social movements and the legal system: A theory of law reform and social change.* New York: Harcourt Brace Jovanovich.
Handler, Joel F., Betsy Ginsberg, and Arthur Snow. 1978. The public interest law industry. In *Public interest law: An economic and institutional analysis,* ed. Burton A. Weisbrod, 42–79. Berkeley: University of California Press.
Houseman, Alan W. 1995. Political lessons: Legal services for the poor—A commentary. *Georgetown Law Journal* 83:1669–1709.
———. 1998. Civil legal assistance for the twenty-first century: Achieving equal justice for all. *Yale Law and Policy Review* 17:369–433.
Issacharoff, Samuel. 1996. Contracting for employment: The limited return of the common law. *Texas Law Review* 74:1783–1812.
Johnson, Denise R. 1998. The legal needs of the poor as a starting point for systematic reform. *Yale Law and Policy Review* 17:479–88.
Johnson, Earl, Jr. 1974. *Justice and reform: The formative years of the OEO Legal Services Program.* New York: Russell Sage Foundation.
Kelly, Lynn M. 1998. Lawyering for poor communities on the cusp of the next century. *Fordham Urban Law Journal* 25:721–28.
Komesar, Neil K., and Burton A. Weisbrod. 1978. The public interest law firm: A behavioral analysis. In *Public interest law: An economic and institutional analysis,* ed. Burton A. Weisbrod, 80–101. Berkeley: University of California Press.
Llewellyn, Karl N. 1930. A realistic jurisprudence—The next step. *Columbia Law Review* 30:431–65.
Lopez, Felix. 1998. Lawyers matter, policy matters: How one small not-for-profit combats discrimination against ex-offenders, people in recovery, and people with AIDS. *Yale Law and Policy Review* 17:443–54.
Maltby, Lewis L. 1998. Private justice: Employment arbitration and civil rights. *Columbia Human Rights Law Review* 30:29–64.
Melnick, R. Shep. 1994. *Between the lines: Interpreting welfare rights.* Washington, D.C.: The Brookings Institution.
National Employment Law Project. 1975. *Legal services manual for Title VII litigation.* Unpublished Manuscript.
O'Connor, Karen, and Lee Epstein. 1989. *Public interest law groups: Institutional profiles.* New York: Greenwood Press.
Paget, Karen. 1990. Citizen organizing: Many movements, no majority. *The American Prospect* (Summer): 115–28.
Parker, Wendy. 1994. The future of school desegregation. *Northwestern University Law Review* 94:1157–1227.
Pound, Roscoe. 1910. Law in books and law in action. *American Law Review* 44: 12–36.
Resnick, Judith, and Emily Bazelon. 1998. Legal services: Then and now. *Yale Law and Policy Review* 17:291–303.
Rutherglen, George. 1995. From race to age: The expanding scope of employment discrimination law. *Journal of Legal Studies* 24:491–521.
Selmi, Michael. 1998. Public vs. private enforcement of civil rights: The case of housing and employment. *UCLA Law Review* 45:1401–59.
Settle, Russell F., and Burton A. Weisbrod. 1978. Occupational safety and health and the public interest. In *Public interest law: An economic and institutional analysis,* ed. Burton A. Weisbrod, 285–312. Berkeley: University of California Press.
Slind-Flor, Victoria. 1998. Workers have right to privacy. *National Law Journal* 20 (February 16): A8.

Spar, Karen. 1996. Legal Services Corporation: Basic facts and current status. Congressional Research Service Report for Congress, October 23.
Sturm, Susan P. 1993a. Lawyers at the prison gates: Organizational structure and corrections advocacy. *University of Michigan Journal of Law Reform* 27:1–129.
———. 1993b. The legacy and future of corrections litigation. *University of Pennsylvania Law Review* 142:639–738.
Trubek, Louise G. 1995. The worst of times . . . and the best of times: Lawyering for poor clients today. *Fordham Urban Law Journal* 22:1123–40.
———. 1996. Embedded practices: Lawyers, clients, and social change. *Harvard Civil Rights-Civil Liberties Law Review* 31:415–41.
———. 1998. Reinvigorating poverty law practice: Sites, skills and collaborations. *Fordham Urban Law Journal* 25:801–11.
Udell, David S. 1998a. Implications of the legal services struggle for other government grants for lawyering for the poor. *Fordham Urban Law Journal* 25:895–922.
———. 1998b. The legal services restrictions: Lawyers in Florida, New York, Virginia, and Oregon describe the costs. *Yale Law and Policy Review* 17:337–68.
Weisbrod, Burton A. 1978. Conceptual perspective on the public interest: An economic analysis. In *Public interest law: An economic and institutional analysis,* ed. Burton A. Weisbrod, 30–41. Berkeley: University of California Press.
White, Lucie E. 1987–88. Mobilization on the margins of the lawsuit: Making space for clients to speak. *New York University Review of Law and Social Change* 16: 535–64.
Willborn, Steven, Stewart Schwab, and John F. Burton. 1998. *Employment law: Cases and materials.* Charlottesville, Va.: Lexis.

II

Studies of Membership-Based Initiatives

5

Unionization of Professional and Technical Workers
The Labor Market and Institutional Transformation

Richard W. Hurd and John Bunge

Changes in control structures and corporate hierarchies are combining with rapid advances in information technology to create intense pressure in labor markets for many professional and technical occupations. Employers face increased incentives to monitor job content while workers experience heightened anxiety about potential obsolescence. These influences are reinforced by developments in the political economy as greater reliance is placed on unrestrained market forces. In a recent article aptly titled "How the Economy Came to Resemble the Model," Alan Blinder (2000) argues that labor is now viewed as "just a commodity" as evidenced in part by the rapid growth of contingent employment and by reduced job security for white-collar workers. In this evolving context, there is evidence that in a broad array of professional and technical occupations, workers are losing their revered control over job content along with the ability to exercise discretion.

In the medical field, the growth of health maintenance organizations, group practice, and managed care has changed the role of medical doctors, leading some social scientists to describe the "deprofessionalization of . . . medicine" (Anderson 1992, 241) and others to call for a new perspective, the "physician as worker" (Hoff 2001, 53). Similarly, pharmacists have transitioned from self-employment to organizational employment and in the process have lost autonomy (McHugh and Bodah 2002). Dramatic change in the structure of work is not limited to healthcare. A trend toward

Richard W. Hurd is professor and director of labor studies at Cornell University. He is coeditor of *Rekindling the Movement* (Cornell University Press, 2001), *Organizing to Win* (Cornell University Press, 1998), and *Restoring the Promise of American Labor Law* (ILR Press, 1994). John Bunge is associate professor in the Department of Statistical Science at Cornell University.

corporate acquisition of certified public accountant (CPA) firms is reducing the independence and discretion associated with accounting (Shafer, Lowe, and Fogarty 2002), while in academia the share of teaching handled by adjuncts and part-time faculty is growing (Rhoades 1998, 131–138). There are developments with similar implications for occupations as diverse as airline pilots whose latitude on the job is restricted by technology and symphony musicians whose work is routinized by management rules and close supervision (Hackman 1998).

And yet, employment continues to grow rapidly in relevant occupations. The Bureau of Labor Statistics projects that jobs for professional specialties will increase by 27 percent from 1998 to 2008, while those for technicians will expand by 22 percent; these are the fastest anticipated growth rates among the major occupational groups (U.S. Department of Labor 2000, 2–5).

Established institutions that serve the interests of white-collar workers find themselves at a critical juncture. On the one hand they can foresee the potential to augment membership and influence. On the other hand, they confront the reality of reconfigured labor markets. Growth (and indeed survival) is contingent upon being able to adapt to the changing needs and interests of professional and technical workers. The combination of technological advances and alterations in the functioning of white-collar markets suggests strategic reconceptualization and institutional transformation. This chapter explores the attitudes of professional and technical workers toward their jobs and labor market organizations in search of information relevant to institutional transformation.

Although primary attention is devoted to unions of white-collar workers, professional associations play an essential role in these markets and serve as an apt source of institutional comparison. While their membership bases often overlap, there are substantial differences in the emphasis and practices of these two types of organizations. Unions focus on relations with the employer, whereas professional associations cater to individual needs and simultaneously foster collegial relationships (within the profession and with the employer). Professionals are drawn to associations because of information, professional development, and networking. They are often drawn to unions because of trouble on the job. As Tina Hovekamp (1997) aptly contrasts in an article about librarians, professional associations bring people together outside of work around common knowledge and expertise, whereas unions bring people together within the workplace based on distinctions in power (242). The character and functions of professional associations are described in greater detail later in this chapter to help facilitate interpretation of statistical results.

5.1 Reflections on the Decline of Unions in the Private Sector

Private-sector union density in the United States has consistently been higher among blue-collar workers, especially in manufacturing, construction, transportation, and communication, and lower among white-collar workers, particularly in the service industries. As the economy has evolved with white-collar employment and the service sector growing disproportionately, unions have struggled to adapt. Nonetheless, scholarly analyses of union decline typically discount standard explanations tied to changing employment patterns. A review article by Chaison and Rose (1991) concludes that no more than one-quarter of the loss in union density in the United States can be accounted for by structural variables.

Freeman (1988) offers a strong critique of structural explanations, explicitly rejecting the increase in white-collar employment as a key influence. Of particular relevance here, he objects to the standard assumption in that line of research that union density in a sector remains fixed over time. As evidence of the flawed nature of this assumption, he refers to union expansion among public employees in the 1970s that featured unionization of white-collar professionals. Freeman then explores government industrial relations policies, employer resistance, and union strategy as more important influences. Since the early 1990s the research on union decline and potential resurgence has concentrated on these three factors, with some attention as well to globalization, deregulation, and public opinion.

In a recent paper, Farber and Western (2001) revisit the structural approach and offer a model that addresses the weakness in the earlier research by incorporating other factors. The implications of their analysis are compelling and pessimistic regarding the future of union density in the private sector. Rather than looking at trends in employment by industry or occupation, Farber and Western divide the private sector into two subsectors—the union sector and the nonunion sector. They argue that because of the combined influences of economic change, public policy, and employer antiunionism, there is a natural tendency for the share of employment in the union sector to fall.

A key observation based on data for 1973–1998 is that most new jobs are created in the nonunion sector. Except for expansion of employment in unionized facilities, the National Labor Relations Board (NLRB) certification process assures that virtually all new jobs are nonunion and must be organized in order to move into the union sector. This is seldom a simple process even when the employer owns unionized facilities elsewhere, given the widely accepted tenet that "deep seated opposition to unions [is] embedded in the ideology of American management and the culture of many American firms" (Kochan, Katz, and McKersie 1994, 56). The combined effects of globalization, deregulation, and the growth of the service sector merely serve to accelerate the pace of relative decline in the union sector.

If the union sector naturally shrinks, then union density can remain stable or increase only if union organizing in the nonunion sector is successful and is quantitatively sufficient to counterbalance or exceed the relative loss of union jobs. Because of the myriad of challenges that make union organizing difficult, private-sector density has fallen steadily for almost fifty years. As Hirsch (1996) notes, the drop in density is pervasive and has affected all industries for 1983–94 (19), a trend that has continued through 2003. Thus, not only have unions failed to penetrate industries and occupations beyond their base, they also have been unable to retain their share in those parts of the private sector where they are established.

In order to assess the potential for union growth, Farber and Western (2001) attempt to estimate the magnitude of union organizing activity that would be required to attain selected steady-state levels of density. Their forecasts are built upon the explicit and reasonable assumptions of fixed government labor relations policy, a union objective of wealth redistribution from employer to worker, and continuing employer antiunionism. A corollary implicit assumption is that labor market institutions (including unions) remain unchanged. Their estimates of the magnitude of increased expenditures on organizing required to reverse the downward trend in density are staggering. In order to halt decline, unions would approximately need to quadruple the share of resources devoted to organizing. In order to achieve a steady state of 12.25 percent (the current density is 9 percent), unions would have to devote resources to organizing that exceed 100 percent of their current total budgets (Farber and Western 2001, 480).

Although Farber and Western (2001) must rely on incomplete information (particularly regarding expenditures on organizing) to make specific forecasts, the logic of their argument is convincing, and in essence their calculations are consistent with an emerging consensus among industrial relations academics. Is the labor movement doomed to obscurity in the private sector, or are there realistic options that could halt or even reverse decline? Unions have limited ability to influence environmental factors such as government industrial relations policy and employer antiunionism. But they do control their own resources and are in a position to reconfigure priorities and initiate internal institutional change.

Since the election of John Sweeney as president of the American Federation of Labor-Congress of Industrial Organization (AFL-CIO) in 1995, virtually all major unions have embraced organizing as a top priority (at least rhetorically). The federation's "change to organizing" effort, though, has emphasized almost exclusively the objective of increasing the resources devoted to the task. After eight years and a major reallocation of funds in many prominent unions, there is little if any progress. Private-sector union density continues to slide. Farber and Western's (2001) analysis helps explain why. With a naturally shrinking base, it becomes increasingly difficult to marshal the resources necessary to reverse momentum.

Perhaps the most important weakness in the "change to organizing" is that a resource shift, *ceteris paribus,* seeks to extend unionism as it exists. This paper accepts, consistent with Farber and Western, that it is unrealistic to presume that a resource shift alone will be sufficient to halt the decline in union density. Unions need to go beyond resources and explore innovations that in effect will increase the demand for their services. As David Brody (1991) argued a decade ago, the labor movement cannot assume that workers will accept unions in their current form, nor can labor define the aspirations of its potential members. The rapid growth of the CIO in the late 1930s was possible because of its capacity to become "the institutional embodiment of the vital job interests of the mass production workers" (308), in this case by offering an industrial union alternative to the AFL. Similarly, the expansion of membership in the public sector during the 1960s and 1970s was facilitated by the ascension of unions willing to adopt an approach more in tune with the experiences of government employees, in part by basing bargaining power on political influence rather than relying on economic weapons like the strike. Any resurgence of labor early in the twenty-first century is likely to depend on the ability of existing or emerging unions to identify and respond to the job related needs of substantial concentrations of workers who have unmet "aspirations for industrial justice" (Brody 1991, 308).

The structural explanations of union decline that were dismissed as insufficient in the late 1980s actually encompassed as a negative a potential route to union survival. To reinterpret the conclusions of that line of research in a more productive light, even if union density is roughly constant in those industries and occupations with relatively high levels of unionization (an unlikely scenario standing alone), long-term stability and growth depend on the ability of unions to appeal to workers in industries and occupations where employment is expanding but union density is low. And as the structural analysis points out, private-sector markets for white-collar workers are crucial because of steady disproportionate employment growth and limited penetration of unions. The changing conditions of professional and technical workers, particularly the loss of control over job content and reduced job security, present an opportunity for unions if they can adapt. Furthermore, the success of public-sector unions among professional workers demonstrates that with the appropriate institutional characteristics there is realistic potential to organize similar workers in the private sector.[1]

The contrast in unionization between the private and public sectors is dramatic for professional workers. As table 5.1 shows, private-sector den-

1. The experience of public school teachers is particularly relevant. The evidence suggest that lack of control in the workplace created incentives for a militant response via unionization (Bacharach, Bamberger, and Conley 1990). And yet teacher unions struggled to find a comfortable identity that combined activism with concern for professionalism (Murphy 1990, 46–60).

Table 5.1 **Professional workers representation gap**

	2000 Private-sector union density (a)	2000 Public-sector union density (b)	Density gap (b – a)	Density ratio (b/a)
Professional workers	6.4	42.9	36.5	6.7:1
All other nonmanagerial workers	10.8	38.0	27.2	3.5:1

Source: Unpublished data from the Current Population Survey (CPS) provided by David Macpherson. For extensive union information based on the CPS, see Hirsch and Macpherson (2001).

sity is substantially lower for professionals than for other workers while public-sector density is higher. The gap in density is greater than for any other major occupational group. In relative terms, public-sector density is nearly seven times private-sector density for professional workers, almost twice the ratio for all other workers. This contrast suggests that there is substantial growth potential among professional workers if unions are able to respond to their concerns.

Success among professional workers would be an important accomplishment in its own right because this is now the largest occupational group. If a foothold can be established among professionals, unions will be in a position to use this as a base to spread into technical and clerical occupations; both of these latter occupational groups share the characteristic of relatively low private-sector unionization. In 2000, there were only 8.8 million union members in the entire private sector; that year there were 11.5 million nonunion professional workers. Add the technical and clerical occupations, and there were 28.4 million nonunion white-collar workers in the private sector. The potential importance of these workers to the future of the labor movement is self-evident.

If labor law and employer antiunionism are fixed, then any appeal by unions to white-collar workers is unlikely to succeed unless unions alter their character and institutional role to match the desires of potential members. The research reported here examines the institutional characteristics preferred by professional and technical workers. It does not offer a blueprint for union renewal, but it does suggest that there is much to be learned by comparing unions with professional associations, which are viewed by many white-collar workers as a more attractive institutional alternative.

5.2 Targeted Survey of Professional and Technical Workers

A survey was designed in cooperation with the AFL-CIO Department for Professional Employees, six national unions, and the Union Privilege Benefits Corporation. The idea behind this research was to interview private-sector white-collar workers who had actually experienced the influences of union and management in the context of a contested organizing campaign. Responses reveal a complex but consistent pattern of attitudes among white-collar workers who are contemplating unionization. Because the interviews were conducted after the respective campaigns were concluded, the responses are grounded in experience and therefore should be more reliable than answers to hypothetical questions typically posed in opinion surveys.

Seven cases were selected in coordination with the participating organizations and represented a mix of close union wins, close union losses, and pullbacks due to lack of support. The survey was subsequently administered for two additional cases in conjunction with one of the participating unions. Among those surveyed were health care providers, librarians, university technical and professional employees, performers, transportation agents, education paraprofessionals, and industrial office and technical employees.

In the nine cases, the units being surveyed range from several hundred to several thousand. Unions provided lists of names, addresses, and phone numbers. Appropriate random samples were drawn for each case, and introductory letters were followed with telephone interviews conducted by Cornell University's Computer Assisted Survey Team. Final authority over survey content and full control over detailed data were retained by the authors and Cornell University. Participating unions received summary data and an analytical report (Hurd 1998). Interviews for the seven original cases were conducted in 1997 and 1998 and for the two subsequent cases in 1999 and 2000. Telephone contact was made with a total of 2,311 workers, and fifteen- to twenty-minute interviews were conducted with 1,751 of them for a 75.7 percent response rate.

Because the survey research is limited to nine cases, it would be inappropriate to assume that the views expressed would be representative of all professional and technical workers. The workplaces studied employ large concentrations of workers from the relevant occupations. The very fact that a contested union organizing campaign took place is itself indicative that collectively the workers interviewed are more interested in securing some type of representation than their counterparts in other nonunion settings, perhaps because of either dissatisfaction or a strong desire to join together with their peers. On the other hand, these characteristics make these workers particularly appropriate for the research at hand. Their views are relevant to the potential for increased unionization among professional and technical workers and to the question of the type of labor market institution that might best meet the needs of workers in an evolving economy. At any rate, because the analysis concentrates on differences among subgroups of those interviewed, whether these subgroups are relatively larger or smaller than they might be in other settings is not a factor that would limit the validity of the findings.

The survey addresses attitudes toward the job, the workplace, the employer, different types of employee organizations, and the organizing campaign. A total of 100 questions are posed: fifteen are about the job and the workplace, eight are about unions, seven refer to employee involvement programs, twenty-three cover characteristics or tactics of employee organizations, nineteen pose possible services offered by employee organizations, twenty-one concern the specific organizing campaigns, and eight relate to demographic information.

Examination of raw survey responses and descriptive summary data suggests that more extensive analysis should center on a question that asks each interviewee to select the type of employee organization most likely to attract his or her support. The following options are offered: union, nonunion workplace association, employee involvement committee, professional association, or no organization. Unions and professional associations are the preferred choices in each of the seven cases that pose this question.[2] Furthermore, the vast majority of those who indicate that they ultimately chose to support unionization in the actual organizing campaign are drawn from these two groups. Combined with interesting patterns in responses to other questions, it is apparent that much can be learned from a comparison that centers on those preferring union and those preferring professional association. Before turning to the detailed analysis, the following section will review summary data to provide context.

5.3 Committed to Their Work

Although specific attitudes differ from one case to another because of varying objective conditions, what is far more impressive is the consistency across the samples and the different occupations. These professional and technical workers are strongly attached to their jobs and professions; 71.4 percent have been employed in the occupation for over ten years, and 71.5 percent anticipate being in the profession five years from the time of the survey. Job satisfaction is unusually high, with 83.4 percent either very satisfied or somewhat satisfied. Commitment to the job and the profession is reflected further in the selection of "freedom to exercise professional judgment" as the most important work-related issue. The group activity of greatest interest to these professionals is "meeting with management to discuss policies," endorsed by 90.9 percent of those interviewed. When asked to identify the key reason to join an employee organization, the top choice is "give workers a voice." The composite picture is a group of workers committed to their professions, confident of their own abilities to exercise independent judgment and interested in finding a way to increase their say in key decisions.

2. This question was omitted from the survey for one sample and posed differently for another.

However, the consistent views regarding work do not translate into consensus regarding the type of workplace institution that would be supported in order to secure voice. There are important variations in attitudes toward employee organizations generally and unions specifically, and it is these differences that largely determine the potential for some type of workplace association. What type of representation appeals to professional and technical workers? When asked what approach they would like to see in their workplace, 80.9 percent indicate preference for an organization that develops "a cooperative relationship with management" rather than one that is "aggressive and stands up to management." This strong preference holds for union supporters and opponents alike. Another question asks interviewees to select a key reason *not* to join an employee organization. The most frequent answer is "creates conflict at work," and the second choice overall is "loss of individual freedom."

The combination of a desire for voice, aversion to conflict, preference for cooperation, and concern about preserving individualism presents a challenging mosaic for any organization that hopes to appeal to professional and technical workers and build consensus for collective action. In order to examine more deeply the organizational opportunities, it is necessary to concentrate on responses to questions regarding institutional form.

Table 5.2 summarizes responses to several relevant questions. The first column reports the type of employee organization preferred. Although unions are the first choice, barely more than one-third select this option. Nearly as many prefer a professional association, with substantially less support for a nonunion workplace association or an employee involvement committee. Only about one-eighth are opposed to any form of employee

Table 5.2 **Organizational preferences and attitudes**

Type of preferred employee organization	Share of total interviewees	E.I. programs address concerns of professionals[a]	Unionized professionals better off[b]	Vote yes[c]	Pro-union[d]
Union	35.2	40.0	93.3	93.6	69.4
Professional association	31.9	46.2	43.5	50.2	27.4
Nonunion workplace association	9.4	46.6	42.0	44.3	12.5
Employee involvement committee	11.3	53.8	25.5	23.6	9.4
No organization	12.2	49.1	34.2	23.7	12.3

Note: Column (1) adds to 100 percent; all other cells are self-contained and report the share of those preferring each type of organization who agree with or match the column heading.

[a]Employee involvement programs effectively address concerns of workers in your occupation.

[b]Workers in your occupation who are represented by a union are better off overall.

[c]Would vote for a union in a hypothetical representation election on day of interview.

[d]Openly supported union during organizing campaign.

organization, a reflection of the degree of interest in some type of forum to voice work-related concerns.

To benchmark these responses, it is useful to compare them to the results of Freeman's and Rogers's (1999) Worker Representation and Participation Survey (WRPS). Because the WRPS involves a national random sample it undoubtedly is more representative of general attitudes than the research reported here, which is targeted to a narrow subset of professional and technical workers. Nonetheless, there are some intriguing parallels and dissimilarities. The WRPS offers a different set of institutional options, but it does include as choices (in slightly different form) union, employee involvement committee, and no organization; a fourth option is "laws that protect employee rights." The overall response is union 27 percent, employee involvement 49 percent, laws 15 percent, and no organization 9 percent (Freeman and Rogers 1999, 150–51).[3]

Freeman and Rogers (1999, 150–51) actually offer two versions of this set of alternatives; half of those surveyed have the opportunity to select "union," while the other half can chose "an employee organization that negotiates or bargains." The 27 percent overall support for union actually combines 23 percent choosing "union" in one-half of the sample and 31 percent choosing "employee association" in the other half. Comparing this to entries in the first column of table 5.2, the 9.4 percent selecting "nonunion workplace association" in the survey reported here is roughly comparable to the 8 percent increase in support for representation Freeman and Rogers find when they replace "union" with "employee association." At any rate, the 35.2 percent support for a union among workers surveyed for this research is clearly higher than would be expected based on the WRPS benchmark. To reiterate, this is not surprising because these workers have experienced the direct influences of a union organizing campaign. Furthermore, this survey does not offer the WRPS's option of laws to protect employee rights, which may be viewed by some workers as a reasonable substitute for union representation.

Of greater interest is the contrast in the level of support for employee involvement committees. To clarify, Freeman and Rogers (1999, 150–51) use slightly different terminology, "joint employee-management committees." Furthermore they mailed to each participant in advance a description of how such committees might function, a step that could have increased interest. It seems highly unlikely, though, that these factors could explain the stark difference in support for employee involvement, 49 percent in the WRPS compared to 11.3 percent here. It seems more likely that the difference results from the preference of these professional and technical work-

3. In a slightly different context, Freeman and Rogers (1999) report that those in professional occupations are less likely to support unions than other nonmanagerial employees (71).

ers to address their work-related concerns through a professional association, an alternative not offered in the WRPS, which was designed for a broad cross section of workers from a diverse set of occupations.

The responses reported in the second column of table 5.2 are relevant in this context. Although only about one-tenth of those interviewed indicate a preference for employee involvement committees as an organizational form, nearly half agree that these programs effectively address the concerns of workers in their occupation. This assessment of the instrumentality of employee involvement committees is remarkably consistent regardless of the type of organization preferred, ranging from two-fifths of those who select union to only a little over one-half of those whose first choice is employee involvement. Contrast this consistency with the responses regarding union instrumentality reported in the third column. Overall there is a more positive assessment for the effectiveness of unions than for employee involvement, but there is considerable variation in opinion. Those who prefer unions are nearly unanimous regarding instrumentality, compared to only one-quarter of those who prefer employee involvement.

Clearly the union option generates a more spirited and diverse reaction than the more benign alternative of employee involvement. The final two columns lend additional texture to the range of attitudes towards unions. The hypothetical vote in a representation election is a staple in research on opinions about unions, and the fourth column shows that responses closely resemble those to the question on union instrumentality. However, union organizers have learned to be skeptical about workers' stated intention to vote yes, either in response to union-sponsored surveys or even to direct questions posed by organizers or co-workers. Given the intensity of management opposition in most campaigns, the current practice of organizers is to consider a yes vote reliable only if the worker publicly demonstrates support. The fifth column reports the "prounion" share of workers, or those who indicate that they openly supported the union during the organizing campaign.

Even among those who select unions as their desired type of organization, actual public support drops compared to hypothetical vote. In relative terms, the decline is even greater for those aligned with other institutional alternatives. Although those who prefer a nonunion workplace association show moderate interest in unions in their responses regarding instrumentality and hypothetical vote, in the actual organizing campaign their level of public support is indistinguishable from those who want no organization. The workers who would rather address concerns through employee involvement committees are actually the least likely to be active on behalf of a union. Workers who choose professional association display greater affinity for unions; they are more than twice as likely to be active supporters compared to those who select other nonunion alternatives. This is actually a positive sign for unions because professional associations attract broad interest and because they operate as independent voluntary membership organizations similar to unions in many respects.

To look at the final two columns in a slightly different light, among the professional and technical workers surveyed, 83 percent of those who were "prounion" during the organizing campaign select either union or professional association as their preferred type of employee organization. If unions hope to extend their appeal among professional and technical workers they must reach beyond the pool of their most ardent supporters and connect with those for whom unionization is in effect a second-best solution. In order to explore how this might be accomplished, the statistical analysis that follows concentrates on comparisons between advocates for unions and professional associations, respectively.

5.4 Statistical Analysis

This chapter draws upon a data set that, though narrow in reach and technically not representative, is rich in information about the attitudes of professional and technical workers toward unions and other labor market institutions. Utilizing inductive statistical techniques, leads are developed and patterns emerge that have the potential to inform unions and other organizations that seek to represent the interests of white-collar workers. This analysis is conducted in the spirit of the methodology pioneered in the early years of the National Bureau of Economic Research by its founder and original research director Wesley C. Mitchell (see, for example, Mitchell 1927). His brand of institutional economics starts with data, and it is through the exploration and analysis of the data that Mitchell discovers explanatory hypotheses (Blaug 1986, 168).

The statistical analysis reported here pools data from the survey and utilizes exploratory inductive techniques.[4] During the first phase of the research, classification trees are constructed in order to examine patterns in the data regarding preference among different types of employee organization. The primary comparison is between union and professional association. Classification tree analysis is an appropriate tool because it allows the data to sort themselves. Of the ninety-two substantive questions included in the survey, thirty-two are relevant to the question of organizational preference, and all of these are considered in the construction of the classification trees.

4. Only six of the cases are included in the detailed analysis. In addition to the two cases that do not pose a choice among organizational forms, another is omitted both because it is the only public-sector sample and because the ultimate choice faced by the workers is between two competing labor unions in a challenge election; thus, the situation is fundamentally different. However, for all three of the omitted cases, examination of the raw data reveal attitudes and patterns similar to those found in the six cases subjected to the more formal analysis.

In order to conduct significance tests, the second phase of the analysis relies on a stepwise logistic regression process to test the variables that emerge as useful in the classification tree sort. As a further check on the results, the third phase of the quantitative research utilizes the stepwise logistic regression methodology with all of the thirty-two variables considered in constructing the classification trees; in addition, six of the demographic variables are used as controls. Though not reported here, in each of the three phases the comparison of union with professional association is supplemented with comparisons of both union and professional association with other organizational forms.

The survey instrument includes five questions that address union instrumentality. One asks about unions in a generic sense, while the other four specifically reference unionized workers in the respondent's occupation in regard to wages and benefits, fair treatment, job security, and overall conditions. Not surprisingly, when all five measures of instrumentality are included, they dominate statistical tests of support for unions in comparison to alternatives. There are two ways to interpret these results. One could argue that union instrumentality in its various forms influences rational choice in a predictable direction and explains union support. An alternative interpretation is that these results are tautological because union supporters will be predisposed to believe that they will be instrumental and, further, that multiple variations of the instrumentality measure will simply reinforce the tautological nature of the test.

In an effort to both capture the role of union instrumentality and avoid the problem of tautology, two steps are taken. First, only one instrumentality measure is included among the thirty-two variables selected for the classification tree and regression analyses. Second, all tests are performed both with and without the instrumentality variable. Systematic omission of the variable has the added advantage of potentially allowing other influences masked by union instrumentality to surface.

With classification tree analysis, observations are sorted among the selected options (in this case union or professional association) based on the variable that does the best job of classification. Once the first sort is accomplished, each subset is sorted again based on the remaining variable that does the best job of classification. Each new branch of the tree is referred to as a "node," and there is a "yes" leaf and a "no" leaf associated with each node. Although the basic sort assumes that "majority rules," some intermediate sorts accomplish this only in a relative sense that conceptually parallels comparative advantage. However, these relative sorts are allowed only if one or more of the remaining variables can further classify the data based on "majority rules." The trees presented in figures 5.1 and 5.2 are based on the 629 individuals from the six relevant cases who select either union or professional association. The trees have been trimmed to remove those branches that do not appreciably improve the sort in that

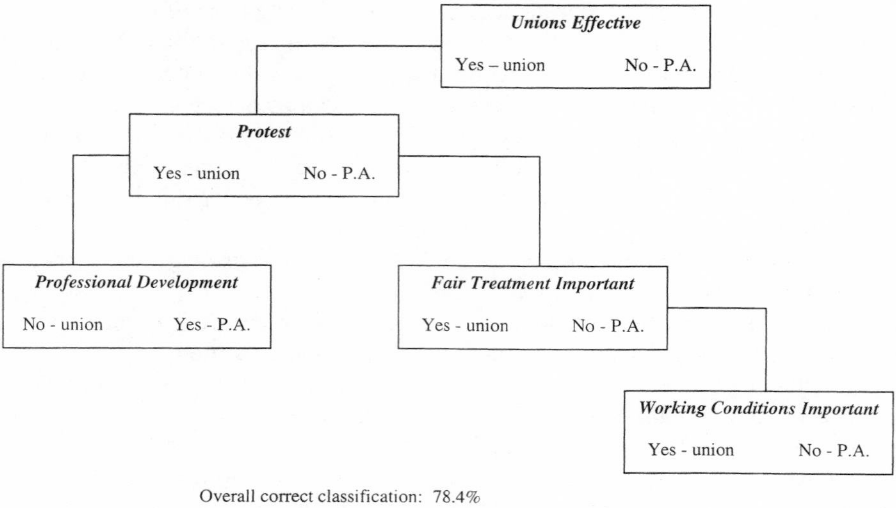

Fig. 5.1 Classification tree, unions vs. professional associations, union effectiveness
Note: Overall correct classification: 78.4 percent.

one or the other leaf has six or fewer observations (six represents 1 percent of total observations).

Figure 5.1 displays the classification tree constructed when the instrumentality variable is included. Not surprisingly, this variable, *unions effective,* does the best job of classifying the data. To avoid clutter, the actual breakdown of each sort is not presented, but it may be instructive to report this data for the initial sort to aid with interpretation. Of the 629 observations, 438 believe that unions are effective; of these, 308 prefer union, while 130 prefer professional association. Thus the "yes" sort is labeled "union." Among the 191 remaining observations (those who believe that unions are ineffective or neutral), 169 prefer professional association while 22 prefer union. Thus the "no" sort is labeled "professional association." In total, *unions effective* by itself correctly classifies 477 of the 629 observations; it is selected under the classification tree methodology because no other variable is as accurate at assigning observations.

Looking first at the right side of the tree, note that there are no further branches. This indicates that among the "nos" there is not another variable in the mix that improves the classification appreciably. On the left side of the tree, however, there are additional branches. Among those who agree that unions are effective, the variable that does the best job of refining the classification is *protest*. Those who would participate in group protests are

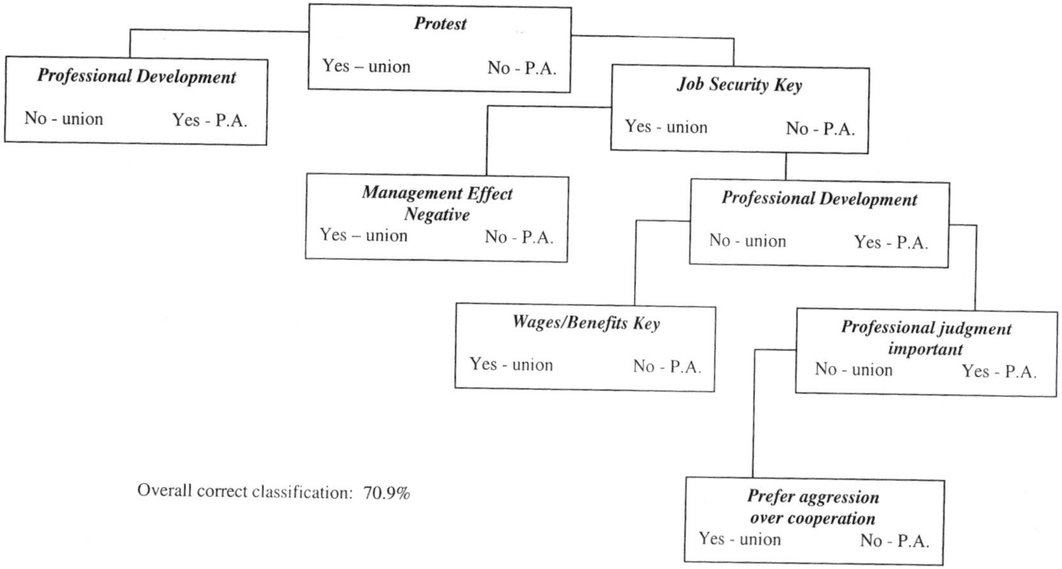

Fig. 5.2 Classification tree, unions vs. professional associations, characteristics of employee organizations
Note: Overall correct classification: 70.9 percent.

more likely to select union, while those who would not are more likely to select professional association.

A further sort of those willing to protest is possible using the variable *professional development.* Those who would participate in professional development activities outside of working hours are more likely to select professional association, while those not interested in professional development select union. Looking now at the right side of the *protest* branch, the classification can be refined using the variable *fair treatment*. Those who believe that procedures to assure fair treatment are especially important tend to select union, while those who do not tend to select professional association.

The final branch on the classification tree involves a further refinement among those associated with the "no" leaf of the *fair treatment* branch. Among this subset, the variable *working conditions* performs a successful sort. Those who agree that a key reason to join an employee association is to improve working conditions are more likely to select union, while those who do not agree are more likely to select professional association.

To summarize the message of figure 5.1, among the professional and technical workers surveyed, union supporters judge unions to be effective, are willing to participate in protests, and are concerned about fair treatment and working conditions. Those who prefer professional associations, on the other hand, are less convinced that unions are effective and shy away from protest but are interested in pursuing professional development opportunities.

Figure 5.2 displays the classification tree constructed when the union instrumentality variable is omitted. Although there is some overlap with figure 5.1 in terms of important variables, a number of other factors come into play. The variable that proves most successful in classifying the observations is *protest*. Following the same logic as applied in the interpretation of the tree in figure 5.1, the information displayed here can be summarized more succinctly. Those who prefer unions tend to support protests, to be concerned about job security, to give top management negative ratings, to believe that employee organizations should address wage and benefit concerns, and to prefer an aggressive approach that stands up to management. Among those surveyed, supporters of professional associations take a contrasting stance on these matters (at least relatively), express interest in pursuing professional development opportunities, indicate particular concern with protecting the freedom to exercise professional judgment, and prefer to be represented by an organization that adopts a cooperative demeanor with management.

Although classification trees help us tell a story about the data (or more accurately, allow the set of data to tell its own story), they are not capable of establishing the significance of relationships. The next stage of the analysis constructs a series of models using a stepwise logistic regression process. As applied, the stepwise process discards all variables with a *p*-value greater than 0.100. All specifications are binary; all variables appearing here and in the additional models presented subsequently are defined in table 5.3. Note that for all of the regression equations the dependent variable is *union* defined as 1 for those selecting union and 0 for those selecting professional association. Thus a positive coefficient indicates that the independent variable is consistent with preference for a union, and a negative coefficient indicates preference for a professional association. In all cases the final logistic regressions fit the data well, according to a variety of goodness-of-fit assessments. For example, *p*-values for the residual chi-square test of goodness of fit range from 0.22 to 0.89.[5]

The first set of equations takes all of the variables that contribute to the construction of the classification trees (i.e., those displayed in figures 5.1 and 5.2) and tests for significance using a stepwise logistic regression process. The results are presented in table 5.4. Model I includes the instrumentality variable (*unions effective*); model II does not. Considering models I and II together, the stepwise regression process largely corroborates the story told by the classification trees. Seven of the ten variables that aid in the classification tree sorting process have a *p*-value of 0.066 or less, and in each case the sign of the coefficient is appropriate.[6]

For one of the six samples used to construct the classification trees, the survey instrument was edited to omit most demographic questions at the request of the sponsoring organization. Thus it is not possible in models I and II to control for race; income; or education; and a proxy (years of experience) is used in place of age. Two additional models were constructed repeating the stepwise regression with the variables from the classification trees but with the data only from the five cases where it is possible to use a full set of demographic controls. Though the details are not reported here, the results for the reduced sample (with full controls) are nearly identical to those of the complete sample (with partial controls). The same seven independent variables are significant with *p*-values of 0.069 or less.

Based on these tests for statistical significance, the story told by the classification trees can be refined. Those who prefer unions are significantly

5. The goodness of fit of a logistic regression model can be assessed by a number of statistics of varying degrees of technical sophistication (and correctness). In our data analyses all of these measures give the same result, namely, that the final models fit the data well. In the tables, we report the simplest statistic, here denoted p^*, which is the *p*-value of the residual chi-square test. Although there are mathematical technicalities regarding the degree of replication within subpopulations in the sample required for the chi-square approximation, here we are using the test as a summary measure of goodness of fit, and in this context, roughly speaking, the larger the *p*-value (which ranges from zero to one), the better the fit of the model. For more information see, for example, chapter 5 of Hosmer and Lemeshow (2000).

6. The stepwise regression methodology eliminated the variable *professional judgment* in model I even though it is retained in model II. In a separate run with all variables identified in the classification tree analysis including *unions effective,* the coefficient for *professional judgment* is –0.31, almost identical to model II, but the chi-square value is only 1.90, which is not significant.

Table 5.3 **Variable definitions**

Variable	Specification (all independent variables binary)[a]	Description
Dependent variable		
UNION	1 = union 0 = professional association	Preference for a union or a professional association
Independent variables		
MGMNT NEG	1 = not positive at all 0 = very/somewhat/not very positive	Effect of top management on workers like you
PROF DEV	1 = yes 0 = no	In order to address work-related concerns, would participate in professional development activities outside of working hours
PROTEST	1 = yes 0 = no	In order to address work-related concerns, would participate in group protests to encourage management to change policies
JOB SEC	1 = key 0 = not key	A key reason to join an employee organization is to improve job security
COOP	1 = cooperate 0 = aggressive	Would like an employee organization to have a cooperative relationship with management or be aggressive and stand up to management
PROF JDG	1 = especially important 0 = not important	Freedom to exercise professional judgment is an especially important workplace issue
UN EFF	1 = better 0 = no difference or worse	Professional workers in your occupation who are represented by a union are better off overall
WRKLD	1 = especially important 0 = not important	Staffing, workload are especially important workplace issues

GOVT	1 = yes 0 = no	In order to address work-related concerns, would participate in appeals to appropriate government agencies
PETN	1 = yes 0 = no	In order to address work-related concerns, would participate in petition campaigns that ask management to change policies
INDV FR	1 = key 0 = not key	A key reason not to join any employee organization is loss of individual freedom
MEET MGMT	1 = yes 0 = no	In order to address work-related concerns, would participate in meetings with management to discuss policies
INFO	1 = key 0 = not key	A key reason to join an employee organization is as a source of information
Control variables[b]		
Unit dummies	1 = unit in question, 0 = all others	
Years of experience	1 = 10 years or longer, 0 = less than 10 years	
Gender	1 = male, 0 = female	
Race	1 = white, 0 = all others	
Age	actual age in years	
Income	1 = over $40,000 annually, 0 = $40,000 or less annually	
Education	1 = four-year college degree or higher, 0 = no four-year college degree	

[a]The binary specification is a reduction from original responses since some questions offered more than two choices. For the independent variables, those few who volunteered that they did not know or refused to answer are grouped with the option assigned a zero.

[b]In the tables that follow, "partial set" of controls indicates that only unit dummies, years of experience, and gender were used; "full set" of controls indicates that all controls except years of experience were used.

Table 5.4 **Union versus professional association (variable selection based on classification trees; full sample)**

	Model I			Model II		
Independent variable	Coefficient (standard error)	Chi^2	*P*-value	Coefficient (standard error)	Chi^2	*P*-value
Mgmnt neg	0.964 (0.274)	12.34	<.001	0.881 (0.244)	13.02	<.001
Prof dev	–1.032 (0.250)	17.09	<.001	–0.909 (0.221)	16.90	<.001
Protest	0.943 (0.216)	19.06	<.001	1.312 (0.194)	45.68	<.001
Job sec	0.579 (0.233)	6.17	.013	0.869 (0.213)	16.59	<.001
Coop	–0.601 (0.249)	5.83	.016	–0.743 (0.229)	10.56	.001
Prof jdg				–0.363 (0.198)	3.38	.066
Un eff	2.538 (0.273)	86.42	<.001	omitted		
Controls						
Unit dummies	yes			yes		
Demographic	partial set			partial set		
Goodness of fit	$p^* = 0.22$			$p^* = 0.24$		

Note: The goodness-of-fit statistic is explained in footnote 4.

more likely to believe that unions are effective, to give management negative ratings, to support protests, and to identify job security as a concern. Supporters of professional associations are significantly more likely to express interest in professional development, to prefer a cooperative approach with the employer, and to identify freedom to exercise professional judgment as a concern.

The next step in the analysis seeks to extend the search for significant relationships beyond the distillation facilitated by the classification tree methodology. An additional set of stepwise logistic regressions is constructed starting with the thirty-two variables potentially relevant to the question of organizational preference. The results are summarized in table 5.5; model III includes *unions effective* in the mix; model IV does not.

Results are consistent with those already described as all but one of the variables from models I and II are significant. Several additional factors also surface. Model III indicates that union advocates are significantly more likely to identify staffing and workload as important issues and to endorse appeals to government agencies to address workplace concerns. Those who prefer professional associations are significantly more likely to be concerned about potential loss of individual freedom and to endorse petitions

Table 5.5 **Union versus professional association (variable selection based on stepwise regression)**

Independent variable	Model III Coefficient (standard error)	Model III Chi²	Model III *P*-value	Model IV Coefficient (standard error)	Model IV Chi²	Model IV *P*-value
Mgmnt neg	0.841 (0.281)	8.95	.003	0.772 (0.251)	9.48	.002
Prof dev	–1.192 (0.266)	20.03	<.001	–1.062 (0.237)	20.02	<.001
Protest	1.064 (0.247)	18.53	<.001	1.290 (0.201)	41.19	<.001
Job sec	0.483 (0.244)	3.93	.048	0.895 (0.234)	14.68	<.001
Coop	–0.652 (0.259)	6.33	.012	–0.810 (0.236)	11.78	<.001
Un eff	2.600 (0.283)	84.45	<.001	omitted	omitted	omitted
Wrkld	0.690 (0.273)	6.38	.012	0.598 (0.242)	6.09	.014
Govt	0.914 (0.247)	13.67	<.001	0.925 (0.225)	16.87	<.001
Petn	–0.484 (0.271)	3.19	.074			
Indv Fr	–0.542 (0.239)	5.14	.023	–0.583 (0.215)	7.37	.007
Meet Mgmt				–0.778 (0.342)	5.17	.023
Info				–0.591 (0.333)	3.16	.076
Controls						
Unit dummies	yes			yes		
Demographic	partial set			partial set		
Goodness of fit	$p^* = .87$			$p^* = .46$		

Note: The goodness-of-fit statistic is explained in footnote 4.

as a way to address workplace concerns (presumably as a more dignified alternative to protests). Model IV reinforces the significance of workload, individual freedom, and appeals to government and also detects two additional variables associated with preference for professional associations—a heightened interest in meeting with management to discuss policies and a tendency to view employee organizations as a source of information.

The inductive statistical techniques used to construct classification trees and regression models have highlighted a total of sixteen variables that help distinguish between those professional and technical workers who prefer unions and those who prefer professional associations. Although different approaches yield somewhat different results, the stories that emerge are extraordinarily similar. Supporters of unions tend to focus on terms and conditions of employment and workplace rights; they are drawn to direct action and aggressive organizations. Advocates for professional associations, on the other hand, appear to be more interested in occupational matters and individual control; they are drawn to organizations that seek influence through cooperation and information sharing.

In spite of the statistical contrasts, there clearly is substantial overlap in support for these two organizational forms. As noted earlier, many professional and technical workers who fit the profile of advocates for professional associations ultimately support union organizing campaigns. Similarly, detailed exploration of the survey responses of union supporters indicates that they too appreciate many of the apparent attributes of professional associations. And yet, questions remain regarding these two options. Are they mutually exclusive organizational forms? Are they viewed as substitutes or compliments by those who purchase their services? In order to gain a more complete understanding of the character of professional associations and thereby lend texture to the comparison, the authors gathered descriptive information on a broad range of professional associations and conducted in-depth interviews with key staff at many of them. The next section summarizes that research.

5.5 The Enterprise of Professional Associations

Professions achieve their standing not solely because of inherent qualities of the work, but also as a product of intentional collective effort among practitioners to elevate the social and labor market status of the occupation.[7] Professional associations are essential to the process of establishing, maintaining, and enhancing professional identity (Ritzer and Walczak 1986). In the early stages of professionalization, a new association typically adopts a strong code of ethics that spells out the expectations of professional behavior and emphasizes service to the public. Based in part on its code of ethics, the association strives to promote a dignified public image for the profession. Simultaneously, it seeks to erect barriers to entry by establishing certification standards (either generally for the profession or for areas of specialty practice), typically through political action designed

7. Unless otherwise referenced, this section is based on documents gathered directly from selected professional associations and from interviews with key national staff members of these organizations. A broad range of associations were selected for study, including several from health care, engineering, and education plus an assortment of others including accountants, architects, social workers, librarians, and golf professionals. A special effort was made to include several associations of technical workers with modest educational requirements. A complete list of associations and interviews is available from the authors. Summary data has been obtained from the American Society of Association Executives, confirming that the information gathered on these associations fits the pattern for comparable organizations (American Society of Association Executives 1996).

to influence state licensure requirements. Ultimately most associations address scope of practice, attempting to delineate the expertise and competence of their members from those of related occupations.

Initial entry into a profession is tied, at least informally, to holding a relevant college degree; this expectation is often a prerequisite for full membership in the relevant association. In addition, successful performance on a licensing exam may be required in order to qualify for the legal right to practice. In some occupations, states establish additional formal requirements that must be met in order to retain licensure. Although national standards for a profession are not unusual, licensing and certification requirements normally are the province of state governments, and there may be substantial variation.[8] Some associations participate in certification directly, and all maintain working relationships with agencies established to confer certification or licenses to those in practice. In this regard, professional associations monitor relevant legislation at the federal and state levels and promote regulations that protect their members' right to practice and that uphold quality standards. In those professions where state regulations include continuing-education expectations, associations offer programs to help meet those requirements.

Professional association members are attracted to events and publications that enhance their own knowledge and earning power by offering access to certification and state-of-the-art information. In those professions and states where licensing and certification are optional, the practitioners' desire for information is often satisfied by technical publications and annual conferences. In those jurisdictions with licensing exams and particularly where there are ongoing certification requirements, professional development takes on an elevated level of importance. The extent and type of continuing education offered by professional associations are largely determined by these intertwined factors of member interest, requirements for entry into practice, and formal procedures for relicensure and recertification.

In addition to professional development activities, most associations offer consumer services such as credit cards, home mortgages, financial advice, and travel bookings and discounts. These services are provided by vendors, and apparently are of only secondary interest to most members. However, associations whose members are in private practice or health care report that malpractice liability insurance is a very popular benefit.

In the context of the changing nature of professional work described early in the paper, many associations are in the process of expanding the labor market services they provide, particularly those related to job search; employment listings in association newspapers and on web sites, salary profiles of members in specific geographic areas and subspecialties, and career counseling services are all common. Some engineering associations

8. For an overview of key issues related to occupational licensing, see Kleiner (2000).

are in the process of setting up a portable pension plan in response to increased turnover and labor market mobility. Nonetheless, associations are reluctant to interfere in the workplace directly or in any way encroach upon employer authority. In most associations, employers are accepted as members and may even encourage their employees to join. At all levels, associations maintain cordial relations and often close collaboration with key employers, especially regarding professional development programs.

With growing concern among professional workers about their labor market status and the changing nature of work, associations are experiencing some pressure to be more proactive. A few publish professional employment guidelines that amount to standards of employer conduct. Others have attempted to open a dialogue with employers. But these efforts are merely suggestive and have no enforcement mechanism. Even such modest initiatives can create problems that most associations would rather avoid. As one association executive explained to us in a conversation that was not for attribution, "We have to be careful not to get our members crosswise with our companies."

Most professional associations are content to focus on what they do best and serve the professional interests of their individual members. They are reluctant to interfere in the workplace and for the most part eschew union like activity. A few associations with large numbers of members who are represented by unions in the public sector actually endorse union representation, although they do not provide collective-bargaining services themselves. And with the American Medical Association's new attention to collective-bargaining options, some associations in health care are reconsidering historic opposition to unions.

By in large, though, unions and professional associations continue to operate in different realms. The research on professional associations summarized here confirms their importance in promoting specific professional and technical occupations. It also points to a clear link between professional development activity and the labor market; indeed, in many occupations, continuing education is necessary to maintain status as a licensed practitioner. By all indications, the pressure on these associations to address labor market deficiencies and to defend professional integrity and authority is increasing. This phenomenon deserves monitoring and further in-depth analytical attention.

5.6 The Potential for Institutional Convergence

In the broad context of their decline in the private sector, unions must address a number of specific challenges if they are to retain their role as influential economic institutions. Perhaps the most important is to determine how to extend membership and influence in labor markets for professional and technical workers. It is unlikely that demand for union representation among these workers will increase without some affirmative action on the part of labor organizations to reconfigure themselves, either by offering a substantially altered set of services or by adopting a markedly different strategic approach. Simply appealing to latent demand for traditional union representation is extraordinarily unlikely to produce a groundswell of interest.

The statistical analysis presented here facilitates inference regarding the type of labor market institution preferred by professional and technical workers. To recap the descriptive overview of survey responses, these workers are satisfied with their jobs, display long-term attachment to the occupation, and are interested in protecting individual autonomy at work. At the same time they want to enhance their role in decision making, preferably through dialogue with management in a cooperative framework rather than through confrontation.

This combination of attitudes does not neatly match existing institutions. Unions offer voice at work but promote collective rather than individual influence and often rely on adversarial tactics. Professional associations offer opportunities to enhance individual expertise and promote the profession, often in collaboration with employers, but do not address workplace concerns or promote influence on the job. Although employee involvement programs seem to fit some of these attitudes, they do not promote occupational concerns and (among those surveyed) are not viewed as a preferred institutional form.

The detailed comparison between those who align with unions and those drawn to professional associations helps guide the analysis. The classification trees and stepwise logistic regressions tell a story on behalf of the professional and technical workers. Union advocates want to address working conditions, wages and benefits, workloads, and job security. They hold relatively negative views towards management, are concerned about fair treatment, and will participate in protests to voice their opinions. Supporters of professional associations, on the other hand, place priority on exercising professional judgment at work and want to protect individual freedom. They are attracted to organizations that provide relevant information and professional development opportunities. At the same time they do have workplace concerns but prefer to address them by meeting with management in a cooperative spirit.

The characteristics of professional associations described in the preceding section are largely consistent with the factors associated with preference for professional association that emerge from the statistical analysis. There are a few factors, however, that go beyond the traditional sphere of associations. Especially important is a desire to address workplace concerns directly by meeting with management to discuss policies. Though the absolute difference is small, it is particularly notable that advocates of professional associations are significantly more interested in meeting with management than are union supporters. Unions do provide mechanisms to address workplace concerns with management; professional associations do not. This indicates a potential for unions to appeal to these workers by offering them voice and simultaneously raises questions about professional associations' resistance to assuming such a role. The message is reinforced by the evidence in one of the statistical models that workers who prefer professional associations are more likely to sign petitions to address workplace concerns. Although a less-assertive stance than the support for protests from union adherents, this willingness to petition the employer again would not fit the culture of most professional associations.

Given the active promotion by associations of government intervention in the context of licensing and certification requirements, it is also notable that union advocates are significantly more likely to endorse appeals to government agencies as a way to address workplace concerns. The model developed by Weil (chap. 1 in this volume) facilitates exploration of this apparent contradiction. Weil describes how labor market institutions can affect workplace regulation, distinguishing between actions to influence regulations and those that affect enforcement. He concentrates on the latter in his model.

The statistical results linking union supporters with appeals to government agencies are consistent with Weil's (chap. 1 in this volume) formulation, which argues that agents such as unions can help resolve the public goods problem inherent in workplace regulation. The fact that it is union supporters that embrace this type of activity is consistent with the overall profile of these workers based on the survey. They are relatively more concerned about terms and conditions of employment, more negative toward management, and more vigilant about fair treatment. These all match their concern for protecting rights in the workplace, which can be addressed by unionization, by appeals to appropriate government agencies, or by both.

Based on survey responses, those who prefer professional associations are less likely to address workplace issues by appealing to government agencies. This is not inconsistent with the political role of professional associations because their focus is on actions to influence regulations regarding *access* to the labor market rather than on enforcing rights in the workplace. To return to Weil's (chap. 1 in this volume) model, by concentrating on enforcement he omits the potential role embraced by associations. Professional and technical workers, though less concerned with fair treatment and workplace rights, may nonetheless be quite supportive of actions that enhance their labor market position. This is clearly consistent with interest in professional development because it offers the potential to increase productivity and market value.

The future of unions and, indeed, of professional associations may lie in the nexus between these two organizational forms. Unions are capable of asserting collective voice in the workplace to exercise rights and promote enforcement of regulations. However, they can play this role only if they gain majority status, a prerequisite under U.S. labor law for establishing the union as bargaining agent. Achieving majority status among professional and technical workers may well depend on the union's ability to attract those who want a voice at work but whose preferences are otherwise more closely aligned with the package of services offered by professional associations. This implies more attention to professional or occupational issues both on the job and in the broader labor market, initiatives to provide access to professional development opportunities, and perhaps a modified demeanor vis-à-vis employers. Professional associations are likely to face pressure simultaneously to move toward unions, especially if professional and technical workers continue to express concern about limitations on their ability to exercise professional judgment.

Professional and technical workers are interested in career development and education, but they are also concerned about what happens on the job. They want information about their profession but also about their employer and their workplace. They are attracted to organizations that serve as advocates, but they also seek a forum to speak out themselves and the ability to control the content of their work. There is a natural tension between the growth in professional and technical employment and the deprofessionalization of the work. In the context of this tension there are incentives for unions and professional associations to find common ground. As labor markets induce convergence, they create the potential for the emergence of institutions capable of addressing the multifaceted needs of the expanding professional and technical workforce.

References

American Society of Association Executives. 1996. *Membership recruitment and retention.* Washington, D.C.: American Society of Association Executives.

Anderson, James. 1992. The deprofessionalization of American medicine. *Current Research on Occupations and the Professions* 7:241–56.

Bacharach, Samuel, Peter Bamberger, and Sharon Conley. 1990. Professionals and workplace control. *Industrial and Labor Relations Review* 43 (5): 570–86.

Blaug, Mark. 1986. *Great economists before Keynes.* Atlantic Highlands, N.J.: Humanities Press International.

Blinder, Alan S. 2000. How the economy came to resemble the model. *Business Economics* 35 (1): 16–25.

Brody, David. 1991. Labor's crisis in historical perspective. In *The state of the unions,* ed. George Strauss, Daniel Gallagher, and Jack Fiorito, 277–311. Madison, Wisc.: Industrial Relations Research Association.

Chaison, Gary N., and Joseph B. Rose. 1991. The macrodynamics of union growth and decline. In *The state of the unions,* ed. George Strauss, Daniel Gallagher, and Jack Fiorito, 3–45. Madison, Wisc.: Industrial Relations Research Association.

Farber, Henry S., and Bruce Western. 2001. Accounting for the decline of unions in the private sector, 1973–1998. *Journal of Labor Research* 22 (3): 459–85.
Freeman, Richard B. 1988. Contraction and expansion: The divergence of private sector and public sector unionism in the United States. *Journal of Economic Perspectives* 2 (2): 63–88.
Freeman, Richard, and Joel Rogers. 1999. *What workers want.* Ithaca, N.Y.: Cornell University Press.
Hackman, J. Richard. 1998. What is happening to professional work? *Perspectives on Work* 2 (1): 44–66.
Hirsch, Barry T. 1996. The Dunlop Commission's premise: A tilted playing field? *Journal of Labor Research* 17 (1): 15–37.
Hirsch, Barry T,. and David Macpherson. 2001. *Union membership and earnings data book* Washington, D.C.: Bureau of National Affairs.
Hoff, Timothy. 2001. The physician as worker. *Health Care Management Review* 26 (4): 53–70.
Hosmer, David W., and Stanley Lemeshow. 2000. *Applied logistic regression.* 2nd. ed. New York: Wiley.
Hovekamp, Tina Maragou. 1997. Professional associations or unions? A comparative look. *Library Trends* 46 (2): 232–44.
Hurd, Richard. 1998. *The organizing challenge: Professional and technical workers seek a voice.* Washington, D.C.: AFL-CIO Department for Professional Employees.
Kleiner, Morris. 2000. Occupational Licensing. *Journal of Economic Perspectives* 14 (4): 189–202.
Kochan, Thomas, Harry Katz, and Robert McKersie. 1994. *The transformation of industrial relations.* Ithaca, N.Y.: ILR Press.
McHugh, Patrick, and Matthew Bodah. 2002. Professionalism and union voting intentions: The case of pharmacists. *Journal of Labor Research* 23 (4): 659–71.
Mitchell, Wesley C. 1927. *Business cycles: The problem and its setting.* New York: National Bureau of Economic Research.
Murphy, Marjorie. 1990. *Blackboard unions.* Ithaca, N.Y.: Cornell University Press.
Rhoades, Gary. 1998. *Managed professionals.* Albany: State University of New York Press.
Ritzer, George, and David Walczak. 1986. *Working: Conflict and change.* Englewood Cliffs, N.J.: Prentice Hall.
Shafer, William, D. Jordan Lowe, and Timothy Fogarty. 2002. The effects of corporate ownership on public accountants' professionalism and ethics. *Accounting Horizons* (June): 109–24.
U.S. Department of Labor, Bureau of Labor Statistics. 2000. *Occupational outlook handbook, 2000–01 edition. Bulletin 2520.* Washington, D.C.: U.S. Department of Labor.

6

A Workers' Lobby to Provide Portable Benefits

Joni Hersch

In 1993, the prominent sociologist Herbert Gans published a four-page article entitled "Time for an Employees' Lobby." Gans advocated the formation of a national lobby to promote the interests of workers. In Gans's vision, this "employees" or "jobs" lobby would be multiclass and trans-ideological and would represent all members of the labor force, including traditional employees as well as managers, the jobless, and contingent and other nonstandard workers. Gans proposed structuring this lobby on the AARP model of individual membership, with a small membership fee.

Inspired by Gans's (1993) article, Sara Horowitz founded an employees' lobby she called Working Today, which was launched on Labor Day 1995. As recommended by Gans, Working Today was initially based on the AARP model of individual membership. Working Today started with an ambitious objective. The *Christian Science Monitor* described the goal of Working Today as "to put jobs back on the public agenda by lobbying for political action on measures to save jobs, create new ones, and explore long-term solutions to the ongoing erosion of good jobs."[1] An editorial in the *Boston Globe* heralded this new organization, noting that "Working Today aims to be a low-dues, broad-based lobbying organization for workers of all sorts—full-time, part-time, the increasingly numerous ranks of

Joni Hersch is adjunct professor at Harvard Law School. The author thanks James Rebitzer for his helpful comments and Mckean Nowlin and Jonathan Patchen for excellent research assistance.

1. Nicole Gaouette, "New Lobby Group Gives Harried Workers a Voice," *The Christian Science Monitor,* February 1, 1996, 8.

contingent workers and the unemployed—patterned on the immensely successful AARP, with its 33 million members."[2]

But the task of operationalizing Gans's (1993) suggestion of a national lobby that would represent all workers proved elusive. As the evolution of Working Today demonstrates, it is difficult to form and sustain an organization with such a broad goal. Working Today has shifted from seeking to represent all workers via a membership organization to providing private services to independent workers, with the primary emphasis on provision of portable benefits. Perhaps in recognition of the changing focus, in September 2001 the slogan posted on the Working Today website changed to "benefiting the way you work" from "a national voice for America's independent workforce."[3] Working Today maintains that access to portable benefits is a first step to building a strong constituency that will push for policy changes to advance the interests of independent workers.

I begin with an overview of how organizations form and survive. Section 6.2 provides additional background on the broad-based workers' lobby suggested by Gans (1993). I follow this in section 6.3 with a discussion of two highly successful membership organizations, AARP and Common Cause, which might serve as potential models for a workers' lobby. This section also provides a description of the evolution of Working Today.

Section 6.4 develops a model of fundraising by a workers' organization. In this model, the founder must allocate resources between the provision of public goods, which attracts foundation grants, and the provision of private goods, which attracts individual members. While the model applies generally to any private good, for concreteness I discuss health insurance as this is the main private good provided by Working Today. In order to examine the market for health insurance supplied by an organization such as Working Today, in section 6.5 I use data from the Current Population Survey (CPS) Contingent Work Supplement to provide statistics on the insurance coverage status and demographic characteristics of nonstandard workers and traditional employees.

Working Today's original focus was on independent workers, and section 6.6 identifies specific policy areas involving independent workers in which a workers' lobby might fruitfully address its efforts. Section 6.7 evaluates the accomplishments and prospects of Working Today. I conclude with an evaluation of the prospects of a broad-based workers' lobby.

2. David Warsh, "Needed: A Lobby for Labor, Like the AARP," *Boston Globe,* September 3, 1995, 73.

3. See http://www.workingtoday.org; accessed January 20, 1999 and September 4, 2001. By October 2003, the slogan changed again, reading "Working Today represents the needs and concerns of the independent workforce through advocacy, information and service" (accessed October 18, 2003). Benefit provision remains the emphasis of Working Today.

6.1 Organizational Formation

Organizations exist to serve the common interests of their members that could not be advanced adequately by individual action. Unions have traditionally provided a collective voice for covered workers (Freeman and Medoff 1984.) Various theories have been proposed to explain the incentives for organizations concerned with the common good to form, with none of the theories being entirely satisfactory. Truman (1951) maintained that groups formed spontaneously out of shared feelings of frustration. This view was challenged by Olson (1965) who argued that because of the basic problem of free riding, members of a large group will not work for the group's interest unless membership is compulsory or unless there is some sufficient selective incentive that is separate from the public (collective) good. The AARP is an interest group that would have been unlikely to form without providing a selective benefit, in particular health insurance for retirees, at rates extremely profitable to AARP's founder.

In contrast, Hirschman (1982) believed that individuals will work for a common good because the act of seeking that good provides a benefit in addition to the good itself. Walker's (1991) empirical analysis of membership groups reveals that while most successful advocacy groups appear to provide private goods as incentives, group leaders do not consider these private benefits as important as collective benefits in attracting members. Indeed, the success of Common Cause provides a compelling counterexample to the notion that selective benefits are necessary to attract and sustain membership.

A workers' lobby can take one of three broadly defined forms: that of a social movement, a special interest lobby, or a service organization. Gans's (1993) vision was that of a social movement, and much of the early interviews with Working Today founder Sara Horowitz emphasized the social movement nature of the lobby.

Social movements, such as those for civil rights, women's rights, or the environment, strive to bring about institutional change by organizing or representing the collective interests of some disadvantaged or underrepresented group. Social movements tend to be one of two kinds: empowerment movements or professional movements. Empowerment movements derive their strength and resources from its intended beneficiaries. This type of movement seeks broad membership and involvement by the group's members. They pursue widespread attention in order to change values, which may in turn be reflected in public policy in the future. Professional movement associations have professional staff and receive resources from institutions and isolated constituencies. These organizations "speak for" rather than organize their nominal beneficiaries. They are likely to lobby federal bureaus or political leaders, such as members of Congress.

A special interest lobby seeks specific benefits for its constituency, such as legal reform and tax reform. There are a large number of organizations that lobby for policy measures affecting the earnings and employment of their members, either directly or indirectly. Indeed, it is hard to imagine any occupational or professional organization that does not seek to benefit its constituency. Existing workers organizations that have documented successes in benefiting their constituencies include the National Writers Union; WashTech; and 9to5, National Association of Working Women.

As a service organization, a workers' organization would provide specific benefits directly, such as education, training, and insurance benefits. In contrast to social movements, service organizations do not seek institutional change. For example, members of the American Economic Association (AEA) receive education and training, disseminated in the form of journals and conferences, but the AEA does not engage in lobbying.

Organizations attempt to ensure their continued existence, which means they must maintain funding, either by appealing to members or potential members or by appealing to principal sources of funding, such as foundations. The funding of any workers' organization depends on both its focus and its constituency. Gans (1993) envisioned a membership organization that would be funded by small membership dues, voluntarily given. However, even if membership dues will ultimately fully finance an organization, start-up funds are necessary. Roughly, start-up funds for social movements tend to come from wealthy patrons or private foundations, although the government has also played a large role; start-up funds for special interest lobbies are often provided by the beneficiaries (and hence are subject to inherent free-riding problems among constituent groups); and service organizations are often funded by government grants (Walker 1991.)

To attract funding, organizations will choose activities such as lobbying or litigation, and strategies such as organized protests and media coverage intended to generate public visibility for the organization, or a combination of these strategies. Common Cause attracted start-up funding because of the visibility of its founder John Gardner. Most professional and occupational organizations pursue their lobbying activities quietly. The National Association for the Advancement of Colored People (NAACP) pursued a successful strategy of selective litigation. Jobs with Justice is a national campaign aimed at raising workers' incomes. This effort is conducted by organized labor as well as community and religious organizations and uses organized protests as one of its strategies.

Most successful interest groups derive substantial funding from members' self-interest or profit motive. Walker (1991) reports that 80 percent of American interest groups have emerged from preexisting occupational or professional committees. The remaining 20 percent arise in the wake of broad social movements such as pollution, civil rights, and women's issues. These groups often are created by political entrepreneurs operating with the support of wealthy individuals, private foundations, or elected political leaders. As Jenkins (1998) documents, the role of foundations in funding social movements historically has been quite modest. Grants to social movements were a minor component of total foundation giving between 1953 and 1980, representing at its peak (in 1977) only 0.69 percent of total foundation giving.

6.2 Herbert Gans's Vision of a Workers' Lobby

In his article "Time for an Employees' Lobby," Gans (1993, 35) suggested that a national lobby of employees be established to encourage President Clinton to keep his campaign promise to do something about the "ever-declining number of full-time, decent jobs." His article included a series of specific policies with the overall focus being to "place the jobs issue high on the public agenda, and educate the public both about the drastic changes our economy is facing and the need to address them politically."

Gans (1993) recommended that the principal purposes of such a lobby would be to develop short-term and long-term policies to save jobs and create new jobs, to begin considering long-term solutions to the erosion of jobs, and to establish income support programs for the underemployed and unemployed. He suggested that the proper organization would be a workers' party, similar to those that exist in Europe, but dismisses this option because the United States has never had an important workers' party, and the long-established parties in Europe have become less effective. Gans likewise considered it unlikely that unions will be able to solve the problems faced by workers because union membership and influence are declining. Further, he did not consider it possible that a single union or a network of unions could represent all workers today.

Gans (1993) suggested that the membership model of the AARP might serve as the model for the organizational structure of the lobby. He anticipated that membership would come from job losers, the unemployed, those threatened by future job loss and their friends and family, as well as those with jobs who recognize that employment no longer offers the job security of the past.

For the most part Gans's (1993) concerns might seem unwarranted in light of the strong economy of the 1990s (although they may invite more attention in periods, such as the early 2000s, in which the economy is weaker). Despite his concern that any jobs lobby represent all workers regardless of political values, his recommendations are highly politically laden and run counter to trends to limit government intervention into the economy. Although he dismisses the possibility that unions can represent all workers, oddly he does not seem to recognize that any lobby is equally unlikely to represent all workers. Nonetheless, while one might quibble over the specific reasons he offers, at the time his paper was published, there was no unified voice offering to speak for all workers.

6.3 The Evolution of Three Organizations: The AARP, Common Cause, and Working Today

Shortly after Gans's (1993) article was published, Sara Horowitz founded the organization Working Today, which offered to provide a unified voice to speak for all workers. As noted in the introduction, Working Today was formed with the ambitious goal "to put jobs back on the public agenda by lobbying for political action on measures to save jobs, create new ones, and explore long-term solutions to the ongoing erosion of good jobs."[4] Horowitz maintains that today's economy represents a third industrial revolution, arguing that in this new economy workers needs were not met because of archaic labor laws.[5]

In this section I describe the evolution of Working Today since its founding in 1995. To understand the options for survival and growth available to an organization such as Working Today, it is useful to examine two successful membership organizations: the AARP and Common Cause. The AARP mainly attracts members by providing individual benefits, while Common Cause offers no selective benefits.

Membership in the AARP is open to anyone aged fifty and older, and as of 2003 the AARP reports over 35 million members.[6] Members do not run it, and it has no legal status to represent the interests of its constituency of individuals aged fifty and older. Yet it is routinely ranked as the most powerful lobbying group in the United States.[7]

How did the AARP evolve into such a powerful force, and can this model be applied to workers?[8] A little bit of background shows the integral role of private goods in attracting and sustaining membership. Ethel Percy Andrus was a retired schoolteacher who had formed a service organization that provided health insurance policies to retired teachers. Observing this popular interest in health insurance among other retired individuals, insurance salesman Leonard Davis provided financial capital to start the AARP in 1958. Insurance sales were integrally tied with the growth of AARP, which were publicly revealed during the 1970s to offer protection well below market norms. Despite this scandal, the AARP retained its strength. Its continued membership is attracted to discounts offered on car rentals, hotels, and package tours, all of which is available with the $12.50 per year membership fee (as of October 2003). Membership also includes a subscription to

4. Nicole Gaouette, "New Lobby Group Gives Harried Workers a Voice," *The Christian Science Monitor,* February 1, 1996, 8. The article does not explain what evidence Horowitz draws on in describing the labor market.

5. Sara Horowitz and Peter DeChiara, "Past Can Teach How to Cope with New Jobs' Uncertainties," *USA Today,* September 1, 1999, 11A.

6. See http://www.aarp.com/what_is.html; accessed October 30, 2003.

7. Jeffrey H. Birnbaum, "Follow the Money," *Fortune,* December 6, 1999, 206.

8. See Van Atta (1998) and Morris (1996).

AARP *The Magazine* (formerly called *Modern Maturity*), the nation's largest circulation magazine.

The AARP model of private goods provision differs from that of Common Cause.[9] Common Cause was formed to be a people's lobby to combat undue power of special interests, that is, a national "good-government" lobby. Common Cause was founded in 1970 by author and ex-U.S. Department of Health, Education, and Welfare (HEW) Secretary John W. Gardner. Gardner had headed the Carnegie Foundation, written two best-selling books, chaired a presidential committee on education policy, and served as secretary of HEW under Lyndon Johnson from July 1965 to January 1968. He then took on the leadership of the Urban Coalition. Gardner felt that the most effective policy tool was the lobbying arm of the Urban Coalition—the Urban Coalition Action Council. Common Cause was formed after the passage of the Tax Reform Act of 1969, which prohibited foundations from contributing to lobbying activities, thereby undermining the financial basis of the Urban Coalition Action Council. In order to secure a mass financial base, from its inception Common Cause took the direction of wide membership. Indeed, their financial support is primarily small contributions as a matter of organizational policy.

Gardner was a highly regarded and politically connected leader, who had both the visibility and credibility to raise $250,000 in start-up funds. To generate membership, Common Cause began with a series of newspaper ads and mass mailings. John Gardner also appeared on *Meet the Press* in 1970. This initial effort was highly effective, yielding 100,000 paying members within the first six months and 200,000 in the next six months. More than thirty years later Common Cause is still a viable organization, with over 200,000 individuals in all fifty states voluntarily paying the $20 annual membership fee.[10]

Working Today began as a mixture of the private goods model of AARP and the public goods model of Common Cause. Like the AARP, from its inception Working Today has offered private goods, such as access to group health insurance, discounts on office supplies, and discounted legal services to individuals who pay a small membership fee (originally $10, now $25 as of October 2003.) Like Common Cause, Working Today was founded by a political entrepreneur and had a broad objective, with "good jobs" substituting for the "good government" agenda of Common Cause. At its founding, Working Today positioned itself as a social movement, which was undoubtedly instrumental in securing initial foundation funding. Like both AARP and Common Cause, Working Today has an open membership policy.

However, individual membership growth was slow, and the organization

9. See McFarland (1984).
10. See http://www.commoncause.org; accessed October 30, 2003.

has largely been supported by foundation and government grants rather than individual membership dues. In contrast to the rapid membership growth of Common Cause, Working Today gained new members gradually. By May 1996, nine months after beginning operations, Working Today had about 700 dues-paying individual members. The remaining source of its $60,000 budget was a grant from the Ms. Foundation and a salary fellowship from Echoing Green, a foundation which supports innovative projects.[11] Foundations continued to provide the bulk of Working Today's funding, with $192,000 in foundation grants and about $17,000 in member dues and contributions after about one year of operation.[12] The number of individual dues-paying members as of January 1999 was 2,072.[13]

By January 1998, Working Today reported that its membership had rocketed to 35,000. However, this leap in membership represented a transformation in organizational structure and accounting technique rather than necessarily an increase in interest among individuals. The organization shifted to linking existing membership groups into one cohesive group under its Working Today Network umbrella, or in the words of Working Today, "joining organic associations and worker organizations into a larger whole, and advancing universal concepts."[14] Working Today counted as a member anyone who was a member of one of the organizations that had joined the network as well as those who paid dues to Working Today individually. Working Today reported in June 2000 that they had 93,000 members who had joined either individually or through one of the twenty-six organizations that have joined their network.[15]

Working Today is currently a mix of a special interest lobby and a service organization, although it still claims an overriding social agenda. As a special interest lobby, the organization lobbies for access to portable benefits for independent workers. As a service organization, Working Today most notably offers group health insurance. The primary visible project is its Portable Benefits Network launched in September 2001 that acts as an intermediary to provide group benefits to workers in New York's new media industry. Like other service organizations, it receives government funding. In particular, the Portable Benefits Network is funded in part by grants

11. Lini S. Kadaba, "Doing A Job for Workers, Call Sara Horowitz a Savvy Idealist. This Former Labor Lawyer has a Cause—A Lobbying Group to Better the Lot and Ease the Pain of American Workers," *Philadelphia Inquirer,* May 23, 1996, G1.

12. Sandra Livingston, "Reaching Out to Workers; Using AARP as a Model, Group Aims to Put Jobs on Nation's Agenda," *The Plain Dealer,* December 8, 1996, 1E.

13. Proposal to the John D. and Catherine T. MacArthur Foundation, Working Today, January 28, 1999, 8.

14. Reported on website accessed June 6, 2000 at http://www.workingtoday.org. This statement no longer appears on the website as of September 6, 2001.

15. Reported on website accessed June 6, 2000. This number is also reported in news articles. See, for example, Carol Gurstelle, "Ideas Web Watch Column," *Saint Paul Pioneer Press,* April 23, 2000.

from the state of New York. In May 2003, the Portable Benefits Network was renamed the Freelancers Union. Working Today reports 2,000 members of the Freelancers Union as of May 2003.[16]

Providing portable benefits is an integral part of Working Today's broader social mission of promoting the interests of independent workers. This role of benefit provision is expressed on the Working Today website in the section "News & Features: Advancing a New Social Agenda" as follows:

> The key to building a strong constituency will be linking services with advocacy—bridging people's economic and political interests to reignite the democratic discussion. . . . In building this model we can serve as a pilot, allowing people not just access to portable benefits, but also to push for a larger set of portable rights. . . . We believe it's imperative to effectively move the "new workforce" agenda forward by setting a cycle in motion: by accessing services, individuals will learn more about the larger policy issues facing them; and by getting active on these issues, they will improve the services they are able to access and make the policy debate reflect their concerns. Services, however, are only a first step . . . by linking people and groups together, we will assemble a constituency that can have its voice heard so we may build a secure and more complete safety net for the future.[17]

As the Portable Benefits Network/Freelancers Union seems to be the key to the continued survival of Working Today as a lobby for workers, it is useful to provide background on the plan. I will be providing information later on the likelihood that this plan will attract a sufficient number of members to form a critical mass to further change social policy. The Portable Benefits Network provides access to health insurance at group rates as well as disability and life insurance. This coverage is currently available to qualifying workers (such as freelance skilled computer users and new media workers) in the New York City area. The health insurance plan is a comprehensive health maintenance organization (HMO) offered through HIP Health Plan of New York. The monthly premiums for the September 1, 2001–August 31, 2002 coverage year were $242.25 for an individual, $434.07 for two persons (individual plus spouse or individual plus child), and $685.08 for a family.

With the more recent emphasis on portable benefits, Working Today no longer includes on its website the statement quoted earlier about linking organic associations and began emphasizing the practical advantages to organizations of joining the Working Today Portable Benefits Network. For example, as of September 2001, the website stated "a surefire way of at-

16. See http://www.workingtoday.org/about/05-01-03.php; accessed October 30, 2003.

17. See http://www.workingtoday.org/advocacy/advancing.html; accessed September 14, 2001.

tracting people to your organization is by making relevant, valuable benefits available."[18]

6.4 A Model of a Financially Viable Workers' Lobby

Working Today has survived by providing a mix of private goods and public goods. The private goods attract individual members, and the public goods, such as offering to be the spokesperson for the independent workforce, attract foundation grants. These two activities are closely linked to the organization's ability to raise funding. This section models the options for raising funds available to a new organization such as Working Today. I assume the founder must allocate resources between private goods efforts and public goods efforts. For specificity, I assume that the private good is health insurance at rates more attractive than available to individuals. However, the model applies more generally to any private good.

The workers' lobby engages in two types of activities, denoted by its expenditures X on private goods efforts and its expenditures Y on public goods efforts. The private good is group health insurance. The workers' lobby does not engage in underwriting insurance policies but instead serves as an intermediary between its members and the insurance company. The contribution of the lobby is forming a group that is eligible for health insurance priced at group rates. The private good is the principal benefit individuals receive from their affiliation. The number of organization members, N, is positively related to the private goods efforts, X. There are several measures a workers' lobby can take to increase membership, including widely advertising that group insurance may be available, holding seminars and educational events, soliciting insurance companies to offer coverage at attractive rates, and soliciting firms to encourage their employees to purchase insurance through the organization. The lobby reaps a net gain from this insurance underwriting given by $I(N[X], X)$.

The public goods expenditures, Y, are on activities that attract foundation funding other than through the insurance operation. These include activities such as lobbying, efforts to draw media attention to the organization, public dissemination of information, or efforts to elicit endorsements that will give the organization greater credibility. Working Today engages in various public goods activities, including lobbying politicians and maintaining a website with information on the legal status of independent workers and links to websites providing information about insurance options.

Foundation grants, F, depend positively on the level of public expenditures, Y, and the number of organization members, N. Each of these vari-

18. See http://64.49.223.100/about/intermediaries2.html; accessed September 4, 2001. This statement no longer appears on the Working Today website.

ables provides a signal that this is a viable organization meriting support and will consequently lead to greater foundation support.

Although the workers' lobby may be a nonprofit organization, for simplicity I model the effort as one that maximizes profits, π. Treating the lobby's objective as profit maximization is consistent with the demonstrable accomplishments to date of Working Today, which has largely consisted of raising revenues in order to provide private benefits rather than any observable impact on broader social objectives. The problem for the lobby is consequently to

$$(1) \qquad \max_{X,Y} \pi = F(Y, N[X]) + I(N[X], X) - X - Y,$$

leading to the first-order conditions that

$$(2) \qquad \pi_X = 0 = F_N N_X + I_N N_X + I_X - 1,$$

and

$$(3) \qquad \pi_Y = 0 = F_Y - 1.$$

Combining these two conditions and rearranging terms leads to

$$(4) \qquad F_Y = (F_N + I_N)N_X + I_X.$$

The marginal productivity of publicly visible efforts in boosting foundation support, which is the term on the left side of equation (4), equals the marginal productivity of the private goods, represented by the terms on the right side of equation (4). Additional expenditures on the private insurance operation have two classes of benefits. First, increasing X will raise the number of affiliated workers, N, which in turn will affect both foundation support, F, and gross revenues from insurance, I. One would expect that F_N is positive. A larger affiliated worker base should make the workers' lobby more attractive to foundations. Similarly, I_N should be positive as well to the extent that greater economies of scale in insurance underwriting and decreased problems of adverse selection makes the workers' lobby more profitable. The second component of the marginal efficiency of expenditures on insurance provision is the marginal effect on insurance operating profits, I_X. The sign of I_X is likely to be positive up to a certain point but eventually may become negative if, for example, increased expenditures on advertising fail to sufficiently increase the number of members. Typically the lobby will want a profitable insurance operation so will operate at the level where I_X is positive. But it will also be possible to offset losses in the insurance effort if doing so will raise the number of subscribers, N, sufficiently to attract additional foundation support.

This model highlights the departures of the Working Today model from Gans's (1993) original vision. The main choice variable is not political effort intended to promote social change but rather private goods provision and observable public activities intended to sustain and attract foundation funding. The source of funds is not workers as a whole but rather foundations that contribute to support the public good and workers who are subscribing to receive a well-defined private service.

6.5 The Market for Working Today's Health Benefits Plan

Provision of health insurance at group rates has been a key feature of many organizations, including AARP and many unions. Portable benefits, which follow workers as they move from job to job, have long been available to members of the Screen Actors Guild and those employed in the unionized construction industry. Recently, Amy Dean of the South Bay Labor Council in California instituted a portable benefits program for employees of the temporary agency she founded.

Thus, the concept of portable benefits for workers who move from job to job is not novel. Because of problems of adverse selection, it will not generally be profitable for insurers to offer health insurance to individuals at group rates. Insurers will enter the group health insurance market only if profitable; this means identifying a profitable group, which is generally formed by a company or some entity other than the insurer. Employees of large firms form a natural group for which group insurance pricing can be made actuarially attractive to insurers. The risks of moral hazard and adverse selection increase if the insurer cannot monitor the riskiness of the insured and if the costs to individuals of entry and exit from the group for the purposes of obtaining insurance are low.

The ultimate success of Working Today in achieving its broader vision relies first on its success in drawing members into its portable benefits plan to form a group that is attractive to insurers and second on energizing these participants to organize for additional policy changes. This section examines the likelihood that a broadly available portable health benefits plan will attract a sufficient number of members that are also desirable to insurers to form a critical mass to further change social policy.

The potential pool of workers for a portable benefits plan could be drawn from three groups: those currently uninsured; those currently buying insurance on their own who might switch plans; and those currently covered by their employer's plan who might switch to a noncovered work status, such as self-employment or part-time employment if they could obtain health insurance from another source at suitably attractive rates. Of course, whether workers will purchase insurance or switch coverage if offered a lower-cost option depends on the responsiveness of demand for insurance to changes in price. There is evidence that the demand for health insurance among the self-employed is price elastic so that lowering the price of health insurance increases the probability that self-employed individuals purchase insurance (Gruber and Poterba 1994). Whether other independent workers, particularly low-income or contingent workers, are likewise price sensitive is unknown.

Whether Working Today is able to generate participation in its Portable Benefits Network in part depends on whether the Working Today plan is a better "value" in terms of either quality of coverage and/or price, relative to the alternatives as well as whether uninsured workers feel coverage is worthwhile. Working Today faces competition for its target market of independent workers. First, coverage at a similar cost is available in the Working Today coverage area.[19] Second, lower-income workers who are sole proprietors, full-time or part-time employees, or employed on an episodic basis are eligible for reduced-cost coverage through the Healthy NY program. In particular, as of September 2001, the plan offered through Working Today is available to workers at a lower cost in the same coverage area.[20]

As independent and other nonstandard workers are the target market for the portable benefits plan, I use data from the February 1999 CPS Contingent Work Supplement to examine their coverage status and characteristics. This survey provides information on who is uninsured as well as demographic information that might suggest which of the uninsured are likely to be able to afford to purchase insurance through a new group plan. In addition to the information provided on the monthly CPS, the Contingent Work Supplements, which have been collected biennially since February 1995, provide data on workers in contingent and alternative work arrangements as well as information on health and pension coverage.

Workers are characterized as contingent if they hold jobs that are temporary or not expected to last for nonpersonal reasons. The CPS provides three estimates of the number of contingent workers, which ranged from 1.7 to 4.0 percent in 2001.[21] The narrowest definition refers to wage and salary workers with less than one year of tenure who expect their jobs to last less than one additional year. The broadest definition counts as contingent any wage and salary worker who does not expect their job to last indefinitely and includes the self-employed and independent contractors with less than one year of work experience as self-employed or as an independent contractor who expect to be in this arrangement for less than an additional year.

19. A search of http://www.ehealthinsurance.com (accessed September 14, 2001) reveals that the GHI Alliance Value Plan is similarly priced in the Working Today coverage area. The GHI plan is a preferred provider organization (PPO) rather than an HMO as offered by Working Today.

20. See http://www.ins.state.ny.us. Healthy NY is a statewide reduced-cost coverage plan that was introduced in New York after the passage of the Health Care Reform Act of 2000. The income limits for eligibility vary with family size. For example, the monthly income cap for a family of four is $3,678. The rates for the HIP Health Plan of New York through Healthy NY are $215.25 for an individual, $430.48 for two parents, $400.35 for parent and child(ren), and $658.44 for family coverage.

21. Reported in Contingent and Alternative Employment Arrangements, February 2001. Available at http://www.bls.gov/news.release/conemp.nr0.htm.

In addition to gathering information on contingent workers, the survey elicited supplemental information on workers in four types of alternative work arrangements: independent contractors (including consultants and freelancers), on-call workers, workers paid by a temporary agency ("temps"), and contract workers. Whether a worker is self-employed is reported in the main CPS survey as is whether a worker works part-time.

I consider the following groups: independent contractors and the self-employed, temporary agency workers, part-time workers, and contingent workers (using the broadest CPS definition of contingent.) Because 88 percent of the independent contractors are self-employed, I combine independent contractors and the self-employed into one group. I also define a "traditional" category that excludes any worker who is contingent, in any alternative arrangement, or works part-time.[22] Under this broad definition, about one-third of the workforce is nontraditional and corresponds to the intended constituency of Working Today. The traditional category is disjoint from the four other categories, and independent contractors and the self-employed are disjoint from temporary agency workers. But these workers may be part-time and/or contingent, and part-time workers may also be contingent.

Of particular importance for this study is information on whether a worker is covered by health insurance and the source of health insurance. This information is available for all employed persons who responded to the supplement. Wage and salary workers were asked if they were insured through their employer's plan and if they were not covered, whether they were eligible for coverage. Insured wage and salary workers who were not covered by their employer were asked the source of their coverage. Self-employed workers were not asked whether their insurance was provided by their employer but were asked the source, with "received through company/work" one of the options.

The CPS includes information on a range of demographic and labor market characteristics that influence insurance coverage, including age, education, marital status, race, hours worked, family income, and earnings. The regular CPS survey includes information on earnings of wage and salary workers in the outgoing rotations (about one-quarter of the sample). Earnings for self-employed workers are not reported in the regular CPS survey. However, the Contingent Work Supplements also request earnings information for all contingent workers and workers in alternative arrangements, including the self-employed, thus providing information on a much larger sample of self-employed and nonstandard workers than would otherwise be available.

22. The survey also requested information for workers in three other alternative arrangements: day laborers, on-call workers, and contract employees. These workers are likewise excluded from the traditional worker category.

The statistics in tables 6.1 and 6.2 exclude respondents who did not provide information on their health coverage status as well as workers aged sixty-five and older as such workers will be eligible for Medicare. For the sample who report earnings, I also restrict the analysis to workers with weekly earnings greater than $25. These restrictions resulted in a sample of 50,126 respondents with information on their health benefit status, with 20,237 also reporting weekly earnings.

The first question is which worker groups are likely to have health insurance coverage, and what is their source of coverage? Table 6.1 presents statistics on health insurance coverage rates and the source of coverage by work arrangement. Traditional employees have the highest coverage rate at 86.6 percent. The coverage rates for independent contractors and the self-employed is also high at 75.7 percent. It is perhaps surprising that part-time and contingent workers also have high coverage rates that are 74 percent and 64.6 percent, respectively. Only temporary agency workers have insurance coverage rates markedly below that of traditional workers, with 41.5 percent covered from some source. As table 6.1 demonstrates, the vast majority of traditional employees with coverage—83 percent—are covered under their employers' plan. Relatively few nontraditional workers are covered under their employers' plan. Over half of the independent contractors and the self-employed are covered either by directly purchasing insurance on their own or through their company. Among those with coverage, temporary, part-time, and contingent workers are more likely to be

Table 6.1 **Health coverage status and work arrangement**

	Independent contractor/ self-employed	Temporary	Part-time	Contingent	Traditional
Work arrangement					
Has health insurance (%)	75.7	41.5	74.0	64.6	86.6
Percent of sample	10.7	0.8	21.5	4.1	67.4
Sample size	5,376	419	10,787	2,045	33,786
Source if covered					
Employer (%)	1.6	21.8	28.9	33.2	82.8
Spouse/family member (%)	35.6	42.5	50.9	43.6	12.6
Company/work (%)	24.2	0	2.5	0.9	0
Buy (%)	28.8	11.5	8.1	6.9	1.5
Other[a]	9.7	24.1	9.7	15.3	3.1

Source: Author's calculations from the 1999 Contingent Work Supplement.

Notes: The categories of traditional, independent contractors and self-employed, and temporary agency workers are mutually exclusive. Workers in other nonstandard arrangements such as on-call workers are not included in this table. Independent workers, self-employed, and temporary agency workers may also be part-time and/or contingent.

[a]Other sources of coverage are other job, previous job, Medicare, Medicaid, labor union, association or club, school or university, and any other source.

Table 6.2 Characteristics of workers by health coverage status and work arrangement

	Independent contractor/ self-employed	Temporary	Part-time	Contingent	Traditional
Without health insurance					
Male (%)	68.0	44.5	43.7	55.3	58.8
Age	41.2	33.1	33.6	32.5	34.9
	(10.8)	(10.8)	(12.6)	(11.4)	(11.2)
Education	12.9	12.6	12.5	12.7	12.0
	(2.6)	(2.3)	(2.5)	(3.0)	(2.8)
Married (%)	57.2	24.5	36.1	31.4	43.6
White (%)	88.5	73.5	82.0	79.5	81.7
Black (%)	6.2	22.4	13.1	13.8	12.7
Hispanic (%)	10.9	14.7	13.8	19.1	21.9
Weekly earnings	578.9	358.2	303.6	335.6	422.2
	(526.7)	(253.8)	(362.9)	(329.3)	(291.9)
Family income (× 1,000)	35.3	26.7	31.0	28.0	31.0
	(23.2)	(20.9)	(23.0)	(22.4)	(20.6)
Household size	3.1	3.1	3.3	3.2	3.3
	(1.7)	(1.5)	(1.7)	(1.6)	(1.6)
Sample size	1,308	245	2,803	723	4,535
With health insurance					
Male (%)	64.4	36.2	37.2	44.8	53.9
Age	45.0	36.9	36.4	33.9	40.2
	(10.3)	(12.8)	(14.0)	(13.0)	(10.8)
Education	14.3	13.5	13.4	14.2	13.9
	(2.8)	(2.2)	(2.6)	(2.8)	(2.6)
Married (%)	79.1	50.0	56.7	45.9	64.5
White (%)	93.0	80.5	90.0	84.3	86.3
Black (%)	3.1	14.9	6.1	7.9	9.2
Hispanic (%)	3.1	8.0	4.9	6.4	6.9
Weekly earnings	784.4	488.0	408.5	423.2	703.7
	(682.1)	(419.9)	(494.1)	(447.8)	(455.5)
Family income (× 1,000)	56.0	42.9	49.6	46.5	51.7
	(23.1)	(25.6)	(24.0)	(24.6)	(22.1)
Household size	3.1	3.0	3.3	3.2	3.0
	(1.4)	(1.6)	(1.4)	(1.6)	(1.4)
Sample size	4,068	174	7,984	1,322	29,251

Source: Author's calculations from the 1999 Continent Work Supplement.
Note: Figures in parentheses are standard deviations.

covered under a family member's policy than to be covered by an employer or to buy insurance on their own or through their company.

To understand some of the sources of variation in coverage rates, table 6.2 presents summary statistics for demographic characteristics and earnings, displayed both by work arrangement and by health coverage status. As shown by table 6.2, the characteristics of workers vary widely by type of work arrangement and by health insurance coverage. Among workers in the same type of work arrangement, uninsured workers are younger, less educated, less likely to be married, and have considerably lower earnings and family incomes than their insured counterparts. Independent contractors and the self-employed are more likely to be white, male, married, and older, and to have higher earnings, relative to workers in traditional arrangements and relative to contingent, temporary, or part-time workers. But part-time and contingent workers who also have high coverage rates are, on average, relatively young with low earnings. Temporary agency workers who have a low coverage rate on average are more likely to be black, Hispanic, female, and younger.

What do these results suggest about the potential pool of workers for a portable benefits plan? As table 6.1 demonstrates, coverage rates for all but temporary agency workers are fairly high, with many workers who are not covered by their employer covered through a family member. Many of the self-employed and independent contractors buy insurance through their company or work; such workers may already be participating in a group health plan available to small businesses. As table 6.2 demonstrates, workers with health insurance from any source earn more and are better educated than the uninsured in the same work status. Earnings among the uninsured workers, on average, are sufficiently low that these workers may continue to remain uninsured even if lower-cost health insurance is available. For example, with the exception of the self-employed and independent contractors, the monthly premium for a family of four under the Working Today plan costs about half the gross monthly earnings of all uninsured workers. Further, there is evidence that despite the lower coverage rate among the self-employed, they are as healthy as wage earners based on both objective and subjective measures of health status (Perry and Rosen 2001). This finding suggests that many workers may feel that insurance is unnecessary.

6.6 The Role of a Lobby for Nontraditional Workers

In forming Working Today, Sara Horowitz's original mission was to provide a unified voice to speak for all workers, especially independent workers. This section summarizes policy areas that affect nontraditional workers that might be influenced by the efforts of a workers' lobby.

The argument that independent and other nonstandard workers need a collective voice and a new form of representation stems from the view that there has been a large-scale shift in the structure of the economy and that the existing labor market structure and political institutions do not serve the needs of the current labor force. As I discuss in the following, workers in nonstandard work arrangements frequently are not protected under existing employment laws. They are also less likely to stay in long-term arrangements with employers from whom they would receive benefits typically requiring waiting periods, such as health insurance or pensions.

A variety of legal rules create a potentially important role for a workers' lobby seeking to provide legal protection and benefits to nonstandard workers. First, the Wagner Act gives the National Labor Relations Board the right to determine the appropriate bargaining unit. The level of such units has generally been interpreted as a single work site.[23] The interpretation of "employee" is also narrow and excludes about half of the workforce from being considered an employee under the National Labor Relations Act.

Second, whether nonstandard workers are covered by employer health or pension plans varies. Employers may exempt part-time workers from health care benefits provided to their full-time employees. Temporary and contract workers are paid by an agency that has a contract with employers and receive benefits, if at all, from the agency that employs them. Self-employed workers, including self-employed independent contractors, pay for their own health insurance and set up their own pension plans.

Third, unemployment insurance and the Family and Medical Leave Act have hours thresholds for eligibility, often making it difficult for nonstandard workers to qualify for protection. Even if they qualify, it is more difficult to enforce and monitor these laws for nonstandard workers, and such workers are less likely to be informed of their rights.

Fourth, whether nonstandard workers are covered under employment discrimination laws is not always well defined. Title VII of the Civil Rights Act prohibits employers with at least fifteen employees, employment agencies, and unions from discriminatory employment practices. However, whether firms are required to comply with employment discrimination laws with respect to their temporary employees is unclear. Companies using agency temps, leased employees, or contract company workers may have obligations under labor and employment laws, since even if they are not the employer they may have "joint employer" status. For example, an individual can be an independent contractor for Internal Revenue Service (IRS) purposes but an employee under antidiscrimination laws.

6.7 Evaluating the Impact and Prospects of Working Today

Working Today has evolved from an organization offering to provide a voice for workers to an organization that provides a well-defined private good. Its success in achieving broader social objectives in part depends on the organization's visibility. Although not a household name, Horowitz has received some highly visible media coverage, including articles in the *New York Times, Boston Globe,* and the *Los Angeles Times.* In 1999 Horowitz was named a MacArthur Foundation Fellow, receiving a grant of $275,000. The media attention following this award likewise brought visibility to Working

23. The success of the Service Employees International Union in gaining representation in 2000 for 74,000 Los Angeles County home-care workers demonstrates that unionization is not limited to a single worksite.

Today. The extent of media coverage indicates not only public interest in the organization's agenda but also the scope of the organization in raising public awareness and changing public perceptions. It is also a mechanism to maintain visibility and gain funding from foundations and from potential individual members.

Success in influencing legislative change is perhaps the most important indicator of success but also the hardest to quantify because it will rarely be possible to identify whether any such change is a direct consequence of the organization's efforts. Working Today reports that their lobbying efforts have had concrete results, noting "in 1999 we convinced Senators Kennedy and Torricelli to call for a GAO study into the size and needs of the independent workforce. Also, in 2000 we successfully worked with the Pataki administration to insure that low-income independent workers be covered by insurance plans created by New York's Health Care Reform Act."[24]

Currently, Working Today's continued survival is closely linked to its portable benefits plan now available to a narrow sector of the labor force—workers in New York's Silicon Alley. If the Portable Benefits Plan proves successful and cost-effective when applied to new media workers in New York, it will provide a new example of portable health benefits outside of the union framework employed in the unionized construction industry and by the Screen Actors Guild. This demonstration may serve an important social goal and demonstrate to private insurers that a profitable group insurance market exists among independent workers.

But it is not clear that the Working Today health insurance plan will be attractive to a large number of members. First, even at group rates, the rates are high enough to discourage participation among lower-income and part-time workers. Working Today notes that only a small fraction of its members participated in the health insurance plan it offered to members since the organization was formed. This plan was available through a partnership with the National Writers Union and provided access to insurance at group rates with Aetna U.S. Healthcare.[25] Eight years later, Working Today reports only 2,000 members of the Freelancers Union who are eligible for group insurance policies through Working Today.[26] Unless the new portable benefits plan can be made sufficiently less expensive, the number of participants is unlikely to increase dramatically.

Second, many of the targeted independent workers are young enough that they forgo health insurance out of either a rational or erroneous belief that health insurance is not economically valuable at their age, and evidence that health status does not differ among the self-employed and wage earners suggests their belief may be rational (Perry and Rosen 2001).

24. See http://64.49.223.100/advocacy/joiningtogether.html; accessed September 4, 2001.

25. Working Today proposal for the New York New Media Portable Benefits Fund, 3 (undated).

26. See http://www.workingtoday.org/about/05-01-03.php; accessed October 30, 2003.

Third, although it is premature to evaluate the success of the Portable Benefits Fund/Freelancers Union after only two years, it is not clear that the adverse selection problem will be solved by a broad-based insurance plan available to all nonstandard workers. Even under the best-case scenario, the administrative and monitoring costs incurred in trying to lower the risk pool and avoid adverse selection are unlikely to lead to insurance premiums that will be affordable to low-income workers, part-time workers, or contingent workers more generally.

But for Working Today, a successful portable benefits plan is only a starting point. The overriding objective is to use access to portable benefits to form a constituency to push for a larger set of portable rights. The viability of Working Today requires that a sufficient number of workers participate in the portable benefits plan and that these workers go on to push for the other components of the Working Today social agenda. Whether Working Today offers a compelling mission remains to be seen. There has been only a small increase in membership eight years after founding, with membership increasing from 700 in May 1996 to 2,000 in May 2003. Even if Working Today's mission is sufficiently compelling to large numbers of independent workers, any efforts to form a new social movement must overcome the declining interest in civic affairs as observed by Robert Putman (2000). But without a social agenda and the membership to support the agenda, it is unlikely that foundations would continue to provide funding.

The prospects of Working Today as a large scale intermediary for health insurance surfaced in conjunction with the devastating events of September 11, 2001. As described in an article in the *New York Times,* the September 11th Fund, which raised money to help victims, wished to provide health insurance to 15,000 people who had lost jobs or had a reduction in income because of the attacks.[27] Working Today seemed to be uniquely positioned to provide group health insurance to such individuals, and a large pool of prospective subscribers potentially provides Working Today with the means to demonstrate the viability of its insurance concept. The *New York Times* article reports that Working Today now has almost 1,000 subscribers. It remains unclear, however, whether the post–September 11 opportunity will be sufficient to jumpstart Working Today into a significant force in the insurance market.

6.8 The Prospects of a Broad-Based Workers' Lobby

There are a number of labor market institutions that are involved in enforcing and administering labor policies. In addition to traditional unions, these institutions include legal service organizations such as the American

27. Stephanie Strom, "Group Health Insurance Offered to Freelancers: A New Focus on Overlooked Workers," *New York Times,* October 2, 2002, A28.

Civil Liberties Union (ACLU) and other legal services centers (as described in Jolls, chap. 4 in this volume), mandated workplace committees, and alternative dispute resolution systems. There are also a vast number of service organizations that exist to help workers, with many organizations involved in improving the well-being of lower-income or lower-skilled individuals. Examples of such organizations include community groups such as Living Wage campaigns and Industrial Areas Foundations. Professional organizations also provide a variety of services to their members that sometimes include lobbying activities. Examples of professional organizations with demonstrated success in lobbying include the National Writers Union and WashTech. Thus, any new lobby would need to fill a void not met by existing labor market institutions or organizations. The void identified by Gans (1993) was a lack of a unified voice to speak for all workers.

The viability of any broad-based workers' lobby requires that funding is maintained. There are three sources of funding: individuals who feel their working lives would improve through the efforts of such a lobby and pay membership dues; existing organizations who feel they would benefit from becoming linked with a central organization and contribute to this central group; and foundations that provide grant funds. But it is doubtful that a single workers' organization could speak for the interests of all workers or even all nonstandard workers. While there are vast differences among conventional employees, the disparities among nonstandard workers may be even greater. The types of skills and the pay of such workers runs the gamut, from highly skilled and paid professionals, such as Microsoft's army of long-term temps, to day laborers. As such, attempting to find a common ground among workers with seemingly little in common appears unduly optimistic. For example, most temporary workers will have little in common with Microsoft permatemps, and labor legislation that improves their status may appear discriminatory against permanent employees. In contrast to their regularly employed exempt counterparts, temporary agency employers are eligible for overtime pay.

It seems likely that having a well-defined constituency with common interests will enhance an organization's success. Most successful worker groups are defined more narrowly by occupation (such as WashTech or the National Writers Union) or by income or training level (such as those targeted by Industrial Areas Foundations and the Wisconsin Regional Training Partnership), and it is not obvious that they would gain by linking to a central organization such as Working Today. In addition to its powerful voting bloc represented by its membership, the AARP's influence derives by focusing on specific issues such as Social Security and Medicare. Thus organizations with a broader membership base with diffuse interests may ultimately be less influential in changing policy.

For any workers' lobby to survive it may likewise be necessary to take the approach of Working Today and provide private goods, such as group health insurance. Although Common Cause thrived without providing selective benefits, provision of private goods was essential to the success of AARP. Ultimately there may not be a viable market niche for a general workers' lobby. What does seem clear at this juncture is that Gans's vision of a broadly based workers' lobby does not appear promising. Rather, success is likely to come through narrowing the substantive focus of the concern to private benefits.

References

Freeman, Richard B., and James Medoff. 1984. *What do unions do?* New York: Basic Books.

Gans, Herbert J. 1993. Time for an employees' lobby. *Social Policy* 24 (Winter): 35–38.

Gruber, Jonathan, and James Poterba. 1994. Tax incentives and the decision to purchase health insurance: Evidence from the self-employed. *Quarterly Journal of Economics* 109 (3): 701–33.

Hirschman, Albert O. 1982. *Shifting involvements: Private interest and public action.* Princeton: Princeton University Press.

Jenkins, J. Craig. 1998. Channeling social protest: Foundation patronage of contemporary social movements. In *Private action and the public good,* ed. Walter W. Powell and Elisabeth S. Clemens, 206–16. New Haven, Conn.: Yale University Press.

McFarland, Andrew S. 1984. *Common cause: Lobbying in the public interest.* Chatham, N.J.: Chatham House Publishers.

Morris, Charles R. 1996. *The AARP: America's most powerful lobby and the clash of the generations.* New York: Times Books.

Olson, Mancur. 1965. *The logic of collective action.* Cambridge, Mass.: Harvard University Press.

Perry, Craig William, and Harvey S. Rosen. 2001. The self-employed are less likely to have health insurance than wage-earners. So what? NBER Working Paper no. 8316. Cambridge, Mass.: National Bureau of Economic Research, June.

Putman, Robert D. 2000. *Bowling alone: The collapse and revival of American community.* New York: Simon and Schuster.

Truman, David. 1951. *The governmental process.* New York: Alfred A. Knopf.

Van Atta, Dale. 1998. *Trust betrayed: Inside the AARP.* Washington, D.C.: Regnery Publishers.

Walker, Jack L. 1991. *Mobilizing interest groups in America: Patrons, professions, and social movements.* Ann Arbor: University of Michigan Press.

III

New Union Opportunities and Initiatives

7

A Submerging Labor Market Institution?
Unions and the Nonwage Aspects of Work

Thomas C. Buchmueller, John E. DiNardo, and Robert G. Valletta

Our understanding of emerging labor market institutions would be incomplete without an understanding of traditional institutions, including apparently diminishing forms such as the American labor union. Our focus in this paper—the effect of labor unions on a variety of nonwage aspects of work—is a small, yet important, aspect of the recent history of American unionism.

The importance of nonwage aspects of jobs to union goals dates back to the origins of the modern labor movement in the United States and other countries. For example, in late nineteenth-century Britain, according to Sidney and Beatrice Webb, "the prospect of securing support in sickness or unemployment [was] a greater inducement [for young men] to join the union . . . than the less obvious advantages to be gained by the trade combination" (Webb and Webb 1897, 158). Similarly, in the United States, to take a prominent example, the American Federation of Labor's resolution that "eight hours shall constitute a legal day's labor from and after May 1st, 1886" was one impetus for the Haymarket Rebellion—an event which is still commemorated in much of the world as International Worker's Day.

Although unions have demonstrated a historical commitment to non-

Thomas C. Buchmueller is a research associate at the National Bureau of Economic Research and associate professor in the Graduate School of Management at the University of California, Irvine. John E. DiNardo is a research associate at the National Bureau of Economic Research and professor of economics and public policy at the University of Michigan, Ann Arbor. Robert G. Valletta is a research advisor at the Federal Reserve Bank of San Francisco. The opinions in this paper are those of the authors and do not represent the views of the Federal Reserve Bank of San Francisco or the Federal Reserve System. The authors would like to thank Janice Hu for valuable research assistance and Eli Berman for comments on a previous draft.

wage aspects of jobs, union goals and impacts may have changed as union density and influence have declined. Using data from a variety of databases, we investigate the following questions: How do the nonwage aspects of union jobs differ from those of nonunion jobs? Have these differences changed during the past several decades? We first document and describe differences in hours worked in union and nonunion jobs. We then provide an updated assessment of union impacts on the provision of various fringe benefits, addressed for an earlier period in various studies (most comprehensively by Freeman and Medoff 1984).

7.1 Background

If only a single bit of context is to be highlighted about the role of today's unions, surely it is the decline in union representation. The fraction of workers currently represented by a labor union is at roughly the same level as it was *before* the passage of the National Labor Relations (Wagner) Act in 1935. The Wagner Act declared that it was U.S. policy "to eliminate the causes of certain substantial obstructions to the free flow of commerce and to mitigate and eliminate these obstructions when they have occurred by encouraging the practice and procedure of collective bargaining" (see the National Labor Relations Board website at http://www.nlrb.gov). After a rapid spurt of growth between 1935 and 1945, unionization rates remained roughly level until the late 1950s. Since the 1960s, unionization rates have fallen almost continuously.[1]

Following the publication of Lewis (1963), a comprehensive study of union/nonunion wage gaps, years of subsequent research provided ample quantitative evidence of wage premia associated with unionization. As to benefits, a simple summary of the findings in the review by Freeman and Medoff (1984) is that ceteris paribus, union jobs provide more generous benefits. Current union density, however, is about half as large as it was at that time, which raises the possibility that union impacts on benefit provision may have changed as well.

Some indirect evidence regarding possibly changing union impacts on benefits comes from recent work on the causes of rising wage inequality (Bound and Johnson 1992; Katz and Murphy 1992; Autor and Katz 2000; Levy and Murnane 1992; Card, Lemieux, and Riddell 2003). Unionization has traditionally been an equalizing influence, reducing both inequality *between* groups with different demographic characteristics and inequality *within* demographically homogeneous groups. Unions have typically reduced between inequality by raising the relative pay of groups with low

1. Although it might be tempting to predict continued declines, the certainty of such a forecast should be tempered by the striking similarity of the recent time series path of unionization to that in 1935. In particular, despite years of decline prior to the Wagner Act, during the subsequent ten years the union membership rate doubled.

earnings; for example, unionization rates typically are higher among the less educated. Given this equalizing effect of unions, declining unionization might be expected to increase between inequality, and the evidence bears this out.[2] Because unions also tend to compress pay schedules within groups, a decline in the power of unions to affect wages also should lead to increased within-group inequality. Indeed, deunionization has coincided with an increase in *within* inequality not only because fewer workers are covered but also because the distribution of wages in the union sector increasingly resembles that of the nonunion sector (DiNardo and Lemieux 1997). That is, the ability of unions to minimize differences in wages between demographically similar workers has declined. The changing impact of unions on the wage distribution suggests the possibility of changing union impacts on nonwage aspects of jobs as well.

7.2 Union Effects on Hours of Work

Comparatively little has been written about union/nonunion differences in hours worked for employed individuals. Neither of Lewis's (1963, 1986) comprehensive surveys address the issue at any length; the same is true for more broadly focused summaries of research on labor unions (Freeman and Medoff 1984; Hirsch and Addison 1986), although Freeman and Medoff investigate the cyclical sensitivity of union employment (see Raisian [1979] for a similar focus). Killingsworth's (1983) extensive survey makes no mention of labor supplied in the presence of unionization. Earle and Pencavel (1990) examine the question with the 1978 Current Population Survey (CPS) and time series data. They find conflicting evidence—negative union impacts on full-time hours worked in time series data but positive union effects on total hours worked for some groups (white male laborers and women) in the cross section. In contrast to their cross-section findings, Trejo (1993) found negative union impacts on hours worked using 1985 CPS data. The most comprehensive study of the question across Organization for Economic Cooperation and Development (OECD) countries is Blanchflower (1996) who found, inter alia, that unions reduce total hours of work in the full set of OECD countries analyzed.

The most severe obstacle to such an analysis is the comparatively poor quality of information on hours worked. Moreover, a fuller analysis would incorporate related aspects of time use, such as commuting time. Unfortunately, we are unaware of any data set that allows for a comparison across time in hours worked of the same quality (and quantity) as, say, the wage data in the CPS.

2. See DiNardo, Fortin, and Lemieux (1996); Card (1992); and Freeman (1993) for the United States and Gosling and Machin (1995) for the United Kingdom.

7.2.1 The Economics of Hours Reductions

Before turning to our empirical analysis, it is helpful to motivate why one might see differences in hours worked between the union and nonunion sectors. The textbook monopoly union model generally is silent regarding the effect of unionization on hours worked, treating hours per worker as fixed, and focusing on the number of workers employed. In this type of model the main consequence of unionization is lower employment.

By contrast, in efficient contract models (Brown and Ashenfelter 1986; MaCurdy and Pencavel 1986) the relationship between the union and the firm is oriented around rent sharing. In these models, the union maximizes the joint revenue of the firm and the workers—the wage is merely an artifact of the division of this revenue between the two groups. In appendix A we present a version of the efficient contract model to motivate the possible economic logic of a difference in hours worked between union and nonunion workers. Our intent is not to test an obviously simplistic model of union hours determination.[3] Instead, we use the model to highlight one possible trade-off that employers and union workers face in collective bargaining—the trade-off between a larger number of members splitting smaller shares of the "economic pie" versus fewer members with larger shares. This trade-off arises because increases in labor supplied to firms can come either through an increase in the number of workers employed or an increase in hours worked per employee. As derived in the model, compared to a nonunion setting, an optimal union contract typically results in (1) fewer hours per worker and (2) union members being constrained to work fewer hours than they would like to at the negotiated wage rate (despite being better off as union members than as nonmembers).

In the model, the magnitude of these effects will depend on the extent to which the wage-setting process differs between the union and nonunion settings. The more union wage setting resembles wage setting in the "competitive" sector (the smaller the difference between union member utility and the nonunion alternative), the smaller is the hours differential and the less "constrained" is the union hours outcome. Thus, given the decline in the level of unionization in the United States and the implied decline in union power, it may be reasonable to expect the size of the union effect to decline over time as well.

7.2.2 The Data

Our analysis of the impact of unions on hours worked relies on two data sources. The Current Population Survey (CPS) is the federal government's

3. Booth (1995), among others, has argued that tests of efficient contract models, such as those employed in Brown and Ashenfelter (1986), are flawed because it is not possible to empirically distinguish between the monopoly union and efficient contracting views using data on employment and wages. She notes that in the absence of such a test, a "pragmatic approach" would rely on studying the texts of collective bargaining agreements instead.

monthly survey of about 60,000 households, which provides information on labor force activities, earnings, and related variables for a rotating cross section designed to be representative of the U.S. population. We use data from the Annual Demographic Supplement (March) to the monthly CPS, which provides information on income and work hours during the complete calendar year preceding the survey. We also use data from the Panel Study of Income Dynamics (PSID), a panel study of 5,000 families initiated in 1968. Each year, the original sample of families and their "splitoffs" (for example, children who leave to form their own households) are reinterviewed; sample attrition has been relatively limited over time, and new families are added when necessary to keep the sample approximately representative of the nation as a whole.[4]

Relative to the March CPS data, the PSID has some unique advantages and disadvantages in regard to estimating the effect of union status on hours worked.

The main advantage of the PSID is its collection of information that provides a complete yearly calendar for each individual; this calendar indicates the total amount of weeks spent at work, on vacation, unemployed, on strike, or away from work due to personal illness or the illness of a family member. Despite some ambiguity in the questions, the response accuracy is enhanced through the survey requirement that the interviewer readminister the questions until the responses add up to fifty-two. This is important given the well-known problems of measurement error in data on hours and weeks worked.[5]

In contrast, the March CPS includes "paid" vacation as part of weeks "worked." This complicates use of the CPS in several ways. Consider a person with two weeks' paid vacation (and no unpaid vacation time). The estimate of annual hours is fifty-two times average hours per week, instead of fifty times average hours per week. Arguably, use of the March CPS leads to systematic underreporting of the hours differential if vacation time is more generous for union workers (as we document in the following, this appears to be the case).

A main disadvantage of the PSID is inconsistency across respondents in their answers to the question regarding "average hours per week"—some respondents appear to base their answer on a "typical" work week rather than a true average. Other problems in the PSID include the comparatively small size of the sample, the lack of information on nonhousehold heads, and the lack of statistical dependence in successive years of data for each panel member.[6]

In the following analyses, we use PSID data for the years 1972–1992 and

4. To enhance our sample's representation of the general U.S. population, we do not include the low-income oversample in the analyses below.

5. See Bound and Krueger (1991) for one illustration.

6. For example, we restrict our analyses to men because most of the detailed information on work time is not available for the "wife" of the household.

CPS data for the years 1983–1997. Although our preference was for an exact match of sample years for both sources, our choice was dictated by data availability constraints in the PSID.[7]

7.2.3 Methodology

An important aspect of the hours data that we analyze in this section is that it is either multimodal (often at 0 and another value) or otherwise distributed in a way that precludes the use of straightforward regression techniques to characterize the conditional distribution. Olson (1998) faced a similar problem in his study of the effects of health insurance on hours worked and found that conventional regression estimates tend to produce misleading results.

Following Olson (1998) and Buchmueller, DiNardo, and Valletta (2002), we apply the reweighting techniques from DiNardo, Fortin, and Lemieux (1996) to adjust the union and nonunion distribution for differences in worker characteristics. That is, we adjust the average hours of a typical worker relative to some base set of characteristics, specifically the characteristics of a typical worker in 1992. This technique, which relies on the estimation of "conditioning weights," allows us to estimate the conditional impact of unionism on hours worked without imposing any misleading distributional assumptions on the data; appendix B describes this method in detail. Stated simply, given our data structure, it is easier to estimate the relationship between union status and related variables and use this relationship to adjust the hours data rather than applying the flexible functional forms needed to directly estimate the conditional impact of union status on hours worked. In the case where our estimated conditioning weights are based on a partition of discrete groups (such as union and nonunion workers), our procedure amounts to calculating simple differences in means for the various groups and then appropriately weighting them to form an overall average. This can be viewed as an application of propensity score weighting as in Rosenbaum and Rubin (1983). We apply this technique to estimate union/nonunion differences for each of the hours measured discussed in this section and listed in tables 7.1–7.5. As discussed in more detail in the appendix, we use a complete set of race dummies, school dummies, marital status dummies, standard metropolitan statistical area (SMSA) dummies, and a cubic in age as explanatory variables for the PSID data. For the CPS data we use five education categories, five age categories, an SMSA dummy, three regional dummies, marital status, and three race categories.

7. We assume that the design changes in the CPS questionnaire after 1993 are ignorable in the context of our analyses.

7.2.4 Results

Hours

Our estimates of the union impact on "average weekly hours" (PSID) and "usual weekly hours" (CPS) are presented in tables 7.1 and 7.2. The first column of table 7.1 lists the mean hours for nonunion workers in a given year in the PSID, *calculated as if they had the characteristics of union workers in the 1992 sample.* The second column lists the mean for union workers in a given year, also calculated as if they had the characteristics of union workers in 1992; our estimate for 1992 union workers, therefore, is the unadjusted mean from the data (using the appropriate population weights). The third column in the table lists the differences between the first two columns; under our estimation procedure, this represents the effect on nonunion status on hours worked, conditional on a set of covariates used to estimate the conditioning weights (we include controls for a standard set of individual characteristics; see the end of appendix B for a complete list). The format for the CPS results is similar. Figures 7.1 and 7.2 display the PSID and CPS results (first two columns) graphically.

Considering the PSID estimates first, in almost all years union workers work fewer hours per week than do nonunion workers; during the years 1972–1984, this difference is about three hours per week. After 1984 the differential begins falling, and by 1992 the situation is reversed, with union workers estimated to work about one hour more per week than nonunion workers. However, the standard errors listed in these tables indicate that the union/nonunion differences generally are not statistically significant after 1984.[8]

In table 7.2, we present results based on the CPS data, again using the 1992 union worker as our basis of comparison. The estimates for nonunion workers (appropriately weighted) hover around 42.2 hours per week, and the estimates for union workers are approximately 0.5 hours per week lower. By comparison with the PSID results, the CPS-based estimates of usual weekly hours for nonunion workers are slightly higher in general, although the differential between the two sectors is relatively constant.[9]

The differences between the PSID and CPS estimates could arise from a number of sources. Part of the difference is surely differences in the wording of the questionnaires as well as sampling error due to the comparatively small size of the PSID. Another salient difference is that with both data sets

8. The standard errors listed probably understate the true sampling errors because they were not adjusted for the uncertainty generated by estimation of the conditioning weights nor for the nonindependence of multiple observations per individual in the PSID data.

9. Although problems of sample selectivity and limitations of scope preclude an extensive analysis here, the relationship between union and nonunion workers is reversed when women are included in the sample (Earle and Pencavel 1990).

Table 7.1 **Mean average hours per week for men with characteristics of 1992 union workers (PSID data)**

Year	Nonunion	Union	Difference
1972	45.16	41.95	3.20
	(0.29)	(0.43)	(0.52)
1973	45.43	42.61	2.81
	(0.27)	(0.41)	(0.49)
1974	45.09	41.82	3.26
	(0.26)	(0.34)	(0.43)
1975	44.89	38.82	6.07
	(0.29)	(0.43)	(0.52)
1976	44.67	40.70	3.97
	(0.28)	(0.38)	(0.47)
1977	44.57	39.60	4.98
	(0.27)	(0.44)	(0.51)
1978	44.39	41.54	2.85
	(0.26)	(0.31)	(0.40)
1979	44.17	41.20	2.97
	(0.26)	(0.34)	(0.43)
1980	44.02	40.21	3.81
	(0.26)	(0.37)	(0.45)
1981	44.00	41.27	2.73
	(0.25)	(0.37)	(0.45)
1982	44.31	40.52	3.79
	(0.23)	(0.41)	(0.47)
1983	44.04	40.32	3.72
	(0.23)	(0.39)	(0.46)
1984	43.71	40.73	2.98
	(0.23)	(0.41)	(0.47)
1985	42.99	41.39	1.60
	(0.27)	(0.37)	(0.46)
1986	42.54	42.65	–0.10
	(0.27)	(0.25)	(0.37)
1987	42.57	42.20	0.38
	(0.27)	(0.33)	(0.43)
1988	42.71	41.75	0.96
	(0.26)	(0.36)	(0.45)
1989	42.56	41.44	1.11
	(0.25)	(0.43)	(0.50)
1990	42.31	42.92	–0.61
	(0.25)	(0.35)	(0.43)
1991	41.98	42.68	–0.70
	(0.25)	(0.37)	(0.45)
1992	41.86	42.92	–1.06
	(0.25)	(0.41)	(0.48)

Notes: Standard errors in parentheses. For description of counterfactual weights see text.

Table 7.2 **Mean average hours per week for men with characteristics of 1997 union workers (CPS data)**

Year	Nonunion	Union	Difference
1983	41.33	40.50	0.83
	(0.04)	(0.04)	(0.06)
1984	41.67	41.03	0.64
	(0.03)	(0.05)	(0.06)
1985	41.82	41.15	0.66
	(0.03)	(0.05)	(0.06)
1986	41.81	41.21	0.60
	(0.03)	(0.05)	(0.06)
1987	42.02	41.37	0.65
	(0.03)	(0.05)	(0.06)
1988	42.05	41.46	0.58
	(0.04)	(0.05)	(0.07)
1989	42.21	41.57	0.63
	(0.04)	(0.06)	(0.07)
1990	42.19	41.47	0.71
	(0.03)	(0.05)	(0.06)
1991	41.88	41.28	0.60
	(0.04)	(0.06)	(0.07)
1992	41.84	41.41	0.43
	(0.04)	(0.06)	(0.07)
1993	41.94	41.61	0.34
	(0.04)	(0.06)	(0.07)
1994	42.15	41.56	0.59
	(0.04)	(0.07)	(0.08)
1995	42.20	41.89	0.32
	(0.04)	(0.07)	(0.08)
1996	42.33	41.76	0.57
	(0.04)	(0.07)	(0.08)
1997	42.30	41.84	0.45
	(0.04)	(0.07)	(0.08)

Notes: Standard errors in parentheses. For description of counterfactual weights see text.

the variability in weekly hours is substantially higher in the nonunion sector. To give the reader some sense of the difference, we display the standard deviation of hours worked from our CPS data in figure 7.3. The variability across workers is fairly constant for the nonunion sector, although it appears to be increasing in the union sector—the relative increase in union sector variance is consistent with other evidence, suggesting that union wage setting is growing more like nonunion wage setting (DiNardo and Lemieux 1997).

Figure 7.4 uses the propensity score (the predicted probability from the logit that we use for our weights) to take a first pass at investigating heterogeneity (e.g., variability) in the union effect across different groups of

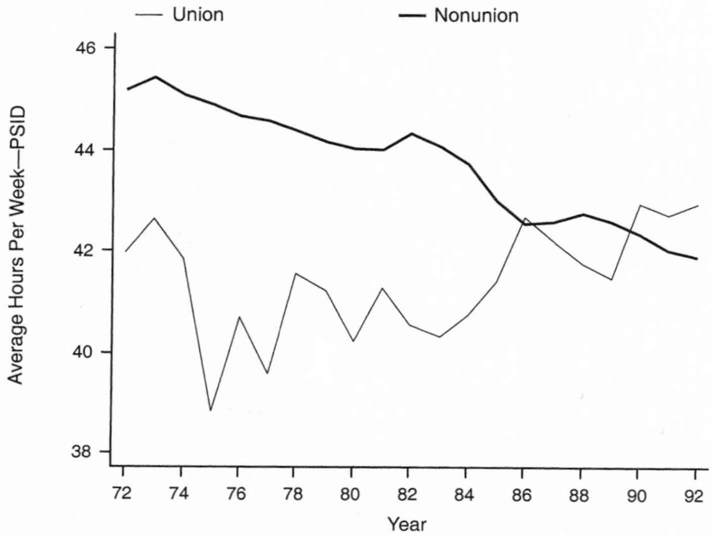

Fig. 7.1 Average hours per week for men with characteristics of 1992 union workers PSID data

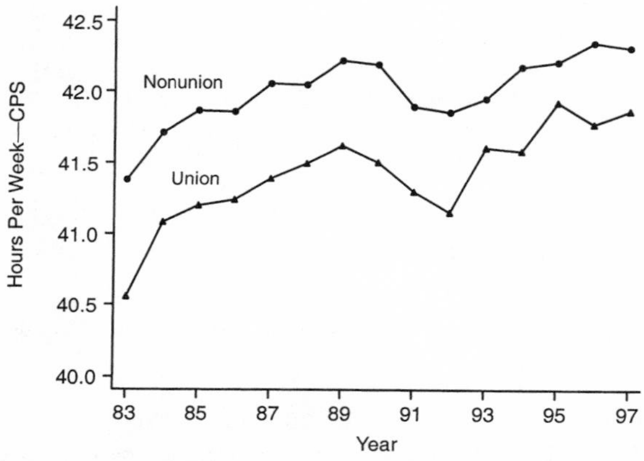

Fig. 7.2 Average hours per week for men with characteristics of 1992 union workers CPS data

male workers in the 1992 CPS cross section. Workers with characteristics "more like" union members have higher values of this propensity score.[10]

10. The actual regression lines are the result of a natural cubic spline with knots at the 33rd and 66th percentile of the observed propensity score. Experimentation with nonparametric estimates and regressograms confirmed the adequacy of the natural cubic spline to fit the data.

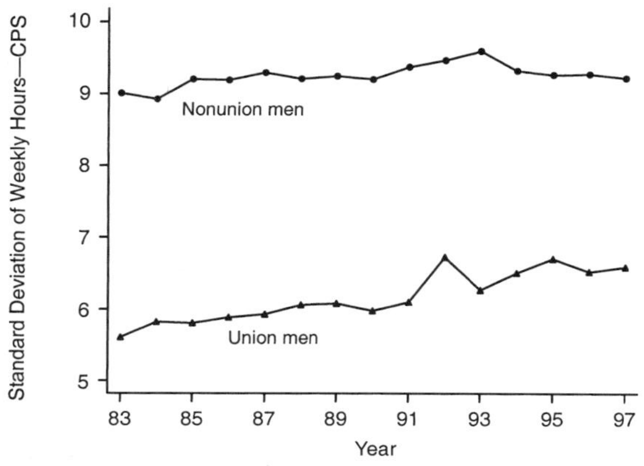

Fig. 7.3 Standard deviation of hours per week men with characteristics of 1992 union workers CPS data

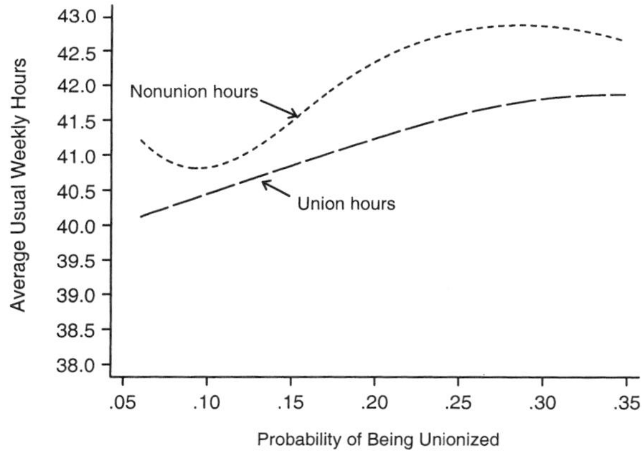

Fig. 7.4 Average weekly hours and union propensity score

Note: Plots are generated with a natural cubic spline with knot points at the 33rd and 66th percentiles of the propensity score.

We restrict our attention in the figure to the domain between the 5th and 95th percentile of propensity scores.[11]

The analysis suggests some variation in the size of the union effect, with the effect being greater for workers who look more like the "typical union worker." On the other hand, the amount of variation explained by the propensity score is tiny. Depending on the precise specification of the pro-

11. Outside this range, the union hours effect is actually reversed; however, our estimates in this range are very unreliable due to the paucity of observations.

pensity score, the total variation in hours explained is typically less than 8 percent. This is not surprising given the fact that the literature on labor supply (see, for example, Killingsworth 1983), which typically conditions on the observed wage in addition to the covariates that we use, has only managed to explain a tiny fraction of the variation in hours worked.

In sum, both the PSID and CPS results suggest that hours are lower in the union sector, although there are some differences in the levels, differences, and trends between the two sets of numbers.

Time Spent Due to Illness (Own or Other)

Based on our PSID data, table 7.3 reports the average number of weeks spent not working due to illness, with the nonunion and union values computed as before (i.e., with the characteristics of union workers in 1992 used as the adjustment base). In general, nonunion workers spend slightly less time away from work due to illness—approximately 1 week per year compared to 1 to 1.4 weeks for union members. This differential is somewhat consistent with our evidence regarding "paid" sick leave, presented in the following (see table 7.10 later in the chapter). While the magnitude of the difference varies from year to year, there is no discernible trend.

Time Spent on Vacation

Recall from our earlier discussion that the treatment of paid vacation time as time spent at work makes the use of the CPS problematic for an analysis of union/nonunion differences: Indeed, as we show later in the chapter (see Table 7.10), there appears to be a difference in the incidence of "paid" vacation time between union and nonunion workers. We therefore use only the PSID—which records all vacation time whether paid or not—for this analysis. These results are listed in table 7.4 (again estimated using our conditioning technique).

Given the relatively small samples, it is noteworthy that the difference between the two groups of workers is fairly constant—union workers typically have one week more vacation time than nonunion workers and, perhaps surprisingly, the level of vacation time in the two groups rose during the years 1972–1992 (albeit slowly).

Hours Constraints

In table 7.5, we list the percentage of workers who report that they "would like to work more" and those who "would like to work less" (the worker is also free to choose neither more nor less.) During the sample period, two trends are immediately evident for both sets of workers—the percentage of workers who say they would like to work more rises, and the percentage of workers who would like to work less falls. Consistent with the previous tables and with our simple model of union behavior, during the

Table 7.3 **Mean weeks not working due to illness for men with characteristics of 1992 union workers (PSID data)**

Year	Nonunion	Union	Difference
1972	0.92	1.23	–0.31
	(0.06)	(0.11)	(0.12)
1973	0.96	1.06	–0.10
	(0.06)	(0.10)	(0.11)
1974	0.83	1.18	–0.35
	(0.05)	(0.12)	(0.13)
1975	1.12	1.23	–0.11
	(0.07)	(0.08)	(0.10)
1976	1.07	1.36	–0.29
	(0.06)	(0.09)	(0.10)
1977	1.06	1.37	–0.31
	(0.05)	(0.09)	(0.10)
1978	1.15	1.27	–0.12
	(0.06)	(0.09)	(0.10)
1979	1.22	1.24	–0.02
	(0.06)	(0.08)	(0.10)
1980	1.12	1.32	–0.20
	(0.05)	(0.09)	(0.10)
1981	1.15	1.32	–0.17
	(0.05)	(0.09)	(0.10)
1982	1.13	1.26	–0.14
	(0.05)	(0.09)	(0.11)
1983	1.15	1.43	–0.29
	(0.05)	(0.11)	(0.12)
1984	1.17	1.56	–0.39
	(0.05)	(0.13)	(0.14)
1985	1.26	1.22	0.04
	(0.07)	(0.09)	(0.11)
1986	1.09	1.34	–0.25
	(0.06)	(0.12)	(0.13)
1987	1.08	1.33	–0.25
	(0.06)	(0.10)	(0.11)
1988	1.05	1.30	–0.25
	(0.05)	(0.11)	(0.12)
1989	1.02	1.27	–0.25
	(0.05)	(0.10)	(0.12)
1990	1.05	1.18	–0.13
	(0.05)	(0.12)	(0.13)
1991	1.10	1.43	–0.34
	(0.05)	(0.15)	(0.16)
1992	1.15	1.21	–0.06
	(0.05)	(0.14)	(0.15)

Notes: Standard errors in parentheses. For description of counterfactual weights see text.

Table 7.4 Mean vacation time in weeks for men with characteristics of 1992 union workers (PSID data)

Year	Nonunion	Union	Difference
1972	1.71	2.17	–0.46
	(0.06)	(0.09)	(0.11)
1973	1.71	2.18	–0.47
	(0.06)	(0.09)	(0.11)
1974	1.77	2.16	–0.39
	(0.06)	(0.09)	(0.11)
1975	1.93	2.37	–0.44
	(0.06)	(0.09)	(0.11)
1976	1.94	2.42	–0.48
	(0.05)	(0.09)	(0.11)
1977	1.99	2.49	–0.50
	(0.05)	(0.10)	(0.11)
1978	1.97	2.55	–0.58
	(0.05)	(0.10)	(0.11)
1979	1.99	2.44	–0.46
	(0.05)	(0.10)	(0.11)
1980	2.03	2.53	–0.50
	(0.05)	(0.10)	(0.11)
1981	2.09	2.46	–0.38
	(0.05)	(0.10)	(0.11)
1982	2.10	2.51	–0.41
	(0.05)	(0.11)	(0.12)
1983	2.09	2.69	–0.59
	(0.05)	(0.12)	(0.13)
1984	2.14	2.56	–0.43
	(0.05)	(0.12)	(0.13)
1985	2.34	2.88	–0.54
	(0.07)	(0.10)	(0.12)
1986	2.35	2.98	–0.63
	(0.07)	(0.12)	(0.13)
1987	2.34	2.96	–0.62
	(0.07)	(0.12)	(0.13)
1988	2.36	2.91	–0.56
	(0.06)	(0.12)	(0.14)
1989	2.40	2.93	–0.53
	(0.06)	(0.12)	(0.14)
1990	2.36	2.87	–0.51
	(0.06)	(0.12)	(0.13)
1991	2.39	2.80	–0.41
	(0.06)	(0.12)	(0.13)
1992	2.31	3.27	–0.96
	(0.05)	(0.15)	(0.15)

Notes: Standard errors in parentheses. For description of counterfactual weights see text.

Table 7.5 **Percent saying "Would like to work more" or "Would like to work less" for men with characteristics of 1992 union workers**

	Would like to work more			Would like to work less		
Year	Nonunion	Union	Difference	Nonunion	Union	Difference
1972	0.17	0.24	–0.06	0.08	0.06	0.03
	(0.01)	(0.02)	(0.02)	(0.01)	(0.01)	(0.01)
1973	0.15	0.26	–0.11	0.10	0.07	0.03
	(0.01)	(0.02)	(0.02)	(0.01)	(0.01)	(0.01)
1974	0.15	0.25	–0.10	0.08	0.07	0.01
	(0.01)	(0.02)	(0.02)	(0.01)	(0.01)	(0.01)
1975	0.17	0.34	–0.16	0.07	0.09	–0.02
	(0.01)	(0.02)	(0.02)	(0.01)	(0.01)	(0.01)
1976	0.25	0.36	–0.12	0.05	0.06	–0.01
	(0.01)	(0.02)	(0.02)	(0.01)	(0.01)	(0.01)
1977	0.24	0.37	–0.13	0.08	0.10	–0.02
	(0.01)	(0.02)	(0.02)	(0.01)	(0.01)	(0.01)
1978	0.18	0.30	–0.12	0.09	0.18	–0.08
	(0.01)	(0.02)	(0.02)	(0.01)	(0.02)	(0.02)
1979	0.20	0.34	–0.15	0.06	0.12	–0.05
	(0.01)	(0.02)	(0.02)	(0.01)	(0.01)	(0.01)
1980	0.22	0.34	–0.12	0.07	0.06	0.01
	(0.01)	(0.02)	(0.02)	(0.01)	(0.01)	(0.01)
1981	0.28	0.36	–0.08	0.03	0.06	–0.02
	(0.01)	(0.02)	(0.02)	(0.00)	(0.01)	(0.01)
1982	0.26	0.39	–0.12	0.04	0.05	–0.01
	(0.01)	(0.02)	(0.02)	(0.00)	(0.01)	(0.01)
1983	0.30	0.39	–0.08	0.05	0.03	0.02
	(0.01)	(0.02)	(0.02)	(0.00)	(0.01)	(0.01)
1984	0.27	0.33	–0.05	0.06	0.08	–0.02
	(0.01)	(0.02)	(0.02)	(0.01)	(0.01)	(0.01)
1985	0.27	0.30	–0.03	0.05	0.03	0.02
	(0.01)	(0.02)	(0.02)	(0.00)	(0.01)	(0.01)
1986	0.31	0.31	–0.00	0.03	0.04	–0.01
	(0.01)	(0.02)	(0.02)	(0.00)	(0.01)	(0.01)
1987	0.31	0.31	0.00	0.04	0.02	0.02
	(0.01)	(0.02)	(0.02)	(0.00)	(0.01)	(0.01)
1988	0.29	0.32	–0.03	0.05	0.02	0.03
	(0.01)	(0.02)	(0.02)	(0.00)	(0.01)	(0.01)
1989	0.30	0.34	–0.05	0.05	0.02	0.03
	(0.01)	(0.02)	(0.02)	(0.00)	(0.01)	(0.01)
1990	0.32	0.31	0.01	0.04	0.02	0.02
	(0.01)	(0.02)	(0.02)	(0.00)	(0.01)	(0.01)
1991	0.32	0.35	–0.02	0.04	0.03	0.01
	(0.01)	(0.02)	(0.02)	(0.00)	(0.01)	(0.01)
1992	0.31	0.34	–0.03	0.04	0.03	0.01
	(0.01)	(0.02)	(0.02)	(0.00)	(0.01)	(0.01)

Notes: Standard errors in parentheses. For description of counterfactual weights see text.

early part of our sample, union workers were more likely than nonunion workers to desire more work hours. However, over the entire sample frame the proportion constrained in this regard rose much more for nonunion workers than for union workers so that beginning in the mid-1980s, the gap between the two groups was numerically and statistically insignificant. Similarly, the final columns of the table show that union workers are slightly less likely to desire fewer work hours; however, the small percentage of workers expressing this view means that the difference between union and nonunion workers is not significantly different from zero at conventional levels.

7.3 Health Insurance, Pensions, and Other Benefits

As suggested by the quote by Sidney and Beatrice Webb (1897) in our introduction, labor unions have long played an important role in securing social insurance benefits for workers. Indeed, according to Munts (1967), many early union organizations were established for the provision of such benefits and only later became engaged in bargaining over wages. Later on, pressure from organized labor provided significant impetus for the growth of pension plans in the 1940s and 1950s (Allen and Clark 1986).

There are several reasons to expect a positive effect of union membership on health insurance, retirement plans, and related benefits.

First, in nonunion workplaces, where entry and exit are the primary adjustment by which worker preferences are expressed, compensation policies will be tailored to suit the "marginal" workers, who tend to be young and mobile and therefore likely to have a low demand for health and retirement benefits. In contrast, the political processes of unionized workplaces often result in greater weight being placed on the preferences of older, less-mobile workers, who are likely to have a greater demand for such benefits.[12]

Second, to the extent that unions play a role in administering benefit programs, they may also lower the actual cost of such programs to employers. In many cases, the union's role involves providing information to employees about the value and tax advantages of nonwage benefits, and thus influencing employee demand. This notion of unions as providing information to employees is consistent with the evidence that union workers are more likely to take up publicly funded benefits, such as workers' compensation and unemployment insurance (Hirsch, Macpherson, and Dumond 1997; Budd and McCall 1997). Also worthy of note is the possibility that in repeated bargaining, established benefits such as health insurance are difficult for the firm to eliminate—they become part of a nonnegotiable "base" as compared to a negotiable "increment."

12. See Goldstein and Pauly (1976) for a more formal treatment.

A number of studies from the 1970s and early 1980s show large union effects on the receipt and quantity of fringe benefits, particularly health insurance and pensions (Freeman 1981; Alpert 1982; Freeman and Medoff 1984; Feldman and Scheffler 1992; Allen and Clark 1986; Belman and Heywood 1990). Pierce (2001) exploited the Bureau of Labor Statistics (BLS) data used to compute the Employment Cost Index (for the years 1981–1997) and found significant union effects on paid leave, pensions, and health insurance. In this section we update this research by estimating the relationship between union membership and health insurance and pensions from the 1980s to the mid-1990s, using data from several special supplements to the CPS. Both benefits are very important from a policy perspective. There is great concern among health economists and other policy analysts over the decline in health insurance coverage over the past several decades (see, for example, Kronick and Gilmer 1999). Likewise, the aging of the baby boom cohort combined with questions concerning the long-run viability of Social Security heighten the policy importance of employer-sponsored retirement programs.

In the last part of this section, we also present union/nonunion differences in the receipt of several other nonwage benefits, using additional data sources besides the CPS supplements. Largely for reasons of data availability, we focus on the offer or receipt of the various benefits rather than the level or generosity of coverage. Because several studies indicate significantly positive union effects on the latter (Freeman 1981; Freeman and Medoff 1984; Allen and Clark 1986; Buchmueller, DiNardo, and Valletta 2002), the estimates we report here can be thought of as lower bounds of sorts.

7.3.1 Health Insurance

Table 7.6 presents estimates of union/nonunion differences in health insurance benefits for four different periods: 1983, 1988, 1993, and 1997. The data are from various supplements to the CPS. The 1983 data is the most limited, providing information only on whether the responding worker received health insurance coverage through his employer. For later years, it is possible to distinguish between whether a worker's employer offers health benefits to any workers and whether the worker is covered.[13] The third column in the table reports unadjusted union/nonunion differences for these outcomes—that is, the difference between the figures in the first two columns. The adjusted differences in the fourth column are the coefficients on an indicator variable for union membership from linear probability models that also include individual characteristics and industry

13. Conditional on firm offers, coverage depends on whether a worker is eligible for benefits and take-up conditional on eligibility. See Buchmueller, DiNardo, and Valletta (2002) for more detail on union/nonunion differences in these intermediate outcomes.

Table 7.6 **Union/nonunion differences in health insurance availability and coverage (CPS benefits supplement data)**

			Difference (union-nonunion)		
	Union	Nonunion	Unadjusted	Adjusted	Adjusted (size)
			A. 1983 (N = 15,637)		
Covered	.929	.655	.274	.211	.151
			(.009)	(.009)	(.008)
			B. 1988 (N = 15,254)		
Available	.938	.816	.122	.095	.039
			(.008)	(.009)	(.009)
Covered	.890	.668	.222	.152	.097
			(.010)	(.010)	(.010)
			C. 1993 (N = 15,179)		
Available	.946	.792	.154	.141	.078
			(.010)	(.009)	(.009)
Covered	.870	.624	.246	.194	.132
			(.012)	(.011)	(.011)
			D. 1997 (N = 8,144)		
Available	.928	.816	.112	.100	n.a.
			(.013)	(.013)	
Covered	.835	.620	.215	.175	n.a.
			(.016)	(.016)	

Notes: All estimates were obtained using the survey supplement weights. Standard errors are in parentheses. The estimates in the fourth column are the union coefficients from linear probability models that also control for education (four category dummies), age, age squared, female, whether married, female by married, race/ethnicity (dummy variables for black and hispanic), a dummy variable for metropolitan statistical area (MSA) residency, three region dummies, and eight major industry dummies. The adjusted differences in the final column are based on a specification that also includes five establishment size dummies (10–24, 25–49, 50–99, and 100–249, 250+; <10 is the omitted category; four dummies in 1983); n.a. = not available.

dummy variables.[14] The fifth column adds controls for firm size. This is our preferred specification as both health insurance coverage and union membership are positively related to firm size. The column (4) specification is reported because we would like to trace union effects over the entire period and information on firm size was not available in the 1997 data.

In each year, the percentage of union workers with health insurance is substantially higher than the corresponding figure for nonunion workers, and for both groups the percent covered fell over time. Since the decline between 1983 and 1997 was greater for union workers (10.3 percentage points versus 5.1 percentage points), the union/nonunion difference also fell. A

14. Using some of the same data we use here, Even and Macpherson (1993) show that estimates of union/nonunion differences in health insurance and pension receipt are fairly robust to alternative econometric specification. We use linear probability models for their ease of interpretation.

comparison of the estimates for 1988 and 1997 suggest that for both sectors the decline in coverage was not driven by a cutback in employer offers but, rather, in the percentage of workers in insurance-providing firms that are covered, a result that has been documented in other studies (Cooper and Schone 1997; Farber and Levy 2000).

Differences in worker and firm characteristics account for roughly half of the union/nonunion difference in health insurance coverage. When the regression controls for firm size, the adjusted difference falls from 15 percentage points in 1983 to 9.7 percentage points in 1988 before increasing to 13.2 percentage points in 1993.[15]

One interesting pattern in table 7.6 is that, for all years, the union effect on coverage is greater than the effect on offers. Unreported regressions reveal that this is due to the fact that within firms where insurance is available there are positive union effects on both the probability of being eligible for coverage and take-up among eligible workers. These two effects have opposing time trends. The adjusted union/nonunion difference in the probability a worker is eligible for coverage, conditional on employer provision, fell from 6 percentage points in 1988 to 2 percentage points in 1997 (without controlling for firm size). The comparable difference in take-up rates (conditional on being eligible for coverage) increases from 3 to 10 percentage points over this same period.

The higher take-up rate for union workers is partly explained by their lower required employee contributions and more generous benefits available in offered plans. Table 7.7 lists the evidence for this, which comes from a 1993 survey of employers conducted by the Robert Wood Johnson Foundation.[16] Adjusting for establishment characteristics (size, industry, state, years in business, and employee demographics), the mean employer premium contribution (expressed as a percentage of the premium) is between 9 and 10 percent higher in unionized establishments. Part of this difference arises from the fact that establishments with union workers are between 15 and 20 percent (depending on coverage tier—i.e., single or family) more likely to pay the full cost of coverage (results not listed).

In terms of plan benefits, indemnity and PPO plans offered to union employees have significantly lower deductibles. For preferred provider organization (PPO) plans, the mean in-network and out-of-network coinsurance rates are 2 percentage points lower for union plans. Among health maintenance organization (HMO) plans, there is no significant difference in office visit co-payments between union and nonunion plans. The likely explanation is that in the case of HMOs, provider panel size and "quality" are more

15. Because insurance provision is essentially universal among firms with 100 or more employees, the union effect on offers reported here represent the average of large effects for small and medium-sized firms and zero effects for larger ones. See Buchmueller, DiNardo, and Valletta (2002).

16. See Buchmueller, DiNardo, and Valletta (2002) for more details on this data set.

Table 7.7 Union effects on employer premium contributions and health plan cost sharing

	Mean (standard deviation)		Difference: union-nonunion (standard error)	
	Union	Nonunion	Unadjusted	Adjusted
Employer premium contribution (as a percent of premium)				
Single coverage (N = 19,450)	88.3	81.8	6.5	9.1
Family coverage (N = 19,102)	76.3	64.9	11.4	10.1
Plan cost sharing: Indemnity plans (N = 8,891)				
Deductible ($)	200.05	300.70	–100.65	–54.32
	(164.10)	(164.10)	(16.71)	(18.69)
Coinsurance (%)	17.22	17.41	–0.19	–0.37
	(9.16)	(9.61)	(1.25)	(1.18)
PPOs (N = 6,543)				
In-network				
Deductible ($)	163.64	206.46	–42.82	–14.17
	(214.64)	(257.48)	(23.32)	(21.05)
Coinsurance (%)	14.55	16.85	–2.31	–2.15
	(10.18)	(8.60)	(1.12)	(1.06)
Out-of-network				
Deductible ($)	275.36	343.90	–68.64	–55.06
	(286.14)	(365.19)	(27.05)	(25.45)
Coinsurance (%)	25.88	27.88	–2.00	–2.23
	(10.26)	(11.25)	(1.19)	(1.08)
HMOs (N = 4,753)				
Office visit copayment ($)	6.62	7.25	–0.64	–0.46
	(4.50)	(4.48)	(0.49)	(0.52)

Notes: All figures are weighted by plan enrollment. Adjusted differences are based on linear probability model regressions. The regression specification includes indicator variables for establishment size (six categories), industry (ten categories), state, and whether or not the firm has another location. The model also includes the percentage of workers in five demographic categories (males under age twenty-five, females under age twenty-five, females aged twenty-five to fifty-four, males aged fifty-five and older, females aged fifty-five and older) and the natural log of the ratio of annual payroll to the number of employees. The regression standard errors have been adjusted to account for establishments that offer multiple plans.

important variables than co-payment rates for distinguishing between more- or less-attractive plans. We have no data on these other plan attributes.

An aspect of employer-provided health insurance that has received somewhat less attention from researchers, but is of increasing policy importance, is retiree health benefits. Because nongroup health insurance is typically quite expensive and in some cases not available at any price for older workers, retiree health benefits make it possible for many workers to retire before the age of sixty-five without suffering a loss of insurance coverage. Also, there are substantial gaps in the coverage offered by Medi-

Table 7.8 **Union-nonunion differences in retiree health benefits (CPS benefits supplement data)**

			Difference (union-nonunion)		
	Union	Nonunion	Unadjusted	Adjusted	Adjusted (size)
		A. 1988 retiree health insurance supplement (N = 1,098)			
Retiree coverage	.740	.639	.101	.045	n.a.
			(.031)	(.034)	
		B. 1993 benefits supplement (N = 1,806)			
Retiree coverage	.766	.598	.167	.146	.128
			(.026)	(.029)	(.028)

Notes: All estimates were obtained using the survey supplement weights. Standard errors are in parentheses. The estimates in the fourth column are the union coefficients from linear probability models that also control for education (four category dummies), age, age squared, female, whether married, female by married, race/ethnicity (dummy variables for black and hispanic), a dummy variable for msa residency, three region dummies, and eight major industry dummies. The adjusted differences in the final column are based on a specification that also includes five establishment size dummies (10–24, 25–49, 50–99, and 100–249, 250+; <10 is the omitted category; four dummies in 1983); n.a. = not available.

care—that is, no coverage for prescription drugs or health insurance from a former employer that supplements Medicare provides significant benefits for retirees over the age of sixty-five.

The 1993 CPS Benefit Supplement and a 1988 supplement focusing on retiree health benefits provide information on whether current workers will be eligible for employer-sponsored health insurance when they retire. Union/nonunion differences estimated using these data are reported in table 7.8. For each year, the sample is limited to workers between the ages of forty-five and sixty-four whose employer offers health insurance to active employees.[17]

The figures in the first panel of table 7.8 show that in 1988 there was a 10 percentage point difference in eligibility for retiree health coverage between union and nonunion workers (74 percent versus 64 percent). Controlling for worker characteristics and employer's industry produces an adjusted difference of roughly half this magnitude. The union/nonunion difference increased between 1988 and 1993 due to an increase in the percentage of union workers with retiree coverage and a decline among nonunion workers. Adjusting for all observables (including firm size) results in a 12.8 percentage point difference in 1993.

To summarize, the data from several CPS supplements show significant, though declining, union effects on health insurance coverage. This trend is

17. It is important to keep the second sample selection criterion (employer health insurance offers) in mind when interpreting the reported union effects. The union effect for all workers combines the retiree coverage effect with the effect on employer offers listed in table 7.6.

consistent with the notion of declining union bargaining power. However, other results suggest a slightly more complicated story in which union efforts are increasingly focused not merely on getting employers to offer health insurance but, rather, on the scope and quality of the benefits that are offered (including the availability of retiree benefits).

7.3.2 Pensions

Table 7.9 presents our results on union/nonunion differences in pension plans. The data are from the same CPS supplements used in the health insurance analysis, and the layout of table 7.9 is the same as table 7.6. As with the health insurance analysis, we examine two outcomes: whether a pension is offered by the worker's firm and, if so, whether he or she is covered.

Table 7.9 **Union/nonunion differences in pension availability and coverage (CPS benefits supplement data)**

			Difference (union-nonunion)		
	Union	Nonunion	Unadjusted	Adjusted	Adjusted (size)
			A. 1983 (N = 15,637)		
Available	.843	.494	.349	.310	.227
			(.009)	(.009)	(.009)
Covered	.766	.388	.378	.303	.236
			(.009)	(.009)	(.009)
			B. 1988 (N = 15,254)		
Available	.868	.536	.333	.302	.212
			(.011)	(.011)	(.010)
Covered	.772	.415	.358	.281	.212
			(.011)	(.011)	(.011)
			C. 1993 (N = 15,179)		
Available	.862	.586	.275	.268	.172
			(.012)	(.012)	(.011)
Covered	.750	.432	.318	.269	.196
			(.012)	(.012)	(.011)
			D. 1997 (N = 8,371)		
Available	.820	.578	.242	.227	n.a.
			(.017)	(.016)	
Covered	.719	.438	.281	.236	n.a.
			(.017)	(.016)	

Notes: All estimates were obtained using the survey supplement weights. Standard errors are in parentheses. The estimates in the fourth column are the union coefficients from linear probability models that also control for education (four category dummies), age, age squared, female, whether married, female by married, race/ethnicity (dummy variables for black and hispanic), a dummy variable for metropolitan statistical area (MSA) residency, three region dummies, and eight major industry dummies. The adjusted differences in the final column are based on a specification that also includes five establishment size dummies (10–24, 25–49, 50–99, and 100–249, 250+; <10 is the omitted category; four dummies in 1983); n.a. = not available.

For all years, the union/nonunion differences for pensions are larger than those for health insurance. In 1983, union workers were nearly twice as likely to participate in an employer-sponsored pension plan: 76.6 percent versus 38.8 percent. This result is due mainly to a large difference in whether the worker's firm offered a pension plan at all (84.3 percent versus 49.4 percent), though there also is a union edge in coverage conditional on employer offers (0.909 versus 0.784, figures not shown). Holding constant worker and firm characteristics (including establishment size), in 1983 union workers were 23.4 percentage points more likely than nonunion workers to participate in a pension plan.

Over time, the coverage rates for the two groups move in opposite directions, generally falling for union workers and increasing steadily for nonunion workers. In 1993, the adjusted union/nonunion difference was 19.6 percentage points according to our preferred specification and 26.9 percentage points when we do not control for firm size. The more restricted specification implies a slightly smaller union effect, though still large, of 23.5 percentage points in 1997.

7.3.3 Other Fringe Benefits

The National Organizational Survey Data

In this section, we examine union effects on a variety of other benefits using data from the 1993 CPS Employee Benefit Supplement and two other surveys conducted in the 1990s–the 1996 Medical Expenditure Panel Survey (MEPS) and the 1991 National Organization Survey (NOS). Of the three data sets we use in this section, only the NOS is not well known to labor and health economists, so a few words are in order.

The 1991 NOS was designed for research on organizational behavior.[18] The sample was drawn in the following way. Employed respondents to the 1991 General Social Survey (GSS), a nationally representative survey of U.S. adults, were asked to provide the names of their employers. These organizations were then contacted, and their representatives were asked about a number of organizational characteristics and policies, including whether the organization provided a number of nonwage employee benefits. While previous researchers using the NOS have treated the organization as the unit of observation,[19] the public-use file contains both organization-level variables and the individual-level variables from the GSS, including whether each respondent is a union member. We treat the combined GSS/NOS as an individual-level data set and estimate the relationship between an individual's union status and the probability that his or her

18. See Kalleberg et al. (1994) for an overview of the objectives of the NOS and Spaeth and O'Rourke (1994) for details on its design and implementation.

19. For example, see Knoke (1994), Knoke and Ishio (1994), and Huffman (1999).

employer offers various benefits. The drawback of these data is our inability to identify whether the employee is eligible for offered benefits.

Results

Table 7.10 presents regression-adjusted union effects on the receipt of several fringe benefits. The econometric specification varies slightly across these data sets due to differences in data availability, though in all cases it is fairly comparable to our preferred specification for the health insurance and pension regressions discussed previously.

Each of the outcomes in this table is dichotomous (provided or not). The top panel presents results for three types of insurance: dental, life, and long-term disability. The results here are similar to what we find for health insurance and pension benefits. For all three types of insurance, the adjusted union/nonunion difference is statistically significant. The difference is largest for dental insurance (16.5 percentage points) and smallest for life insurance (4.5 percentage points). In the case of long-term disability, our two data sources provide fairly similar estimates—9 percentage points for the 1991 NOS and 6 percentage points for the 1996 MEPS.[20]

The estimated union effects on the various types of paid leave are generally smaller. All three of the surveys have information on paid sick leave. The largest union effect, and the only one that is statistically significant at conventional levels, is estimated using the 1993 CPS Employee Benefit Supplement. The estimate from the NOS is of a comparable magnitude but, because of a much smaller sample size, is not statistically significant.

In the NOS, the employers of union members are 6 percentage points more likely to offer some type of maternity leave. Unfortunately, the data set provides no further details on the nature of that coverage—that is, paid versus unpaid or length of time. There is a similarly sized union effect on vacation coverage from the 1996 MEPS. This is consistent with our previous evidence from the PSID. Union workers are more likely than nonunion workers to have *any* paid vacation.

The last panel presents union/nonunion differences in dependent care benefits from the NOS. Those results indicate no significant difference in the percentage of union and nonunion workers receiving employer-sponsored child care or elder care benefits. Given the unfortunately vague way in which these last two outcomes are defined—child care benefits could include anything from subsidized on-site day care to Section 125 benefit programs that allow employees to pay child care expenses with their money on a pretax basis—we are reluctant to read too much into these results.

Finally, because the NOS and MEPS also contain information on pen-

20. Given differences in survey design, we are reluctant to interpret differences across these sources as reflecting time trends.

Table 7.10 **Union effects of fringe benefits other than health insurance in the 1990s**

Outcome	Data set	Adjusted union-nonunion
Other insurance		
Dental	1991 NOS	0.165
		(.045)
Life	1991 NOS	0.047
		(0.037)
Long-term disability	1991 NOS	0.092
		(0.045)
Pension/retirement plan		
Offered	1991 NOS	0.187
		(0.041)
	1993 CPS Benefit Supplement	0.172
		(0.011)
	1996 MEPS	0.197
		(0.017)
Leave		
Paid sick leave	1991 NOS	0.052
		(0.042)
	1996 MEPS	0.014
		(0.018)
Maternity leave	1991 NOS	0.065
		(0.037)
Paid vacation	1996 MEPS	0.062
		(0.017)
Dependent care		
Child care benefits	1991 NOS	–0.021
		(0.040)
Elder care benefits	1991 NOS	–0.023
		(0.041)

Notes: Estimated union-nonunion differences are based on linear probability models. All regressions control for the following: age (and age squared), years of education (and education squared), and indicator variables for gender, marital status (married/not married), gender × marital status, firm size (five categories), geographic region (four categories) and race/ethnicity. The NOS and CPS regressions also control for industry. The CPS and MEPS regression controls for whether the individual lives in an MSA. The NOS sample sizes range from 636 to 650, depending on the outcome. Standard errors are in parentheses.

sions and retirement plans, we also compute estimates similar to those in section 7.3.2. The similarity of the estimates from all three data sets is reassuring.

7.4 Conclusions and Discussion

Consistent with other research, and with the comprehensive review in Freeman and Medoff (1984), we find generally significant union effects on the large variety of nonwage aspects of work that we can measure. For a worker with the attributes of a typical union member, a union job offers more vacation, fewer hours per week, the greater likelihood of dental, health, maternity, retirement, and pension benefits, inter alia. We also uncover evidence that there has been a decline in the magnitude of the various differentials over time. This is consistent with the decline in the extent of unionization and possibly a decline in their influence within unionized workplaces, although the inconsistency in measurement across our different data sets makes this conclusion tentative in some cases.

One open question is the extent to which our findings reflect a direct causal impact of unionization on nonwage outcomes. For example, the results may instead reflect systematic worker sorting between union and nonunion workplaces (endogenous unionization) so that omitted worker characteristics and choices rather that unionization per se are the cause of differences in benefit outcomes.

Although our estimates did not account for endogenous unionization, estimates of the union wage effect using data on individuals that attempt to account for endogeneity indicate a substantial positive, causal impact of union status (see, for example, Robinson 1989). Moreover, Blau and Kahn (2000) observe that the impacts of unionization are much the same whether measured within countries over time or across countries subject to similar global influences but with differences in unionization.

A related issue is the mechanism by which unions provide these "premiums." In most variants of the monopoly union model, union gains come exclusively at the expense of nonunion workers and the level of economic activity in the economy. The mechanism is straightforward—unions raise the cost of inputs to the firms. Profit maximizing firms respond by lowering output and substituting away from the higher-priced input. Although this view is widespread among economists, direct supporting evidence is quite scarce. Indeed, the presence of a "deadweight welfare loss" to unionization is a staple of textbook treatments of unionization. Even Freeman and Medoff (1984) who, inter alia, highlight the potential for allocation improvements under unionization, essentially stipulate the existence of such a welfare loss, although they note that their estimate of this loss is small.[21] More recent evidence from DiNardo and Lee (2001) suggests that the employment losses resulting from union impacts on establishment closure are quite small.

Overall, our results suggest that unions have had substantive allocative

21. The "Harberger triangle" in this setting equals one-half the product of the union wage effect, the associated employment decline in the union sector, the fraction of the workforce unionized, and the fraction of total costs associated with labor. Assuming an elasticity of demand for labor of –2/3, an upper bound to the union wage effect of 25 percent, a union share of the workforce of 25 percent in 1981, and a labor share of gross national product (GNP) of 3/4, Freeman and Medoff (1989) estimate the efficiency loss as a share of GNP is $1/2 \times 0.20 \times 0.13 \times 0.25 \times 0.75 = 0.0040$. They note that this estimate is very close to the calculations in Rees (1962).

impact on important nonwage aspects of jobs. These include key benefits, such as health insurance and pensions, for which market conditions for their provision have changed substantially in recent decades. The apparent continuing union impact on these key benefits may both provide a link to the historical origins of the labor movement and a means by which unions may continue to have important impacts on the terms and conditions of employment in the future despite the decline in unionization.

Appendix A
A Simple Model

In this appendix we discuss a parameterization of a simple theoretical model, due to Johnson (1990), of hours determination in a unionized setting. The point of departure is the work of Pencavel and MaCurdy (1986) and Brown and Ashenfelter (1986) and the class of models sometimes referred to as "contract curve" models (hereafter CC models), which constitute an alternative to standard "labor demand" models of union behavior. In the labor demand model, the effect of unions is similar to that of the minimum wage: the union raises the wage above the competitive level, leading to a decrease in employment (assuming hours per worker are fixed). In the basic CC model, however, the union is aware that its wage demands affect employment and takes that effect into account when formulating its bargaining stance. In Brown and Ashenfelter (1986), for example, the union's optimal choice for the level of employment maximizes firm profits, and any resulting rents are divided between the union and the owners of the firm. As in implicit contract models, this process implies that the wage no longer plays the allocative role it does in the simple textbook model and that it is not possible to consider hours worked as the outcome solely of individual preferences interacting with a fixed wage rate.

Johnson (1990) develops a variant of the basic CC model where hours per worker are not fixed and where the union negotiates jointly over wages, employment levels, and hours worked per worker. As it is hard to rationalize hours of work decisions by union members as labor supply responses to higher wages, this model provides a potentially useful framework for understanding the differences between hours worked in union and nonunion environments.[22]

Profits to a firm are given by a revenue function, $V(\cdot)$, that depends on

22. Estimating a standard labor supply equation, with union status used to instrument for the wage, typically results in labor supply elasticity estimates that are much larger than those found in other studies. See DiNardo (1992).

total man-hours and labor costs, which equal the (average) wage rate times total man-hours employed.[23]

$$\pi = V[f(hN)] - whN, \tag{A1}$$

where π is profits, h is hours per worker, N is numbers of workers, and w is average wage rate.

The union has preferences over individual worker utility as well as the total number of employed members:

$$R = [U(wh, -h) - U_a]^{\beta} N \tag{A2}$$

It is convenient to specify a specific (Stone-Geary) utility function with utility increasing in earnings and decreasing in the number of hours worked.

$$U(wh, -h) = (wh)^{\theta}(T - c - h)^{1-\theta}, \tag{A3}$$

where $R(\cdot)$ is the union objective function, T is total hours, c is committed leisure, β is parameter of union preferences, θ is parameter of individual preferences, and U_a is nonunion utility.

Equation (A1) defines profits for employers, equation (A2) defines union utility, and equation (A3) is a simple characterization of individual preferences.

When $\beta = 0$, this model is a standard competitive model, and as $\beta \rightarrow \infty$, the union cares more about wages and hours per worker. If unions and firms negotiate over w, N, and h, the observed values of h and N for a given contract should satisfy the following conditions.

$$\frac{\partial \pi}{\partial h}\bigg|_{\pi = \pi_0} = \frac{\partial R}{\partial h}\bigg|_{R = R_0} \tag{A4}$$

$$\frac{\partial \pi}{\partial N}\bigg|_{\pi = \pi_0} = \frac{\partial R}{\partial N}\bigg|_{R = R_0} \tag{A5}$$

These two equations imply the following:

$$(V'f' - w)N = \beta[U(wh, -h) - U_a]^{\beta-1}N(U_1 w - U_2) \tag{A6}$$

$$(V'f' - w)h = [U(wh, -h) - U_a]^{\beta} \tag{A7}$$

Together, equations (6) and (7) imply that

$$\frac{U_2}{U_1} = w\left\{1 - \left[\frac{U_a\mu}{(U_1\beta h)}\right]\right\}, \text{ where } \mu = \frac{[U(wh, -h) - U_a]}{U_a}, \tag{A8}$$

23. A fuller analysis might treat labor as a quasi-fixed factor as in Oi (1962) so that firms might prefer fewer workers and greater hours per work. However, our simplifying assumption suffices for characterizing differences between union and nonunion workers.

or, to write it in a more intuitive way,

$$\frac{U_2}{U_1} = w\left\{1 - \frac{\mu}{(1 + \mu)\beta E}\right\}, \tag{A9}$$

where E is elasticity of utility with respect to income.

Recall that in the absence of a union, a utility-maximizing individual worker would set

$$\frac{U_2}{U_1} = w. \tag{A10}$$

The condition that $\mu > 0$ (unions place some emphasis on hours and wages, and union workers are better off than their nonunion worker counterparts) implies that union workers would prefer to work more hours at the actual wage rate. The intuition underlying this result is straightforward. In this model, the firm is indifferent between combinations of N and h that yield the same amount of labor. By contrast, the union faces a trade-off between more members and higher utility per member.

Several implications that we can compare with the data include:

1. Union work hours generally will be less than nonunion hours.[24]
2. In addition to working less, union workers will be more likely to report being constrained and desiring to work more hours at the union wage rate.
3. The more union wage setting resembles wage setting in the "competitive" sector (the smaller the difference between union member utility and the nonunion alternative), the smaller is the hours differential and the less "constrained" is the union hours outcome.

Appendix B
Statistical Methods for Reweighting

The procedure described here is a straightforward application of "propensity score" weighting (Rosenbaum and Rubin 1983). The exposition follows the discussion in DiNardo, Fortin, and Lemieux (1996) and Johnston and DiNardo (1997). Let the conditional distribution of hours in year i and sector j be given by $f^{i,j}(h \mid X = x_b)$, let x_b denote the characteristics of our base sample and $x_{i,j}$ the characteristics of the sample that we wish to reweight to have the same distribution of characteristics as the base sample. We are interested in computing the counterfactual distribution

24. This is not true for all possible utility functions; the key is that the worker's utility-constant "income effect" of the higher wage should not be too large.

$$\int h \cdot f^{i,j}(h \mid X = x_b)dx,$$

by means of a reweighting of the actul distribution:

$$\int \theta h \cdot f^{i,j}(h \mid X = x_{i,j})dx,$$

where θ is the appropriate weight, and $f^{i,j}(\cdot)$ is the distribution given the structure of hours in year i. The counterfactual distribution yields the distribution of hours that would have obtained in year i for sector j had the distribution of relevant characteristics in the population been x_b instead of $x_{i,j}$. We can use this distribution to characterize the counterfactual mean (or any other moment of the distribution).

Consider calculating θ when we wish to reweight the 1972 distribution of hours of nonunion members so that they have the same distribution of characteristics as union workers in 1992.

We derive the appropriate weight by noting that the distribution of hours worked among union workers in 1992 is given by

$$\int f^{92,U=1}(h \mid X = x_b)dx \equiv \int f^{92}(h \mid X)g(X \mid U = 1, t = 1992)dx,$$

where the term $g(X \mid U = 1, t = 1992)$ denotes the multivariate distribution of X in the union sector in 1992.

The appropriate counterfactual distribution is given by

$$\int f^{72,U=0}(h \mid X = x_b)dx \equiv \int f^{72,U=0}(h \mid X)g(X \mid U = 1, t = 1992)dx,$$

where the term $f^{72,U=0}$ denotes the structure of hours (i.e., the relationship between hours and characteristics) in the nonunion sector in 1972.

The actual distribution of hours in the nonunion sector in 1972 is given by

$$\int f^{72,U=0}(h \mid X)dx \equiv \int f^{72,U=0}(h \mid X)g(X \mid U = 0, t = 1972)dx.$$

We merely need to solve for the value of θ such that

$$\int f^{72,U=0}(h \mid X = x_b)dx \equiv \int \theta f^{72,U=0}(h \mid X)g(X \mid U = 0, t = 1972)dx.$$

A simple application of Bayes law shows that

$$\theta \propto \frac{\Pr[(U = 1, t = 1992) \mid X]}{\Pr[(U = 0, t = 1972) \mid X]} = \frac{\Pr[(U = 1, t = 1992) \mid X]}{1 - \Pr[(U = 1, t = 1992) \mid X]}.$$

We then compute the sequence of these counterfactual means, say, $\int h \cdot f^{72,j}(h \mid X = x_{1992,U=1})dx$, $\int h \cdot f^{73,j}(h \mid X = x_{92,U=1})dx$, $\int h \cdot f^{74,j}(h \mid X = x_{92,U=1})dx$, $\ldots \int h \cdot f^{92,j}(h \mid X = x_{92,U=1})dx$, for both union and nonunion sectors.

Holding X constant allows us to make a sensible ceteris paribus comparison—comparing the "same" individuals through time we look at changes in the "structure of hours." One advantage relative to a standard regression framework is that if there is significant "treatment-effect heterogeneity," the analysis holds constant the comparison group so that the relative "strength" of the union effect over time can be easily gleaned from the estimates.

As a practical matter, we compute the probabilities in the previous expression using a logit pooling the 1992 union member sample with the 1972 nonunion member sample. We use a complete set of race dummies, school dummies, marital status dummies, SMSA dummies, and a cubic in age as explanatory variables for the PSID data. For the CPS data we use five education categories, five age categories, an SMSA dummy, three regional dummies, marital status, and three race categories.

References

Allen, Steven G., and Robert L. Clark. 1986. Unions, pension wealth, and age-compensation profiles. *Industrial and Labor Relations Review* 39 (4): 502–18.

Alpert, William T. 1982. Unions and private wage supplements. *Journal of Labor Research* 3 (2): 179–99.

Autor, David, and Lawrence Katz. 2000. Changes in the wage structure and earnings inequality. In *Handbook of labor economics,* ed. Orley Ashenfelter and David Card, 1463–1555. Amsterdam: North Holland.

Belman, Dale, and John S. Heywood. 1990. Application of the Oaxaca decomposition to probit estimates—The cases of unions and fringe benefit provision. *Economics Letters* 32 (1): 101–4.

Blanchflower, David G. 1996. The role and influence of trade unions in the OECD. Centre for Economic Performance Discussion Paper no. 310. London: London School of Economics, CEP.

Blau, Francine, and Lawrence H. Kahn. 2000. Institutions and laws in the labor market. In *Handbook of labor economics,* ed. Orley Ashenfelter and David Card, 1399–1462. Amsterdam: North Holland.

Booth, Alison Lee. 1995. *The economics of the trade union.* Cambridge: Cambridge University Press.

Bound, John, and Alan Krueger. 1991. The extent of measurement error in longitudinal earnings data—Do two wrongs make a right? *Journal of Labor Economics* 9 (1): 1–24.

Bound, John, and George Johnson. 1992. Changes in the structure of wages in the 1980s: An evaluation of alternative explanations. *American Economic Review* 82:371–92.

Brown, James N., and Orley Ashenfelter. 1986. Testing the efficiency of employment contracts. *Journal of Political Economy* 94:S40–S87.

Buchmueller, Thomas C., John DiNardo, and Robert G. Valletta. 2002. Union effects on health insurance provision and coverage in the United States. *Industrial and Labor Relations Review* 55 (4): 610–27.

Budd, John W., and Brian P. McCall. 1997. The effect of unions on the receipt of unemployment insurance benefits. *Industrial and Labor Relations Review* 50 (3): 478–92.

Card, David. 1992. The effect of unions on the distribution of wages: Redistribution or relabelling? NBER Working Paper no. 4195. Cambridge, Mass.: National Bureau of Economic Research, October.

Card, David, Thomas Lemieux, and Craig W. Riddell. 2003. Unionization and wage inequality: A comparative study of the U.S., U.K. and Canada. NBER Working Paper no. 9473. Cambridge, Mass.: National Bureau of Economic Research, February.

Cooper, Phillip F., and Barbara Steinberg Schone. 1997. More offers, fewer takers for employment-based health insurance: 1987 and 1996. *Health Affairs* 16 (6): 142–49.

DiNardo, John. 1992. Union employment effects: An empirical analysis. University of California, Irvine, Department of Economics, Working Paper no. 11.

DiNardo, John, Nicole Fortin, and Thomas Lemieux. 1996. Labor market institutions and the distribution of wages, 1973–1993: A semi-parametric approach. *Econometrica* 64 (5): 1001–45.

DiNardo, John, and David S. Lee. 2001. The impact of unionization on establishment closure: A regression discontinuity analysis of representation elections. CLE Working Paper no. 38. University of California, Berkeley, Center for Labor Economics, October.

DiNardo, John, and Thomas Lemieux. 1997. Diverging male wage inequality in the United States and Canada, 1981–1988: Do institutions explain the difference? *Industrial and Labor Relations Review* 50 (5): 629–51.

Earle, John, and John Pencavel. 1990. Hours of work and trade unionism. *Journal of Labor Economics* 8 (1): S150–S174.

Even, William E., and David A. Macpherson. 1993. The decline of private-sector unionism and the gender wage gap. *Journal of Human Resources* 28 (2): 279–96.

Farber, Henry S., and Helen Levy. 2000. Recent trends in employer-sponsored health insurance coverage: Are bad jobs getting worse? *Journal of Health Economics* (1): 93–119.

Feldman, Roger, and Richard Scheffler. 1992. The union impact on hospital wages and fringe benefits. *Industrial and Labor Relations Review* 35 (2): 196–206.

Freeman, Richard B. 1981. The effect of unionism on fringe benefits. *Industrial and Labor Relations Review* 34 (4): 489–509.

———. 1993. How much has de-unionization contributed to the rise in male earnings inequality? In *Uneven tides: Rising inequality in America,* ed. Sheldon Danziger and Peter Gottschalk, 133–63. New York: Russell Sage Foundation.

Freeman, Richard B., and James L. Medoff. 1984. *What do unions do?* New York: Basic Books.

Goldstein, Gerald S., and Mark V. Pauly. 1976. Group health insurance as a local public good. In *The role of health insurance in the health services sector,* ed. Robert Rosett, 73–110. Cambridge, Mass.: National Bureau of Economic Research.

Gosling, Amanda, and Steve Machin. 1995. Trade unions and the dispersion of earnings in British establishments, 1980–90. *Oxford Bulletin of Economics and Statistics* 57 (2): 167–84.

Hirsch, Barry T., and John T. Addison. 1986. *The economic analysis of unions: New approaches and evidence.* Boston: Allen & Unwin.

Hirsch, Barry T., David A. Macpherson, and Michael J. Dumond. 1997. Workers' compensation recipiency in union and nonunion workplaces. *Industrial and Labor Relations Review* 50 (2): 213–36.

Huffman, Matt L. 1999. Who's in charge? Organizational influences on women's representation in managerial positions. *Social Science Quarterly* 80 (4): 738–56.

Johnson, George. 1990. Work rules, featherbedding, and Pareto-optimal union-management bargaining. *Journal of Labor Economics* 8 (1): S237–S259.

Johnston, Jack, and John DiNardo. 1997. *Econometric methods.* 4th ed. Cambridge, Mass.: McGraw-Hill.

Kalleberg, Arne L., David Knoke, Peter V. Mardsen, and Joe L. Spaeth. 1994. The National Organizations Study. *American Behavioral Scientist* 37 (7): 860–71.

Katz, Lawrence, and Kevin Murphy. 1992. Changes in relative wages, 1963–1987—Supply and demand factors. *Quarterly Journal of Economics* 107 (1): 35–78.

Killingsworth, Mark. 1983. *Labor supply.* New York: Cambridge University Press.

Knoke, David. 1994. Cui bono? Employment benefit packages. *American Behavioral Scientist* 37 (7): 963–78.

Knoke, David, and Yoshito Ishio. 1994. Occupational training, unions and internal labor markets. *American Behavioral Scientist* 37 (7): 992–1016.

Kronick, Richard, and Todd Gilmer. 1999. Explaining the decline in health insurance coverage, 1979–1995. *Health Affairs* 18 (2): 30–47.

Levy, Frank, and Richard Murnane. 1992. U.S. earnings levels and earnings inequality: A review of recent trends and proposed explanations. *Journal of Economic Literature* 30:1331–81.

Lewis, H. Gregg. 1963. *Unionism and relative wages in the United States.* Chicago: University of Chicago Press.

———. 1986. Union relative wage effects. In *Handbook of labor economics,* ed. Orley Ashenfelter and Richard Layard, 1139–81. New York: Elsevier Science.

MaCurdy, Thomas, and John Pencavel. 1986. Testing between competing models of wage and determination in unionized markets. *Journal of Political Economy* 94 (3): S3–S39.

Munts, Raymond. 1967. *Bargaining for health: Labor unions, health insurance, and medical care,* Madison: University of Wisconsin Press.

Oi, Walter. 1962. Labor as a quasi-fixed factor of production. *Journal of Political Economy* 70 (6): 538–55.

Olson, Craig A. 1998. A comparison of parametric and semiparametric estimates of the effects of spousal health insurance coverage on weekly hours worked by wives. *Journal of Applied Econometrics* 13:543–65.

Pierce, Brooks. 2001. Compensation inequality. *Quarterly Journal of Economics* 116 (4): 1459–1525.

Raisian, John. 1979. Cyclic patterns in weeks and wages. *Economic Inquiry* 17 (4): 475–95.

Rees, Albert. 1962. *The economics of trade unions.* Chicago: University of Chicago Press.

Robinson, Chris. 1989. The joint determination of union status and union wage effects: Some tests of alternative models. *Journal of Political Economy* 97:639–67.

Rosenbaum, Paul, and Donald Rubin. 1983. The central role of the propensity score in observational studies for causal effects. *Biometrika* 70 (1): 41–55.

Spaeth, Joe L., and Diane O'Rourke. 1994. Designing and implementing the National Organizations Study. *American Behavioral Scientist* 37 (7): 872–90.

Trejo, Steve. 1993. Overtime pay, overtime hours, and labor unions. *Journal of Labor Economics* 11 (2): 253–78.

Webb, Sidney, and Beatrice Webb. 1897. *Industrial democracy.* London: Longmans, Green, and Co.

8

Union Participation in Strategic Decisions of Corporations

Eileen Appelbaum and Larry W. Hunter

8.1 Introduction

In the United States, the explicit representation of workforce interests in strategic decision-making processes of corporations is rare. Participation in strategic decisions—those that affect the basic direction of the company—is unusual even when workforce interests are represented collectively through unions. In this chapter, we consider U.S. labor-management experiments with two institutions through which strategic participation for unions might be realized: negotiated union-management partnership agreements and union representation on corporate boards.

Legal mandates for works councils and workforce representation on corporate boards of directors (or "codetermination") are characteristic of many European countries. In contrast, there are no legal structures that require American firms to engage workers in participation at either the workplace or the corporate board. Strategic participation for U.S. unions has emerged from an ad hoc set of private initiatives. In this chapter, we examine these initiatives. We begin by considering the problem of corporate governance and reviewing the rationale for strategic partnerships. The next section discusses the prevalence of partnerships in the United States. The following sections report on negotiated partnerships and on union involvement in corporate boards of directors. We discuss the challenges and dilemmas unions face in seeking strategic partnerships and conclude with observations on public policy.

Eileen Appelbaum is the director of the Center for Women and Work at Rutgers University. Larry W. Hunter is assistant professor of management and human resources at the School of Business of the University of Wisconsin, Madison.

8.2 Corporate Governance in the United States

Corporate governance is generally understood to refer to the legal and organizational structures that govern the relationship between corporate executives and the shareholders that are the ultimate owners of the company. Through corporate governance structures, firms make decisions about investments in plant and equipment, levels of staff and deployment of workers, location of operations, the allocation of resources, and the distribution of earnings. In theories of the firm that dominate U.S. legal and economic discourse, the purpose of corporate governance structures is to align the interests of corporate executives with those of the shareholders and to assure that managers act in shareholders' best interests (Shleifer and Vishny 1997). Shareholders have legally recognized rights to be represented on corporate boards of directors and to have their assets protected from misuse or misappropriation by the careless or opportunistic behavior of managers.

Shareholder-focused conceptions of the firm and their supporting legal structures sharply differentiate decision-making managers from workers who do not make decisions. Some states have allowed directors to consider the interests of workers and other stakeholders (Orts 1992), but most American corporate boards of directors owe a fiduciary responsibility to the companies' shareholders. Workers typically have no legally guaranteed rights to participation in corporate governance structures or to have their interests taken into account when strategic decisions are made. Shareholder-based theories reduce the relationship between owners and workers to an employment contract that specifies the wage–work effort bargain.

Contemporary practice, however, suggests that effective management requires more than the specification of this bargain because workers also make important decisions about the ways in which work gets done. Workers' engagement in decision making began on a reasonably large scale in the United States with Quality of Work Life (QWL) programs in the 1970s (Appelbaum and Batt 1994). Subsequent competitive pressures and technological developments led firms to adopt self-directed work teams and an array of other practices that facilitated worker participation in operational decisions at work sites. These practices began slowly in the 1980s and became increasingly prevalent in the 1990s (Lawler, Ledford, and Mohrman 1989; Lawler, Mohrman, and Ledford 1992; Osterman 1994; Lawler, Mohrman, and Ledford 1995; Gittleman, Horrigan, and Joyce 1998; Osterman 2000).

At the operational level, the benefits of involvement typically outweigh costs associated with joint decision making. Empirical evidence demonstrates improvements in productivity, quality, delivery times, and even financial performance as a result of worker participation in operational decisions of the enterprise (Katz, Kochan, and Weber 1985; MacDuffie 1995;

Ichniowski, Shaw, and Prennushi 1997; Appelbaum et al. 2000; Rubinstein 2000). (Becker and Gerhart [1996], Ichniowski et al. [1996], and Baker [1999] also review the evidence.) These studies suggest that corporate management has an interest in implementing what have been termed "high-performance work systems." Workers in high-performance work systems also generally find that their jobs are more intrinsically satisfying and rewarding—more challenging and able to make better use of their skills (Appelbaum et al. 2000).

At decision-making levels above that of the day-to-day workplace, however, participation and partnership typically remain the prerogative of management. Managers have resisted calls for joint decision-making forums for decisions that might require downsizing, divesting of parts or whole divisions, or shifting operations to new locations or to other (often nonunion) subsidiaries, for example. Shareholders, similarly, may oppose decision-making processes that make it more difficult for owners to capture rents associated with innovations in technology, work systems, products, or services. Managerial opposition to strategic participation by unions has often been strident (for an example, see Loughran 1985).

Traditional collective bargaining by unions, within the existing framework of labor law, provides some constraints on managerial discretion. Unions have legally protected rights to negotiate over the effects of strategic decisions (though not the decisions themselves), and collective bargaining creates governance structures within firms that affect the distribution of resources, including the extent to which the firm's revenue is shared with the workforce and the ways in which pay is allocated across workers. Unions may also negotiate to establish grievance procedures that provide a voice mechanism for workers who feel they have been treated unfairly by management and for job rules and employment security arrangements that limit employers' ability to hire and fire at will.

Union leaders have been historically reluctant to involve themselves any more deeply in strategic decision making than is called for under traditional collective bargaining. Such involvement might require them to assume responsibility for the performance of the company or to participate in business decisions that may have disparate effects on different groups of union members, and labor leaders have not embraced such a role. Thomas Donahue, then American Federation of Labor-Congress of Industrial Organization (AFL-CIO) secretary-treasurer, summarized the traditional viewpoint in a 1976 speech:

> Because American unions have won equality at the bargaining table, we have not sought it in corporate boardrooms. We do not seek to be a partner in management—to be, most likely, the junior partner in success and the senior partner in failure. We do not want to blur in any way the distinctions between the respective roles of management and labor in the plant. We guard our independence fiercely—independent of govern-

ment, independent of any political party, and independent of management.

8.2.1 The Rationale for Strategic Partnerships

Even as new work practices diffused over the 1980s and 1990s, some union leaders came to believe that neither employee involvement nor collective bargaining provided unions with the means to deal with the turbulence associated with increasingly mobile capital, global competition, and corporate restructuring. For example, some evidence on the diffusion of new work practices suggests that such practices were not typically accompanied by provisions for employment security (Osterman 1994) and that firms that adopted them were, in fact, more likely than others to lay off workers in the 1990s (Osterman 2000).

Workers tended to be favorably inclined toward new work systems, but their responses were less enthusiastic when reforms were coupled with corporate strategies that made jobs more precarious rather than more secure (Hunter, MacDuffie, and Doucet 2002). Union leaders observe that downsizing and restructuring threatened their members even as the work practices they had negotiated were delivering higher performance. These threats prompted more vigorous interest representation through collective bargaining and more skeptical attitudes toward high-performance work systems.

Some unions also began to seek venues for engaging the strategic decisions themselves, looking for influence over the direction of the business, the allocation of resources, and the distribution of revenues, and for access to the financial information and business records upon which such decisions were based. While risky, these strategic partnerships may prove to be popular with union members: the Workplace Representation and Participation Survey (Freeman and Rogers 1999) provides evidence that union members would support such institutions. Past opposition to such involvement may also have been overstated; an earlier survey by Fatehi-Sadeh and Safizadeh (1986), for example, showed that Illinois United Auto Workers (UAW) and AFL-CIO officials were favorably inclined toward strategic engagement.

Strategic partnership not only commands some support among workers but also has an underlying economic rationale. Workers who invest in firm-specific skills—skills that do not transfer easily to other jobs—have a vested interest in the long-term performance of the firm that employs them. This rationale is intensified in the current competitive environment, which features both continued downsizing and increasing use of high-performance work practices; these practices require that workers make large investments in firm-specific skills (Appelbaum and Berg 2000). As with investments by shareholders in firm-specific physical capital, the returns to investments in these skills are earned over an extended time period as the company employs these skills to generate revenue. Should strategic considerations lead companies to lay off workers before they have the chance to recover the value of their investments in skills, U.S. workers, unlike their counterparts in many European countries, have no legally enforceable means to protect their investments. A role for unions in these decisions may therefore enhance the credibility of commitments made by managers, who themselves may be employed for relatively short periods and who may have incentives focused heavily on short-term performance.

8.2.2 The Prevalence of Strategic Labor-Management Partnerships

Gray, Myers, and Myers's (1999) review of the Bureau of Labor Statistics file on contemporary collective-bargaining agreements (those expiring between September 1, 1997 and September 30, 2007 and covering more than 1,000 employees) found that nearly 47 percent of U.S. collective-bargaining agreements contained some form of "partnership." In this chapter, we focus on partnerships that include strategic engagement—negotiated agreements that provide the union with a voice in high-level decisions and with some influence over the governance of the company. Strategic partnerships enable unions to participate along with management in financial planning, in determining competitive strategy, and in decisions governing investments, technology, and production processes.

Gray, Myers, and Myers (1999) located the strategic partnerships that we discuss here at one end of a cooperation continuum, with modest arrangements (such as language indicating the intention of the parties to cooperate) at the other end, and provisions for employee involvement and information sharing somewhere between. A review of the collective-bargaining agreements showed that strategic partnerships were extremely rare: only 27 of 1,041 contracts contained provisions for what Gray, Myers, and Myers termed "full partnership"; these contracts covered about 200,000 workers.

The history of some relatively high-profile labor-management partnerships, such as the one that developed between Xerox and the Amalgamated Clothing and Textile Workers Union ([ACTWU] now the Union of Needletrades, Industrial and Textile Employees [UNITE]), implies that strategic partnerships might evolve from shop-floor cooperation as a result of a sort of natural progression (see Appelbaum and Batt [1994] for an overview of this case). Gray, Myers, and Myers (1999) similarly suggest that partnerships may progress from low levels of cooperation, through more elaborate channels for employee involvement, to full strategic partnership.

We used this premise as a starting point for a small-sample inquiry. In the summer of 1999, we surveyed twenty-five researchers in management, human resources, and labor studies. Each had published studies examining negotiated labor-management cooperation; the studies covered twenty-four different companies.[1] Many of these studies were assessments, negative as well as positive, of "high-performance workplace" practices implemented through negotiated agreements.

Our survey focused on the extent to which negotiated cooperation, or lower-level partnerships, served as a precursor to subsequent involvement of the union in strategic decisions. Because the researchers were well positioned to provide a perspective with a longitudinal element, we asked them to describe the evolution of cooperation in the union-management relationship and the extent to which strategic partnership had developed, emerged, or been negotiated.

We received usable responses from twelve researchers. Of these, five researchers reported that the union-management partnerships they studied led to no strategic participation for the union. At an information technology manufacturing company, for example, a partnership formed between corporate executives at company headquarters and the top levels of the union resulted in no high-level joint decision making at the plant being studied. Similarly, a telephone company that had negotiated more cooperative work practices with its union "never approached [strategic involvement]," according to the researcher who studied it.

Three researchers reported on companies and unions that negotiated cooperative relations, but not strategic partnerships, with the relationship blurring into discussions and consultation on strategic issues. The cooperative relation between the local union and management at one auto plant, for example, was described by a researcher as based on information sharing on business and operational matters. However, the relationship was never meant to be a strategic partnership. On the contrary, the researcher reported that "both parties jealously guard their rights and their obligations to their respective constituencies." This sort of partnership included communication, trust, consultation, and advance notice of changes; there was, however, no shared decision making or union involvement in decisions relating to financial planning, investments, pricing, competitive strategies, or production processes.

Another researcher characterized an auto agreement similarly:

> Dialogue is not the same as negotiation. Above all, it doesn't authorize any claim by the union to a legitimate place at the table. . . . In my opinion, management has been savvy and consistent in its efforts to promote worker participation (and not merely symbolic participation) while at the same time limiting the union to a fairly traditional role.

1. The companies include GTE, NYNEX, NUMMI, AT&T, Lucent, NCR, Saturn, Chrysler, US West, Pac Bell, GM Linden, Alcoa, Levi Strauss, Xerox, Harrison Radiator, Ford, Chrysler Canada, US Steel, Bethlehem Steel, Inland Steel, and companies in semiconductors, trucking, airlines, and steel that wished to remain unidentified.

Here, the union was informed and consulted prior to implementation of management decisions but rarely involved in joint decision making. For example, the company had already decided to adopt participatory workplace practices before it began any discussion with the union. It then involved the workforce extensively in the implementation of these practices.

The remaining four researchers reported on full strategic labor-management agreements that accompanied other kinds of cooperation at five companies. Differences in the origins and evolution of these agreements are instructive. In the steel industry, strategic participation was driven by the United Steelworkers of America (USWA) national bargaining agenda (discussed in more detail in the following). The agenda includes a commitment to build strategic labor-management partnerships wherever possible in order to gain increased control over company decision making. Researchers reported that companies in the steel and aluminum industries entered into strategic partnership agreements with the USWA because they needed to introduce new workplace practices in order to meet heightened global competition. The companies sought to redesign work processes, to increase discretionary effort, and, by doing so, to improve operational performance at the plant level; this required union participation. In practice, these partnerships have been implemented differently across companies and even across plants in the same company.

Telecommunications researchers described a contrasting case. Competition from nonunion companies led one large company to enter into strategic partnership with the Communication Workers of America (CWA). The company wanted union support for favorable legislation and administrative rulings domestically as well as union help when it sought approval to participate in a foreign telephone company. This, it believed, would help the company compete and grow; the union supported these efforts because they were likely to result in more union jobs. The union made company neutrality in union organizing drives and card check recognition for the union key requirements for its participation in a strategic alliance at this and other telecom companies. According to the researchers,

> The striking aspect of the union security clauses is that while the union began to demand [them] soon after divestiture, it met with limited success until the companies began needing union support in the regulatory arena. . . . The union supported their efforts in return for some guarantees for union and job security. . . . The union won the union security clauses by linking regulatory and collective bargaining activities.

Researchers suggested, however, that while CWA is involved in an alliance with the company about strategic issues, unlike the steelworkers, the union does not necessarily see shared decision-making authority as a key piece of its bargaining agenda.

Our survey of researchers is consistent with the data that show that strategic labor-management partnerships are rare. Even in cases where labor and management made commitments to cooperation at other levels, strategic involvement was unusual and did not typically follow other kinds of cooperation as part of an unfolding process. The survey suggested further that where such partnerships exist, they need not necessarily have evolved out of earlier experiences with negotiated cooperative relationships. Rather, there are a variety of paths to strategic partnership. We turn our attention to these paths next.

8.2.3 The Shape of Strategic Engagement: Negotiated Partnerships

Some union leaders and companies have established strategic partnerships through negotiation. In the following we consider in more detail the content of these partnerships as well as the reasons that different unions and firms agreed to construct them. We do so with reference to four different partnerships, negotiated by unions in electrical contracting, telecommunications, steel, and manufacturing.

Two primary kinds of interests—company growth (or stability) and new work practices—have brought companies and their workers' unions together in strategic partnerships. In the following we consider examples of each. First, as competitive pressures continue to intensify, companies and unions may find that they have a common interest in seeing the company grow. Growth of the company and expansion of union jobs, when these are mutually agreed upon goals, can be advanced by a partnership relationship. The cooperation of the union can help management preserve or increase market share, while the union sees involvement in defense or expansion of market share as an opportunity to protect and promote union jobs.

Second, at many companies increased competition also leads managers to introduce participatory management and high-performance workplace practices. Strategic involvement can complement these practices. An active union role in decisions about workplace practices provides workers with a further voice and a forum for addressing the context in which the organization introduces new practices. Unions, like companies, have an interest in the adoption of practices that contribute to organizational viability and success. Mutual respect for both company and union goals can also be advanced by partnership relationships.

Cooperative Efforts in the Electrical Construction Industry

Perhaps the longest standing labor-management joint relationship in the United States is in the electrical contracting industry between the International Brotherhood of Electrical Workers (IBEW) and the National Electrical Contractors Association (NECA). Composed of an equal number of representatives from the IBEW and NECA, the Council on Industrial Relations was established in 1920 as a judicial body to handle labor-management disputes in the electrical construction industry. Disputes are submitted voluntarily, and all decisions are unanimous. The Council on Industrial Relations attempts to keep the industry free of strikes, serves as binding arbitrator for the industry, and meets to discuss safety and training matters. The NECA and the IBEW also jointly operate the National Joint Apprenticeship and Training Committee for the electrical industry. This program was established in 1947 as the national coordinating arm for apprenticeship training. With a budget of approximately $80 million a year, it operates more than 300 local apprenticeship training programs as well as in-service skill-improvement training for electricians.

Building on these experiences with joint programs, NECA and the IBEW responded to competition from nonunion electrical contractors by establishing the National Labor Management Cooperation Committee (NLMCC) in 1995. In addition to more traditional functions, such as promoting mutual-gains bargaining, the NLMCC functions as a strategic partnership between the thousands of union electrical contractors associated with NECA and the IBEW, which represents more than 300,000 electrical construction workers. About 4,200 electrical contractors are members of NECA, and nearly 12,000 other union electrical contractors are "signatory" contractors who have indicated that they would like to be covered by the NECA contract. The NLMCC is funded at one cent per person-hour worked, or at about $3.5 million per year.

Five years ago, in the context of its "Blueprint for the 90s," the NLMCC developed a "market recovery program" to take back market share from the vast number of small, nonunion contractors in the construction industry. Local NECA and IBEW groups work together to administer surveys to determine how much construction work is carried out by union contractors and union workers and to develop programs for increasing the share of union work; the NLMCC helps to finance and conduct the surveys.

The program also includes joint campaigns to increase the number of apprentices, to create pride in the industry and union, and, especially, to promote the advantages of using union contractors. The NECA and the IBEW jointly advertise union contractors and jointly hire sales people to market union contractors to builders and architects. Advertising emphasizes the skills and versatility of union electricians and the pride they take in doing their jobs well. *Quality Connection,* an industry magazine published by the NLMCC, also supports this effort.

The IBEW described the market recovery program and the NLMCC as successful partnerships, noting that the number of union apprentices in the industry rose from 25,000 to 40,000 in the last half of the 1990s. Further, in 1987 only about 28 percent of the electrical construction market was unionized. By 1999, according to IBEW, the market share of union contractors had risen to 37 percent of workers in the electrical construction industry.

The Workplace of the Future in Telecommunications

Concerns over market share and jobs also drove unions to seek strategic engagement in the telecommunications industry. One example comes from AT&T, where the loss of monopoly protection in 1984 and the breakup of the Bell System led to a dramatic decline in union jobs. AT&T eliminated over 60 percent of its unionized workforce between 1984 and 1992, while the regional Bell companies reduced the number of employees by about 30 percent through attrition (Batt, Katz, and Keefe 1999).

More than 100,000 CWA jobs were lost, and union leadership came to believe that traditional collective bargaining was limited in its ability to prevent further job losses. The smaller IBEW presence was also weakened: all IBEW jobs in some units, such as sales, were lost. The unions were concerned not only about the effects of restructuring on their membership but about their own institutional security. In 1991, after acquiring NCR, a company that had aggressively used plant closures and other policies to avoid unionization, AT&T allowed NCR to go forward with a full range of antiunion tactics. This occurred simultaneously with discussions AT&T had begun with CWA about a code of conduct that would commit both the company and union to nonhostile behaviors during union organizing drives (Nissen 1998).

On the management side, AT&T came to believe it would be able to compete more successfully if its union relationships were cooperative rather than adversarial. The company hoped that more cooperative relations with its unions would help it to expand its market share: unionized workers were heavily involved in customer service, and the company found it difficult, in a competitive environment, to gain new business and to retain customers while engaging in adversarial relationships with these workers and their representatives.

The partnership model negotiated between AT&T and its unions, the CWA and the IBEW, known as the Workplace of the Future, was intended to help all parties move from an adversarial to a more cooperative relationship. The partnership was kicked off in March 1993. The agreement states that "[t]he parties share the goals of establishing a world class, high performance organization and protecting employment security through market success," and recognizes that market success will require the company to target customer satisfaction and market flexibility (Communications Workers of America [CWA] 1993, 1). Further, the agreement recognized that "[j]oint training, jointly designed, will be essential to develop common understandings, describe business strategies, and develop union expertise in new technology" (CWA 1993, 1).

The partnership structure of the Workplace of the Future had four components. Workplace models, to be jointly defined by the company and its unions, were charged with identifying and managing the implementation of workplace practices that enhance quality, customer satisfaction, quality of work life, and competitiveness. Business Unit/Division Planning Councils were intended to facilitate participation by the unions in business decisions regarding technology, work organization, job content, training, employment, and in the development of cooperative work and leadership styles. The Constructive Relationship Council, established through bargaining in 1989, would continue to function and would facilitate the work of the Workplace Models and Business Unit/Division Planning Councils. Finally, a Human Resources Board, consisting of three AT&T executives, one union leader each from the CWA and the IBEW, and two distinguished leaders in the field of human resources, was established. The Human Resource Board was to address "broad, strategic, global human resources and business issues within the context of the external environment over long range time frames" (CWA 1993, 1).

The various partnership structures called for in the Workplace of the Future agreement have provided the unions and workers with increased opportunities for participation, but the record has been uneven. The joint committees have not met the unions' expectations. The top-level Human Resources Board has provided only limited opportunities for union participation in strategic decisions. It functions mainly as a means for the unions to obtain information from AT&T.

The record of the partnership in promoting greater security for the workforce and for the union has also been mixed. Employment security language remains weak, and restructuring continues to cause great insecurity for workers. This problem has been especially acute for IBEW; CWA has had more opportunities to try to save jobs by suggesting alternatives to the company or to mitigate the effects of downsizing on workers. The company, however, has not always accepted the unions' job-saving recommendations.

The partnership has been further strained by the unions' perception that AT&T is hostile to the unions' institutional interests. For example, when CWA successfully organized a majority of the potential members at AT&T's American Transtech to sign union cards, the company backed down on its neutrality pledge, embarking on an antiunion campaign. The union lost the 1995 representation election. More recently, the company has been buying into parts of the telecommunications industry that are nonunion and resisting the unions' attempts to organize these workers. For example, AT&T acquired Tele-Communication, Inc. (TCI) and Media One in order to get into the cable business, but these acquisitions were not discussed in the partnership. The long-term prospects of the partnership, in CWA's view, depend largely on whether AT&T agrees to neutrality when the unions undertake organizing drives to represent workers in its cable operations.

New Directions Bargaining in Steel

In the decade following the 1982 collapse of steel production in the United States, integrated steel mills were idled, employment fell, and wage and benefit concessions led to sharp declines in real compensation for steelworkers. In 1992, the USWA adopted its New Directions bargaining program, seeking "an ongoing voice for itself and its members in managerial decisions affecting shop-floor, plant, and corporate performance, all with an eye toward producing business success sufficiently sustained and shared as to serve both company and worker interests on a continuing basis." (Frankel 1997, 3). The program, according to USWA President George Becker, calls for "employment security guarantees and partnership agreements providing for union and worker involvement at every level from a seat on the Board of Directors to problem-solving on the shop floor." (Becker 1998, 120).

Building on its 1986 partnership agreement with National Steel, the USWA introduced New Directions bargaining in the 1993–1994 round of contract negotiations. The main provisions of the New Directions program include a no-layoff guarantee; union involvement in workplace and corporate decision making; restructuring the work place to increase flexibility, improve productivity, and reduce costs; and neutrality and card check recognition when the union seeks to organize nonrepresented employees (Frankel 1997). The program also included a strategic alliance between the company and the union with respect to public policy and joint company and union responses to industry trends. The union successfully negotiated contracts that included these partnership provisions with the major integrated steel companies—Inland, National, Bethlehem, USX, and LTV. Contracts with other companies, including Wheeling-Pittsburgh, Republic Engineered Steels, USS/Kobe, Acme, J&L Specialty, Lukens Steel, Gulf States, and Northwestern Steel and Wire, contained many of the substantive features of the New Directions program. The agreements were for six years and have been renegotiated since August 1, 1999. Partnership agreements remain an important part of the unions' bargaining agenda and have been renegotiated with the major integrated steel companies.

The partnership agreement provides the union with the right to participate, along with company managers, in decisions at multiple levels. At the corporate level, joint strategic partnership committees bring union leaders and company executives together to consider strategic plans, technological change, staffing levels, customer evaluations, major organizational issues, and facilities utilization. The agreements also include mechanisms by which union and plant officials can negotiate over instituting modern work practices; plant steering committees investigate alternative approaches to safety, work redesign, work assignments and scheduling, planning for technological change, training, and process improvement.

The New Directions Bargaining Pattern contains provisions that require the steel companies to remain neutral when the USWA seeks to organize their nonrepresented employees and, in most cases, to recognize the union once a majority of workers has signed union cards. The strength of these provisions was tested quickly after their adoption: in the 1993–1994 contracts, such provisions covered only those affiliates in which the steel company directly or indirectly owned more than 50 percent of the voting power. Subsequently, LTV took exactly a 50 percent stake in a minimill in Gadsden, Alabama—in the union's view, to evade the neutrality provisions—and the USWA put the partnership it had negotiated with the company in 1993 on hold. Both workers and the union refused to participate in problem-solving and decision-making activities. In the 1999 bargaining round, the neutrality provisions were extended to cover any entity in which the steel company owns a material interest and whose business involves steel raw materials or steel production and distribution; LTV agreed to accept these provisions and to withdraw from its joint venture in the Alabama steel mill if its partners refused to remain neutral during a USWA organizing drive.

The acquiescence of LTV to the neutrality provisions suggests that the withdrawal of the workers and union from involvement in decision making and from cooperation in plant committees had consequences for performance at LTV's integrated mills. More generally, Appelbaum and Berg (2000) report that the partnership program of the USWA played an important role in increasing the legitimacy of worker involvement on the shop floor from the perspectives of both workers and managers, observing that employment security provisions assure individual workers that they will not work themselves out of a job if they use their capacities to innovate to contribute to increased productivity. The new workplace practices, these authors show, were associated with significantly higher productivity and contributed heavily to the return to profitability of the integrated mills and to the turnaround in the steel industry.

The extent to which these partnership agreements have been implemented by union and management officials varies widely as does the extent to which union officials participate in strategic decisions at the corporate level. Some local unions and managers have been able to use the partnership agreement to engage in mutual-gains bargaining, but other facilities have experienced resistance from union officials or local managers to the basic elements of cooperation and partnership. Both union officials and managers express skepticism about whether the New Directions partnerships in steel live up to expectations about union participation in top-level strategic decisions. But the partnerships have proven valuable to both steel companies and the USWA as a means to modernize workplace practices, improve the economic viability of the integrated steel mills and the strength of the union as an institution, and preserve or expand union jobs in the industry.

High-Performance Work Organization (HPWO) Partnerships

The International Association of Machinists and Aerospace Workers (IAMAW) has successfully launched HPWO partnerships, or is far along in the process, at approximately fifty (out of several thousand) of the facilities at which it represents workers. Union locals and managers at a far larger number of work sites have taken early steps toward partnerships. Partnerships are being developed not only at leading companies such as Harley Davidson or Weyerhauser, but at smaller companies, often family owned. The union intends the HPWO Partnerships to enhance employers' competitive position and thus its members' job security and welfare. Partnerships have been developed with companies that wanted to increase market share in the face of intense competition as well as with those facing financial problems that pose a threat to their survival.

The IAMAW observes that partnerships must begin with the commitment of management to growth; this commitment enables the union's participation in developing and implementing plans to achieve that growth. In the view of the union, if all management and the union do "is increase productivity and efficiency and do not develop strategies to stabilize and grow the business and get control of costs, employees may improve their way out of employment" (International Association of Machinists and Aerospace Workers [IAMAW] 1999, 1).

In addition to growth, the IAMAW has several other aims for its high performance work organizations. These include agreement on employment security, development of an education and communication plan for all employees, and an implementation plan for replacing traditional top-down decision making by managers with joint decision making by labor and management at the appropriate levels of the organization. The union expects to be "recognized as a valued and trusted partner by management." At the same time, "the institutional support and protection provided by the union for the Partnership helps employees accept new roles and explore new work methods" (IAMAW 1999, 5). The IAMAW thus identifies three components of a successful partnership: a business plan that incorporates long-term returns, market expansion, and growth of the workforce; accurate costing-out of the activities that support production of the firm's products and services; and changes in the work process that improve quality and productivity.

Extensive education, training, and planning go into developing partnerships. Several years may elapse between the time the union and company agree to explore a partnership relationship and the time an agreement is implemented. Partnership agreements establish governance structures to guide the development of a growth strategy. The corporate partnership committee at Harley Davidson, for example, comprises four union and two company representatives. Only after the union and management have agreed on a growth strategy and a system for costing activities will the union agree to assess work processes jointly and to propose improvements. The introduction of high-performance workplace practices follows, rather than precedes, the development of the partnership.

Partnership structures also include decision-making bodies at the workplace, such as business-unit or plant-level teams. These teams determine appropriate performance measures and guide implementation of new in work practices. Shop stewards meet daily with their salaried counterparts, and natural work groups gather and share information, solve problems, and make daily operational decisions. (IAMAW 1999). To assist its local unions, the IAMAW also has a five-person department that provides consulting and training and seven field staff that provide support services. Particularly in smaller companies, top managers have welcomed advice on business-process improvement and the development of alternative products and workplace practices.

Many of the partnerships have been established in firms and plants that have the inefficiencies typical of older manufacturing systems. The trying circumstances have provided a motivation for cooperation but have also made it difficult to establish trust, develop joint decision making, or to make fundamental changes in work processes. Obstacles to successful partnerships include the difficulty of taking on new roles for managers, professionals, other salaried employees, union leaders, and workers. For example, engineers and supervisors may fear that they have much to lose from the partnerships and may be reluctant to participate. Further, under competitive duress, managers experience more pressure to turn to layoffs, and the union may interpret consideration of such options as less than trustworthy. Shop-floor frustration with the pace of change or skepticism about management's motives can lead to rejection of union leaders or of contracts that include partnership agreements.

Yet a partnership that provides a commitment by management and the union to jointly developing a proactive approach to addressing competitive pressures may be the key both to survival for the company and to employment security for workers. The partnership may also increase the union's strength as it comes to be seen by its members as providing real leadership to ensure the employer's long-term survival and growth, thereby preserving jobs.

8.3 Union Representatives on Corporate Boards of Directors

Our reviews and descriptions of partnerships are consistent with the finding that fewer than 3 percent of major collective-bargaining agreements feature these arrangements: full partnerships appear to be extremely difficult for unions to establish and maintain. Negotiated strategic partnerships occupy precarious ground. They are vulnerable to collapse where union members are skeptical of the value of such involvement. Their survival and effectiveness also depend heavily on management commitment to the partnership because information sharing and joint decision making are integral parts of strategic involvement. What is less clear is whether unions can force such commitment upon management given sufficient bargaining power or whether commitment depends in part on the good faith of management.

Several American unions, aware of the tenuous nature of negotiated partnerships, have sought to bolster their strategic influence further by seeking seats on the boards of directors of companies where they represent members. Board seats for unions are not necessarily coupled with other joint approaches or a commitment to partnership in decision making. Throughout the 1970s and 1980s, for example, union-nominated directorships resulted chiefly from negotiations over the institution of Employee Stock Ownership Plans [ESOPs] (Hunter 1998). In these cases, protection of the workers' ownership interests, rather than an increased commitment to shared strategic decision making, motivated union leaders to seek board representation. But board seats can be particularly valuable in strategic partnerships because directorships come with statutory rights to information and involvement in decisions. Such seats have emerged as a target of collective bargaining in programs such as the USWA's New Directions and the IAMAW's HPWO partnerships.

Hunter (1998) identifies three important constraints on union-nominated directors' abilities to use the corporate board to represent workers' interests in strategic decisions. First, union nominees, like all directors on American corporate boards, are required to represent the interests of shareholders (for a more complete description of this responsibility, see Johnson, Daily, and Ellstrand 1996), and are legally liable should they fail to do so effectively. Their fiduciary duties typically proscribe directors from explicit representation of union interests, except where they can argue that meeting such interests is consistent with protecting shareholders' investments.

A second constraint on interest representation in the boardroom is normative: the view of the proper role of corporate boards that pervades American managerial and directors' communities. On typical boards, outside directors—those not part of the executive team—rarely involve themselves with issues of day-to-day governance. Only major events, such as takeovers or changes in top executives, bring forth outside director activism (Useem 1993). Board functioning in less-dramatic circumstances relies on consensus rather than constituency representation or explicit negotiation among competing interests.

Third, managers' interests are not always aligned with those of the firms' shareholders, and managerial opposition to shared control can derail strategic engagement even when it is to the benefit of shareholders. Here the experiences of the International Brotherhood of Teamsters (IBT) with board nominees are instructive. Following deregulation and the weakening of pattern bargaining in the 1980s, trucking companies sought wage concessions. In several firms, workers accepted stock in return for wage concessions; the IBT insisted on board seats to accompany the stock plans. Several of the Teamster-nominated directors envisioned these seats as vehicles to foster joint discussion of the strategic issues facing the firm and union, but this never developed. Instead, the boards became the venues through which the IBT attempted to protect its members' financial investments as the firms struggled. The managers guarded information closely and made as many decisions as possible outside the boardroom. Most of the IBT boards were characterized by considerable mistrust between outside directors and inside managers: one Teamster-nominated director actually sued the managers of his firm. All of the Teamster board schemes eventually disappeared as the firms were acquired or went bankrupt in the fierce competition that followed deregulation.

Awareness of these legal, normative, and practical constraints has dimmed union enthusiasm in board representation as a forum for strategic engagement. Chrysler, for example, was the first large American company to have a union representative on its board, with UAW President Douglas Fraser obtaining a seat following the concessions associated with Chrysler's near bankruptcy in 1980. In 1984, after some wrangling, Fraser's successor as president, Owen Bieber, assumed the seat. The Chrysler-UAW experience illustrated the limits of board representation: both Fraser and Bieber found it difficult to influence management policy in this venue. After several years, the UAW did not emphasize preservation of the board seat as a bargaining objective. The corporation restructured its board, dropping Bieber in 1991.

Nevertheless, experiments with board representation continue. Table 8.1 lists American firms in which union representatives have recently served on corporate boards of directors. Typically, these boards have one or more directors, but fewer than a majority, nominated by a union; the board seats are written into either the collective-bargaining contract or, where backed by share ownership, the ESOP agreement. With the exception of the airlines, the firms have directors representing members of only one union; airline boards comprise members of both the Airline Pilots Association (ALPA) and the IAMAW. In addition to the American firms listed in table 8.1, the UAW is represented on the twenty-person supervisory board of directors of at the German company Daimler-Chrysler. Under German law, the unions that represent Daimler-Chrysler workers in Germany are entitled to three seats; the German union IG Metall has allowed a UAW representative to assume one of the seats.

Though union officials (including presidents of international unions such as Bieber and Fraser) have held directorships, union board represen-

Table 8.1 **Some U.S. companies with union-nominated board directors (circa 2000)**

Algoma Steel
Allegheny Teledyne
Bethlehem Steel
Cable Systems International
Cleveland Cliffs
Hawaiian Airlines
J&L Specialty
LTV
Maryland Brush Co.
National Steel
Northwest Airlines
TWA
United Airlines
Weirton Steel
Wheeling Pittsburgh

tation does not imply that directors must be active unionists or workers. The IAMAW, for example, discourages active union leaders from serving on boards; among its representatives are a number of retired union officials. Another common approach is the nomination of friendly "neutrals"—consultants, lawyers, even college professors—to serve as directors. Some of these union-nominated directors have been effective in improving firm governance in the interests of shareholders (Hunter 1998). Many union-nominated directors have characteristics that, according to corporate governance theorists, should make directors effective: a strong interest in the well-being of the company; sources of information; independence from management; and ties to important stakeholders (Patton and Baker 1987). Union nominees with the right skills, commitment, and support can be as effective contributors to governance as other outside directors.

A few of the boards of companies in table 8.1 have established themselves as forums for strategic partnerships between labor and management. Most typically, this occurs when the board seats are seen by the parties as part of a broader approach to labor-management cooperation, and the parties have strong reasons for cooperation rooted in the demands of the competitive market. Wever's (1989) case study of the Western Airlines board, for example, showed that board participation was stronger when accompanied by further forms of employee involvement and that all these forms of involvement were stronger when unions were more powerful and secure. As with other partnerships, the institutional security of the union and the perception of the union that management will not (or is not powerful enough to) undermine that security are important prerequisites for success.

Union-nominated directors have had influence on strategic decision making in a number of areas. Cagy, experienced directors can use norms of consensus to stall or delay decisions by withholding approval, for example. Union-nominated directors may discourage managers from implementing plans that will be perceived by the unions as divisive or destructive. Typically, they can do so by using their board positions to raise issues for discussion and by requiring managers to address the argument that plans that provoke union opposition may be bad for the company (and its shareholders) in the long term.

Directors also affect the selection and compensation of top executives. Union nominees can push to hire managers who are relatively more committed to partnership and to protecting the institutional interests of the union, for example, and may be able to stall or block the appointments of managers that they believe would be hostile. Directors can also ensure that executive pay packages are established (and explained to the workforce) in ways consistent with the preservation of partnership rather than in ways that breed distrust or discontent.

Board representatives can also be helpful in preserving a role for collective bargaining while placing it in strategic context. The presence of union representatives on corporate boards can help each side make its position credible to the other: books are relatively more open, for example, and directors can establish additional channels for communication.

While board representation can facilitate aspects of partnership, such as information sharing, it is clear that such representation provides no guarantees that the parties will work together to address joint concerns amicably. In addition to the difficulties at Chrysler and the problems the Teamsters had, there have been other well-publicized fiascos with union board seats. At the Rath Packing Company, the boardroom became yet another locus of destructive labor-management conflict (Hammer and Stern 1986), with the union eventually calling a strike against the firm its members owned. At Hyatt-Clark, similarly, the boardroom featured fierce battles over the distribution of wages and dividends ("Hyatt-Clark ESOP" 1985). At Eastern Airlines, labor-management battles raged even as the company plummeted into bankruptcy (Smaby 1988).

United Airlines provides a recent example of the challenges that union-nominated directorships face. The ALPA and the IAMAW obtained one seat each on the board of directors, along with share ownership, in 1994. (The flight attendants did not join in the plan, though nonunion employees also took partial ownership and one board seat.) Directors struggled to establish their roles. The union nominees owed fiduciary responsibilities to all shareholders. Yet they owed their seats, and their loyalties, to the unions that had nominated them. On the board, directors formally represented employees' ownership interests. In practice, the distinction between these interests; the interests of employees in their jobs, wages, and working conditions; and the interests of the unions as institutions tended to get tangled up.

Following the employee buyout, board representation did not emerge as a catalyst for further cooperative approaches to labor-management relations. Over time, the likelihood that an effective partnership would be established diminished as trust between top managers and the unions eroded. A difficult round of bargaining in 1997 was followed by a dispute over the IAMAW's organizing of passenger service agents. An on again–off again proposal for a merger with USAirways provided further controversy. Eventually, the difficulties in the relationship began to have detrimental effects on company performance. In summer 2000 pilots were accused of engaging in work slowdowns (the pilots' spokesmen denied the accusations), and the 2001 round of bargaining between United and the IAMAW was bitter even by industry standards. The airline's performance did not improve relative to its competitors after the buyout (Gittell, von Nordenflycht, and Kochan 2004), and none of the parties saw the ESOP as a success story.

8.3.1 Dilemmas for Unions

In the United States, it seems unlikely that managers or public policy will act to establish joint participation. Thus strategic partnerships will depend primarily on union initiatives. We therefore turn next to the dilemmas that such partnerships pose for unions and consider the ways in which unions have addressed these challenges.

Unions have brought three different orientations to strategic partnerships. First, where workers have invested in the firm through stock purchases and ESOPs, unions can negotiate for ways to monitor managers more carefully from an investor's point of view. Second, partnerships can be defensive, focused on company growth or stability and on the preservation of union jobs. Third, the partnership may be part of an overall attempt by the union to involve itself more deeply in the management of the firm in which the union and its members seek to deploy their expertise to promote firm performance.

Strategic participation from any orientation, whether exercised through negotiated partnerships or through board seats, raises difficult challenges for unions. Problems with participation at the local level are relatively well understood (Frost 2000): the commitment of local representatives to labor-management participation enhances their chances for success, but such commitment requires local unionists to redefine their roles and to convince their members of the value associated with cooperation (Kochan 1985). At the strategic level, the stakes are high. Issues taken up at the strategic level affect job security and the survival of the firm and the union. Historically, union leaders have been averse to accepting even partial responsibility for managerial decisions. They remain skeptical that partnerships will provide true influence, believing that managers are not willing to share decision-making authority. Successful strategic partnerships therefore require unions to determine either that management is committed to participation or can be forced to engage in partnership.

To gain workers' support, strategic partnerships must protect not only workers' investments but also the institutional security of the union itself. American managers enjoy considerable freedom to oppose workers' right to organize and to move work from union to nonunion settings through outsourcing or investment strategies. This aspect of U.S. industrial relations shapes union leaders' reactions to partnerships. On the one hand, because union leaders are centrally concerned with preserving union jobs, they have incentives to seek a variety of strategies, including partnerships, that might be effective in doing so. On the other hand, continued attention to institutional security on the part of the union leaders can distract from other issues that might be considered jointly. The ability of managers to walk away from labor-management relationships, and, in some cases, their demonstrated willingness to do so, can erode the mutual trust necessary to make partnerships effective.

Union leaders are likely to see any purported benefits of partnership as vacuous in the presence of threats to the continued vitality of labor representation for the firms' workers. One promising area for further research is the relationship between union organizing and strategic partnerships. Through strategic partnerships, unions have sought to establish conditions of neutrality toward further organizing and toward treatment of acquisitions. Where partnerships have floundered, on the other hand, it is often because the unions have been unable to forge this kind of arrangement. Keeping union jobs inside the firm rather than outsourcing them may be a similar precondition for success.

Even where the parties have enough common interests to warrant cooperation, further factors also mitigate against the success of strategic partnerships. Effectiveness of strategic partnerships can be greatly enhanced by the support and involvement of the broader union. International unions have more resources to train and guide local leaders, and they can provide directors and local leaders in partnerships with information and expert advice. International unions, however, are also charged with setting industry frameworks for bargaining and with the establishment of common standards and principles. This creates problems for the international with respect to strategic participation. As one union leader remarked,

> When I talk about a conflict of interest I'm not really talking about the simple union-management problem. The issue is really single enterprise loyalty. I don't want me or the [international] union to be in a position of playing God, to be picking winners in the industry. (Hunter 1998, 564)

Strategic engagement and partnerships confront competitive issues in which decisions that help one firm may harm another. A dilemma for international union leaders is to establish principles for support of partnerships that will enable them to avoid being caught up in such intraindustry competition. Internationals, and hence partnerships, are more likely to be effective where circumstances permit the partnership to focus on competitive challenges that do not raise such internal problems for the union (for example, attacking the nonunion sector in electrical contracting).

Successful partnerships require the commitment of substantial union resources, both to the achievement of the partnership (because management is often opposed) and to its support and maintenance. With the benefits of strategic engagement unclear, unions may be reluctant to provide the required levels of support; few unions besides the USWA, IAMAW, and ALPA, for example, have identified strategic partnerships as an objective of collective bargaining, and the USWA is currently reassessing the prominence it has assigned to this goal. Within the CWA, similarly, the future of partnerships is being debated, with skeptics questioning the commitment of union resources to participation at the expense of activities such as organizing.

Union-management strategic partnerships also may exclude from the discussion parties that are necessary to the long-term success of the firm (Heckscher and Shurman 1997). For example, inside the firm, middle managers and supervisors go unrepresented, yet their reactions strongly affect the success of strategic initiatives or the introduction of new work systems. Further, partnerships must be matched to the appropriate level of organizational decision making: corporate-level partnerships may be ineffectual in a highly decentralized management structure, for example, while effective division- or plant-level partnerships may be undone with a single decision made at corporate headquarters.

Table 8.2 brings together in summary form a range of choices available to unions in the design of these institutions. The choices union leaders make will depend on a number of factors: internal union politics and structure; the particular features of the competitive markets in which the firms seek to compete (the extent of unionization, global competition, or competition on the basis of price, for example); the bargaining power of the union at the local and international levels; and the relationship and history union leaders have with local and corporate-level management.

8.4 Concluding Remarks

Few firms have actively sought the involvement of union leaders in strategic decisions. Rather, the construction of these forums has required unusual circumstances, strong common interests in surviving in difficult competitive environments, and determined union leadership. Nor have strategic partnerships in the United States evolved naturally from other kinds of partnerships or employee involvement programs. Though managers will

Table 8.2 Choices facing union leaders in the design of institutions for strategic partnership

Type of choice	International union	International or local union	Local union
Establishment of partnership	• Does the international union advocate partnerships as a matter of policy? • Does the union support board seats? • Does the union support negotiated strategic partnerships? • What policy should the union demand of the company with respect to subsequent organizing campaigns?	• Does the union bargain for partnership structures? • If management is reluctant to agree, how much is partnership worth? • How should future organizing campaigns and acquisition of nonunion operations be handled?	• Should workers buy stock in their own company? • Should partnerships accompany concession bargaining? • What role should employment security guarantees play in the partnership agreement?
Identity of union representatives in strategic level decisions	• Should active international union leaders be permitted to involve themselves in governance decisions of individual companies?	• What criteria will be used to select representatives?	• Who will the representatives be?
Continuing support for representatives	• Will the international union provide training and technical support for the representatives?	• Will the union attempt to coordinate with or instruct the representatives?	• Will structures be established for communication between representatives, local union leaders, and local members?

continue to seek performance advantages from employee involvement in the workplace, they seem less likely to invite unions into the executive suite or other arenas for strategic partnership.

The primary rationale for union-management partnerships is to promote the long-term competitive position of the firm in directions consistent with protection of the workers' investments in the firm, whether in financial or in human capital. In some environments, the parties may not have enough common interests to make partnership viable. As Heckscher and Shurman (1997) note, a potentially "fatal problem" with partnerships is that they cannot address the turbulence outside the firm that seems to be endemic to the current economy.

Management opposition to partnerships may derive from the calculation that the benefits from cooperation are outweighed by the potential costs. There is a self-reinforcing quality to this calculation: the less cooperative the relationship between labor and management, the more likely it is that the parties will not be able to discover or realize joint gains. Nor is it clear that opposition is purely economic. In the absence of clear evidence of advantages, managers may oppose shared control for ideological reasons or believe that partnerships reflect poorly on their ability to manage.

A further consideration is that American labor laws provide relatively weak protection of workers' rights to organize. Even in unionized firms, managers typically oppose vigorously any attempts to extend union representation and seek opportunities to move work from union to nonunion environments. Preserving this ability to oppose unionization also provides another reason for managers' reluctance to purse partnership. Union involvement in strategic decision making tends, on the other hand, to be concentrated heavily on preserving membership. In the absence of such security, union leaders find it difficult to engage in the kinds of cooperation that would permit the parties to confront the kinds of threats to employees' job security and earnings that could be addressed by joint efforts such as those directed toward training or the implementation of high-performance work practices.

More generally, public policy developments that would mandate, or even encourage, strategic partnerships between unions and management also seem exceedingly unlikely. In fact, American unions now confront the issue of strategic participation in a legal environment that fits union-management partnerships poorly. Little legal guidance exists on how partnerships should be conducted even where the parties find ways to establish them—on the extent to which union leaders might compromise their duty of fair representation to their members in the exercise of their fiduciary duties as board directors, for example, or how they might reconcile duties of representation with decisions made in the process of strategic planning. Directors also enjoy little legal guidance on the extent to which they are allowed to share information with the unions that nominate them to boards.

Management lawyers tend to advise union nominees to share nothing, which is hardly consistent with the spirit of the arrangements. Antitrust law governing interlocking directorates is also vague in its application to these contexts and with respect to whether international unions can send representatives to multiple firms. Further, the extent to which conflicts of interest require union-nominated directors to remove themselves from discussions is debatable both in theory and practice. Several boards have considered, with different results, whether the presence of the union representatives in the boardroom is appropriate during discussions of collective-bargaining strategy. Negotiated partnerships, while less burdened by legal requirements than are directorships, operate in a legal vacuum. The further emergence of both these forms of partnership should be considered in the surrounding legal context, and changes in that context merit close attention for those interested in strategic participation.

References

Appelbaum, E., T. Bailey, P. Berg, and A. Kalleberg. 2000. *Manufacturing advantage: Why high performance work systems pay off.* Ithaca, N.Y.: Cornell University Press.

Appelbaum, E., and R. Batt. 1994. *The new American workplace: Transforming work systems in the United States.* Ithaca, N.Y.: Cornell University Press.

Appelbaum, E., and P. Berg. 2000. High-performance work systems: Giving workers a stake. In *The new relationship: Human capital in the American corporation,* ed. M. M. Blair and T. A. Kochan, 102–44. Washington, D.C.: Brookings Institution.

Baker, T. 1999. *Doing well by doing good: The bottom line on workplace practices.* Washington, D.C.: Economic Policy Institute.

Batt, R., H. C. Katz, and J. Keefe. 1999. The strategic initiatives of the CWA: Organizing, politics, and collective bargaining. Paper presented at symposium, Changing Employment Relations and New Institutions of Representation. 25–26 May, Ithaca, N.Y.

Becker, B., and B. Gerhart. 1996. The impact of human resource management on organizational performance: Progress and prospects. *The Academy of Management Journal* 39 (4): 779–801.

Becker, G. 1998. A history of advocating labor/management cooperation. *New Steel* 14 (March): 120.

Communications Workers of America (CWA) 1993. *Workplace of the future.* Washington, D.C.: WA.

Donahue, T. 1976. Speech presented at conference, International Conference on Trends in Industrial and Labor Relations. 26 May, Montreal, Quebec, Canada.

Fatehi-Sadeh, K., and H. Safizadeh. 1986. Labor union leaders and codetermination: An evaluation of attitudes. *Employee Relations Law Journal* 12 (2): 188–204.

Frankel, C. B. 1997. *New directions bargaining in the American steel industry.* Pittsburgh, Pa.: United Steelworkers of America.

Freeman, R. B., and J. Rogers. 1999. *What workers want.* Ithaca, N.Y.: ILR Press.
Frost, A. C. 2000. Explaining variation in workplace restructuring: The role of local union capabilities. *Industrial and Labor Relations Review* 53 (4): 559–78.
Gittell, J. H., A. von Nordenflycht, and T. Kochan. 2004. Mutual gains or zero sum? Labor relations and firm performance in the airline industry. *Industrial and Labor Relations Review* 57 (2): 163–79.
Gittleman, M., M. Horrigan, and M. Joyce. 1998. "Flexible" workplace practices: Evidence from a nationally representative survey. *Industrial and Labor Relations Review* 52 (1): 99–115.
Gray, G., D. W. Myers, and P. S. Myers. 1999. Cooperative provisions in labor agreements: A new paradigm. *Monthly Labor Review* 122 (1): 29.
Hammer, T. H., and R. N. Stern. 1986. A yo-yo model of cooperation: Union participation in management at the Rath Packing Company. *Industrial and Labor Relations Review* 39 (3): 337–49.
Heckscher, C., and S. Shurman. 1997. Can labour-management cooperation deliver jobs and justice. *Industrial Relations Journal* 28 (4): 323–30.
Hunter, L. W. 1998. Can strategic participation be institutionalized? Union representation on American corporate boards. *Industrial and Labor Relations Review* 51 (4): 557–78.
Hunter, L. W., J. P. MacDuffie, and L. Doucet. 2002. What makes teams take? Employee reactions to work reforms. *Industrial and Labor Relations Review* 55 (3): 448–72.
The Hyatt-Clark ESOP: An interview with Jim May. 1985. *Labor Research Review* 1 (6): 25–33.
Ichniowski, C., T. A. Kochan, D. Levine, C. Olson, and G. Strauss. 1996. What works at work: Overview and assessment. *Industrial Relations* 35 (3): 299–333.
Ichniowski, C., K. Shaw, and G. Prennushi. 1997. The effects of human resource management practices on productivity: A study of steel finishing lines. *The American Economic Review* 87 (3): 291–313.
International Association of Machinists and Aerospace Workers (IAMAW). 1999. *High performance work organization partnerships: Field manual.* Upper Marlboro, Md.: IAMAW.
Johnson, J. L., C. M. Daily, and A. E. Ellstrand. 1996. Boards of directors: A review and research agenda. *Journal of Management* 22 (3): 409–38.
Katz, H. C., T. A. Kochan, and M. R. Weber. 1985. Assessing the effects of industrial relations systems and efforts to improve the quality of working life on organizational effectiveness. *Academy of Management Journal* 28 (3): 509–26.
Kochan, T. A., ed. 1985. *Challenges and choices facing American labor.* Cambridge, Mass.: MIT Press.
Lawler, E. E., III, G. E. Ledford Jr., and S. A. Mohrman. 1989. *Employee involvement in America: A study of contemporary practices.* Houston, Tex.: American Productivity and Quality Center.
Lawler, E. E., III, S. A. Mohrman, and G. E. Ledford Jr. 1992. *Employee involvement and total quality management.* San Francisco: Jossey-Bass.
———. 1995. *Creating high performance organizations.* San Francisco: Jossey-Bass.
Loughran, C. S. 1985. Union officials as corporate directors: What price survival? *Directors and Boards* 10 (1).
MacDuffie, J. P. 1995. Human resource bundles and manufacturing performance: Organizational logic and flexible production systems in the world auto industry. *Industrial and Labor Relations Review* 48 (2): 197–221.

Nissen, B. 1998. Fighting the union in a "union friendly" company: The AT&T/NCR case. *Labor Studies Journal* 23 (3): 3.

Orts, E. W. 1992. Beyond shareholders: Interpreting corporate constituency statutes. *George Washington Law Review* 61 (1): 14–135.

Osterman, P. 1994. How common is workplace transformation and who adopts it? *Industrial and Labor Relations Review* 47 (2): 173–88.

———. 2000. Work reorganization in an era of restructuring: Trends in diffusion and effects on employee welfare. *Industrial and Labor Relations Review* 53 (2): 179–96.

Patton, A., and J. C. Baker. 1987. Why won't directors rock the boat? *Harvard Business Review* 87 (6): 10–21.

Rubinstein, S. 2000. The impact of co-management on quality performance: The case of the Saturn Corporation. *Industrial and Labor Relations Review* 53 (2): 197–218.

Shleifer, A., and R. Vishny. 1997. A survey of corporate governance. *Journal of Finance* 52:737–83.

Smaby, B. 1988. Labor-management cooperation at Eastern Air Lines. Washington, D.C.: U.S. Bureau of Labor-Management Cooperation.

Useem, M. 1993. *Executive defense: Shareholder power and corporate reorganization.* Cambridge, Mass.: Harvard University Press.

Wever, K. R. 1989. Toward a structural account of union participation in management: The case of Western Airlines. *Industrial and Labor Relations Review* 42 (4): 600–609.

9 Development Intermediaries and the Training of Low-Wage Workers

Lisa M. Lynch

9.1 Background Discussion

During the latter half of the 1990s the unemployment rate in the United States reached a thirty-year low, a major influx of former welfare recipients entered the labor market, and employers in the high-tech sector demanded immigration reform to import skilled labor in order to meet their hiring needs. The time seemed ripe for increased job training in the United States, yet in spite of increasing returns to education and training over the last twenty years and high skill needs, the United States still seems to invest much less in postschool training than many other advanced industrialized economies. This chapter examines how various labor market intermediaries have intervened in the creation of training programs for low-wage workers to address the so-called "skills gap" of the past two decades. By describing the characteristics of different types of training intermediaries, it is hoped that some light might be shed on the potential longevity of these institutions, their capacity to achieve larger scale in the U.S. economy, and ultimately their ability to have a significant impact on the skill development of low-wage workers.

Before examining the role of labor market intermediaries in the provision of training to low-wage workers it is useful to briefly summarize what is known about the need for and supply of skills in the United States. In a nationally representative survey of U.S. businesses (see Black and Lynch

Lisa M. Lynch is the William L. Clayton Professor of International Economic Affairs and academic dean at the Fletcher School of Law and Diplomacy at Tufts University and a research associate at the National Bureau of Economic Research.

I would like to thank Richard Murnane for helpful comments on a previous version of this paper.

[2001] for more details) 53 percent of nonmanufacturing and 46 percent of manufacturing employers reported that skills associated with the work of production or front-line employees increased over the period 1993–1996. As discussed in Lynch and Black (1998), this rising skill demand and the training associated with it appears to be related to the diffusion of computerization and the reorganization of work to increase employee involvement in problem solving and decision making. However, in this same national survey, more than one-third of U.S. employers reported that 25 percent or more of their workers were not fully proficient in their current job. In a separate survey of U.S. firms, the American Management Association reported in 1999 that over 38 percent of job applicants tested for basic skills by U.S. corporations lacked the necessary reading, writing, and math skills to do the jobs they sought. The share of skills-deficient applicants, the survey said, had increased from 22.8 percent in 1997. Even in the depressed labor market of 2003, the Association reported that 31 percent of the employers it surveyed thought the availability of skilled labor they needed to recruit was in scarce supply.[1] It is not just employers who say that U.S. workers are not prepared for their jobs. Workers recognize this as well. For example, a recent study by Leuven and Oosterbeek (1999) found that one in four workers in the United States reported they were under trained. Finally, in an international survey of adult literacy, the Organization for Economic Cooperation and Development ([OECD] 1997) reported that almost one in five employed youth aged sixteen–twenty-five in the United States had minimal math skills compared to less than 5 percent of youth in countries such as Germany and Sweden.

Part of the reason why employers faced more skills-deficient applicants may have been because they had to hire further down in the distribution of skills given the overall strength of the economy during the latter half of the 1990s. So what have employers been doing in terms of addressing skill needs in the workplace? Research has shown (see Lynch [1994] for a review) that firm-provided training is much more likely to be obtained by more educated employees. This results in the creation of both a "virtuous" circle and a "vicious" circle of human capital accumulation. Individuals who acquire more schooling are also more likely to receive postschool employer-provided training, while those with minimal education find it extremely difficult to make up this deficiency in human capital once they enter the labor market. Workers in unionized firms are more likely to receive training than those in nonunionized establishments (see Lynch 1992; Lynch 1994). Large firms are more likely to provide training than small firms (see, for example, Lynch and Black 1998; Frazis, Herz, and Horrigan 1995), and, as shown in table 9.1, the firms that do invest in training are

1. See http://www.amanet.org/research/pdfs/2002_joboutlook.pdfhttp://www.amanet.org/research/pdfs/2002_joboutlook.pd.

Table 9.1 **Which workers get employer-provided job skills training? (percent of firms offering job skills training to indicated occupational category)**

Category of worker	All employers	Smaller employers	Larger employers
Management	50	46	80
Professional or technical	38	38	42
Computer	53	51	71
Sales	58	56	69
Clerical	35	33	48
Services	17	16	29
Production	36	34	47

Source: Bureau of Labor Statistics Employer Training Survey, 1993.

more likely to provide it to their managers and professionals than to workers farther down the skills ladder. Because low-wage workers are typically employed in smaller firms and in service occupations, the figures in this table suggest that they are very unlikely to find additional support for skills upgrading from their employer. Only 16 percent of smaller firms offer training to service workers, while 80 percent of the largest employers offer training to their managerial workers.

Economists have discussed extensively why, in spite of apparently high returns to employer provided training, employers may not provide training to meet all skills needs. A firm's decision to invest in workforce training, especially more general training, is likely influenced by the characteristics of the workers they employ. Employees who are perceived to have higher turnover rates, such as low-wage and low-skilled workers, are less likely to receive employer-provided training. In addition, training itself may contribute to employee turnover: if new skills are of value to other employers, then firms risk having their trained employee hired away (the poaching or "cherry-picking" problem). Therefore, investments in nonportable firm-specific training are more attractive to firms than are investments in general training unless employers can find some ways to "capture" their investment in general training. If firms invest in general skills of workers and workers then leave a firm, employers may end up investing in a suboptimal level of training.

In addition, smaller firms may have higher training costs per employee than larger firms because they cannot spread fixed costs of training over a large group of employees. The loss in production from having one additional worker in off-site training is probably much higher for a small firm than for a larger one. Smaller firms are also less likely to have developed extensive internal labor markets that allow them to better retain and promote employees within a firm.

But training is a different type of investment decision than the one to invest in new physical capital. There are two players in the training decision—the employer and the worker. Therefore, even if employers were reluctant to invest in general skills training, we would not necessarily see underinvestment in training in the economy as a whole. If capital markets were perfect so that workers could borrow to finance more general training, if the government subsidized general training, or if workers accepted lower wages during training spells, training would still occur. However, capital markets are far from perfect, and workers differ from employers in their attitudes toward risk and time horizons. As a result, there may be a market failure in the provision of general training and the proportion of workers trained in more general skills.

Theoretical work by Stevens (1994) and Acemoglu and Pischke (1998, 1999) has reexamined the issue of market failure in the delivery of training in the context of imperfect competition in the labor market. More specifically, Acemoglu and Pischke show how a firm can exhibit ex post monopsony power, and, as a result, workers decide not to invest in general training because they realize that part of the return will be appropriated by the firm. A key feature of their model is that workers could end up not investing in general training even if they were not credit constrained and firms might underinvest in training as well. Acemoglu and Pischke (1998) argue that, depending on institutional features of the labor market, there may be multiple training equilibriums—low training and high quit rates or low quit rates and high training with the United States representing a high quit rate and low training equilibrium and Germany and Japan representing a low quit rate and high training equilibrium. They propose a variety of possible policy solutions to raise the equilibrium level of training in a noncompetitive labor market. These include training subsidies to employers, government-provided training, and training subsidies supplemented with regulation of the provision of training. They argue that subsidies on their own may result in a windfall gain to employers if the government ends up paying for training that employers would have provided anyway. Government training programs that do not involve employers in the development and updating of curriculum could become irrelevant in meeting the needs of employers. However, they argue that subsidies with regulation where the quality of training programs was monitored and the skills provided were certified could minimize this risk. But they do not discuss the institutional structure that might provide this monitoring and skill certification in the case of the United States.

Booth and Chatterji (1998) show that unions, in the context of firm ex post monopsonistic power, can increase social welfare by counterbalancing the firm's ex post monopsonistic power in wage determination. As a result, local union-firm wage bargaining ensures that the post-training wage is set sufficiently high to deter at least some quits so that the number of workers that the firm trains is nearer the social optimum. The perceived longevity of a union provides the union with critical power to enforce multiperiod contract agreements, reducing the possibility that an employer reneges on wage increases linked to human capital investments ex post.

Empirically we see (see Lynch and Black 1998) that unionized establishments in the United States are more likely to provide training to workers than nonunionized businesses even after controlling for a wide range of firm and worker characteristics. So labor market institutions, especially unions, can play a potentially important role in ensuring that there is not a market failure in training and move a country in the direction of a high training equilibrium. But even in countries with high unionization rates, the existence of unions alone does not appear to be a sufficient condition to overcome the potential of a market failure in training. As discussed in Lynch (1994), many countries, such as Sweden, Japan, and Germany, have pursued very different yet ultimately successful institutional systems to overcome the potential market failure inherent in firm-based general training. For example, business, labor, and government in Germany have designed an institutional training system characterized by three features—codetermination, coinvestment, and certification of training. These features, along with enforcement pressure provided by chambers of commerce (see Soskice [1994] for a more detailed discussion of this) to minimize "unfair" poaching of workers by employers, have produced a high training equilibrium in Germany. There is substantial *coinvestment* in training in Germany because apprentices in Germany work at substantially lower wages during their apprenticeship. At the same time, employers contribute large sums to apprenticeship programs and the government funds extensive classroom training. The content of apprenticeship programs in Germany is *codetermined* with unions, employers groups, and the government to ensure relevance and generality of skills. Finally, the *certification* of skills makes it worthwhile for young workers to accept lower wages, maintains uniform quality standards, and makes identifying skills much easier for employers. In addition, German employers have created incentives for youths who do not obtain a university degree to perform well in secondary school by linking placement into "better" apprenticeships with their school record.

Whether or not Germany can continue with this model remains to be seen because the German model depends on a broad consensus among the social partners that has been increasingly challenged in the context of unification. But in the United States, with less than 10 percent of all workers represented by unions in the private sector and little tradition of labor-management-government cooperation, the potential for business, labor, and government to intervene a la the German model and push the economy toward a higher training equilibrium seems bleak.

So how might we increase the amount of postschool training provided beyond what single employers may be willing to do (in either a unionized or nonunionized context)? Are there institutions, in addition to unions, in the United States that may be able to play a role in solving this market failure in the delivery of training and move us to a higher training equilibrium? In particular, how could these institutions take on the characteristics that unions or labor market systems in Germany and Japan have historically done to ensure a higher training/wage equilibrium?

I would like to posit that there are several features that any such institution would need to acquire if they are to succeed in addressing the current skills issues facing the U.S. economy. If one of the ways in which unions raise the equilibrium level of training is through enforcement of long-term agreements between employers and workers, then other types of labor market intermediaries would need to be able to negotiate with employers in a similar way. This requires that they are sufficiently powerful to engage in such discussions. Now in union models we typically think of unions having bargaining power because they can organize workers to withhold their labor. However, the sources of power for labor market intermediaries that are based outside of the workplace are not so clear. Potential sources of power for these institutions might include the ability to influence public opinion or consumer buying power or political influence that in turn could bring pressure to bear on employers. In addition, when unemployment is low, as it was at the end of the 1990s, labor market intermediaries have another possible leverage point—their ability to identify and screen new workers from social networks that were not part of employers' traditional recruiting networks. Finally, regardless of the state of the labor market, with welfare reform there is a rising demand from those who have been disconnected from the labor market for a considerable period of time to get reconnected. So the ability of intermediaries to bridge asymmetries in information in the labor market could increase their bargaining power.

In order to avoid the problem of paying for training programs that private-sector employers would have been willing to do anyway, these institutions would also have to have the capacity to design training strategies that go beyond individual employers. To do this they would need to be well connected with employers to ensure that training is relevant and portable.

Employers' perception of the permanency of the intermediary will also affect labor market intermediaries' ability to successfully negotiate with local employers and government. A nonunion organization that wants to be a training intermediary will need to be able to establish a reputation that it is not an institution that might be focused on training issues today but something quite different tomorrow. If the primary basis of its ability to negotiate with local employers is a tight labor market then when demand conditions change they run the risk of not surviving. Therefore, they would need to have a steady and predictable source of funding that would serve to enhance their negotiating power as they bargain with local employers to reach a new training equilibrium. This funding should be sufficient to allow the organization to grow so that it can benefit from returns to scale in the provision of training (just as larger private-sector firms do).

In sum, in order to effectively raise the training equilibrium of an economy, an intermediary would need to act as a broker between employers and workers in the provision of skills, have the ability to enforce contractual agreements over multiple periods, be able to monitor the quality of training provided, and, finally, have the capacity to go to scale. To increase the probability that training intermediaries can raise the equilibrium level of training, they need to be structured in such a way as to ensure that there is codetermination, coinvestment, and certification of training. The next section of this chapter identifies some examples of how labor market intermediaries in the United States have tried to create at the local and national level a new training system targeted at low-wage workers.

9.2 Examples of Emerging Training Intermediaries for Low-Wage Workers

The role of third party intermediaries in the labor market to provide training is certainly not something new—there are numerous for-profit training providers that market their ability to provide skilled training and/or skilled workers to a firm. In addition, under the federal Workforce Investment Act, workforce development boards have been created all over the country to implement federally funded training programs through partnerships with labor, management, and government. Many of these boards have built upon successful partnerships that were previously formed in local private industry councils. However, what I am focusing on in this chapter are primarily not-for-profit social institutions (some have called them development intermediaries) that have attempted to establish new partnerships focused on raising the skills equilibrium in a particular geographic area or for a demographic group rather than for the needs of a single specific employer. This is not meant to be an exhaustive list of all of the many such efforts currently under way in the United States. Instead, I have tried to identify emerging institutions that are geographically diverse; have established different types of partnership relationships between community groups, training providers, employers, and government; have used different sources of funding; and have impacted varying industries.

9.2.1 Union-Management Collaborative Efforts

There are numerous examples of union-management collaborative efforts to increase training (see, for example, American Federation of Labor–Congress of Industrial Organization [AFL-CIO] Working for American Institute 2000). What is special about the following examples is how they have created unique sectoral and regional partnerships between labor and management to raise skills standards. These are all multiemployer partnerships with either a single or multiple unions. I have chosen quite different sectors for my examples—the electrical contracting sector, the hotel and hospitality sector, temporary workers in Silicon Valley, and the garment industry. These are sectors that potentially could provide opportunities for currently low-skilled workers to find jobs with wages and benefits that can support a family. They are also sectors undergoing tremendous change. In electrical contracting and the temporary help business in Silicon Valley, skill needs are being driven by new technologies; in the hotel industry, skill needs are being driven by competitive pressure from nonunion hotels; and in the garment industry, the ability to maintain jobs within the United States with global competition will depend on the ability of employers to use innovative new technology.

The IBEW/NECA Joint Apprentice and Training Committee for the Electrical Contracting Industry of Greater Boston

This program was established in 1947 as a quasi-independent organization and qualifies under Internal Revenue Service (IRS) rules as an educational institution. This is part of a broader national program. The Boston program is funded through several collective-bargaining agreements between the Boston Chapter of the National Electrical Contractors Association (NECA) and Local Union 103 of the International Brotherhood of Electrical Workers (IBEW). It represents approximately 150 major contracting firms and over 4,000 skilled workers. This program is unique because it is responsible for the selection, education, and training of all apprentices entering the units covered by the collective-bargaining agreements of these 150 firms. It is also a collaborative effort in an industry that has been transformed by technological change but one that represents a potentially rewarding career path for currently lower-skilled individuals. This center has all of the features described previously as critical to a successful training system—coinvestment, codetermination, and certification. The program has clearly established a reputation for longevity, and its funding stream is relatively predictable.

Working Partnerships USA

Working Partnerships was founded in 1995 as a collaboration between community-based organizations and the South Bay AFL-CIO Labor Council in San Jose, California. Its objective is to act as a labor market intermediary in the area of temporary help workers. They have established the Temporary Worker's Employment Project (see their website at http://www.atwork.org for more details) that is focused on assisting temporary workers to find jobs at better wages along with creating a skills standard for contingent workers in the clerical field. The project is made up of two components: together@work is a membership-based organization for contingent workers that provides portable benefits and financial services, and solutions@work is an employee-governed staffing company that trains and places clerical workers throughout Silicon Valley. An example of their partnership efforts is their collaboration with Service Employees International Union (SEIU) Local 715 and West Valley Community College to provide skills certification, job rights training, and job placement for temporary workers seeking clerical employment with the county of Santa Clara. As part of this effort they administer portable benefits and provide ongoing job referrals to participants. Their funding sources have included private foundations, such as the Charles Stewart Mott Foundation; union support; and fees they charge to private-sector employers. They have also been very active in reaching out to social institutions in the area to support their activities. For example, they staff the Interfaith Council on Religion, Race, Economic and Social Justice in San Jose and have been involved in local private-industry councils. While their efforts have focused on workers in the Silicon Valley, they have partnered with national organizations such as the National Interfaith Committee on Working Justice. Again, this organization's training development strategy includes the three features of coinvestment, certification, and codetermination. Their institutional structure is unusual due to the decision to not only partner with local employers but also to become an employer as well. While the crash of the high-tech sector has had a large impact on the local employment conditions, it appears that the strategies of this organization remain unchanged, and there are even discussions to try to create a national version of this organization. The charismatic head of this organization, Amy Dean, left her position as executive officer of South Bay Labor Council in the summer of 2003 to go to Chicago and create a national version of this organization. It will be interesting to see how the organization responds to this change in leadership.

The San Francisco Hotel Partnership

In 1994 a group of the major hotel chains in San Francisco banded together to form the San Francisco Multiemployer Group and negotiated a new labor contract (called a Living Contract) with the local union (Hotel Employees and Restaurant Employees [HERE] Local 2) to improve service and productivity in order to better compete with nonunion hotels. Stuart Korshak (2000), who was the general counsel hired by the hotel group to help them negotiate this agreement, argues that a critical component of the 1994 contract was the training program created within the agreement. The training program is focused on improving communication skills between workers and guests and workers and managers along with improving critical thinking skills, team building, problem solving, English as a second language, and craft-specific technical skills. It is sixty times larger in scope than any previous joint training program in the hotel industry in

San Francisco and is funded jointly by the unions, management, and funds from the state of California. Union and management jointly designed the curriculum. Korshak (2000) states that this was critical to overcome fears among some employees that the program was merely a way for management to weed out workers or just some fad. Finally, the training of workers within the hotels was extended to the hiring hall to raise skills for banquet servers, including classes in French service, wine appreciation, and food carving along with training in sanitation and safety issues. The training component of this agreement was an important complement to another unique dimension of this agreement, which was greater employee involvement. At the end of the five-year contract, the hotels and unions, as described by Korshak (2000), have gone from a confrontational relationship to a partnership based on mutual gains. Again, this is a good example of an institutional structure that is characterized by coinvestment, codetermination, and certification of skills. The fact that the contract was recently renewed and kept these unique features suggests that this increased investment in workers' skills will remain a permanent feature of the hotel industry in San Francisco. It will be interesting to watch, however, what happens if employee turnover is such that the partnership finds itself providing much of the training for the nonunion hotels as well.

The Garment Industry Development Corporation

This is a nonprofit consortium established in 1984 by labor, industry, and government focused on improving the competitiveness of the apparel industry in New York City. In the area of training, the Union of Needletrades, Industrial, and Textile Employees (UNITE), representing over 30,000 workers, in collaboration with hundreds of local employers, has established the Fashion Industry Modernization Center located in the garment district in New York City. Its facility includes the latest in computerized sewing machines, state-of-the-art presses, and a computer lab carrying Computer Aided Design and Computer Aided Machining (CAD/CAM) software. More specifically, it offers skills training for dislocated sewing machine operators as well as English as a second language and health and safety instruction. A unique feature of this training center is that it trains not only workers in the industry but also garment contractor and manufacturers in the latest techniques and innovations. In this way the center hopes that it will train employers in techniques that will ensure that they will be able to compete successfully and therefore retain jobs in the city. Again this is a good example of the three Cs, with financial support coming from labor, management, and government. However, what is unusual in this collaboration is the nature of the codetermination of the training content. When we usually think of codetermination, we think of employers being involved in curriculum design to ensure that the skills content of courses is sufficiently up to date to meet their needs. Instead, in this example the training center is focused in part on educating employers about technology options that will enable them to remain competitive.

9.2.2 Community Based Organizations

Perhaps the most important new form of training intermediaries has been the rise of community-based organizations taking on activities in economic development. In particular, more interfaith organizations have become involved in efforts to increase the training opportunities provided by local employers for low-wage workers. The interfaith organizations are place-based, and so they build upon a preexisting institutional structure. But this structure has not historically been involved in economic development issues. Therefore, a first challenge faced by these organizations is to develop the human capital within the organization to allow it to prepare a strategy for economic development issues, such as training. If they "contract out" this expertise, they run the risk of losing an important source of their power—broad-based grassroots support. Their source of leverage is their diversity and ability to bring together a broad political coalition. A challenge for these organizations, however, is to maintain support (both financial and public) for an issue like training that may not generate the same sense of urgency as housing or school quality. In addition, some of the organizations have struggled to create a governance structure that ensures that the institutional partnerships that they broker can deliver a training system that is characterized by coinvestment, codetermination, and certification. The examples in the following include interfaith community-based organizations along with other examples that have been chosen for the sectors they target or unique sources of funding.

San Antonio, Texas Industrial Areas Foundation

A considerable amount has already been written about the Industrial Areas Foundation (IAF), especially its experience in Texas. As discussed by Ernesto Cortés (1994), the IAF is a national network of broad-based, multi-ethnic interfaith organizations in primarily poor and moderate-income communities. It was created over fifty years ago by Saul Alinsky, and it provides leadership training for nearly forty organizations representing over 1,000 institutions and one million families principally in New York, Texas, California, Arizona, New Mexico, Nebraska, Maryland, Tennessee, and the United Kingdom. One of the best-documented experiences of the IAF and training for low-wage workers is Project QUEST in San Antonio, Texas. Project QUEST grew out of a new social compact among employers, workers, and the community at large. It was engineered by two IAF organizations—Communities Organized for Public Service (COPS), one of the oldest and most established IAFs, and Metro Alliance. Brett

Campbell (1994) describes this compact as a new kind of labor market intermediary.

As Campbell (1994) discusses, the IAF, through its involvement in Project QUEST, "operates as a mediating institution to bring families back into relationships with employers, training institutions and social service providers." This has a certain ring of "codetermination." In addition to this structure that provides codetermination, the IAF's philosophy and experience in Project QUEST emphasizes coinvestment in training with workers contributing "sweat equity," state and local governments providing funds, local employers committing to 650 jobs, and employer involvement in curriculum design and funding support for training programs at local community colleges. Finally, in the studies by Campbell (1994) and Osterman and Lautsch (1996), it is clear that Project QUEST focused much of its attention on redesigning the role that community colleges played in the local labor market. This included certification of training programs as seen, for example, with a customer-service–accredited certificate program they developed in conjunction with a local community college and the American Institute of Banking.

However, before concluding that the Texas IAFs are the new magic elixir for worker voice and worker protection, it should be pointed out that there have been difficulties. Mark Warren (1996), in his detailed study of the Fort Worth IAF, points out that the Fort Worth IAF has had difficulty in recruiting large numbers of affluent whites in mainstream denominations to work cooperatively with leaders of African-American and Hispanic communities. In addition, in their evaluation of Project QUEST, Osterman and Lautsch discuss how employers have supported Project QUEST by providing input on training programs development and forecasts of future staffing needs. But they argue that few employers have made dramatic changes in their hiring practices in response to Project QUEST. In addition, unstable government funding has at times undermined the sense of permanency of Project QUEST. Although employers were "coinvesting" by making employment pledges, the length of Project QUEST training programs meant that employers found themselves making a pledge of a job placement that would not occur for two years. Project QUEST has also struggled to attract clients given Texas's "work first" mandate that stresses work over skills training.

Osterman and Lautsch (1996) also raise concerns about how successful the program would be in meeting the needs of displaced workers from Kelly Air Force Base in San Antonio, which closed in August 2001. On this front, the IAF worked to broker a deal whereby in April of 1997, Boeing signed a twenty-year lease (four five-year options) for 1.3 million square feet of space at Kelly to create a world-class maintenance and modification center for large, primarily military aircraft. Part of the agreement between the city of San Antonio, the Greater Kelly Development Corporation, and

Boeing included $7 million of warehouse improvements for the facilities that Boeing occupies that are Boeing-specific upgrades on top of another $25 million of general improvements. In addition, incentives were included to reward Boeing for the number of Kelly workers hired and the wages and benefits paid to them.

As part of the master plan to redevelop the Kelly Air Force Base, a high-tech training center has also been established. In July 2002, the Alamo Community College District (ACCD) opened the Advanced Technology Center (ATC) at the former Kelly Air Force Base. This training center partners the ACCD with Lockheed-Martin, Boeing Aerospace, Standard Aero, Chromalloy, Pratt & Whitney, Defense Aerospace Industry, a range of industrial technology (IT) companies, and ARC Information Assurance Institute. The center provides customized training taught by faculty from the ACCD colleges in the areas of aerospace industries, computer technologies and e-commerce, and telecommunications. The center is projected to train 2,000 people on site each year, with an additional 800 trained via distance learning. One of the four community colleges that make up the ACCD is St. Philips College. St. Philips College, a historically black and Hispanic serving institution, was the first Texas community college to be designated a One-Stop Workforce Center. It serves to link welfare recipients and displaced Kelly employees to area education and employment opportunities. It has worked very closely with the IAF to revamp its course offerings to meet the needs of local workers and employers and is a good example of a transformed labor market institution.

Jane Addams Resource Corporation

This not-for-profit community development organization was founded in 1985 to promote retention and growth of local metal working firms on Chicago's north side. One of their primary activities has been their Metalworking Skills Training Program to provide literacy and technical training for low-wage workers, but they also have programs in computer skills training and adult basic learning. As described in a report for the National Governors Association (see Brown et al. 1998), this training program is undergoing an extensive evaluation and assessment effort. While this program appears to have been highly successful, it is still relatively small. More generally, the challenge for many community development organizations is how to broaden their impact and achieve greater scale. But this organization has tried to achieve larger scale through a recent collaboration with other Chicago-based community-based training providers. In 1999 the U.S. Department of Labor (DOL) funded a two year one million dollar demonstration project (this was one of ten such projects funded by the DOL) in Chicago called the Regional Manufacturing Training System (RMTS). This project links the metal working program training provided by the Jane Addams Resource Corporation with wood working training programs developed by the community-based organization Greater West Town Project and manufacturing training for machine operators, electroplaters, and industrial maintenance mechanics developed by the Chicago Manufacturing Institute and targets over 300 workers in Chicago. There is active involvement in standards and curriculum development by local employers, local government, community colleges, and universities in the RMTS. But the real challenge for this new organization will be its ability to become self-sustaining in the face of federal cuts in job training. How they do this will be informative of the issues facing other CBOs as they try to go to scale.

National Urban League

One community-based program that has gone to scale and has a well-developed national presence is the National Urban League (NUL). Founded in 1910 with affiliates in over 100 cities in thirty-two states and the District of Columbia, the mission of the NUL has been to enable African Americans to secure economic self-reliance, parity and power, and civil rights. Local affiliates have organized and developed numerous job training programs over the years. For example, with technical assistance from companies such as IBM, the San Diego Urban League has established the Training Institute, which provides training programs for careers in computing such as clerical and administrative assistants, electronic assemblers, mechanical assemblers, systems coordinators, systems maintenance analysts, technical support specialists, installers, quality assurance specialists, and equipment testers. The programs range from 120 to 480 hours long and are specialized for beginner, intermediate, and advanced learners using a mixture of computer-based and instructor-led training. In addition to training, the San Diego Urban League has an extensive employment service that places over 2,000 people annually in unsubsidized employment. The league has worked with local employers to develop employment networks, get their involvement in training design, and even conduct mock interviews. The sources of funding for the San Diego Urban League include local employers, foundations, and local government. So the San Diego Urban League's institutional structure has covered the three Cs of training. But the NUL has been able to do what few other community-based groups have done and that is to pull together local efforts into a national strategy to share and build on successful programs. Through this coordination the NUL has built a powerful political base that helps it negotiate workforce development issues at the local and national level.

Annie E. Casey Foundation Jobs Initiative

One of the important funding sources for many not-for-profit training intermediaries has been foundations. This support has been critical for the creation and survival of many of these organizations. For example, in 1995 the Annie E. Casey Foundation began an eight-year six-site $30 million demonstration project to help low-income residents in designated neighborhoods find jobs that paid family-supporting wages. All of the six sites (located in Denver, Milwaukee, New Orleans, Philadelphia, St. Louis, and Seattle) are managed by what the foundation calls "entrepreneurial intermediaries." The general philosophy of the foundation's efforts appears to be a catalyst to bring together employers, elected officials, community-based organizations, low-income residents, and other stakeholders in the design and creation of new job-related initiatives.

By 2003, this jobs initiative had served over 17,000 people of which 40 percent were single parents, 35 percent had less than a high school degree, 20 percent did not speak English as their primary language, the median income for participants who had ever worked was $6,000, and 45 percent received public assistance at the time of enrollment. The model is a sectoral-based approach in that the intermediaries target specific sectors of the local economy in which they develop employment and training opportunities. The sites have varied greatly in the composition of these managing intermediaries. The two examples in the following have been chosen because of the different governance structures chosen, the diversity of the targeted participants, and the range of sectors for placement.

The Milwaukee example is typical of the problems facing many large urban areas. When this jobs initiative began in 1997, the city's unemployment rate was around 3 percent, but in the poorest neighborhoods it was 23 percent, with many long-term unemployed. The Milwaukee Jobs Initiative chose to partner with an existing training program, the Milwaukee Graphic Arts Institute (MGAI) to develop training for low-wage workers with no previous experience in an industry that has been rapidly transformed by computerization. As described in an initial report by the Annie E. Casey Foundation (2000), the Milwaukee Jobs Initiative worked quickly to get money from agencies receiving Temporary Assistance for Needy Families (TANF) grants to fund and implement training programs for entry-level workers. This allowed MGAI to recruit more broadly, provide customized training, and get people into jobs quickly. As a result, MGAI was able to establish a track record that they used to approach new industries and employers. They also worked closely with the local private industry council to streamline its funding process to get resources into training more quickly.

The Milwaukee Jobs Initiative has also been active in two other sectors—manufacturing and construction. In manufacturing they are working with the preexisting Wisconsin Regional Training Partnership (a consortium of unions and employers) to develop vocational education, including the provision of instructors for on-the-job training from the Milwaukee Area Technical College. In construction, the Campaign for a Sustainable Milwaukee has opened a construction workers' center in a neighborhood church where job seekers can meet contractors and union officials to find out about training and other support services to help them build a career in the construction trades. This effort is especially focused on recruiting more African Americans into this sector.

The New Orleans Job Initiative had a difficult start and has some of the greatest challenges of the six sites. In fact, the demonstration project almost fell apart initially. In 1997 the New Orleans Jobs Initiative faced an organizational crisis. On the one hand, they realized that in order to succeed they needed to include more representatives from major businesses on their governing board. But, on the other hand, because the initiative was a grassroots effort, how could community control be maintained if the board was expanded to include employers? What lurked behind this discussion was, according to the Abt Associates and the New School for Social Research (1999) initial evaluation report, a long history of racially charged tension between representatives of the impact community and the city's business community. This issue was ultimately resolved by increasing employer representation on the board but giving veto power to three principal community groups over all board policies and actions. Because of the delay in resolving governance issues, this site has only just begun to organize its training activities.

They are targeting four sectors—construction, manufacturing (in particular, machining), health care, and office sectors. Employee referrals come from community-based organizations. Once recruited, enrollees receive technical skills training at a local community college, which in turn works closely with employers to design curricula to meet their skill needs. In the construction area, the initiative is developing a program with community groups, contractors, and a labor union to recruit job seekers and place them in a 100-hour training program and then in jobs paying $7 to start. In the area of machinists, the program has developed a training program for entry-level workers where an employer will provide a six-month training program. At the end of the training, the individuals are placed in jobs at other machine shops. Community organizations have been engaged to help workers with transportation and other social supports. One of the innovations of this program has been a twenty-one-day job-readiness program that focuses on the development of "soft skills" of work (such as coping with stress and work attitude) to complement the technical training.

However, there have been tensions in the relations between the local private industry council and the New Orleans Jobs Initiative. The private industry council decided that the training models the New Orleans Jobs Initiative developed did not meet federal funding guidelines. This affected funding for the New Orleans Jobs Initiative. In addition, the initiative had difficulty early on with the local community college it was working with to provide the type of technical skills training the New Orleans Jobs Initiative clients needed and the time constraints they faced. Only two people completed the manufacturing program in the first two years of the initiative. However, as reported in its most recent update,[2] the number of participants who have completed the machinist program is twenty-five, and fifty have completed the construction program.

Clearly the New Orleans Jobs Initiative has struggled and is a good example of the tensions underlying the concept of codetermination. It is not necessarily easy to get all parties to agree to codetermine the content of programs if there is not sufficient trust among all the partners. The city of New Orleans has also created a new Office of Workforce Development that will manage and administer federal training funds. Establishing a successful relationship with this new office will be critical for the survival and ultimate success of the New Orleans Jobs Initiative.

WorkSource Staffing Partnership, Inc.

While this chapter has focused on not-for-profit efforts in training programs, there has been another avenue in which not-for-profit institutions have tried to expand the development of training programs targeted at low-wage workers. This is through the use of federally sponsored Community Development Financial Institution Funds that link low-income areas with financial capital to spur economic development. An example of this activity is WorkSource Staffing Partnership, Inc. in Boston, Massachusetts. The initial funding source for this for-profit firm was venture capital from the Boston Community Venture Fund, which was created as part of the federally sponsored Community Development Financial Institutions Fund. Established in 1995 as a for-profit firm, WorkSource Staffing Partnership, Inc. has developed partnerships between community-based organizations and employers based in Boston. The focus of this firm has been to help underemployed low-wage workers and former welfare recipients obtain job training and access to better career paths. At the same time it has provided local employers in a tight labor market the ability to identify potential employees outside their traditional recruiting networks. The success of the firm depends critically on its ability to establish a reputation for identifying and preparing motivated and work-ready employees. They do this by working closely with community-based organizations to identify motivated individuals who they then help obtain appropriate training and employment. WorkSource Staffing Partnership, Inc. also provides follow-up support for child care, transportation, housing, and personal management issues. Their employer partnerships have been primarily in the health care sector, such as the Joslin Diabetes Center and Partners Health Care. In this

2. See http://www.aecf.org/initiatives/jobsinitiatives/neworleans.htm; accessed November 14, 2003.

case, a not-for-profit social investment fund supported the creation of a for-profit firm to deliver training to economically disadvantaged workers. By focusing on the health care sector, which has continued to grow even during the most recent recession, this organization has established a successful track record of working with welfare recipients and successfully placing them in the health care sector. In fact, Partners Healthcare has decided to privately fund its Project RISE (Reaching Individuals Striving for Excellence). In the longer term it will be interesting to see how this firm is able to continue to serve its current client base compared to other more traditional for-profit placement firms and not-for-profit community-based organizations. Will its for-profit status drive it away from low-wage workers once not-for-profit funding support is gone? So far this does not seem to be the case.

9.3 The Future of Emerging Training Intermediaries

As outlined in the examples detailed previously, one of the biggest challenges to the capacity of these emerging labor market intermediaries has been funding. For those programs supported by joint labor management agreements, funding for the training programs will likely be determined in large part by the economic fortunes of the sector for which the training is done. For many of the programs examined in this study that are sponsored by venture capital money or private foundation support, the hope is that once the programs are up and running that alternative sources of funding would be identified. These would include employers in the private sector paying a fee for the ability to recruit skilled work-ready individuals outside their traditional networks or state or federal funds to support workforce development of low-wage workers.

However, as these programs are pushed to become more self-sufficient and depend primarily on private employer funding, will they be able to maintain their focus on the most disadvantaged workers? If they instead rely on federal funds to maintain their activities, they run the risk of competing for increasingly scarce funds given a special problem with federal funding formulas. A state's share of funds from the Workforce Investment Act is heavily based on unemployment rates and concentrated joblessness. This works against a state like Massachusetts, for example, that is more plagued by earnings shortfalls among the working poor than by pockets of high unemployment. Second, in principle, the Workforce Investment Act allows states to target not only unemployed but also low-wage working individuals for training. But if we look at the inflation-adjusted federal training funds per civilian labor force member over the period of 1993–1999, we see that this number has fallen almost 20 percent (see Donahue, Lynch, and Whitehead 2000). So the federal government is an unlikely source for increased training funds, especially when economic conditions are relatively good. More federal funds are available when the economy goes into a recession, but this is also the toughest time to place those with the lowest skills into employment.

As a result of this trend in federal funding of training, what states chose to do will have an important impact on the eventual success of these different types of intermediaries. It will be up to individual states to decide whether they will allocate additional funds for the creation of a workforce development system that will meet the needs of the working poor along with those without employment. The most recent economic downturn has put enormous pressure on state-funded workforce development programs as requirements to balance state budgets resulted in substantial cuts in state funding. This will mean that many of the organizations described in this chapter will need to engage in the political process to ensure that funds are allocated to their activities. Their success will be driven by their political power and reputation, the success of current activities, and the general economic climate of the state/community they are in.

A second issue is employer involvement. While it is critical to ensure that there is employer involvement in these emerging intermediaries, there is also a tension about how much of a role employers should play in the governance of these institutions. In the Abt Associates and the New School for Social Research's (1999) study of the Annie E. Casey Foundation's six-site jobs initiative, there is considerable discussion of reasons why employers were willing to participate in these programs and why they weren't. Participation was usually driven by employers playing a "leadership" role on advisory boards or a "placement" role where they are recruited as customers of the jobs initiative. In tight labor markets it is easier to attract employers into a placement role, but this has not always been so. Stereotypes of the impact communities persist, and one wonders about the fortunes of some of the programs described in this chapter as the economy suffers an economic downturn.

This chapter has tried to outline some of the basic characteristics of emerging intermediaries in the provision of training to low-wage workers (see table 9.2).[3] The examples cited are not meant to be exhaustive of all the ongoing efforts, but I think that they highlight some key features and challenges of these institutions. Their probability of success in the longer term will certainly be affected by economic conditions but also by the ability of these newly emerging institutions to build a track record that establishes them as a permanent fixture that must be negotiated with in the local labor market. These challenges are not unfamiliar to unions. The key to the sur-

3. See table 9.2 for a summary of the programs discussed in this chapter along with their key features.

Table 9.2 **Summary of emerging training intermediaries**

Type of structure	Industry	Location	Source of funding	Date started
	Union/Management consortiums			
IBEW/NECA Joint Apprentice and Training Committee	Electrical contractors	Dorchester, MA	Jointly funded union, firms	1947
San Francisco Hotel Partnership	Hotel	San Francisco, CA	Union, firms, state of California CET	1994
Working Partnerships USA	Temp help	San Jose, CA	Fees paid by firms, union funds	1995
Garment Industry Development Corporation	Garment industry	New York, NY	Union, industry assoc., state government, JTPA	1984
	Community-based organizations			
Project Quest/IAF (www.questsa.com)	Health care, aircraft maintenance, IT, business services	San Antonio, TX	Private donations, JTPA, state of Texas	1993
Jane Addams Resource Corporation	SME manufacturers	Chicago, IL	Local government grants, foundations, firms	1985
National Urban League	Diverse sectors	100+ cities	Foundations, government, fees	1910
Annie E. Casey Foundation Jobs Initiative			Matched foundation local money, TANF	1995
Milwaukee	Manufacturing, construction, printing			
New Orleans	Construction, machining, office jobs, health care			
WorkSource Partners	Health care	Boston, MA	Venture capital	1995

vival and impact of these organizations will be their ability to construct the social cohesion and common vision necessary to bring about the consensus that we see in other countries in a high training equilibrium.

References

Abt Associates and The New School for Social Research. 1999. *Private interests, shared concerns: The relationship between employers and the AECF Jobs Initiative.* Final report prepared for the Annie E. Casey Foundation. Baltimore, Md.: Annie E. Casey Foundation.

Acemoglu, Daron and Jorn-Steffen Pischke. 1998. The structure of wages and investment in general training. NBER Working Paper no. 6357. Cambridge, Mass.: National Bureau of Economic Research, January.

———. 1999. Beyond Becker: Training in imperfect labor markets. *Economic Journal* 109:F112–F142.

American Federation of Labor–Congress of Industrial Organization (AFL-CIO) Working for America Institute. 2000. *High road partnerships report.* Washington, D.C.: AFL-CIO Working for America Institute.

Annie E. Casey Foundation. 2000. *Stronger links: New ways to connect low-skilled workers to better jobs.* Baltimore, Md.: Annie E. Casey Foundation.

Black, Sandra E., and Lisa M. Lynch. 2001. How to compete: The impact of workplace practices and information technology on productivity. *Review of Economics and Statistics* 83 (3): 434–45.

Booth, Alison, and Monojit Chatterji. 1998. Unions and efficient training. *Economic Journal* 108 (447): 328–43.

Brown, Rebecca, Evelyn Ganzglass, Susan Golonks, Jill Hyland, and Martin Simon. 1998. Working out of poverty: Employment retention and career advancement for welfare recipients. Available at [http://www.nga.org/Welfare/Employment Retention.htm].

Campbell, Brett. 1994. *Investing in people: The story of Project QUEST.* San Antonio, Tex.: Communities Organized for Public Service (COPS) and Metro Alliance. Available at [http://www.cpn.org/topics/work/quest6-7.html].

Cortés, Ernesto. 1994. Reweaving the social fabric. *The Boston Review* 19 (3). Available at [http://www.bostonreview.net/BR19.3/Cortes.html].

Donahue, John D., Lisa M. Lynch, and Ralph Whitehead Jr. 2000. *Opportunity knocks: Training the commonwealth's workers for the new economy.* Boston: MassINC.

Frazis, Harley J., Diane E. Herz, and Michael W. Horrigan. 1995. Employer-provided training: Results from a new survey. *Monthly Labor Review* 118 (5): 3–17.

Korshak, Stuart R. 2000. A labor management partnership: San Francisco's hotels and the employees' union try a new approach. *Cornell Hotel and Restaurant Administration Quarterly* 41 (2): 14–29.

Leuven, E., and Hessel Oosterbeek. 1999. Demand and supply of work-related training: Evidence from four countries. *Research in Labor Economics* 18:303–30.

Lynch, Lisa M. 1992. Private sector training and its impact on the earnings of young workers. *American Economic Review* 82 (1): 299–312.

Lynch, Lisa M., ed. 1994. *Training and the private sector: International comparisons.* Chicago: University of Chicago Press.

Lynch, Lisa M., and Sandra E. Black. 1998. Beyond the incidence of employer-provided training. *Industrial and Labor Relations Review* 52 (1): 64–81.

Organization for Economic Cooperation and Development (OECD). 1997. *Literacy skills for the knowledge economy.* Paris: OECD.

Osterman, Paul, and Brenda Lautsch. 1996. Project QUEST: A report to the Ford Foundation. MIT, Sloan School of Management. Mimeograph.

Soskice, David. 1994. Reconciling markets and institutions: The German apprenticeship system. In *Training and the private sector,* ed. Lisa M. Lynch, 25–60. Chicago: University of Chicago Press.

Stevens, M. 1994. A theoretical model of on-the-job training with imperfect competition. *Oxford Economic Papers* 46:537–62.

Warren, Mark. 1996. Creating a multi-racial democratic community: A case study of the Texas Industrial Areas Foundation. Paper presented at conference, Social Networks and Urban Poverty. 1–2 March, New York.

Contributors

Eileen Appelbaum
Center for Women and Work
Rutgers, The State University of New Jersey
162 Ryders Lane
New Brunswick, NJ 08901

Jared Bernstein
Economic Policy Institute
1660 L Street, NW
Suite 1200
Washington, DC 20036

Thomas C. Buchmueller
Graduate School of Management
University of California, Irvine
Irvine, CA 92697-3125

John Bunge
Cornell University
358 Ives Hall
Ithaca, NY 14853

John E. DiNardo
Ford School of Public Policy
University of Michigan, Ann Arbor
440 Lorch Hall
Ann Arbor, MI 48109-1220

Kimberly Ann Elliott
Institute for International Economics
1750 Massachusetts Avenue, NW
Washington, DC 20036-1903

Richard B. Freeman
National Bureau of Economic Research
1050 Massachusetts Avenue
Cambridge, MA 02138

Joni Hersch
Harvard Law School
1557 Massachusetts Avenue
Cambridge, MA 02138

Larry W. Hunter
School of Business Management and Human Resources Department
University of Wisconsin, Madison
4114 Grainger Hall
975 University Avenue
Madison, WI 53706

Richard W. Hurd
Cornell University
208 ILR Conference Center
Garden Avenue
Ithaca, NY 14853-3901

Christine Jolls
Harvard Law School
Griswold 504
Cambridge, MA 02138

Lisa M. Lynch
Fletcher School of Law and Diplomacy
Tufts University
Medford, MA 02155

Lawrence Mishel
Economic Policy Institute
1660 L Street, NW
Suite 1200
Washington, DC 20036

Robert G. Valletta
Economic Research Department
Federal Reserve Bank of San Francisco
101 Market Street
San Francisco, CA 94105

David Weil
School of Management
Boston University
595 Commonwealth Avenue
Boston, MA 02215

Author Index

Subject Index